Richness and solidity ... beauty and energy ... the wide ... miles, great shops — cafes — great boulevards — where does it come from? what's here?

---

Frankfurt Ex. M. Sunday Sept 2 — wrote part of letter to Celine last night — today up late for coffee — fine cool sunny day — sparkle of early autumn in the air — this is a fine city — as all the German cities — and — lately see ... fl garden under the broad ... three trees (?) — already ... turn yellow ... Picture Museum this

... Boston ... who is become ... ... (the Fight ... with the ... er)

— Stocke ... others

# THE NOTEBOOKS OF
# *Thomas Wolfe*

*"Here then, picked out at random from the ferment of ten thousand pages, and a million words—put down just as they were written, in fragments, jots, or splintered flashes, without order or coherence—here with all its vanity, faith, despair, joy, and anguish, with all its falseness, error, and pretension, and with all its desperate sincerity, its incredible hope, its insane desire, is a picture of a man's soul and heart—the image of his infuriate desire—caught hot and instant, drawn flaming from the forge of his soul's agony."*

THOMAS WOLFE, *Of Time and the River*

# *THE NOTEBOOKS OF*
# *Thomas Wolfe*

*Edited by*
RICHARD S. KENNEDY
*and*
PASCHAL REEVES

*Volume I*

*THE UNIVERSITY OF*
*NORTH CAROLINA PRESS*
***Chapel Hill***

*Manufactured in the United States of America*
*Printed by Kingsport Press, Inc.*
*Library of Congress Catalog Card Number 70-80917*

*For*

ELLA KENNEDY

*and*

SUZANNE REEVES

# *Preface*

The story of the publication of these notebooks begins in January, 1937, when Thomas Wolfe met William Wisdom in New Orleans. "An autograph collector," Wolfe jotted in his current pocket notebook, "but he likes me." Liked him so well, one must add, that after the death of the author he purchased the entire two-ton collection of Wolfe papers and books and deposited it in the Harvard Library, where it became the center of the largest single collection devoted to any major American writer. In this amazingly rich accumulation the most fascinating body of material is the series of thirty-five pocket notebooks that Wolfe carried intermittently from 1926, when he was just beginning his first novel, *Look Homeward, Angel,* until just before his death in 1938.

Only one of them, Wolfe's last notebook (which recorded his impressions of a trip through a dozen national parks in the West), has been published before. A few scattered notebook entries were published by Wolfe himself as Eugene Gant's Paris notebook in *Of Time and the River*. But the preponderant bulk of the material is here published for the first time. Some years ago Elizabeth Nowell had planned an edition of selections from Wolfe's notebooks, but her tragic death halted the project very near its outset. Richard Kennedy, who had become familiar with all the Wolfe manuscripts in the 1950's, made plans in 1963 for a full-scale publication of the notebooks plus supplementary material from the Wolfe papers which would illuminate obscure portions and enrich sparse stretches. The idea was to provide sufficient notes and commentary and to go back far enough with Wolfe's scattered jottings so that the edition would present a kind of interior biography of Wolfe beginning with his years at Harvard, the time of his first serious literary endeavors. Paschal Reeves, who not only had lived in North Carolina but was writing a book on Wolfe's social attitudes, joined this project in 1964. The two editors then worked together for five years in what has been both an exciting literary experience and an exacting and tedious task.

As in other editions of materials that were not intended by the author for publication, editorial decisions have had their impact on the final appearance of the material in print. An initial decision was made to prepare an edition for the general reader, especially the college student—an edition that would have its place on any library shelf, not an edition designed exclusively as a research tool. At the same time, the editors determined to present a reliable text for scholars and critics to use and a text full enough so that there would be scarcely any need to go beyond it. Where such a need might exist, an examination of the Harvard Library microfilm of the notebooks should quickly clear up any questions.

With such an edition in mind, we have reproduced about nine-tenths of the total material in the notebooks. Except for representative samples, we have omitted such entries as these: grocery lists, train schedules, American Express check numbers, names and addresses, lists of things to do, lecture notes from Dean James Munn's course in Literature and the Bible, and many of the notes Wolfe set down in connection with his own teaching at New York University. We have also left out repetitions of literary outlines, some of the astounding number of statistical lists (e.g. of cities he had visited, people he had met in the last month, or books seen in store windows), many records of conversations overheard in bars and lunch counters, and a few short passages which were incoherent and mostly illegible, which Wolfe wrote when he was deep in his cups. Three brief passages were omitted to avoid offense to living persons.

We have placed periods at the ends of sentences and capitalized the beginning word of each entry, but otherwise we have supplied a minimum of punctuation, mostly apostrophes for possessives and contractions: we have closed quotations and parentheses; we have occasionally added a missing comma or dash for clarity. We have corrected inadvertent misspellings ("teeth" for "teeeth," "talk" for "tallk," "bicycle" for "bycicle"), and we have corrected most misspellings of names or places, especially in foreign languages (thus the restaurant Wolfe always calls the "Cicogne" becomes the "Cigogne"). We have left misspellings which seemed to indicate the way Wolfe pronounced a word (e.g. "track" for "tract," "breath" for "breadth"), and we have not normalized Wolfe's characteristic spellings of such words as "fulness" or "prolog." We have added the proper accent marks in French or German words (which Wolfe omitted half of the time) in the same way that we have dotted his "i"s and crossed his "t"s. We have supplied omitted words and placed them in brackets. We have left abbreviations when they were clear ("Tues.") but spelled them out when they might not be ("yest" becomes "yesterday"). We have rendered passages which Wolfe crossed out, unless he rewrote or restated the matter.

We have rearranged the order of the material when continuity or chronology was interrupted, or when it was necessary because Wolfe himself had been haphazard about the order of his entries. We have done some paragraphing when the matter ran too long without it (notably in the Western Journal) and have followed normal usage when rendering dialogue. On the whole, the aim has been to provide a readable page rather than one festooned with [*sic*]'s, arrows, daggers, cancellations, and other intrusions.

We have identified, the first time it appears, each name that Wolfe mentioned, except for a few people whom we were unable to track down. We have pointed out most of the pertinent references to Wolfe's published works by title and page number, but we have restrained ouselves, we hope, from excessive annotation of this kind.

In many places Wolfe's script was very difficult to read—for a number of reasons: because he was scribbling in furious haste, because he was writing on a subway or a train, because he had been drinking heavily, because the writing had become faint with the wear of too much handling of a page, or because the penciled pages had become smudged from rubbing together in Wolfe's pocket. At times, only the context could guide the right guess at a word: a short squiggle that was high at the beginning and had one high loop before drooping below the line could be "holy," "body," "lovely," "lively," "hiding," "daily," "clearly," or "looking," depending on the sentence in which it appeared. At other times, when context was an insufficient guide, readers have come up independently with extremely different readings of a troublesome word: at one point, one word was interpreted as "glimpses," "starlight," and "stonework." Thus, the two editors have spent an inordinate amount of time, magnifying glass in hand, puzzling over a doubtful passage, and some passages have been scrutinized by four different readers who were expert in deciphering Wolfe's hand. There are, no doubt, some misreadings, but we have striven beyond reasonable expectations in order to avoid them.

In developing this edition we have been aided by many generous-hearted people, and it is a pleasure to acknowledge their help publicly: W. H. Bond, director of the Houghton Library at Harvard, where the Wisdom Collection is housed; Miss Carolyn Jakeman and her capable staff in the Houghton Library Reading Room; Miss Myra Champion of the Pack Memorial Library, Asheville, North Carolina; Miss Eleanor Devlin and her staff of the Temple University Library; and Porter Kellam, John W. Bonner, Jr., Mrs. Christine Burroughs, and Mrs. Vivian Phillips of the University of Georgia Library.

Mr. Fred W. Wolfe answered many questions about the Wolfe

family; Mr. William Wisdom was a helpful guide in reading Wolfe's smudged pages about New Orleans; Herman Gundersheimer, professor of art history at Temple University and former director of the Rothschild Museum in Frankfurt, Germany, was an invaluable consultant about Wolfe's German references and his visits to European museums; C. DeWitt Eldridge, professor of French at Temple University, has aided us in reading Wolfe's French references and in guiding our understanding of Wolfe's European travels, especially in Paris. Professor Walter Grossman of the University of Massachusetts, Boston, also helped us greatly with the European sections, especially those relating to Austria. For specific information we are indebted to Professors Nicholas A. Beadles, Calvin S. Brown, J. Woodrow Hassell, Jr., Rayburn S. Moore, and the late Edd Winfield Parks of the University of Georgia; Harry C. Rutledge of the University of Tennessee; Erika W. Davis and Wolfgang Freitag of Harvard University; Klaus Lanzinger of the University of Innsbruck; and Hans Helmcke of the University of Mainz.

We are grateful to Paul Gitlin, administrator of the estate of Thomas Wolfe, for permission to publish the Wolfe notebooks and for his encouragement of the project from the start. We especially appreciate the manuscript reading and legal advice of Melville Cane, who was Thomas Wolfe's lawyer and a long-time friend of the Bernstein family. We wish to express special thanks to Richard Walser of North Carolina State University for his painstaking scrutiny of the manuscript, and to Andrew Turnbull for answering a number of questions about Wolfe's acquaintances.

The editors owe a special debt of gratitude to their universities for the encouragement and support of this project over a five-year period. Both institutions were generous in financial aid for typing and photographing and for travel expenses. In addition, Temple University provided a summer research grant and a one-semester study leave, and the University of Georgia provided three summer research grants and a reduced teaching load to assist the editors in carrying out the task. We wish to direct special thanks for this help to Deans Rhoten Smith and George Johnson, Professors William Rossky and Jacob Gruber of Temple University and to Deans John O. Eidson and Robert A. McRorie, and Professor Robert H. West of the University of Georgia. The University of Georgia also provided the able services of Leon Austin Wilson and Mrs. Vicky J. Statham as research assistants for part of the project.

In preparing the manuscript, we have had help from many hands and our thanks are certainly due to Mrs. Rosemary Maher and Miss

Carla Anderson for their skill and perception in transcribing from Wolfe's manuscript and for their patience in preparing the final typescript. To the members of the staff of The University of North Carolina Press we are deeply indebted for aid and concern that extended over many months. Finally, we wish to thank Professor C. Hugh Holman, who acted as a consultant throughout the project, and to express our regret that his activities were so demanding that he was unable to be one of the editors of this work.

RICHARD S. KENNEDY

PASCHAL REEVES

# *Abbreviations*

| | |
|---|---|
| FDTM | *From Death to Morning* (New York, 1935). |
| HB | *The Hills Beyond* (New York, 1941). |
| *Letters* | *The Letters of Thomas Wolfe*, ed. Elizabeth Nowell (New York, 1956). |
| LHA | *Look Homeward, Angel* (New York, 1929). |
| LTM | *The Letters of Thomas Wolfe to His Mother*, ed. C. Hugh Holman and Sue Fields Ross (Chapel Hill, 1968). |
| OT&R | *Of Time and the River* (New York, 1935). |
| PN | Pocket Notebook. There are thirty-five pocket notebooks, HCL*46AM-7(69), in the Wisdom Collection at Harvard. |
| SN | *The Story of a Novel* (New York, 1936). |
| *Short Novels* | *The Short Novels of Thomas Wolfe*, ed. C. Hugh Holman (New York, 1961). |
| W&R | *The Web and the Rock* (New York, 1939). |
| YCGHA | *You Can't Go Home Again* (New York, 1940). |

# *Contents*

## *Volume I*



## *Volume II*

# *Introduction*

Thomas Wolfe first became acquainted with the notebooks of a literary man in 1920 during his study under John Livingston Lowes at Harvard. Professor Lowes and his seminar students were giving close attention to Coleridge's 1795–98 notebook and studying the way in which Coleridge's reading fused in his imagination to re-emerge in the images of "Kubla Khan" and "The Ancient Mariner." In fact, Wolfe tried at this time to imitate Coleridge's practice: he began to read widely and haphazardly in the Harvard Library in the hope that a full reservoir of images and the activity of some "unconscious cerebration" would help him to become a great literary artist. But despite his identification with Coleridge he did not begin keeping a notebook—probably because he was a very unsystematic person.

Not until 1926, when he set down, in a series of short phrases, the memories of his childhood and youth, did he begin to collect notes in a single place. He filled two writing tablets full of a working outline for an autobiographical novel and then began to make narrative entries in several large accounting ledgers that Aline Bernstein had bought him. She felt that this was the only way she could prevent him from losing track of what he wrote.[1] It was in this way that Wolfe began to accumulate the story of Eugene Gant and his family that became *Look Homeward, Angel.*

At the same time, Wolfe began carrying small pocket notebooks

1. Miss Nowell has published Wolfe's application for a Guggenheim Fellowship in *Letters*, pp. 210–12, but Wolfe had scratched out some parts of his statement that reveal how disorderly his writing habits had been before he discovered notebooks and ledgers. The following sentences are in paragraph four; the italicized portions are those that Wolfe deleted: "I was quite unhappy about my writing—nothing I did ever saw the light of day: I wrote at random, but all the time; *I wrote on loose sheets of paper, and lost, or got hopelessly confused what I had written.* When I had finished something, a powerful inertia settled upon me—I would not show what I had written to anyone, I would not send it out for publication, I did not know what to do, or how to go about it. *I mention the loose sheets on which I wrote because one of the most important events in my life as a writer came when I began to write, at the suggestion of a friend, in big bound ledgers. The discovery gave me joy and hope: I could no longer lose the pages, because they were bound together.*"

in which to jot random ideas and observations as well as to set down drafts of material when he was away from his accounting ledgers. From that year until the time of his death, Wolfe carried pocket notebooks. They are not like Coleridge's, though parts of them resemble Coleridge's very much. Nor are they diaries, or journals for recording daily thoughts, or commonplace books for recording the thoughts of others. They are the informal records of a literary career, mixed in with the jottings of a man talking to himself and frequently interspersed with evidences of daily living. To be specific, the notebooks are a jumble (in the way that life is a jumble and that the human memory is a jumble) of literary ideas, outlines of literary projects, character sketches, first drafts of passages that later turn up in published work, observations jotted down while traveling, diary passages, first drafts of letters (some of which he never mailed), opinions on social questions (politics, religion, race, etc.), meditations and generalizations about his own life and about human behavior, opinions on contemporary literary figures, notes on books that he read, records of dreams, records of conversations overheard in restaurants or bars, notes on telephone conversations, lists (of mountains seen, rivers crossed, states and countries visited, women he slept with, books read, restaurants dined in, people met), jottings in which he is using his notebook as a way of arguing with himself, lists of books to buy, grocery lists, laundry lists, telephone numbers, American Express check numbers, assignments for his New York University students, and so on. In other words, the notebooks reflect the experience both trivial and valuable of a writer's life. Further, they show Wolfe in a variety of moods: he is sometimes exuberant, other times in despair; he is often as good-humored as Falstaff but soon after as mean-spirited as Jason Compson.

At times, especially when Wolfe was traveling, the notebooks are very full. Again, perhaps during some extraordinarily creative period, the notebooks contain very few entries. The editors have tried to deal with this unevenness by drawing on other and similar materials available in scattered fashion among Wolfe's manuscripts. The big accounting ledgers that he filled with unfinished works such as "The October Fair," "The Good Child's River," and "The Hound of Darkness" were especially useful for showing his literary activities. Unpublished letters and other miscellaneous jottings and fragments served to reflect his personal concerns. Since some loose sheets of notes went back as far as Wolfe's days at Harvard, it was possible to collect representative materials that reveal Wolfe's thoughts and tendencies as early as his twentieth year. In the end, we have been able to put together materials that provide an unusual acquaintance with the inner life of a major American writer and a fascinating glimpse of the artist in his workshop.

The notebooks and supplementary materials give us as close a look as possible at the creative process that transformed Wolfe's experience into fiction. We see, for example, in Pocket Notebook 13 that a few notes recording a scene in a speak-easy can become a satiric rendering of the Americans who patronize later immigrant groups. Or we can see in Pocket Notebook 11 the account of a train race outside Elizabeth, New Jersey, which Wolfe developed into an episode for "K 19" and later reworked into "The Train and the City." The literary raw materials range from the account of a man's death in a subway, part of which went verbatim into "Death the Proud Brother," all the way to remote words or references that can scarcely be recognized as the origin of a particular scene or passage in one of his fictional works. Of greatest interest is the record of statements and outlines that allow us to trace the development of stories and major sections of Wolfe's work. At the same time, these notes and outlines tell us of the struggle that Wolfe had with the composition of book-length narrative. They show, too, the difficulties that the autobiographical method created for him in ever-expanding, ever-detailed proliferation of material.

These notebooks, while full of details about Wolfe's personal life that are already known, also contain a number of new crisis documents and unusual psychic reflectors. One finds, for example, among the Harvard notes Wolfe's covenant with God written on the approach of his twenty-first birthday and in Pocket Notebook 11 his anguished recognition that he has lost his connection with home and family and that he belongs nowhere and to no one. Indeed, Wolfe tries to be so open and honest with himself that reading his notebooks is like a plunge into his psyche, and as a result we find them chaotic, puzzling, amoral. He lays bare his guilts, anxieties, hostilities, obsessions, his sexual selfishness, his self-aggrandizement, his self-pity. He reveals the spiritual meagerness of his sex life and the ultimate fear of women which prevents his forming any lasting relationships. Because his liason with Mrs. Bernstein was the one experience with love that meant the most to him and since it caused, at the same time, his deepest emotional distress, we have added a number of excerpts from the unpublished correspondence, and we have provided more commentary than usual on their intermittent association. It is a painful situation to become acquainted with, and Wolfe's treatment of her is reprehensible. But only by a full and frank presentation of the material can this all-important portion of Wolfe's life be understood in all its intensity. It was for him a second Oedipal ordeal.

These introductory remarks have, so far, been pointing out the ways in which the notebooks reflect Wolfe's life and literary work in areas in which one might expect to find illustration. But there are other areas in which the notes illuminate characteristic features of Wolfe's work in surprising ways. Wolfe is not an ordinary novelist. His work is largely autobiographical fiction, narrative written in a highly elevated style about the adventures of a superhuman character named Eugene Gant or George Webber. It has always been difficult for critics to call these works novels, for each one is, to some extent, an encyclopedic assembly of literary phenomena—encyclopedic in the sense that Melville's *Moby Dick* is an encyclopedic prose work and Whitman's *Song of Myself* is an encyclopedic work in verse. Also Thomas Wolfe's writings have been regarded as having an "American" quality, just as we think of the work of Jean-Paul Sartre as distinctly French, or of John Galsworthy as distinctly British, or of J. M. Synge as distinctly Irish.

Wolfe's notebooks provide a new perspective on some of these features of his work. They show in great detail how an American artist, who was as naïvely self-conscious of his national identity as if he were a contemporary of George Bancroft or Daniel Webster, equipped himself to be a writer and strove to cope with what he conceived to be the problems of an American writer.

His national consciousness is continually expressed in his notebook. Sometimes it is as abrupt and enigmatic as his jotting "My name is Wolfe. I am an American." [2] When he is in Europe, he expresses his homesickness in physical terms, "A man belongs to his country as an arm belongs to its socket. Any permanent separation from it is an amputation," [3] and he devotes many pages to comparing the virtues of his own nation to one European country or another. Pocket Notebooks 3 to 9, kept during his European tour of 1928, are full of comparisons, some of them rather childish.

But in spite of the nationalistic chauvinism he sometimes expresses, his entries in his notebooks reveal a sense of cultural insecurity. The search for roots and for tradition is a common feature of American literary history. But Wolfe's concern, which is unusual for an American writer of his generation (i.e., one who was too young to be in World War I), shows a renewed, twentieth-century worry about being a representative American writer. He jots down what he calls "An Inquiry Into the State of My Culture" and considers what he

2. PN 3.
3. PN 8.

knows about the literatures of Greece, Rome, France, Germany, England, and America.[4] He is very much aware of the European foundation of American culture. When he draws up "A Library For a Young Man of Today," he begins with Plato and Herodotus and comes up to Joyce and Mann—but there is not one American work on the list.[5] On his many European journeys he gluts himself on museums and exhausts his energy prowling through the bookshops. Sometimes he recognizes that he is displaying a kind of cultural megalomania. In 1928, he scribbles, ". . . I am tired—the desire for it *All* comes from an evil gluttony in me—a weakness, a lack of belief." [6] But most of the time, he keeps up his compulsive search for cultural props as well as his pursuit of meaningful personal experiences. In fact, at the end of one of his European voyages he rededicates himself: "But deeper study always, sharper senses, profounder living: *Never* an end to curiosity! The fruit of all this comes later—I must think. I must mix it all with myself and with America. I have caught much of it on paper. But infinitely the greater part is in the wash of my brain and blood." [7]

Still these are only manifestations of national awareness and a sense of cultural responsibility. They do not indicate a conscious purpose of giving expression to American life. The dedication to this literary goal developed only after Wolfe's first novel was published. Reviewers of *Look Homeward, Angel* had praised it and declared that it was in the tradition of Melville and Whitman. That same year America's first Nobel Prize winner in literature, Sinclair Lewis, mentioned Wolfe's novel in his acceptance speech, pointing to it as evidence of the great promise of the American literature of the future. Wolfe felt a new responsibility: he had to live up to the best in the American literary tradition. This sense of purpose was something he had been gradually becoming conscious of, and at the end of a lecture at the Colorado Writers Conference in 1935 he put the situation in this way, giving voice at the same time to what he conceived to be the special problems of the American writer:

> The life of the artist at any epoch of man's history has not been an easy one. And here in America, it has often seemed to me, it well may be the hardest that man has ever known. . . . It seems to me that the task [of the

4. PN 5.
5. PN 5.
6. PN 5.
7. PN 8.

> artist] is one whose physical proportions are vaster and more difficult here than in any other nation on the earth. It is not merely that in the cultures of Europe and the Orient the American artist can find no antecedent scheme, no structural plan, no body of tradition that can give his own work the validity and truth that it must have. It is not merely that he must make somehow a new tradition for himself, derived from his own life and from the enormous space and energy of American life . . . it is even more than this: that the labor of a complete and whole articulation, the discovery of an entire universe and of a complete language, is the task that lies before him.
>
> Such is the nature of the struggle to which henceforth our lives must be devoted. Out of the billion forms of America; out of the savage violence and the dense complexity of all its swarming life; from the unique and single substance of this land and life of ours, must we draw the power and energy of our own life, the articulation of our speech, the substance of our art.

Since Wolfe saw multiplicity and diversity of experience as an American problem and since he wanted to be an American spokesman, he set himself to capture and subdue the multiplicity and diversity of American life.

Already he felt he represented some of this diversity in his own background and experience. His mother's people were Southerners long established in North Carolina; his father was a Northerner from Pennsylvania. Forebears on each side had shed blood in the Civil War. He was a Southerner, yet he came from the mountain area of western North Carolina, which was characteristic of another whole region. He had the small town experience of Asheville, North Carolina, but he spent his adult life in Boston and New York. The examples accumulate easily.

But it is in his notebooks that his sense of the multiplicity and diversity of American life appears in staggering evidence, for Wolfe had gradually begun to look upon his note-taking as his own kind of research method. Some of it reflects research in books, documents, records, some of it is deep-sea diving into his memory, and some of it is field research (observations of human behavior that he meets in his travels, records of conversations he had with various people, and so on). But to give it such a description is to over-intellectualize and perhaps falsify this activity. What he is actually trying to do has varying purposes but all intended to help him in writing his books. What he is doing, for the most part, is attempting to set down fleeting words or impressions that come to his ear or eye as he roams about, or to reel in elusive memories that swim up, or to sort out a jumble of facts that are jostling each other in his mind.

Pages and pages of his notebooks record conversations that he overheard at lunch counters or in bars—the talk of businessmen, salesmen, college boys, office workers, vaudeville performers, construction workers, taxi drivers, policemen, waiters. At any point in a notebook one can come on an entry like this:

> I saw your friend last night.
> Who's that?
> Joe Kelly.
> That bastard's no friend of mine.
> I t'ought you and him was friends.
> Naw—we uster be.[8]

Sometimes they are long conversations, sometimes only single statements that someone has dropped. At times, he only jots down typical phrases and omits the subject matter of the conversation: "I checked them off . . . I didn't like it a bit, see . . . an' I said. . . . It's impossible that I didn't . . . when I *knew* it. He threw it up to me in such a sarcastic way, you know . . . well, I *undoubtedly* will find out. Leave it, just leave it, leave it." [9] What he is after are the authentic evidences of American language and American speech patterns. Working with notes like these, Wolfe is later able to produce genuine American idiom for such pieces as the "Only the Dead Know Brooklyn" or "The Voice of the City" passages in *Of Time and the River.*

In the same way he catches the city scene and the great variety of its actors by setting down notes of a particular occasion. One night on a subway going to Brooklyn at 3 A.M., he describes all the passengers.[10] Another time he records all the people who came into a diner while he was there.[11] Frequently he will list all the shops and places of business along a street or all the people he passes on the way from his apartment to the subway. More often, he describes scenes when he is on his travels. They are usually unimportant scenes but are characteristic of the place whether it be Amsterdam or Budapest,

8. PN 20.
9. PN 13.
10. PN 22.
11. PN 21.

Boston or Yellowstone National Park. Most of them were set down during his European jaunts but a large accumulation of them make up the last notebook, The Western Journal.

Sometimes, he turns to written sources. He looks over newspapers. He is not interested in the principal events in the news; he is interested in the whole social scene. "If a man who lived a solitary life in some primitive place," he asks, "but who nevertheless spoke and read English easily, must form his entire opinion of the modern world . . . from reading daily *The Times* newspaper or *The Telegraph*—What sort of picture would he get?" [12]

When he jots down notes, they cover a great range of items. One set from the *New York Times*, May 2, 1928, contains a record of the weather and the temperature, notes on how May Day was observed by the workers of the world, notes about some bloodshed in Poland over the May Day celebration, about Al Smith's victory in a California primary election, about Macy's department store advertisements, about advertisements for razor blades and Squibbs shaving cream, about the circulation figures for *Delineator* magazine, from the sports page about Babe Ruth, something about Coolidge going to the circus to scrutinize a sea elephant.[13]

Then, of course, there are the lists and tabulations that are abbreviations of his experience. At times this listing seems a kind of lonely man's game or a ritualistic conjuring up of the past, as when he sets down the names of people he knows best, or people he has met on board ship on a particular voyage, or when he scribbles out the names of cities in Central Europe that he has visited, or lists of the states of the United States he has entered. These lists are barren of comment. But at other times he will have some notations that give us a clue as to what he is trying to do. One list of various family groups he knows is headed "The Way Men Live," and he has noted their sources of income, whether they are on relief or not, and a few phrases. For example, one family is described as "a pale sunless stricken lot—no sun, no air, no light in their lives—they look as if they have always lived in basements;" another, "A good family gone to seed." [14] At times his lists are clearly arranged for literary use. He set down the deaths he had witnessed in New York and later developed the notes into "Death the Proud Brother." [15] He searched his memory for incidents that could be accumulated for George Webber's mental parade during a fit of insane jealousy, and he put them down under the heading "Shame." [16]

12. PN 6.
13. PN 19.
14. PN 26.
15. PN 18.
16. PN 18.

In summary, one might say that notes like these indicate the means by which Wolfe made his work superior to the usual autobiographical fiction. He selected among the details and illustrations of the life peripheral to his own and arranged them to convey the tone, the color, the richness of the American experience. The adventures of his central character are seen as only a part of a larger life. The experience becomes, then, not personal but national, and the literary mode becomes epic.

But Wolfe wanted also to reach back into the past to display the same kind of living social organism in the 1870's and 1880's. He wanted to create a milieu for Esther Jack and her father, Joe Linder, the characters based on Aline Bernstein and her father, Joseph Frankau, who was an actor on the New York stage in the late nineteenth century. Although Wolfe did not have his own experience to fall back on, he employed the same method. But he now had to depend on written records and photographs. The pocket notebooks reveal that Wolfe looked up in the old city directories the addresses of Joseph Frankau and Theodore Bernstein. He then went out to take a look at these houses and apartments, and he checked old photographs of Times Square and Herald Square at the New York Public Library. The notebooks show that he read through a biography of Steele MacKaye because Joseph Frankau's best role was in MacKaye's *Hazel Kirke.* He thumbed through old copies of *Life* and *Leslie's.* He went through old issues of the *New York Times* taking notes that show the same kind of wide-spread interest with which he read the newspapers of the 1930's.[17]

But there was another kind of American problem that he had to deal with successfully if he were to reflect the national life. There was another sort of multiplicity and diversity: the immense variety of human kind that make up the American nation, a diversity in national origin and religious difference as well as some wide cleavages of class and caste. In this area of the American experience Wolfe failed to qualify as the epic spokesman because he lacked the wide embrace of a Whitman. The notebooks confirm and strengthen the evidence already present in Wolfe's fiction that he was, for most of his career, narrow and intolerant of human diversity, fearful and suspicious of the stranger or the representative of the minority group.[18]

The attitude he expresses toward the Jews is often offensive. Nor was this merely a neurotic by-product of his troubled love affair

17. PN 16.

18. For a full discussion see Paschal Reeves, *Thomas Wolfe's Albatross: Race and Nationality in America* (Athens: The University of Georgia Press, 1969).

with Mrs. Bernstein or a resentful outcome of the rejection of his plays by her friends in the New York theatre. We have included a fragment we discovered among his scribblings at Harvard which exhibits anti-Semitic folklore about the Jews' love of money, long before he ever encountered Mrs. Bernstein. The sensitive reader will be even more distressed, however, at an anti-Jewish coloration throughout his association with Mrs. Bernstein. His pet name for her was "my Jew," but even the term of endearment indicates his consciousness of her as strange, different, other. More often, the notebook entries merely refer to her as "the Jew," and references to her family or her friends often identify them as Jewish in a depreciatory tone. After his break with her, he occasionally takes anti-Semitic postures to help ward her off. It is not until late in his career and his second trip to Hitler's Germany that he finally recognized the inhuman dangers of this form of group prejudice.

In addition to this, he displays other traits of the "nativism" that characterize late nineteenth- and early twentieth-century American life, especially urban life. His notebooks are full of identifications of Americans as belonging to national or racial groups. A person is an Irishman or a Swede or a Dutchman and so on. Often, the references to these groups are slighting or even contemptuous. He is aware, too, that this is the American mixture: when he sailed into New York harbor in 1928 on a ship that carried many immigrants, we find this observation, "This boat too is America—this swarthy stew of Italians, Greeks, and God knows what other combinations." [19] And a Negro is usually dismissed as a "nigger." It is clear that Wolfe found it harder to adapt to the human diversity in his country than to other kinds of variety in the American scene, and this troubles the epic presentation that he attempted. The mid-century reader can look at the incongruous panorama that he created from the "billion forms of America" in a work like *Of Time and the River,* and he can perceive with pleasure authentic, orderly units. But all too often he comes upon offensive social attitudes that mar these impressions, for Thomas Wolfe here reflects a limited America, a white middle-class America with ethnic suspicions and hostilities. Such attitudes disturb the epic tone, which cannot admit littleness of mind.

One can see a source of these limitations in Wolfe's neurotic fears and instabilities, which are manifest throughout the notebooks. Or one can point to Wolfe's background in the largely homogeneous population of western North Carolina in order to account for his

19. PN 8.

patronizing or scornful attitudes toward the ethnic minorities in the Northern urban centers. But this does not make the xenophobic revelations any less unpleasant. What is of more salutary interest, however, is to consider that Wolfe went on to become an American literary spokesman in spite of these shortcomings. This was possible for two reasons. First of all, he consciously struggled to thrust aside his early-learned prejudices so that at the end of his brief career he could write a piece like "The Promise of America," which combined his feeling about the American earth and his faith in American social opportunity and included a vision of a Negro, a Jew, and a poor-white Southerner, each of them addressed as brother, achieving their success in American life.[20] Wolfe was on his way to overcoming his restrictive prejudices and accepting in human terms the deepest meaning of our motto "E Pluribus Unum."

A second reason lay in his becoming more socially conscious and more critical of American culture in the last three years of his life. This led to a more mature view of the American experience but one still envigorated by a powerful desire to give expression to the national spirit. The shift is perceptible in his accumulating plans to write about the activities of life in nighttime America. It is present, possibly as early as 1933, in notes and in his work on "Death the Proud Brother," but it becomes fully clear in 1935 in a project he referred to as "The Book of the Night." Later he called it "The Hound of Darkness" and he planned to show a whole series of scenes taking place all over America on the same night.

Wolfe's preoccupation with the idea of writing about American nighttime life went far beyond physical activity in the darkness. This was to be a dark view with all its implications—dark in the sense of exploring the unconscious of America or giving images that would suggest it; dark also in the sense of depicting the things that were wrong with America; or if not just to present the dark side of American life, at least to give expression to a view of the American experience that was real and complex enough to show a duality of good and evil, serenity and turbulence, beauty and ugliness.

It was in this way that Wolfe began to use the symbol of the American wound or hurt. It appeared for the first time in a draft he composed for his Colorado lecture on the importance of giving the truest picture of life: he spoke about the South as wounded and about readers in the South fearing his books because they laid bare the unpleasant truths. In Pocket Notebook 28, where we have included some

20. YCGHA, pp. 501–8.

excerpts from this material, one may see this metaphor change from that of a wounded South to that of a wounded America which the artist must try to depict: "We must not look alone on the overwhelming evidences of ugliness, savagery, violence, and injustice in the life around us, we must look straight into the ugliness in our own lives and spirits which created them. We must, in short, probe to the bottom of our dark and twisted wound; as men, as artists, as Americans, we can no longer cringe away and lie."

Although Wolfe did not use this passage in his lecture,[21] he did not forget the image of the wound. Since he wrote of it energetically but vaguely, it appears that he cannot really be sure of what he is talking about, but his manner suggests a sense of guilt. It could be personal; it could be regional and his identification with the South just makes it appear to be personal. But it could also be national and Wolfe's sense of identification with all of American life could make him express it with such personal intensity. It seems to be an anxious worry that American life has not worked out the way Wolfe felt it should, that the American Dream has not moved far enough toward reality. Some notes from the last year of his life imply this, as once again he speaks of the American wound:

> But so agreeing, that however bad or hidden our great hurt may be . . . let me ask you this: is it not true that we are all ashamed? Is it not true that there is in our hearts the knowledge of betrayal—vicious, cowardly betrayal—self-betrayal of ourselves, America's betrayal of her self? Is it not true that all of us are conscious in our hearts that there was hope of high and glorious fulfillment in America—and that that high and glorious fulfillment has not only never been achieved but that even the *promise* of that high and glorious fulfillment has been so aborted, corrupted, made dropsical with disease, that its ancient and primeval lineaments are no more to be seen? Is it not true that we were given here for the enrichment and improvement of man's life a golden wilderness, and that we have made of it a wilderness of horror, ugliness and confusion?"[22]

The time is, of course, the middle of the Great Depression, the time when the greatest doubts were raised about the future of the

21. But he used it in a dictated draft entitled "You Can't Go Home Again," which Aswell later revised and worked into YCGHA, Chapter 26, pp. 327–28.

22. Political and Social Notes 1937–1938.

political and economic system in the United States. But even so, the bleakness of the view and the revulsion displayed by Wolfe's language show a feeling running deeper than the usual political or economic criticism. It seems to be a genuine result of identification with the national life, something seldom found in the twentieth century, something more frequently encountered in the nineteenth-century writers. He can say, for instance, "We've got to *loathe* America, as we loathe ourselves; with loathing, horror, shame, and anguish of soul unspeakable—as well as with love—we've got to face the total horror of our self-betrayal, the way America has betrayed herself." [23]

Wolfe displays here an intense self-consciousness of the national life plus the tension that developed as he perceived the dualities of American life. This combination seems to be the source of the special vigor that he gave to the national theme the few times he touched on it in his later writing. Emotional tides like those reflected in the passages above run beneath his fictional treatment of these dilemmas. For example, his unpublished story "No More Rivers" shows his grappling with this dual vision. The story is about a man from Minnesota who was brought up near the Mississippi River and who is extremely conscious of his American identity. He now lives in an apartment in New York overlooking the East River. At one point in the story he looks out the window at the river and sees the morning light flashing on the sewage-filled river and the sun transforming the grimness of factories and warehouses on the opposite bank. He meditates on the paradox of beauty in ugliness, which he finds in American industrial cities. As he attempts to resolve the paradox he watches a tugboat pulling a barge loaded with freight cars. In his meditation the tug becomes an image of the ugliness and beauty of American life because it suggests grime, work, endurance, harbors, travel, the lights of the American coastline, and a place in a larger order of things. Then his attention shifts to the freight cars and their cracked, sun-baked, dull redness. He is moved by thoughts of their commonness, their constant availability for carrying out a task, their movement in all weathers, their presence in and out of every town in the land. They become for him the ultimate image of American life: "He had thundered past unending strings of them, lined up across the midlands of the country, and he had seen them for a fleeting instant, from the windows of a speeding train, curved back upon a spur of rusty track in lonely pine lands of the South, at red and waning sunset in the month of March, empty, open and deserted, yet curiously and indefinably thrilling, filled somehow

23. *Ibid.*

with all the wildness, loneliness, the promise of unknown joy, the message of enormous distance, that is America." [24]

This is for Wolfe the answer to present darkness, ugliness, doubt in American life—the idea of promise, potential, openness, readiness to move. It is a resolution that crops up in his later writings and especially in the posthumous book *You Can't Go Home Again.* This willingness to change, this look to the future rather than the past is the essence of liberalism. The fact that a basically conservative, tradition-prone man like Wolfe could adopt this position in his later career diminishes some of the misgivings one has about his view of the American people in *Of Time and the River.* This new attitude is clearly becoming a dominant one as he turns in his last year to develop the theme, "You Can't Go Home Again." As a result, he is able, in his latest writing, to restore the true epic tone when he manipulates idea and image to express the national theme in such pieces as "So Soon the Morning," [25] "Prologue to America," [26] and "The Promise of America." More than this, the notes and fragments from his last months allow us to see further evidences of the direction his mind was taking, and raw though the material may be, it affords us a glimpse of the achievement that might have been.

24. PN 30.

25. Wolfe prepared the piece with this title for Miss Nowell to sell to a periodical but it was unsold at the time of his death. Aswell worked some of it into W&R, pp. 471–75.

26. This cinematographic piece drawn from "The Hound of Darkness" was the last publication during Wolfe's lifetime. It appeared in *Vogue,* XCI (February, 1938), "Americana Number," 63–66, 150–53, 161.

## *A Chronology*

| | | |
|---|---|---|
| 1900 | Oct. 3 | Born in Asheville, N.C., at 92 Woodfin St. |
| 1904 | Spring | Went with his mother to St. Louis, Missouri, where she operated a boarding house, "The North Carolina," 5095 Fairmont Avenue, during the World's Fair. |
| | Nov. 16 | His brother Grover died in St. Louis. |
| 1906 | Aug. 30 | His mother bought the Old Kentucky Home, 48 Spruce St., Asheville. |
| | Sept. | Entered the Orange Street (public) School, Asheville. |
| 1912 | Sept. | Entered the North State Fitting School, a private school operated by Mr. and Mrs. J. M. Roberts. |
| 1913 | March | Went with his mother to Washington, D.C., to attend the inauguration of Woodrow Wilson. |
| 1916 | Sept. | Entered the University of North Carolina, Chapel Hill. |
| 1917 | June | Romance with Clara Paul. |
| | Nov. | First published creative effort, "A Field in Flanders," a poem in the University of North Carolina *Magazine*. |
| 1918 | March | First published fiction, "A Cullenden of Virginia," a story in the University of North Carolina *Magazine*. |
| | Summer | Civilian war work in Norfolk, Virginia. |
| | Fall | Enrolled in Professor Frederick H. Koch's course in playwriting. |
| | Oct. 19 | His brother Ben died in Asheville. |
| 1919 | March 14 & 15 | *The Return of Buck Gavin*, a one-act play, performed by the Carolina Playmakers with Wolfe in the title role. |
| | Spring | Won the Worth Prize in philosophy for his essay, *The Crisis in Industry*, which was published as a pamphlet by the University of North Carolina. |

| | | |
|---|---|---|
| | Fall | Editor-in-chief of *The Tar Heel*, University of North Carolina student newspaper. |
| | Dec. 12 & 13 | *The Third Night: A Mountain Play of the Supernatural* performed by the Carolina Playmakers. |
| 1920 | June | Received B.A. degree from University of North Carolina. |
| | | Declined teaching job at the Bingham School, a private preparatory school in Asheville. |
| | Sept. | Entered the Graduate School of Arts and Sciences, Harvard University, to work for M.A. degree in English and to study playwriting with George Pierce Baker. |
| 1921 | Jan. 25 | "The Mountains," a one-act play, given trial performance in the 47 Workshop Rehearsal Room. |
| | Oct. 21 & 22 | "The Mountains" produced by the 47 Workshop at Agassiz Theatre, Radcliffe College. |
| 1922 | June | Received M.A. degree from Harvard University. |
| | | Offered an instructorship in English at Northwestern University. |
| | June 20 | Returned to Asheville at the death of his father. |
| | Sept. | Went to Harvard to work with Baker another year. |
| 1923 | May 11 & 12 | *Welcome to Our City*, a ten-scene play, produced by the 47 Workshop, Agassiz Theatre. |
| | Aug. | Revised *Welcome to Our City* and submitted it to Theatre Guild. |
| | Fall | Remained in Asheville awaiting Guild's decision. |
| | Nov. | Went to New York and took temporary job soliciting contributions from University of North Carolina alumni. |
| | Dec. | *Welcome to Our City* rejected by the Theatre Guild. |
| 1924 | Feb. 6 | Began teaching English as an instructor in the Washington Square College of New York University. |
| | Oct. 25 | Sailed aboard the *Lancastria* on first trip to Europe. |
| | Nov. 5 | Landed in England. |
| | Dec. | Went to Paris. |
| | | Lost manuscript of his play, *Mannerhouse*. |
| 1925 | Jan. | Toured Paris with Kenneth Raisbeck, Marjorie Fairbanks, and Helen Harding. |

| | | |
|---|---|---|
| | March | Traveled alone in France. |
| | June | Traveled in Italy, Switzerland, and returned to England. |
| | Aug. | Sailed home aboard the *Olympic*. |
| | | Met Aline Bernstein. |
| | Aug. 26 | Landed in New York. |
| | Sept. | Resumed his teaching at New York University. |
| 1926 | Jan. | Submitted *Mannerhouse* to Neighborhood Playhouse. |
| | Spring | Vain attempts to sell *Welcome to Our City* and *Mannerhouse*. |
| | June 23 | Sailed aboard the *Berengaria* on second trip to Europe. |
| | July | In Paris began an autobiographical outline for a projected novel. |
| | | Traveled with Aline Bernstein in France and England. |
| | | Met James Joyce in London. |
| | Aug. | Settled in London and began work on the first version of *Look Homeward, Angel.* |
| | Sept. 13 | Went to Brussels for ten days. |
| | Fall | Continued work on the novel in London and Oxford. |
| | Dec. | First visit to Germany. |
| | | Sailed home aboard the *Majestic*. |
| | Dec. 28 | Arrived in New York. |
| 1927 | Jan. | Continued work on novel in New York. |
| | March | Went to Boston and brought back his copy of *Ulysses*. |
| | June | Wrote at Olin Dows's home, Foxhollow Farm, Rhinebeck, New York. |
| | July 12 | Sailed aboard the *George Washington* on third trip to Europe. |
| | | Traveled with Aline Bernstein in France, Germany, Austria, Czechoslovakia, and Switzerland. |
| | Sept. | Sailed home aboard the *Belgenland.* |
| | Sept. 18 | Arrived in New York. |
| | | Resumed his teaching at New York University and continued working on novel. |
| 1928 | March | Completed the manuscript of the novel, then called "O Lost." |

| | | |
|---|---|---|
| | May | Began work on a new novel, "The River People." |
| | | "O Lost" rejected by Boni and Liveright. |
| | May 20 | Madeleine Boyd became his agent. |
| | | "O Lost" rejected by Covici-Friede, and Longmans, Green and Company. |
| | June 30 | Sailed aboard the *Rotterdam* on fourth trip to Europe. |
| | July 9 | Landed at Boulogne. |
| | Summer | Aimlessly wandered in France, Belgium, and Germany and continued work on "The River People." |
| | Sept. 30 | Injured in a fight at the Oktoberfest in Munich and was hospitalized. |
| | Oct. | Released from the hospital and visited Oberammergau. |
| | Oct. 19 | Arrived in Vienna and continued work on "The River People." |
| | Nov. 2 | Arrived in Budapest. |
| | Nov. 16 | Returned to Vienna where he found a letter from Maxwell Perkins of Scribner's expressing interest in "O Lost." |
| | Dec. | Traveled in Italy. |
| | Dec. 21 | Sailed home from Naples aboard the *Vulcania.* |
| | Dec. 31 | Arrived in New York. |
| 1929 | Jan. 2 | First meeting with Maxwell Perkins. |
| | Jan. 7 | Scribner's agreed to publish "O Lost." Began revising the manuscript. |
| | Feb. 5 | Resumed part-time teaching at New York University for the spring term. |
| | April | Changed the title from "O Lost" to *Look Homeward, Angel.* |
| | Summer | Corrected proofs of the book in Maine and Canada. |
| | August | "An Angel on the Porch" published in *Scribner's Magazine.* |
| | | Began making notes for "The October Fair." |
| | Sept. 7 | Visited Asheville. |
| | Sept. 24 | Resumed full-time teaching at New York University. |
| | Oct. 18 | *Look Homeward, Angel* published. |
| | Dec. | Applied for a Guggenheim Fellowship. |
| 1930 | Jan. | Resigned from New York University. |

| | | |
|---|---|---|
| | | Met A. S. Frere-Reeves, editor of William Heinemann Ltd., in New York. |
| | | Continued making notes for "The October Fair." |
| | March | Awarded John Simon Guggenheim Memorial Fellowship. |
| | April | Increased tension with Aline Bernstein. |
| | May 9 | Sailed aboard the *Volendam* on fifth trip to Europe. |
| | May 19 | Arrived in Paris. |
| | June 6 | Began writing "The October Fair." |
| | June 29 | Met Scott Fitzgerald in Paris. |
| | July 14 | *Look Homeward, Angel* published in London by Heinemann. |
| | Summer | Traveled in Switzerland, France, and Germany. |
| | Oct. | Settled in a flat at 75 Ebury St., London. |
| | Fall | Maintained steady regime of writing. |
| | Dec. 12 | Praised by Sinclair Lewis in his Nobel Prize Acceptance Speech, Stockholm. |
| 1931 | Feb. | Met Sinclair Lewis in London. |
| | | Visited Holland. |
| | Feb. 26 | Sailed home aboard the *Europa.* |
| | March 4 | Arrived in New York. |
| | March 11 | Began living in Brooklyn. |
| | March | Aline Bernstein hospitalized for dizziness and fainting spells. |
| | Spring & Summer | Worked on "The Good Child's River." |
| | Fall | Wrote steadily on assorted projects. |
| | Dec. | Rewrote "Uncle Emerson" material as a short novel, "A Portrait of Bascom Hawke." |
| 1932 | | *Look Homeward, Angel* published in Germany by Rowohlt and in Sweden by Albert Bonnier. |
| | Jan. | His mother visited him in New York. |
| | | Broke with Aline Bernstein. |
| | | Began writing "The Web of Earth." |
| | April | "A Portrait of Bascom Hawke" published in *Scribner's Magazine* and tied for $5,000 Short Novel Prize. |
| | Spring | Worked on "K 19" and "Death the Proud Brother." |
| | July | "The Web of Earth" published in *Scribner's Magazine.* |

| | | |
|---|---|---|
| | Summer | Perkins rejected "K 19." |
| | | Worked on "A Vision of Death in April." |
| | Sept. | Spent Labor Day weekend in Montreal. |
| | Oct. 20 | Visited Bermuda briefly. |
| | Fall & Winter | Worked on material that eventually went into "The Party at Jack's." |
| 1933 | Feb. | Finished "No Door," a short novel. |
| | March | Attended the inauguration of Franklin D. Roosevelt. |
| | April | Delivered a long portion of his manuscript to Perkins and changed the title of his book from "The October Fair" to "Time and the River." |
| | May | "The Train and the City" published in *Scribner's Magazine.* |
| | | Wrote the discourse on loneliness that was eventually printed as "God's Lonely Man." |
| | | Signed a contract for "Time and the River" that called for fall publication. |
| | June | "Death the Proud Brother" published in *Scribner's Magazine.* |
| | July | "No Door" published in *Scribner's Magazine.* |
| | Fall | Wrote feverishly filling narrative gaps in his huge manuscript and expanding various episodes. |
| | Dec. 14 | Delivered an incomplete manuscript to Perkins and asked for his advice. |
| | Dec. | Perkins persuaded Wolfe to postpone the love story and concentrate on the first portion. |
| 1934 | Jan. | Began working with Perkins on the revision of the manuscript. |
| | | *Look Homeward, Angel* published in Modern Library edition. |
| | | Elizabeth Nowell became his agent for magazine pieces. |
| | Feb. | "The Four Lost Men" published in *Scribner's Magazine.* |
| | May | "Boom Town" published in *American Mercury.* |
| | | "The Sun and the Rain" published in *Scribner's Magazine.* |
| | Summer | Aline Bernstein attempted suicide with an overdose of sleeping pills at her summer home, Armonk, N.Y. |

| | | |
|---|---|---|
| | August | "The House of the Far and the Lost," published in *Scribner's Magazine.* |
| | Sept. | Visited the World's Fair in Chicago, and the last portion of the manuscript was sent to the printer in his absence. |
| | Nov. | "Dark in the Forest, Strange as Time," published in *Scribner's Magazine.* |
| | Dec. | "The Names of the Nation" published in *Modern Monthly.* |
| | | Added new materials to the concluding parts of his book. |
| 1935 | | *Look Homeward, Angel* published in Norway by Steenske. |
| | Jan. | "For Professional Appearance" published in *Modern Monthly.* |
| | | "One of the Girls in Our Party" published in *Scribner's Magazine.* |
| | | Made first outline of "The Book of the Night" ("The Hound of Darkness"). |
| | March | "Circus at Dawn" published in *Modern Monthly.* |
| | March 2 | Sailed aboard the *Ile de France* on sixth trip to Europe. |
| | March 8 | *Of Time and the River* published by Scribner's. Arrived in Paris. |
| | March 14 | Received reassuring cablegram from Perkins about reviews. |
| | March 24 | Arrived in London and took flat at 26 Hanover Square. |
| | April | "His Father's Earth" published in *Modern Monthly.* |
| | | "Old Catawba" published in *Virginia Quarterly Review.* |
| | April 23 | Left London and toured Norfolk and Suffolk. |
| | April 29 | Left England and visited Holland en route to Berlin. |
| | May 7 | Arrived in Berlin, where he was lionized. |
| | May 26 | Learned of Madeleine Boyd's impending lawsuit. |
| | June | "The Face of War" published in *Modern Monthly.* |
| | | "Polyphemus" published in *North American Review.* |
| | | "In the Park" published in *Harper's Bazaar.* |

| | | |
|---|---|---|
| | | "Gulliver" published in *Scribner's Magazine.* |
| | | "Arnold Pentland" published in *Esquire.* |
| | June 11 | "Only the Dead Know Brooklyn" published in *New Yorker.* |
| | June 16 | Went to Denmark. |
| | June 27 | Sailed home aboard the *Bremen.* |
| | July 4 | Arrived in New York. |
| | July | "Cottage by the Tracks" published in *Cosmopolitan.* |
| | July 22 to Aug. 7 | Participated in the Writers' Conference at Boulder, Colorado. |
| | Aug. 19 | *Of Time and the River* published in London by Heinemann. |
| | Aug. & Sept. | Toured the West. |
| | Oct. | "The Bums at Sunset" published in *Vanity Fair.* |
| | | Worked on "The Hound of Darkness." |
| | Nov. 14 | *From Death to Morning* published by Scribner's. |
| | Dec. | "The Story of a Novel" serialized in *Saturday Review of Literature*, issues of the 14th, 21st, and 28th. |
| 1936 | | *Of Time and the River* published in Germany by Rowohlt. |
| | March | Began "The Vision of Spangler's Paul." |
| | March 16 | *From Death to Morning* published in London by Heinemann. |
| | April 21 | *The Story of a Novel* published by Scribner's. |
| | | The rift with Scribner's began. |
| | April 25 | Bernard DeVoto's attack, "Genius Is Not Enough," published in *Saturday Review of Literature.* |
| | May 6 | *Look Homeward, Angel* published in Czechoslovakia by Evropsky Literarni Klub. |
| | May | Wrote character sketches of "James Rodney and Company." |
| | June | Worked on the character Nebraska Crane. |
| | | Took trip to Chicago. |
| | July | Began to consider changing publishers. |
| | July 23 | Sailed aboard the *Europa* on seventh trip to Europe. |
| | Aug. | Attended Olympic Games in Berlin. |
| | | Visited Austria with Thea Voelcker. |

| | | |
|---|---|---|
| | | "The Bell Remembered" published in *American Mercury.* |
| | Sept. 8 | Left Berlin by train for Paris. |
| | | Witnessed the arrest of a fellow passenger at Aachen. |
| | | Began writing "I Have a Thing to Tell You." |
| | Sept. 17 | Sailed home aboard the *Paris.* |
| | Sept. 24 | Arrived in New York. |
| | | Began quarreling with Perkins. |
| | Oct. | "Fame and the Poet" published in *American Mercury.* |
| | Fall | Began dictating his material to a secretary. |
| | | Wrote three versions of "I Have a Thing to Tell You," "The Child by Tiger," the bulk of the State College material, the account of the Southerners in New York, the Oktoberfest material, and his protagonist's European travels. |
| | Nov. 9 | *The Story of a Novel* published in London by Heinemann. |
| | Nov. | Libel suit brought against Wolfe and Scribner's by the Dorman family over "No Door." |
| | Dec. 26 | Left New York on trip to New Orleans, where he met William B. Wisdom. |
| 1937 | | *From Death to Morning* published in Germany by Rowohlt. |
| | Jan. | Mailed letter from New Orleans severing his relations with Scribner's. |
| | Jan. 25 | Arrived in New York after brief stopover in Chapel Hill. |
| | Feb. 7 | Dorman libel suit settled out of court. |
| | March | "I Have a Thing to Tell You" serialized in *New Republic*, issues of 10th, 17th, and 24th. |
| | Spring | Began a new book, "The Life and Times of Joseph Doaks." |
| | May | First visit to Asheville since the publication of *Look Homeward, Angel.* |
| | | Wrote "Chickamauga" and continued working on Doaks material. |
| | May 29 | "Mr. Malone" published in *New Yorker.* |
| | June | "Oktoberfest" published in *Scribner's Magazine.* |
| | July 17 | " 'E: A Recollection" published in *New Yorker.* |
| | Summer | Returned to North Carolina and rented cabin at |

| | | |
|---|---|---|
| | | Oteen, near Asheville. Worked on "The Party at Jack's." |
| | Sept. 2 | Left Asheville and returned to New York. |
| | Sept. 11 | "The Child by Tiger" published in *Saturday Evening Post.* |
| | Sept. | "April, Late April" published in *American Mercury.* |
| | | His break with Scribner's became public knowledge. |
| | Oct. | Searched for a new publisher. |
| | | "Katamoto" published in *Harper's Bazaar.* |
| | Nov. | "The Lost Boy" published in *Redbook Magazine.* |
| | Dec. | Selected Harper & Brothers as his new publisher. |
| | | "Chickamauga" published in *Yale Review.* |
| 1938 | Jan. 11 | "The Company" published in *New Masses.* |
| | Jan. | Wrote about Asheville scandals in the failure of its main bank in 1930. |
| | Feb. 8 | Won lawsuit against Murdach Dooher to recover his manuscripts. Saw Perkins for the last time. |
| | Feb. 14 | Wrote a long but incomplete synopsis of the "Doaks" book for Edward C. Aswell, his new editor. |
| | Feb. | "A Prologue to America" published in *Vogue.* |
| | March | Changed mind about new book and decided on a life-long autobiographical chronicle with George Webber as the protagonist. |
| | April 2 | His letter to *Nation* published, in which he opposed American isolationism. |
| | May 17 | Delivered his enormous manuscript to Aswell. |
| | May 19 | Lecture at Purdue University: "Writing and Living." |
| | June | Made tour of the western National Parks. |
| | July 3 | Became ill in Vancouver. |
| | July | Hospitalized in Seattle. |
| | Aug. 12 | Wrote last letter, a note to Maxwell Perkins. |
| | Sept. 12 | Operated on at Johns Hopkins Hospital. |
| | Sept. 15 | Died in Baltimore. |

# *PART ONE~*

# *THE LONG APPRENTICESHIP*

## *Notes from the Harvard Years*

## *1920–1923*

*Thomas Wolfe left the South for the first time when he was nineteen years old. He had been born October 3, 1900, and brought up in Asheville, North Carolina, a small city beautifully situated in the southern Appalachians. He was the youngest of the eight children of Julia Elizabeth Westall and William Oliver Wolfe, a prosperous mason and stonecutter who owned a monument shop in the central square of the city. Mrs. Wolfe owned and operated the "Old Kentucky Home" boarding house from the time Thomas was six years old. Because she lived separately from her husband most of the time after she began her business venture, the Wolfe children lived a divided existence between the family home and the boarding house.*

*After attending the North State Fitting School, young Thomas went to the University of North Carolina at Chapel Hill. Though he was not yet sixteen years old, he was well prepared in English and Latin and had some training in Greek and German. At Chapel Hill he concentrated in classics and in English literature, but he expended much of his energy in a lively campus life as a debater, as editor of the campus newspaper, and as a member of Professor Frederick Koch's Carolina Playmakers. Although he was too young to serve in World War I, he brushed against the wartime activity one summer when he worked at Langley Field near Norfolk.*

*He began graduate study at Harvard in September, 1920, and earned a Master's degree in English, with seminars in Renaissance literature and in the Romantic poets, but his principal interest was in Professor George Pierce Baker's English 47, a workshop for practice in play-writing. Wolfe was enrolled in the workshop for three years, 1920 to 1923, during which time he developed a genuine talent for literary expression and determined to become a professional writer. After his play* Welcome to Our City *was produced by the 47 Workshop Players in May, 1923, he left Harvard in hopes that the Theatre Guild would give his play a New York production.*

*At Harvard, Wolfe not only began to devote more time to writing but also, away from home and friends, had more time for reflection and introspection. Thus, the earliest significant body of notes and papers which he accumulated in his career comes from the Harvard years. Some of the notes and the drafts of literary work are in academic exercise books, but most of them are on loose sheets of paper of various sizes. He was then making no attempt to keep records of his ideas or his life; he simply began his habit of thinking aloud on paper and his habit of jotting down imagination projections of all sorts—scenes, speeches, phrases, themes.*

*Some of these random notes have been selected as examples of his ideas and interests during this period of literary and intellectual awakening.*

---

[*As a Southerner away from home, Wolfe developed a new awareness of his region. Although he sometimes emphasized the cultural limitations of the Southern writer, he was always ultimately ready to be the defender of and the spokesman for his region.*

*The selection of notes grouped together here at the beginning reflect ideas he was later to work with dramatically in* Welcome to Our City. *Some of them seem to be in preparation for an essay, never written, on the South and modern literature.*]

Tendency to sentimentalize.
Cf. John Fox.
Even Joel Chandler Harris.
Thomas Nelson Page—hasn't got austerity.
Romanticists—not classicists.
Realism not wanted.
Priest-ridden standards of morality.
No conception of the drama.
No conception of art.
Love of organization.
Individualism has gone into bankruptcy.
Puerile nature of intellectual life.

APOLOGIA PRO MEA PATRIA

We have few poets in the South who write about the Spring, or of her coming, but she undoubtedly comes heralded by pomp, magnificence, and glory. After two years residence in New England I am painfully aware of many poets who write about the Spring; who sing her praises metrically or polyphonically, dilate on her quickening influences on poetic imagination, since she is their own sweet chuck and mistress; but who, living in New England, have never seen, felt, or experienced her presence in any way whatsoever. The truth, stated with brutal frankness, is that Spring abides in the South, where there are no poets and, with the utmost scrupulosity, avoids letting even the hem of her white robe touch New England, where there are many poets.

It is with difficulty that we renounce the charms of this pleasing sentiment. There is an atmosphere to it, a kind of old and musty fragrance. Your Southerner in northern states soon learns what is expected of him, and is not unlikely to surrender and become professional. His words crawl and drip with syrupy reluctance from his mouth, the most commonplace facts of his existence become rosy in this romantic glow, and, if he is not careful, he is apt to be found referring to his own father as "the colonel."

In the literature that has so far appeared about our section, our old friends, Snivel and Drivel, have forced us along the tides of sadness and sentiment from which we are wont to survey our past history.

In education we are still suffering from what the redoubtable Mencken has called "the Baptist seminary standard." There is a shocking over-plus of priest-ridden schools. Frequently one will find men with college degrees, presumably with the foundations of a liberal education, who deny the theory of evolution, using, as the basis of their denial, the bible, a book which is used so flexibly as to provide the final and inevitable word on geology, anthropology, or economics.

The venerable priestly tradition is exercised on every hand; the proud uses of the reason are deplored and one is exhorted to forego the wicked privilege of thinking for oneself, for a more godly humility to revealed authority, lest the devil fly away with him.

I think you will find there the reason why men for over a century have loved the university. It is, and has been, the one known haven within our boundaries for individualism; the one place where the spirit of free inquiry has been maintained and fostered.

A gentleman of my acquaintance, a college professor, in making a criticism of the philosophy as taught by a distinguished professor, pointed out that it encouraged the individual to set himself in opposition to the group. For himself, he said, he preferred the fostering of the idea of *harmony;* the social order and the happiness of the individual demanded less friction and a more agreeable relation. In brief, the individual should be taught the policy of *acquiescence.*

A student of the professor of philosophy under discussion, my friend continued, had developed individualism to such a degree that life in his own state became intolerable, and he became a voluntary exile.

A dead weight of despair oppresses one when he realizes that over sixty years after *The Origin of the Species* intelligent people may be found, in what he had always considered an enlightened community, who look upon one who professes belief in the theory of evolution as a "radical" or "advanced" thinker. And the utterly hopeless circumstance in the whole business is that these people, who rather pride themselves on some certain quality they call broad-mindedness, persist in regarding scientific truth as a debatable matter. Without going into the matter farther, evolution is an historic fact, and its existence is no more a subject for debate than the existence of the Atlantic Ocean.

There is a question to be asked and seriously considered to which I have been driven steadily and inexorably, after long and painful consideration, and after many futile attempts to escape its omnipresence. Can there be any advanced intellectual life where a condition exists, where people look furtively about before even arguing the existence of truths which have been known and accepted for over a half a century?

The Middle West is at the present supplying the full quota of rebels. Few, if any, are coming from the South or New England.

To judge from the literature that has lately come from the Mid-Western states, such a book, for example, as *Main Street,* such a play as *Lulu Bett* [by Zona Gale], the texture of life is of a flat, unbroken greyness.

But life in the South, however akin to the elements of life in *Main Street,* still possesses color, fragrance, charm, and a certain variety, produced in part by the warmth and generous temperament of the people, and partly by the shifting panorama of color and light and beauty on Southern hills and meadows.

There are kinds and kinds of provincialism: New England is provincial and doesn't know it; the Middle West is provincial and knows it, and is ashamed; but, God help us, the South is provincial, knows it, and doesn't care.

Literature is, in any sense, a criticism of life. That criticism is either actual or implied. Especially does this hold true of the drama. If we really desire literature, the artist must be given full scope in which to exercise his talent. He must not be withheld from writing a play dealing with the race problem because it is a "tender subject." Any attempt to make him the creature of public squeamishness will kill him and his art. If we are not willing to meet these conditions, we are not ready for art; we are not worthy of literature.

If what we want is not the significant play, but the "good show," the thing that is fashioned out of the stuff of the theatre and is false and hollow, and brittle to its heart, by all means let us make no bones about it.

It has been said that a just and merciful order of things prevents people from really knowing what is happening to them. This is certainly true of the negro. But it makes it very difficult to write a play about him. It is hard to pierce through his eternal buffoonery to reach his tragedy. A ridiculous or absurd occurrence at a funeral can make the mourners laugh.

Russia created a literature out of pain. Can we create another out of complacency? Does the desire to create an art in the South today arise from a passionate desire to create beauty, or from chagrin at our barrenness and a desire to "get back" at H. L. Mencken, who has given our home the title of "The Sahara of the Bozart"?

I venture to think that the South will witness an awakening of culture and will make its own particular and local contribution to the creative arts only when the importance of the artist within the social scheme is recognized, is recognized as fully and as importantly as the position of the politician, the engineer, the farmer, and the doctor.

If somewhere now, on Southern hill or plain, he is toiling painfully toward perfection of his art, if, even, he is diffusing his light, and it is striking through fogs and glooms, at no time and place has the position Shelley attributed to him been better fulfilled; he is indeed "the unacknowledged legislator of mankind."

Suppose, for instance, someone writes a book or a play in which he says: "See here! Your pulpit and your press when it engages in discussions of morality confines itself to attacks on the young. Evidently they are trying to tell us civilization is going to rack and ruin because of cigarettes, pool-rooms, short skirts, bobbed hair, and modern dances. But we are intelligent people: we know these things are trifles. But here's another thing. All about us are members of a savage and inferior race. When they were brought here their skins were black. Now the skins of some—a great many—are yellow; those of a few are almost white. Can you deny it? What folly! It walks by you in the streets like a great plague. It is, and is everywhere. Simply look around you and begin to count. You know this thing, you know many others like it; why then do you confine your conversation to decorous trifling; why do you skim along the surface when the great dark, passionate currents of life are sweeping on down there beneath your feet."

If you listen to such a man, or to a group of men who say these things, if you reflect deeply and earnestly on what they have said, and consider the justice of their statements, then you have provided the fruitful soil from which a great art may be produced.

But if you turn on him and rend him, with savage cries of "Judas" and "traitor," you will drive him into other lands—as did the people of Ibsen. You will bring untold misery and woe to him but if he is an artist, you will not stop him from writing.

[*Wolfe did a good deal of theorizing about literature, especially about the drama, as he prepared term papers for his courses and worked at his play-writing. On the whole, it is of rather poor quality. The following notes are samples, in some of the better expressed statements, of positions Wolfe frequently took—for realism or expression of truth in literature; for emotional intensity controlled by form; against preciosity*.]

But can we seriously maintain the superiority of "natural passion" expressing itself in an expansive and unregulated fury, over "natural passion" disciplined and controlled by an imagination working within the limits of probability and decorum. I do not think we can. As examples of the two methods it is only necessary to mention the names of Rousseau and Sophocles. Although Rousseau rules the roost at present, it were better for us if we had more of Sophocles.

Follow emotionalism to its most violent excesses, and the artist becomes no more than an amanuensis of the popular fervor, a kind of public secretary who stands watchfully by, with his quill in hand, ready to transcribe each new outpouring of sound which bursts from the throat of the People. In some mysterious way, but by what intermediation the romanticists will not venture to say, a ballad or an epic poem grows or accumulates from age to age, constantly shaped and moulded by the unconscious creative force of a people until, at length, Homer appears, trims off the ragged edges, in order that the parts may dove-tail, and offers up the *Iliad* as his own, or as Samuel Butler thought, *her* own.

But do ideas have that permanence the philosopher attributes to them? Are they not variable to custom, usage, and the shifting currents of time? The idea of Beauty! There's a case for you. It is one of the three separate but inter-penetrable unities: Truth, Goodness, and Beauty. But a group of new poets and new painters get together and change your idea of Beauty. Is that permanence? Perhaps it will be said the idea of Beauty is absolute and unchangeable; that the difficulty lies in the false testimony of our senses, in the inability of our little, lone, bounded brains to possess it. In that case it can be shown such an idea does not exist, since the essence of an idea is that it shall find its source within the mind.

A society of aesthetes, a society of beauty-snatchers, is surely as undesirable as a society of money grubbers. Oh, but it is!

Let him be definite.[1] It is the test of the true artist. The challenge should set the mind on fire. The play has feeling—in a vague, unrealized sense it has thought—or the nebulous stuff from which thought may form and drop. But it can never realize itself as long as we talk of "dreams," and explain life with a wide mysterious gesture. Neither can we satisfy when our characters are tremendously stirred by the energies of life but confess, as Angelo does, that they cannot explain (through the low un-spiritual medium of language) what it is that moves them.

[*Other notes show the emotional groping in matters of religion and morality, especially sexual morality, which is characteristic of young people. The most remarkable piece of soul-wrestling is the covenant with God, which reflects Wolfe's Presbyterian upbringing as well as his youthful idealism.*]

I, Thomas Wolfe, having arrived at the end of my twentieth year, with that period that legally marks the beginning of manhood but two weeks off, do look back with bitter and intense sorrow at my manner of living these past four years, for I know that tho I have gained somewhat in certain respects I have been loose, weak, and totally lax in

1. Wolfe is commenting on a play by one of his fellow members of the 47 Workshop.

a moral way. I call to God to give me strength to utterly forget the sorrow and misery of that period and to give to me also to draw henceforth only strength and determination from a contemplation of it. Tonight I make unto me a covenant and I call infinite and all mighty God to witness that I hereby abjure the mental and carnal fleshpots—beasts which have well-nigh destroyed me—that henceforth I will try to see life cleanly and with increased and sympathetic understanding that by virtue of my own bitter knowledge, He may grant it to me to be honest without prudery, clean without hypocrisy. Help me to keep clean, O God, help me to be a man! Give me something to love passionately but cleanly—something that will fire me, thrill me, enrich me. If I must lose myself to find myself, O God, grant that that in which I lose myself may be altogether fine.

Help me to grow, O God. Grant that growth may never stop.

My faith has been cruelly battered. I was taught that God is,—as a child—and that He created Man in His image. But from God the creator my attention, my whole belief has been fastened and focused on Man the creator. Within a few years I have seen men create God in their image. I refer to the process that has unfolded itself within my own family. I want to believe. I want to, but a deadly, horrible conviction deep down—yea, deeper within me than that which once I called my faith—tells me it is so, that what I have seen here among a small group has cheated and defrauded this poor twisted humanity through countless thousands of years and centuries since first among the hairy brute-men of our past the great desire to live forever made itself conscious and articulate.

My family could not be termed a religious family. As children, starched and ironed and washed and curled, on Sundays we made our way to Sunday school. Attendance at church was advocated mainly because it gave one business and social "standing" in a small community such as ours. The best people belonged to the church. If one was to live here one simply couldn't afford not to belong. Religion thus came to serve a utilitarian purpose.

We were all young then and death seemed far away and horribly unreal. It still does. How strange that the most real experience in our lives should thus invest itself with such unreality when it comes home to us! Yet it does. I have never looked upon the face of a corpse without that feeling: twelve hours before, this body was yet warm with life, these pale eyelids fluttered, and more, that cold blue vein beat up and down under the measure of its tiny pulse. People pass by and view the body, uttering the usual banalities. "How natural he looks," they say. No. No. No. How unnatural, how horribly unnatural.

For I am a stranger in the land, a despiser of the empty-headed women of my South, yet longing for their embraces and endowed seductiveness, a mocker of the hard knowingness of the women of the North—God forbid I should touch them with a ten-foot pole—yet an admirer of a certain vigor and an independence that they have. These are the women I know. These are the women I have seen and put my arms around. Shall I, with the rest of the rabble rout, abase the decency of my manhood, and weep maudlin tears on the fates of trulls like these. God forbid!

Shall I write the lie upon the paper—uttering what I know in my heart is false; asserting that the cheap glass of their virtue is a gem of priceless worth, and that the world should weep when it is gone.

This world is a honeycomb, tissued of falsehood and deceit. And the greatest scoundrels of the lot are those who cry "Revolt!" My God, my God. Why hast thou forsaken us! Or dost thou, too, traverse the round of thy creation, and pausest where thou art, on other whirling spheres of vanity! O God, be merciful, and think of us again!

A *virgin* conceived and gave birth to a son, whose Father was the deity. Now we know the world has gone on its way for millions of years and that the laws of nature have never once been suspended. Deep in our inmost hearts, if we pause to look there, we know the thing is not true, that it is a priestly superstition. But we are afraid to look in our inmost hearts, we are afraid to get alone with ourselves, we are afraid of the raw, naked, terrible but glorious truth. Therefore, we huddle together in churches with the other sheep, and bleat and baa at each other and repeat these superstitions over to each other rapidly in order that we may not think about them too deeply. Thus by a kind of "spiritual massage," we become what is technically known as a Christian.

It is a most important thing to be a good Christian, as my dear friend, Jesse Law [2] told me this summer. "No man, Tom, can get along in business here until he accepts Jesus Christ as his saviour." You see that is all that is necessary, he is washed in the blood of the lamb, and made pure, and is straightway entitled to all the privileges of Christianity—namely, to go out and cheat his neighbor and put the first $100 of a real estate track [*sic*] in his own pocket. It is a good club to belong to, especially if one wants to go into business.

The love of money:—whether such a love is degrading. Consider well.

2. A real estate dealer in Asheville.

Is it not [*as*] natural for a man who has made his way from rude beginnings to love that which he has acquired through his shrewdness and industry as it is for a man to love his children or a poet his poems?

In another way is not wealth the legitimate child of industry as poetry is the legitimate child of genius? I think so.

Utilitarianism is not a new thing; it was not invented yesterday. Greece and Rome must have known it. But the utilitarianism we know today is something which has destroyed all proportion, upset all balance.

. . . Life, at its pinnacle, of pain and ugliness; or of tragedy and beauty—escapes us. We never escape life save on an inferior landing stage—romantic escape is mean, base, and transitory: it cannot rise to meet the great facts. Our sensory equipment is inadequate in moments of crisis—our emotions are not so great as the facts of life—death itself, the most magnificent, the most inexorable fact, has always overstepped the poor dignity of human emotion. For, we scuttle away from death's presence with a horrifying sense that the play is greater than the actors —that we have bungled the lines—maimed a brilliant scene. So when Samuel Butler writes of the elder Pontifex [in *The Way of All Flesh*], when his wife of thirty years has died, "He covered his face with his hands to hide the fact that he felt no grief," he was writing a line with unversal applications, if he had added but a single word, "to hide the fact that he felt no *more* grief."

We never know when we are right. We stab into the dark and then, perhaps, there is a cry. I have spent nights and days crying "Lord, I am here! here!" and there is no answer. We have to search out our own paths. "The heart of the king is inscrutable."

It is not for us to write "Why" across the firmament, and then to try and answer it. It is rather for us to write "Why" across the scroll of our being, and there to answer the question we have raised.

Are you not an artist? Then begin with your own life.

[*At Harvard Wolfe began the self-conscious tabulating and recording of his activities and achievements which he continued for the rest of his career. A few examples here will illustrate the value he placed on quantity. The first is a list of modern American, British, and Continental plays he has read.*]

4 Fitch
1 Moody
2 Howard
2 Gillette
2 Walter
3 MacKaye
2 Thomas
1 Peabody
4 O'Neill
2 A. E. Thomas
1 Craven
2 Smith

———

26

3 Wilde
4 Pinero
1 Sutro
6 Jones
2 Houghton
12 Shaw
8 Barrie
1 Phillips
6 Galsworthy
2 Dale
4 Masefield
3 Drinkwater
3 Yeats
2 Synge
5 Gregory
1 St. John Ervine
1 St. John Hankin
3 Housman

———

67

6 Brieux
4 Augier
2 Dumas fils
1 Bataille
2 Rostand
1 Halevy
1 Labiche
1 Guitry
1 Hervieu
4 Maeterlinck
1 Sardou

———

24

8 Ibsen
1 Bjornsen
1 Tolstoi
3 Chekov
4 Andreyev
1 Molnar
6 Hauptmann
2 Sudermann
1 D'Annunzio
4 Benavente
1 Echegaray

———

32

67
26
23 [*sic*]
32

———

148

How many of the people in this country can I touch before I'm thirty:

1000 a day = 365,000 a year
x 8
2920000
∴ 3000000
—Not enough.

People I have seen and noted to-day (M'ch 9, 1923)—From Morn to Midnight.

Up and to the Libe.
The Old Maid Librarian
Prof. Rand—at Emerson [*Hall*]
The thin Libe.
The R. H. Libe.
The Jap at desk
The ugly coed
The class
The Boys on Each Side Of Me
The Des[*k*]
The Boy who argued with Prof.
Those who laughed at boy
Langfeld [3]—my talk with him
The Greek from whom I bought paper
The Book Store Man
The Dentist
The cafeteria people
The four lit. women
The chair
The man at table
The class at 47
Kenneth
P. Baker
Fritz
Ken [4]
The boys in Leavitt's
The newsboys

3. Professor Herbert S. Langfeld, under whom Wolfe was taking the course Philosophy 10, Aesthetics.

4. Kenneth Raisbeck and Frederick (Fritz) Day were members of Professor Baker's 47 Workshop group.

The girl who went down to subway
The subway
The two drunks who sang "green grass grew all around"
Those who looked at them and smiled
The giant negro
The subway guard
The rest.—the waitresses—the six construction engineers
The girl who smiled at me
The cashier—the waitresses at desk—the man phoning
The gray-haired waiter
The three girls downstairs
The woman going down St.
The two who passed me
The subway again

Kenneth—our walk—the policemen—automobiles—Return—the little girl who shouted at us—boys and girls on the st.—then Merle [5]—our talk—those who came in—the workshop again—those there—my talk with Prof. Baker.

Friday, May 11 [*1923*] at 5:55 in the afternoon:

With the first Workshop performance of my play less than two and one quarter hours distant I want to record here, for my personal satisfaction, my belief that the play which I have written has no better show than that of the snowball in the infernal regions. I can only hope that the cast and producing organization will give a performance superlatively better than any they have previously given. And even then? And even then??

"Hope springs eternal"—but let me resolutely abandon it now and henceforth.

[*During his three years in the 47 Workshop, Wolfe wrote two full-length plays: "The Mountains" and* Welcome to Our City, *and began a third,* Mannerhouse. *The first, a play about a family feud, shows Wolfe still writing in the spirit of the Carolina Playmakers. But the second is a work of distinct maturity and modernity, and it was selected for performance by the 47 Workshop Players in May, 1923. We give here the opening scene, an expressionistic prelude which introduces succinctly the themes of race relations and of commercial double-dealing. The high piping tune, which recurs throughout the play, is a mocking commentary on human absurdity.*]

5. Probably Merlin Taylor, another member of the Workshop group.

## WELCOME TO OUR CITY

A PLAY IN TEN SCENES

BY THOMAS CLAYTON WOLFE

SCENE I

A street in Niggertown. One looks across at a ragged line of white-washed shacks and cheap one- and two-story buildings of brick. In the center is a vacant lot between the buildings. It is littered with rubbish, bottles, horseshoes, wagon wheels, and junk of every description.

A group of young negro men is pitching horseshoes in one part of the lot. In another, two young men are playing ball. Still elsewhere, another group is pitching pennies at a line drawn in the earth. To the right, there is a filthy looking restaurant. Through its dirty windows may be seen a long, greasy counter piled with quantities of fried food —chicken, fish and meat. There are smeared glass cases, as well, which contain thick, pasty looking pies.

A negro man and a stout negress are in attendance within.

Next door—divided only by a flimsy board partition—is a pool-room. It is a dark, fathomless place, in which men, seeming like ghosts move through dense clouds of tobacco smoke around the green tables, under shaded lamps which cast wedges of sickly light upon them.

Farther up to the left, on the opposite side of the lot, is a moving picture theater, housed in a cheap building of whitewashed brick. The front of the theater is plastered with immense garish posters. One shows a woman jumping from a bridge on to a moving train; in another a horseman is taking a prodigious leap across the gap that yawns between two towering cliffs. A tinny automatic piano plays, ceases with a spasmodic jerk, hums ominously, and, without warning, commences again.

At the extreme left is the side of a large brick building, which apparently fronts on a street in the white section. It is pierced by windows, doors, and steps which lead down respectively into a barber shop, a pressing club, and a shoe-repair shop.

On the street are clustered groups of young negroes, some in shirtsleeves and suspenders, others more fashionably attired in box coats with heavy stripes, flaring peg-top trousers and club-foot shoes of a screaming yellow. Young negro women, attired in slouchy finery, in which lavender predominates, and wearing coarse white stockings and down-at-the-heel shoes, stroll by. The men make remarks which the girls answer freely. There is much ogling back and forth, much laughter, a great deal of noise.

They are creatures of sudden whim, and do unexpected things. Gales of merriment seize them; one will suddenly commence a shuffling dance, and as suddenly end it. There is much rough horseplay among the young men on the lot.

Up and down the street pass many people. Most of them are young. Now and then, a more dignified or prosperous looking citizen walks by. A stout, middle-aged negro, wearing a long frock coat of good cloth and an expensive white vest, with a heavy gold chain, passes. He addresses people right and left, bestowing genial greetings or benedictions with a fat hand.

These circumstances, coupled with a pious smirk and the oiled smugness of his bearing, cause us to suspect he is a minister of the gospel. His thick lips are wreathed in smiles of sacrificial humility. They move and murmur constantly. We do not hear what he is saying to the people, but his mouth ever fashions and pronounces the word "brother." And as he walks, from somewhere in the distance, a foolish, futile, ever-recurrent little tune is whistled, to which he appears to keep step in his march onward across the stage. He comes; he passes; and he goes; a leaping spark of rumour stills the crowd, and treading on the heels of silence, the mortal kings and captains of this earth march slowly past.

MR. HENRY (H. C.) SORRELL (*White*)
(*Dictating at once to two stenographers*)

She's a bargain; she's a buy; and she's a daisy! It can be done, if you have Vision—the motto of this office. Twenty-two hundred dollars a front inch until Thursday; price advances to three thousand then.

MR. J. C. DUNBAR (*The Tailor*)

Done! I take it. How much down?

MR. HENRY SORRELL

$2.47—the rest in thirty days. (*Money is passed*)

MR. BURTON WEBB (*Attorney and publisher*)

I'll give you twenty five hundred, Jim. How much for a binder?

MR. J. C. DUNBAR

$1.63.

MR. BURTON WEBB

The trade's on. (*Money is passed*) She'll hit three thousand before the summer's over.

GOVERNOR PRESTON CARR

The state is a mighty empire, self-sufficient to all her needs.

MR. J. C. DUNBAR

(*laggard behind the host, drops farther back, turns, bangs, returns; with prankish schoolboy grin he enters too the corridor, hiding his face with his hat.*)
(*Voice half up-stairs, neighing and palpitant*)
Ess-see—who-o do-o you-u lo-o-ve?
(*The foolish, futile, ever-recurrent little tune is whistled over again. The people, suspended in their acts, now break to movement. And suddenly above the tumult of the crowd, one feels a great throbbing in the upper air, which is filled with the noise of whistles, the piercing blast of a siren, and the heavy, booming strokes of the courthouse bell. It is six o'clock.*

*Soon the workmen begin to come by. They are big, strong men, with stooped, burly shoulders, and there is in their manner a solid weariness.*

*They march heavily and solidly on, each bearing a dinner pail or a lard bucket in his hand. They pay no attention to those on either side of them. Their hands and faces are covered with the dust of lime and cement, trenched and engraved by little streams of sweat, and their shoes and the bottoms of their trousers are stiff with mortar.*
*One of their number—a young negro—turns aside, going into the poolroom. Another pauses to talk to a negro in the vacant lot. The rest go solidly past, with an implacable, an animal power, paying no attention to those on either side of them.*)

CURTAIN

[*The following passages are notes and fragments of other plays that Wolfe was working with during his Harvard years. We include them here as illustrations of the range and variety of his experiments in the drama. We have not included any sample from* Mannerhouse, *Wolfe's Civil War drama, the only play which has been published in book form.*

*Wolfe worked intermittently on a play about Horace Williams, his philosophy professor at the University of North Carolina.*

*Drawing on the ideas of H. G. Wells's novel* The Undying Fire, *he planned a modern version of the Job story, in which God allows Satan to afflict Professor Weldon with cancer. In some fragments Weldon dies, in others he recovers. Some scattered pages have Satan speaking in blank verse. One early plan is developed as a prose narrative rather than a play.*]

May 3:

Eleven o'clock at night. I have just returned from the house of Professor Tasker Weldon. He died tonight at nine-thirty following an operation two weeks ago for malignant cancer. He talked plainly and quietly up to the moment of his death. His mind exhibited to the end its accustomed vigor and clarity of perception. His death left us all with a sense of appalling and unrestorable vacancy.

So significant do I consider these conversations of the past two weeks that I hasten to set them down now while they are still fresh in my memory. The knowledge of death was within him even as he spoke; he displayed a curiosity that was not far short of eagerness when he thought of the great experience. As long as he could articulate his words tonight he explained the sensations death awoke in him. Rarely, I believe, has so close, and on that account, so teasing a record, of the experience of death been given to any man.

First I propose to write a brief biography of his life, followed by the culminating experiences of this last fortnight. This it seems to me is more essential in his life than in anyone's I have ever known or read about. For, to an amazing degree, he succeeded in making his life a unity. A realistic novelist, I believe, could write a novel of power and meaning simply by recording the events of his life. Most of us do not make a unity out of our lives; if it is true that each of us are novels bound up in covers of skin and bone, it is equally true that we must be subjected to the selective winnowings of art before the history of our lives may be made to possess a meaning or interest.

But Professor Weldon lived consciously with one aim, that was (in his own phrase) to make his life prevail. His life was a unity because he lived with that intent. Whether he succeeded or not in that intent is a question the reader must decide.

He has a visitor?
Yes, Lucifer is here.
Lucifer. But I thought Michael threw him out some time ago.
Oh, he's back. He comes often.
What does he come for?

Oh, he's a great traveller. He goes everywhere.

Does the Master let him come?

Of course. He is delighted to have him. He is such good company. He's been everywhere and seen everything. He knows so many delightful stories. Really we couldn't get along without him.

What does he do when he comes?

Oh, he just talks, usually. The Master likes to talk with him. He is so quick-witted. Sometimes they argue with each other. (The sound of voices within) Listen, they are talking now.

THE VOICE OF LUCIFER: "There was a man in the land of Uz, whose name was Job."

He's telling a story. See: they're all crowding around him. He has a great gift for narrative.

Satan appears there in the role of a critic. He is given leave by God to afflict man and to try to break his spirit but he is told to spare his life. That life is precious, for the spirit of God is in it.

(Satan leaps suddenly among them. They draw back in terror. He wheels with a dramatic whirl of the red cloak and addresses them with uplifted hand):

Ye ministers and harbingers of light,
Bright tokens of the essence increate,
By what audacious motive came ye hence,
In whose intrepid footprints hast thou followed,
Forsakest thou the gilded minarets,
The deep, cool woods, the meadow-lands of heaven,
The pavement of the stars, the sun's bright face,
Which smiles eternally within thy courts
For these Plutonian depths? Or knowest thou [*end of page*]

[*Many undeveloped literary ideas like the following are found among Wolfe's papers from the Harvard years.*]

Pirandello

Write your own version of Six Characters, etc.

In one scene have the characters ushered into a scene furnished by the mechanics of the stage—a scene representing the vast and infinite—say, the sea, a cliff, mountains, or a great desert—but ridiculous in its theatrical execution—i.e. you are convinced they are stage mountains, a canvas sea, etc. *But* they represent reality to these six characters and they discuss the solemn grandeur of the scene with all the seriousness, let us say, of Alpine tourists.

*Then* while these characters are uttering weighty and ponderous sentiments—palpably artificial—like the scenery—but as real to them as the scenery is—while they are engaged in this self-deception, I say, invisible hands behind the scenes move them away. In the twinkling of an eye these poor characters see their false world crumbling around them—their sea, their mountains, their whole visible external reality is whisked away from their sight—they are left trembling and bewildered on the bare planks. What would they do?

*Today's Golden Thought.* What would *we* do if the stage properties of our existence were whirled away before us? This is as much as to say, is there such a thing as an absolute and self-dependent reality?

[*It has usually been assumed that Wolfe's scornful attitude toward the Jews developed out of the frustrations of his later love affair with Aline Bernstein and the resentment against the New York theatrical groups, who refused to accept his plays. It is pertinent, therefore, to include the following fragment, which reflects early in Wolfe's career a full-blown mythology of anti-Semitism, but at the same time turns into an ironic thrust at anti-Semitic clichés as well as at American competitiveness.*]

Artistically, at any rate, the Jew is a menace. He controls the theatre in New York. If this were all, he might be compelled, by properly enlightened audiences, to advance his standards and improve in the quality of his dramatic selections. But the character of New York audiences is itself determined, in large measure, by the members of his race. They dominate the occasion and their demand is ever for the sensual, the thinly veiled, or the materialistic. The explanation for our country's noble and unique contribution to drama—the "success play"—that is, the play where the brisk and breezy young "American" shows his employer how to double the sale of dill pickles, and thereby wins the old man's daughter, may be found in the strong zest the Semitic audience has for this type of play.

We are prone to chafe at the vast success which attends the Jew in all his efforts. In our small towns, we see our small tradesmen steadily driven to the wall, outwitted and outreached on every side by their Jewish competitor. One fine morning during the Jewish New Year, we awake to walk the streets of an almost deserted business section. And we realize, with a shock, how great an inroad the Jew has made in our financial life. But we rarely pause to reflect that the reason for this lies in the fact we have erected a civilization which fits the Jew like a glove, far better, indeed, than it fits the members of our own race. The chief tenets of its faith are directed toward keeping an eye on the main chance—a regulation the Jew observes with an iron pertinacity compared to which our own efforts seem futile and unavailing.

"My Gott," said my Norwegian lady, apropos of this, "how dose Yews can make de money. I vish dey'd teach me sometings about it. Dot's all dey tinks of. Evryday you sees dem, an' its alvays de same: To de bank, to de bank, to de bank."

And the Jew, under the flush of success, does not become what one would define as an enchanting personality. Rather he pushes the harder, grows more boldly insolent and asserts his right to a hearing loudly and frequently. You are in a crowd, there is a loud voice, and a jostling behind. You need not turn to see who it is. His botanical selection is ever the sun-flower, never the violet. Indeed, I am becoming convinced that he gained his title of "chosen of God" because of the many good things he had to say of himself, oft-repeated before the Lord. Even God must surrender.

Enter two Jews, arm in arm, gesticulating and exhorting each other loudly. Each bears a money bag in his free hand.

TO ONE ANOTHER: To de bank, to de bank, to de bank.

(They rush across the stage and exit).

Angry mutterings and suspicious, discontented glances from the people follow them.

DIFFERENT VOICES:

—Those damned Jews!
—They'll own us body and soul some day.
—They've got the clothing business.
—They've driven me to the wall.
—They control the theaters.
—They're getting hold of the banking.
—I can't compete with them. They undersell me.
—They stick together and gang up on us.
—You can't go in a restaurant but you find them.
—They're everywhere on the streets. In the city they outnumber us.
—We've got to do something about it. They're after nothing but the Almighty Dollar.

(Jeering laughter from the One. They direct their angry muttering against him.)

THE ONE: And what are you all after, my good, respectable friends?

[*A few pages scattered here and there show work on scenes which suggest Eugene Gant ingurgitating the volumes of the Harvard Library in* Of Time and the River.]

The interior of a great library—the shelves are lost in darkness above, and to either side they run off to infinity. They bend over, over, over as if they will whelm and crush the figure of Eugene who sits at a small table in the center with a white wedge of light which falls upon him. Books are piled high upon the table before him. Many lie open around him, and the one which he holds in his hand, he reads with savage voracity, with inconceivable rapidity, with terrific intensity. He throws it aside and plunges into another.

EUGENE. Of Shakespeare's plays alone in this library there are hundreds of editions, over five thousand separate copies. If I read one edition, I have read them all. Now there are here one million books in all—5000 into a million goes but 200 times. But I am reading 10 a day. In 20 days I would have finished. That won't do it.

Other men read books—I read libraries. Other men read books—I invade them. Other men taste—I swallow the whole.

I shall make one globe, not of my learning but of all learning. I shall make one globe, not of my life but of all life. I shall seize and possess the whole.

On the street today I must have passed a full hundred thousand of people. How [able?] were all the things they said! In a year's time that would be 36,000,000. In three years I would have touched the country.

My brain is giddy, my senses numbed, but my heart is filled with exulting joy. O God, O God, let me taste and know all life; make me the reed through which all winds must blow, the silver horn which plays both high and low.

As swift as a swallow,
As light as a flame,
What melodious sweetness,
What harmonious joy
Strange symphonies of [*breaks off*]

[*Among Wolfe's papers of this period are many fragments, some in prose narrative, some in dramatic form, about a family like his own. They are named variously, Broody, Breen, Whitby, or Bateson, and characters very much like his father and mother, his brothers Ben and Fred, and his sister Mabel appear. "The House of Bateson" is the only title Wolfe tries out. A number of scenes prefigure material he developed later in* Look Homeward, Angel. *The following selections are representative of the scattered remains of this project.*]

The Broody's were a strange family.[6] They never saw each other's good points till one of their number died. Then they were lavish in their affection. In their cooperative maudlinism they became almost affectionate in their regard for one another, differences were forgotten in their common intoxication of tears, the dear departed went through a gradual process of canonization, little inhumorous details of his life and habits were sloughed off until finally he stood forth in all the crackling starchiness of brand-new sainthood.

They were a passionate, tempestuous, erratic, irascible family and yet it is doubtful if they were capable of any real profundity of thought or feeling. They were always quarreling and cursing one another with varying degrees of intensity, and what is worse, in large unhappy families of this sort, they were continually splitting up into parties among themselves. Factionalism reigned supreme. This was the rotten spot, this destroyed them. For all large families quarrel. But when the quarreling and the cursing and the fighting is impartially distributed, while there is leaven of sympathy or condolence or mutual understanding between all there is hope.

But when a family divides itself against itself it can't stand. This happened in the Broody family. Slowly, imperceptibly, just like the slow poisonous growth of a rotten spot within the body the factional spirit grew within the family. It grew rotten ripe, then passed into dry decay and hardened. Joe and Sarah had aligned themselves against Seth and Eugene. They cursed each other privately now—party to party. Their talk was all of each other, bitter, acrimonious speech which poisoned speaker and listener alike and a deadly little snake uncoiled himself in the heart of each.

[*Two pages torn out here*]

At the time we begin our story there were seven members of the Groody family. The father, Will Groody,[7] was a man of sixty-five years, tall, with a great bony rack of a frame that still told of a once powerful physique. He had been a great animal of a man with the

6. This material appears in the back of Wolfe's academic notebook for History S9, a course in British History which he took in the summer of 1921. It was probably written in August or September, for the "Covenant with God," which is dated September, 1921, was also written in back of the history notebook.

7. Note that the name has changed from Broody to Groody.

passion and capacity of an animal but earlier excesses had told on him. Now he was wasted by a disease, a slow, creeping, unstoppable thing, that would some day destroy him. Not yet. Perhaps not for a long time, for the doctor had told Sarah the youngest daughter: "He's a creaking gate, Miss Sarah! A creaking gate hanging by one rusty hinge. He looks feeble, he *is* feeble but he may be creaking away twenty years from now."

"Does that mean he will live twenty years?" asked Sarah.

"Not at all," the doctor answered, pausing to take a big black cigar from his coat pocket and light it, professionally unaware of Sarah's pounding heart and nervously clenched fingers. "Not at all. He might not live a year." Having released this infallible information the doctor puffed his cigar with increased appreciation. Poor man! He told all he knew and in two sentences. What doctor could do more?

Benton grew more sullen and more silent day by day.[8] About him the family emotion seethed and surged. Their raw nerves cut him more deeply than he cared to admit—even to himself. How long was this to keep up? he asked himself. A year? Five years? Good God, they'd be mad by that time; he wondered if they weren't already mad. Their rantings, their hysteria, the continual morbidness with which their thoughts were now invested humiliated him. He considered it cowardice, maudlinism. What would death seem to be when it came? Would there be any dignity of feeling? Was this anything but a common prostitution of emotion which would all be decayed and flaccid when it was needed?

It is early morning in the home of William Breen, contractor and dealer in monument and stone.[9] The master of the house, according to custom, is up early, and stirring about in the living room of his residence, or "sitting room," as it is called.

The room is warm and comfortable in its appearance, and very masculine. There is a smooth, leather sofa at the left near a window; on the other side a marble-topped table with heavy books below; to the back, at the left, a glass-panelled door which leads out on the side verandah; center back, a door to a closet; right back, a fire place, and mantel; in the corner by the fire, a child's chair; before the fire two rockers with leather bottoms, to the right, a large combination book-

8. This brief passage, also found in the history notebook, is the only example of a version of the narrative in which the family is named Benton.

9. This and the other dramatic versions were probably written after the death of Wolfe's father in June, 1922.

case and secretary, lower down to the right, a door leading to the dining room and other parts of the house. The woodwork is of a light brown; around on the hearth it has swollen in great blisters, due to the heat, and peeled off. Brass-headed tongs, shovel, and poker, all dented and used, lean against racks in the woodwork. On the mantel is a wooden clock, two tall vases, an engineer's iron match box, and a cigar holder in the shape of a tree-trunk, with holes in the stumps of the limbs.

On the wall is a picture of Cynthia, William's first wife, who died in the late seventies. She is a very homely woman with a protruding mouth, and wears ugly-looking clothes of the period.

William Breen at this time is a man in his mid-fifties. He is of great stature, four inches above six feet, with tremendous big bones: his physique is gaunt but powerful. His hair is thin but not bald, save for a small place on top: It is iron-grey in color, his eyes are grey and clear, but not overly large, and they are sunken under great bushy eyebrows, the nose is a big sharp wedge, very thin but as forceful and decisive as a hawk's: it is the thinnest *big* nose you ever saw. The mouth is thin and straight with a little circular indentation at one corner where he fell and cut himself as a boy, the chin is very stubbornly moulded, and above the lip there is a stiff grey moustache.

He carries himself very erect but without stiffness; he gestures freely and naturally with his big, long, and powerful hands. They are remarkable hands: they are heavily veined and sinewy: the hands of a man who has worked but not the hands of a working-man, which are commonly short and stubby.

When we first see him he is laying and building the fire. It is early April and the mornings are still sharp. He is a man of the most tremendous nervous energy who does nothing by halves. He doesn't know what moderation means. He dramatizes all of his emotions: even his utterance is dramatized and quite often melodramatized in a way that almost passes belief.

He is holding an imaginary dialog with his wife as he builds the fire, and his voice rises and falls in a rapid drone, though we don't hear what he is saying. The rehearsal over his wife and his children will presently bear the performance.

He lays a goodly net-work of kindling inside the hearth, then pours kerosene oil lavishly, muttering to himself all the while. He then ignites the fire, it leaps up the chimney with a roar, and with savage mutterings, he seizes a scuttleful of coal, half of which he hurls upon the blaze. It is almost extinguished by the onslaught and he seizes the oil can again fairly drenching the fire with oil, so that it springs out at him. He turns to depart kitchenwards with his oil can, growling fiercely under his breath, takes a few powerful strides across the room, pauses and turns suddenly, muttering at the fire, and rushes back to it with his oil-can cocked, makes a long swinging motion and pours on more oil.

Mrs. Breen enters the room at this moment, and attempts to take the oil can.

MRS. BREEN. Law, Mr. Breen. What on earth are you doing? You'll blow us all up some day.

BREEN. Leave me alone, woman. I've made fires since I was five years old. (He seizes a heavy poker and hammers on the ceiling with it, punctuating it with heavy stamps from his boots. Muttering he goes to the door and roars toward the upper regions.) Fred! Ben! Tom! Get up! Get up! Merciful God, what will you ever amount to! Grown men and in bed at this hour. Are you going to spend your lives in bed! Look at your old grey-haired Father—up at six o'clock building the fires. When I was your age, I was up at four o'clock every morning. Get up —all of you! (His diatribe delivered in a roaring voice is answered presently by a sleepy grunt: then someone above says "What did you say, papa?"

Presently there is the sound of feet hitting the floor above, rapid movements and sudden footfalls down the stairs and through the hall. The two older boys, 16 and 14, rush in in their underwear with their clothes in their arms. They rush for the best places in front of the fire and dress. Presently there is the scudding of smaller feet, and a little boy of eight years, naked and with his clothes before him, scuttles in. Breen slaps him smartly on his little heeny as he scuttles past to the fire.)

BREEN. Get in there by the corner, boy, and get those clothes on! (The little boy runs to his chair which is occupied temporarily by brother Fred.)

THE L.B. Papa, make him give me my chair.

BREEN. Give him his chair, son. (Fred quickly gets up, and there is peace.)

[*In the version in which the family is called Whitby, there is a fragmentary scene in which Ralph Whitby gives his little brother Henry a watch for his birthday. It continues as follows:*]

HELEN. And we have big times together sometime, don't we, Hen?

HENRY. (eagerly to Ralph.) You bet we do, Ralph. Most every

Sunday we take a hike together, an' take our lunch and stay out all day. (Ralph regards the two again with the same tender little smile, marked now perhaps with a tinge of sadness.)

HENRY. (briskly—looking at his new watch.) Well, I'll be hiking. It's opening up time. So long, folks. (He goes out.)

RALPH. (looking after him—almost to himself.) Poor kid.

HELEN. What, Ralph?

RALPH. Poor kid—he doesn't get lonely, he works too hard. Wouldn't that get you? Sixteen years old today and already started at his drudgery. Yanked out of school, and put to the grindstone when he ought to be playing baseball. What do you know about it?

HELEN. (faltering) Oh, Ralph, Papa's getting old and—and maybe he needs Hen.

RALPH. (bitterly) Huh! Needs him. He's saving a clerk's pay, that's all. That's all Zeb Whitby ever thought of and ever will. Money—for himself. He's the most selfish man I ever knew.

HELEN. (shocked) Ralph, how can you talk about your own father that way?

RALPH. He's been a father to me now, hasn't he? To you? To the kid out there? Does he ever give unless he expects a bigger return? You save him a housekeeper's bill, and more than pay for your keep. The kid pays for himself. What's he ever given us? I've been through it all, Helen. That's why I left eight years ago—ran away. He yanked me out of school, too. I only got as far as the eighth grade.

HELEN. Perhaps you never understood papa, Ralph?

RALPH. Understood him! Why I know his nature from A to Z. I started my education when I was twelve years old going into the bar-room and bringing him home when he was so drunk he could hardly stand. At that he usually had strength enough to knock me clean across the room when we got home and to top it off by beating me with a leather strap. After he got tired out, I'd undress him and put him to bed to sleep.

[*Fragment from "The House of Bateson: A Play in Three Acts by Thomas Wolfe"*]

. . . of the head and wink of the eye. Occasionally he takes up one thread of the recitation himself with a deep booming bass or comments on the meaning of the text as his son proceeds)

JIM. To be or not to be, that is the question.

BATESON. Ay, there's the rub—He never spoke a truer word. Go on, Jim. Go on, my boy. (He raises a commanding arm and says "Psh-h" with a noise like the hiss of steam exhaust, but they are silent.)

[*A part of "The House of Bateson" in which old Mr. Bateson is brought home drunk.*]

BATESON. Where's your Mother?

JIM. (carelessly). Oh, she's around somewhere. Have a cigar, papa. (He takes one from a box on the table and puts it in his father's mouth. He strikes a match and holds it. Then he kneels and begins to unlace his father's shoes.)

BATESON. What are you doing?

JIM. It's all right, papa. Yes, sir, it's all right. We'll get these shoes off and put on your nice easy bedroom slippers. (He pulls off the shoes and puts on the slippers. He keeps a watchful eye on the free foot ready to dodge any whimsical kicks his parent might direct at him. He goes on talking in a soothing tone.) Yes sir, papa, it's all right. We'll have you fixed in a minute. (pulling gently at his coat) Now just a minute and we'll get this off. Just hold your arms up, papa.

BATESON. (struggling). Damn it, let go my coat. I can undress myself if I want to.

JIM. (removing the coat deftly.) Yes sir, papa, it's all right. Everything shall be as you say. (He gently unfastens his father's collar and tie and takes it off.)

BATESON. (roaring like a maddened bull.) You scoundrel, what are you trying to do—undress me? Let me go, I tell you. I don't want my clothes off.

JIM. (tactfully). All right, papa. Just as you say. It's going to be all right just as soon as I get you some nice hot supper. (He unbuttons the shirt quickly and pulls it off.) Yes sir, we'll be all right in a minute. (He comes in front again and begins to pull at the bottom of his father's trousers. Bateson levels a clumsy blow at the boy and half falls from his chair.) Yes sir, papa, it's all right.

BATESON. Where's your mother? Where [*breaks off*]

[*Scattered among Wolfe's papers are many attempts at verse, most of them unfinished. The following examples are typical of both the comic and the serious efforts. Shelley and Byron seem to be the chief models.*]

Wherever one in Boston looks
The people all are writing books

And those that aren't are writing plays
Unless their penchant's for essays.
The children of each household sit in
Each night to hear what mother's written.
True to her glorious fame pristine,
Old Boston's what she's always bean.
Her skirts are clean around the hem;
Her culture is a polished gem;
And for her learning she has caught
"The best that has been said and thought."
Her mental traits are circumspect
Her writing ever most correct [*breaks off*]

### EPITAPH ON A PH.D. MAN

Here lies a noble scholar
  More musty than his books,
A tireless grubber after facts
  A layman overlooks,
Who sucked the works of dead men dry,
  Of new ones a despiser:
He left the world a duller place
  But not one whit the wiser.

A son of the tented night,
Child of Apollo's track,
Treader of pathless light,
Spinning the bright world's back,
Part of the infinite urge,
Tongue of the wave uncurled,
Beating with animate surge,
In the shores of the world.
Is there an animate cause
Radiant ceaseless and warm
Imaged in us and our form?
Spirit that strainest the leash
The which was the gross flesh weak
O, thou who guidest
                    shapest
                    madest
                    mouldest

wroughteth
me, speak!

FROM DOUBLE TOP [10]

Oh, my masters! Ye that the ages have passed
Unchanged and proud
Ye that knew that your strength would outlast
Each ultimate shroud
That the boldness of youth and the strength of the man
Were ashes and dust
And the sad process of growth had curved in its span
To weakness and rust
And we that had thought we were learning to live
Were learning to die
Could have one swift moment of flame and could give
One passionate cry
Could peer into darkness seeking upon
Its inscrutable face
The gleam of a light [*breaks off*]

I shall not follow, though I remember.
I shall remember, though I may not come.
Eagle, my brother, of eagles brother,
Thou has winnowed thin air with thy mighty wings
And the savage winds thou has reft asunder;
And the airs that foul, the fires that smother
And the ravenous grip of the tainted things
Thou has soared above and left thereunder.

10. A mountain near Asheville.

# *Notes from the European Tour*

## *1924–1925*

*After spending the summer of 1923 at home in Asheville, Wolfe received word that the Theatre Guild would not produce his play. He took a temporary job in New York soliciting money for the University of North Carolina Alumni Fund. In February, 1924, he got an instructorship in English at New York University, teaching freshman composition during the spring and summer terms. In October he took the remainder of his year's salary and embarked on a tour of Europe, intending to finish* Mannerhouse *and to work on stories or sketches that his travels or his memory would inspire. He spent a year wandering in England, France, and Italy, working in random fashion at a variety of projects before he returned to teaching in the fall of 1925.*

*On the voyage home in August, he met Mrs. Aline Bernstein, a New York theatrical designer, and fell deeply in love with her, although she was almost twenty years older than he, married, and the mother of two children. During the next year, under her influence and with her encouragement he planned to write an autobiographical novel. She also made it possible for him to take a year off from teaching and go to Europe with her to begin the new project in the summer of 1926.*

*From this two-year span comes the next congruent body of writings that mark Wolfe's literary development. He began to work with prose narrative now, mostly autobiographical sketches. At first he tried a series of vignettes based on his ocean voyage. Later he took in hand his observations and adventures in Europe. Finally his thoughts turned to home and childhood memories, until the plan for the autobiographical novel emerged during the year of his association with Mrs. Bernstein.*

*The following notes and excerpts have been selected from the manuscripts of "Passage to England" and from a heap of loose pages which remain from his experiments with travel sketches. They represent the three main areas of subject matter, plus a few of the notes which reflect Wolfe's views on literary matters and on American culture. The material is roughly in chronological order.*

Sunday, Oct. 26 [*1924*]:

Today, for the first time in my life, I am beginning a more or less methodical record of the events which impinge on my own experience. I do this, I believe, because for the first time in my life I feel an utter isolation from such reality as I have known; because I know that I must live a good week longer with the people on this ship and that try as we may, we cannot get away from one another. The opportunities for observation are humorously unique.

The weather is magnificent—warm, bright, clear—there is no sea; the boat is perfectly steady.

There are less than one hundred of us on the cabin list. Let us see how thoroughly we can dislike one another before the voyage is over. Nine days with your companions is a long time, when the laws of accident govern their selection. I tried to leave New York yesterday as casually as if I had been taking a ferry ride to Hoboken; I was, nevertheless, in a tremendous state of excitement.

At eight o'clock I arose, had breakfast, sweated over my three bulging cases, and at eleven o'clock rode over to the Cunard piers at the foot of West 14th St. in a taxicab.

That was an hour before the *Lancastria* sailed. I went into the ship's writing room and scribbled four rather frantic letters to members of my family. Then I went on deck.

The space around the gang plank was thronged with people—passengers and their friends. I had avoided having anyone come on board to see me off; at the last minute two Jewish boys, students in my classes of Freshman composition at New York University, appeared. I gave one of them my letters to mail.

They were fascinated with the ship. They came on board and made a thorough inspection. In the writing room they appropriated sheets of the ship's stationery: in the smoking lounge they took huge boxes of the ship's safety matches.

My last view of an American crowd, of a New York crowd, was emphasized curiously and fittingly enough—as the ship slid backwards out of her slip, the crowd on the pier moving up constantly from one opening to another to look as long as they were able—by those two broad-nosed, grinning, friendly kike faces,—antithetic types: the one the face of an emotionalist and a sentimentalist, the other an intellectual, the best example of Semitic intelligence I have ever seen. And this is the brain of a high-grade Jew:—hard, cold, brilliant and unsympathetic, ashamed secretly of his own emotion, and deriding it in others; but capable of fierce and amorous devotion to an idea; able to achieve incredible sharpness but rarely able to be mellowed. They have learned to be wise without being gentle; as religious emotionalists they were engaged chiefly in calling down the vengeance of a subsidized God upon greedy and rapacious enemies. I can think of but one supremely great prophet of their race who had learned to be compassionate, and Him they disowned, and scourged through the streets into the hands of alien executioners. . . .

[*The diary passage continues for another four pages with a discussion of the Jews. When Wolfe revised his diary into the eleven installments of "Passage to England; The Log of a Voyage That Was Never Made," he scratched out the last sentence above and expanded the material into thirty-five pages of digressive and tedious commentary on the Jews, the poverty of American intellectual life, Calvin Coolidge, the Ku Klux Klan, and the stupidity of social radicals. It also contained a tentative characterization of his student, Abe Smith, as a dedicated intellectual and an account of a visit to his home for dinner.*

*The following paragraphs are a sample of this material, which may be compared with Wolfe's full development of the character Abe Jones in* Of Time and the River: ]

But how fine and honest and subtle an instrument is the mind of my broad-nosed friend. He is now twenty, but he has arrived at a devotion of which few of us are ever capable—a devotion to thought for its own sake.

Such consecration to thought, as an end in itself, and as existing for nothing else, is not usual to our life. We have not acquired the habit of detached speculation: we care not for the idea, but for the device. Thus there have been few of our nation yet who would lie extended under an apple tree, and meditate upon the laws which govern the descent of a falling pippin. This seems a quite useless waste of time: it has resulted quite literally that a great many of our thinkers have had wheels in their heads—or plans for the invention of wheels. That, you see, is getting somewhere.

And that is why we are all properly convinced of the intellectual stature of Mr. Edison. [*A long satiric sketch follows—about Calvin Coolidge, "the strong silent man in the White House."*]

Perhaps the Jew, one day, may write some words upon a paper —and only a word may live.

The Jew must forget some things. He must forget to bite his nails when he is alone. He must forget a great deal of cant: he spoke to me one time of the "unbearable beauty" of something. Another Jew had said it in a dramatic criticism. A great many Jews and Gentiles have said it before and after. But he must forget it: it is cant.

The Jew must perform a surgical operation on himself. He must cut his whine out. He must never, never say of himself "I'm an artist" until he is forty; and then he must not say it until he is eighty—even if it should be true. And if it should be true when he is eighty, all the young Jews of thirty will deny it.

The Jew must never, never talk loosely about the Philistines, until he knows what they are. He must never speak of "materialists" scornfully until he can find a greater materialist than a poet; he must never picture himself as a wounded stag with the hounds of the earth upon him. He must not talk too much of "beauty;" he must not decorate his room with a rusty tapestry, two Japanese prints, and a small bowl of hammered brass, because he cannot do without it. Finally, he should read Spinoza, Isaiah, and Heinrich Heine persistently.

He must learn to keep the ladies of his tribe in suspension, or he will be suspended by them—those young Rebeccas with the fine curves, and the low foreheads, and the black, hot eyes, who think too early, and too long, and too much about the same thing.

The Jew took me upon a Saturday to his home for dinner. He lived in a tenement on the East Side, noisy and encumbered with a great many small children, but otherwise not an unpleasant place. The family held the top floor: there was a straight chain of ample large rooms running from front to back. The inner rooms were dark.

His mother had prepared an excellent meal of greasy, heavy, odorous food: all the meat, he told me, had been cooked the day before. He was tolerantly amused with the orthodoxy of his parents.

As I remember, he said it was "the bunk."

The mother, an old woman with a friendly, sharp face, and a single, wistful tooth around which swarmed a strange melange of phrases in Russian, Yiddish, with an occasional recognizable splinter of our native tongue, served the meal, but would not eat with us. His conversation with her was confined to friendly, remote monosyllables. They had, I believe, a great deal of affection, but they knew very little about each other. Certainly she did not know him.

Of course, the strong silent man has said that no one knows a man like his mother. At least, he should have . . . .

Monday, Oct. 27:

The mountains were my masters, the unyielding mountains which were beyond the necessity for growth and change.

Upon a ship, attention is focused on two targets—on people and on the sea. If I could represent the effect the sea had on these people—that interpenetration of its influence which Joseph Conrad noticed in its action on the lives of Englishmen—I might have represented here something that is of importance and beauty.

Unfortunately (the deficit being distributed evenly, no doubt, between the people and the observer) the most noticeable direct action of the sea upon the voyagers was to make some of them very sick.

And it did this: it severed them from earth, from towns, from walls; it broke the mould of one hundred little patterns of existence; it removed one hundred people suddenly and violently from the contrived web of habit and custom and association their lives had fashioned. The sea had found men in chains and it had set them free. Was the result, then, social revolution?

It is all a trifle, I suppose, but rightly considered everything is. And I have come to have belief in the tremendousness of a trifle, and to know that men may look in at the world quite as well through a peep-hole as through a window.

And though I come again to London a hundred times, I shall come no more as first, when I was twenty-four; and when a strange wild incoherent pain and joy was in me as I heard the noises of England on shore, drowsy and faint, as if muffled in that yellow fog, the far dim creakings and rattlings, and the subdued muffled whistles of the little boats, not loud and sharp and acrid as in New York; and I shall catch no more as then, half perhaps in imagination, the smell of the river and the fog and land; nor see, as then, the misty radiance of the brave bright sun, so smoked by fog that one could see its yellow circle with the naked eye; now will again this mad inchoate mixture of sounds and sights and odors, those floating and pungent exhalations of sea and land, be staged as background to the ship's straight sides framing, in little circles edged with brass, the evil line of hard white staring faces, faces that hated us.

So I believe in harbors at the end, and in the fence round heaven. I have had proof this day that there's a port for every ship; and I believe in this sea tonight because I know it has a shore.

"We have conquered the sea," says the fat man, taking his wet cigar between his short fingers. "The next thing we shall do is conquer the air."

Poor fool: he never conquered anything; at the end he will not be able successfully to maintain his tenancy of six short feet of earth, for the little crawling inhabitants will make short shrift of him.

I do not know where the fat man will be one hundred years from now—it seems absurd to think of him as either in heaven or hell, he doesn't fit. But I am perfectly sure where the sea will be.

It will be dividing itself gracefully before the cleaving prows of ships, and now and then it will strike with its strong paw and break the back of one of these ships.

[*One of the "installments" of Wolfe's "Passage to England" is "The Tall Young Man's Story," which takes up the problem of the giant as misfit in an unreal and absurd world, a theme which ten years later he developed into the sketch "Gulliver." The following selection is a sample of this experiment in fictional self-projection, as well as being representative of "Passage to England" as a whole.*]

I had forgotten to mention that there is a young man on this ship who is too tall.

I had seen him making the promenade of the decks with three-foot strides; occasionally elderly gentlemen would stop him, and in the kindest tone imaginable, say: "My boy, how tall are you?", to which he would mumble some unintelligible reply, and rush angrily away. Once or twice I found him engaged in brief and rather impersonal conversation with some of the passengers, but for the most part he kept to himself.

My active sympathy and interest was aroused only when I saw this young man fall victim to a series of appalling accidents, all attendant on his height. On two occasions, descending the main stairway to the dining saloon, he cracked his head with painful violence against the woodwork of the upper landing. How often this had happened to him I cannot say, but I saw it happen twice. At another time, after a belated appearance for dinner, in the course of his extraordinary contortions to place his legs comfortably under the table, he upset the water bottle, two glasses, and a bottle of Nuits St. Georges which belonged to his angry neighbor. Two days later he passed me limping painfully, and in answer to my friendly inquiry, he answered rather bitterly that he had barked his shin in the most barbarous fashion against the sideboard of his bunk.

There was in his manner a kind of brooding and subdued excitement; his eyes gleamed madly and, from time to time, darted sidelong glances; and though he spoke little at first, he was liberal in passionate and half arrested gestures, as if he were already making preparations for an eloquence yet to come.

I thought the time was ripe for conversation; and extending my legs to their last capacity, I managed to keep abreast of him. Presently he began to speak:

"It is to be wondered at," he said, "if no one has ever written a book of a man for whom most of the contrivances of the earth are just uncomfortably a little too small; the beds a trifle too short, the tables a bit too low, the food and the drink a mite too scanty. It is in this poignant submission to things that are not quite large enough that the shocking differences of life are felt; one comes to realize the black curse of the three inches too much, to appreciate the awful distances that lie between the fractional separations—the only real distances.

"To be Gulliver, to be a giant in a world of tiny creatures—that is quite a different matter, for to a giant there are no giants, but only dwarfs and brothers.

"And even those poor stunted giants of our own times, who find their way ultimately into circuses and travelling carnivals, those two-by-two eight and nine feet titans, generally, I believe, the children of rather middling-sized parents, who doubtless look on them with much the same terror with which a hen might regard an ostrich egg, are inexorably separated from participation in a world of five feet eight, and cheerfully resigned to that separation.

"They dream, perhaps, of the heroic ages of their ancestors when giants grew to ample stature and pelted ships of mariners with stones the size of mountains, of times when the hills trembled at their approach, and rivers were bridged in a step. And dreaming so, perhaps, these starveling titans of our times erect a world behind the canvas—a mad and merry world in which all the laws of symmetry are broken; they marry the doll lady, or the fat woman, and sit at table with Jo-Jo-What-Is-It?, with the living skeleton, and with the clown. And that, too, is quite a different matter.

"For they have been touched by the lights of carnival, and all beyond the lights are phantom. They see the world vaguely as audience, which makes a stir and a noise beyond, and which pays its fee to look upon them.

"And to be a dwarf—that too is another thing, for it is to sit in a giant chair as a child of ten, to live delightedly in a world in which there is too much of everything. And a dwarf may sleep quite comfortably in a grown man's bed.

"But from these shapes of things, these patterns which pinch like a tight shoe, into which I would willingly mould my life, if I only could—how terribly am I removed!—not by a league or a world or the distance of a star, but Tantalus-like, by the tragic fraction that keeps the bending fruit and the flowing spring just from my lips.

"It is the men who are too tall, I believe, who think most about their childhood, who see and feel most poignantly those crowding phantoms of themselves which follow at their heels, like spectral hounds. Already, before I have come to twenty-five, I am the father of a large family: of a child no higher than my knee, of another youngster whose head comes half way up my belly, and of a boy of sixteen years, all legs and hands and awkwardness, who is just on six feet, and in whose eyes may be read the secret terror of his heart: he reaches just above my shoulder, and he has sprouted a good three inches in a year. Already his elders are telling him that he will grow certainly until he is twenty-two, and that few men stop before they are twenty-five. In his tortured brain the poisonous figures race like vermin in a cage: six times three is eighteen; nine times three is twenty seven. Then, he is to be eight feet and three inches tall when he is twenty five! Who will have him then?—for he is sixteen, and he is thinking of these things. My God, if he but knew that freedom lies in eight feet three, and that he might do what he always wanted to do as a child—go off with a circus.

"Yes, I remember these smaller sizes of myself very well, and I believe it is the sense of departure from my past, so much greater with me than with men who stop at a reasonable limit, that has informed me with a sense of loneliness, a sense of strangeness to all the things of earth, a sense never of possession of anything, but of transitory passage and occupancy.

"You may read in a book or a poem of a man who has grown old, and who speaks of the years so many and sweet of his youth, and who does not believe that that thing may be gone with which he was identified; or you may read of another who contrasts the freedom of other years to his long confinement in a prison cell, and this too seems incredible to him, and all this you will consider of a fine and moving poignancy: you will believe in it. Yet, within a space of six small years, I can tell you of a change more incredible than these, of which you have never thought, and you will see in it nothing but a fantasticality. Six years ago I might sleep extended at my ease in a good-sized bed: the very closeness of that blessed period gives it a weird unreality now, when I awake of mornings, and in that growing twilight of my consciousness, stare with awe and horror across my angled shanks to where my distant toes sprawl on the footboards. I do not believe that they are mine: they seem detached, remote, left there perhaps by another person.

"And then I move, and the toes move with me, and I know again that I am proprietor of the whole abominable distance that lies between. This is my daily legacy of horror. Now, damn you, (he said fiercely) pun!

"I do not understand the principle of growth: I shall never understand it. The biologist seems to think it is all comprehensible enough, and the philosopher once explained it to me in a way which apparently was satisfactory to him, but so far from having a sense of evolution and possession in the boy of six years back who came to my shoulder, or the boy before who came to my belly, these are ghosts, ghosts, incredible now, remote and lost to me, and no part of me.

"And in the same weird fashion all of the physical external objects of my childhood have undergone incomprehensible transformations. I have seen tables, chairs, and ceiling, where once you might have seated kings and marched the Cyclops under, submit year by year to these terrifying lessenings. Nothing is as big as it was, and nothing is small enough to be quaint and useless. The mountains may become hills, but they may not be stepped over, and all the doll houses must be lived in. The burlesque of the comedian who returns to the old home after a long absence and exclaims 'I remember that chair when it was nothing but a little stool,' elicits no mirth from me who remember all the little stools when they were chairs!

"And even now a hope, a touching faith which persists in spite of every crippling and denying circumstance, permits me yet to gallop through doors, or to plunge down stairs with the same belief in my security as I had when I was ten. If you are of a speculative turn of mind you may draw some valuable conclusion here as to the value of experience as a teacher. A consecutive and monotonous series of cracked heads and bloody shins will show you how pitifully I have profited by my teaching.

"The uses of things have been horribly converted: a door is no longer a means of passage, but a means of impeding passage, a bed no longer a means of repose, but a means of hindering repose.

"It is not strange, then, that all my rebellions are turned inward; that my efforts are directed not toward escape but toward admission. I have a passionate fidelity to fences, and I abhor our treachery to them and all the hypocrisies of the little rascal poets who have never cared for poetry and who write about the tyranny of barriers. . . ."

[*Wolfe continued to carry out a random note-taking in England, some of which is preserved in a writing tablet. A sample of these notes follow, concluding with his first impressions of France:*]

The distinction of such men is that having come from the common people, they have themselves become most uncommon persons. Rightly considered, therefore, Lincoln is no more a man of the people than Louis XIV. The natural tendency of a people in a democracy is to resent palpable superiority in its leadership; to resist it; to "knock his blooming head off" if it sticks too far above the herd-level; and after a period of such service, to send forth frantic howls for "one of our kind;" for someone who is not too great, not too wise, and whose ideas might be perfectly intelligible to the average reader of the *American Magazine;* who likes baseball, poker, and smiles affectionately on all little children as they march by in the parade.

For the great artist, I believe, there can be no better beginning than one from the middle class. The blood of the aristocracy vitiates itself by intermixture and tradition; it produces at the end young exquisites of faultless taste but they can't bear the smell of blood; they surrender themselves to moonlight pangs and quivers and take to writing poetry for the *Dial;* having gone in for "real" or "vital" things, they are lost.

Friday—Nov—

Today I bought a pair of English boots: we call them shoes. My toes had begun to protrude through crevices in my American low quarters, and I thought the time for decisive action had come. I went into a shop of modest appearance near Southampton Row, and asked the bowing salesman for his largest pair. He brought me a pair of size eleven triple E's. I am now wearing them with mingled pride and comfort.

Let me describe them to you, for I believe that in these boots one is able to discern certain qualities of the English character—a certain broad, blunt, John Bullishness. They are broad, shiny with straight square toes, and very heavy. As soon as one puts them on, one acquires renewed confidence in his power to subdue all hostile forces. The thick soles and the heavy leather heels make an amazing clatter as one clumps sturdily down the *street*, or up the stairs. In short, there is no secret diplomacy about them—none of your sneaking, squeaking, soft, and cat-like qualities of, let us say, the French shoe. These British boots announce their arrival from afar. They say: "Here I come; old John Bull; get out of my way! clumpety—clumpety—clump!"

## THE LADIES OF LISLE STREET

There is, just North of Coventry Street, and running as approximately parallel as any public way can in London, a narrow dingy pavement, flanked on one side by the stage doors of theatres and by grog shops, and on the other by a squalid huddled row of two and three story brick buildings which house the shops of small tradesmen, tobacconists, and "tea rooms" or tiny Italian and French restaurants with glazed and curtained windows. This place is called Lisle Street; it is on the lower fringes of Soho.

And this is what they say to me these ladies of Lisle Street:

" 'Ullo, Sugar,"

"Hello"—one always answers one's name.

"W'ere you goin'?"

"Oh—nowhere much. Where are you?"

"Home."

"Yes, and where's home?"

"Tottenham Court Road."

"Got a room there?"

"Yes."

"How much do you want?"

" 'Ow much can you give?"

"Oh, you'll take all you can get, won't you?"

"Well, why not? It's 'ard work walkin' these streets. W'ere you from, Sugar?"

"I'm a Yank,"

" 'Ow! Been 'ere long?"

"A week or so. I don't know much about your city or your way. Name a price won't you?"

" 'Ow long would you stay?"

"All night."

A small isle, gentlemen, but packed with incident. There's the trouble. A glance at a map of England presents a mass of bewildering detail: there are places in every quarter that one should see. But I can't afford it.

I resolved, therefore, since I had seen a little of the East of England to see a little of the West. A guide book of the ancient city of Bath fell into my hands. I examined it and resolved to go there.

The city is no longer in the bloom of its glory, but it is one of the most ancient cities of the kingdom. Here the Romans had a settlement and made fortifications and built baths. Here was the fabulous land of King Arthur and his knights; here was the site of ancient Camelot.

And I remembered as well a certain story of a Wife of Bath by a merry poet named Chaucer; and countless details of the tight-packed history of but a century gone—of Sheridan's *Rivals*, which was written here and set here. Of the *School for Scandal*, the materials of which he gathered here; of Beau Nash, who came here ragged and became the lord of fashion and made the seedy old town to live in the eyes of the great again; of Dickens who wrote part of his *Pickwick Papers* at the Saracen's Head Inn . . . .

Indeed what established religion has been saying to science for the past fifty years, with naive disregard of the important means to its growth, through the media of such profound interpreters as the Rev. Dr. John Roach Straton,[1] and the Hon. William Jennings Bryan is: "You can't make a monkey out of me."

They do not like us—in spite of the vigorous assertions of the old ladies of both sexes, and the professors of English literature, and the envoys and plenipotentaries who make speeches before the Pilgrim's Club; yes, even in spite of His Royal Highness, the Prince of Wales, they do not like us.

All of the acquired and inherited superstition and prejudice of the centuries—the dislikes of Samuel Johnson, and Dickens, and Matthew Arnold, all of whom represented quite solidly, on their respective levels, qualities of head and heart indubitably English—have been riveted into the solid masonry of British opinion; and these people are solid in their opinions, lacking the capacity of sudden change.

Quite bluntly it seems that we once did the unpardonable—beat them in a war, and declared our independence of them. This as a matter of fact, was one of the best things that every happened to them. As Seely, one of their historians, indicates: it caused the radical and very intelligent revision in their colonial policy which has made the governance of their vast empire thus far possible.

But beat them we did—whether it was as sound a thrashing as our own schoolbook histories would have us think, or, as theirs insist, an unlucky accident, the result of poor leadership at home, and a great war with France, which diverted the national energies. It seems reasonable to suppose, however, that the colonists did not win the war simply by running away, and that the land we live on was not given us with a royal blessing from the third of the dunder-pated Georges. We possess, after all, the rather conclusive final argument of "Here we are. We got here somehow, you know."

1. A fundamentalist leader, who preached his fiery sermons at the Calvary Baptist Church in New York.

Bristol at night—Little traffic—Wind—effect of crowds tramping through narrow streets. Church window lighted down alley [*sketch here*]. Wine St. Corn St. Narrow Wine St. Old Market. Tram lanterns. The Pub—Voice singing "Til the sands of the desert grow cold." The high-gabled houses—Toy shop in one—Fitness of this. Clifton Down—Nightingale Valley. Leigh Woods. Museums. The Gate with the Church upon it. The Two Maids. St. Stephens. The Bells of Bristol.

And the effect of these great sweet chimes upon the imagination is incalculable: ringing at night there, high above the vast dark huddled town; above the tiled roofs; and gabled eaves; and wet narrow winding streets: these bells ring back the century and throng those ancient ways with phantoms—of men who worked great Bristol glory on their ships, of knights, adventurers, burghers, lords and ladies—smells of musty trade, of the fragrant East, of wine, and of the splendid toilsome commerce of the great slow boats. For supreme irony, it is only in the here and now that trade grows hateful; when it throttles beauty.

Monday, Dec. 8:

Someone has advised young men to see Paris before they reach the age of twenty five. I am here, therefore, in good season; and everything that has been said or written about Paris is true.

It is evil; it is beautiful; it is fascinating; it is bewildering. For the first time in several years I am faced with an utter suspension of all my faculties. I speak French only a little—and very badly. I read it slowly: —a terrible and devastating impotence has possessed me these past two days—life is passing me by which I am unable to grasp but superficially. I am in possession of a beautiful fruit which I am unable to taste.

In two days, however, a certain confidence has come to me in speaking the language. The words I have read, I hear spoken on the streets, and the [*breaks off*].

[*A sampling of Wolfe's notes on literature and culture:*]

Among the innumerable books, the commentaries, criticisms, and observations on American life which have been written by European voyagers, generally by Englishmen, I know of not one which has succeeded in arriving at any genuine understanding of us: I know of only one that seems to have a certain merit of thoughtfulness, of penetration, and it is generally wrong. I refer to certain chapters in *A Modern Symposium* by Mr. G. Lowes Dickinson.

It must be said that the Americans of this time had very little snobbishness about money. No nation in the world's history had known such enormous wealth; no nation had become so habituated to money. There were over thirty thousand millionaires in the country, and there were many times this number with the incomes of millionaires. Money was a commonplace—to those who had it; it was no longer the infallible means of entry into the most desirable and cultivated society.

And there was now in America a most desirable and cultivated society—the most truly elegant and modern society in the world. Its culture was new and urbane—since it had few traditions of its own it had drawn sustenance from its own time and had thus saved itself from that terrible mockery of culture which prowls helplessly by the relics of a mummied past. The new American culture was living; it was not profound. Its roots spread wide and far, but did not go down deep.

There was therefore a lack of profound conviction and belief. While these new people far surpassed the people of the Victorian age in direct and honest judgments, they were inferior to them in their passionate loyalties or hostilities of the nineteenth century. They could no more have echoed the conventional raptures which the Victorians were taught, such as false rapture over Mont Blanc, Raphael, The Last Supper, St. Peters, the Sistine Chapel, etc. than they could have walked on their fingers, but neither had they ever been stirred by anything as deeply as were the Victorians [*by*] Darwin and the Oxford Movement. Many a hoary piece of aesthetic claptrap went down before the cool ennui of these people, but many an idol of their own making also went down after a year's worship. These people had very little faith, and no loyalty. Their false god was not money, but success. They could stick to nothing for long, and they never rallied to a fallen standard.

The New York theatre at this time illustrated this fault. It was the most brilliant and intelligent theatre in the world. Upon its stage at all times were to be seen plays translated from a half dozen languages and representing a dozen cultures. In the course of a single season, its finest single producing group, the Theatre Guild, might present an American play, an English, an Austrian, an Italian, an Hungarian. Yet, brilliant as these productions usually were, there was something terribly unhumorous about this culture quest—something that, in spite of all its outward elegance, stank faintly of the stew and disgust.

I think Mr. Vachell [*sic*] Lindsay is a very fine poet. Likewise, Mr. E. A. Robinson is a very fine poet, and Miss Edna St. Vincent

Millay, whose sonnets, declared a New York columnist, are as good as, if not better than, any of Shelley's. I do not believe Lindsay or Robinson or Edna Millay or even T. S. Eliot have yet written as good a poem as "Ulysses;" I do not believe either of them has yet shown poetic energy equal to that of the regretted Alfred, Lord Tennyson, who did some things very well indeed, and who was very likely to do something extraordinary as long as he was not impressed with the necessity of meeting his pilot face to face, or in assisting at the coronation of the Queen of the May.

On [*Joyce's*] *Ulysses:*

"In his apparent formlessness he achieves a form"—and that of a blot of ink upon a paper is no less definite than that of *Oedipus the King*. The important thing is that this form achieve the dignity of great craftsmanship; this *Ulysses* fails to do, and in this it fails to win consideration as an important and beautiful work of art. If it is important it is as a symptom, not as a fact. The dunces having waited at the feet of the Man from Vienna, were ready for it; and it came.

At least two of the captains of invective, Swift and Voltaire, have used the method of infinite enlargement as a telescope through which to look upon their little crawling worlds of men and cities.

That banal journalism of taste which must live always in its year and month, and which seems to be the special possession of the mediocre. It cannot read Tennyson without thinking of 1875; Swinburne without being reminded of the Queen's Jubilee; Rostand of 1900; Brieux of 1910; Shaw of 1914; Pirandello of 1922. It strings everything on a rosary of days, months, years—and the last pearl is always the largest and best. It mouths certain terms as "modern," "Victorian," "romantic," "classic;" it pleads for the isolation of the "work of art," and it is able to isolate nothing: it is only able to change its shirt.

It writes books with such titles as "From Proust to Dada."

It's a poor rose which blooms for the gardeners alone.

The rarest perfume is not the faintest; the greatest triumph is to render the exquisite comprehensible; when it is rendered comprehensible to the exquisite alone, it is a great triumph, but not the greatest.

The answer I believe is merely this:—art, particularly the art of the theatre, must have a perfectly definite connection with morality even if, as the scoffers say, the standard of morality is not universal and absolute but purely local, determined more by geography than by anything else—it must have this connection, I believe, for the most practical reason in the world:—the influence of ethical standards upon conduct. The reasons why a useful burgher may be allowed six wives in Turkey and one in America may not have been formulated by the Almighty, but the circumstances produced by such custom, by rebellion against it or painful submission to it, has furnished the motive power for more thousands of plays than I should care to read. In fact it has been responsible for almost the whole of the modern French theatre.

For the romantic aesthetician to protest indignantly, therefore, that art has no relation to morality is as absurd as for a very angry man to bellow that he has a very fine sense of humor, much better in fact than the other fellows. They provide their contradiction by their arguments.

Manifestly, the whole course and purport of my intent is to fashion in English prose a personal and distinctive style. If I am to write at all it is to be in the language of the tongue I speak, and not in Chinese, Italian, or Greek. It is far more to the point, therefore, that I imitate,—aye, in the straight, literal sense,—the prose of Thomas DeQuincey, than the prose of Cicero, Renan, or Thucydides.

. . . *Marius the Epicurean*, that if experience could be selected, so that it might meet the life of a man at the time it would have most meaning, the importance and the quality of the man would be vastly increased. This, says Pater, happened to Marius when a certain book came into his hands at a certain time.

[*In Paris, early in 1925, Wolfe finished his play* Mannerhouse *and began to look about for other projects. The following notes and fragments represent his literary activity in the spring of 1925. The first is a diary fragment written in March which describes the experience that Wolfe later developed for "The Sun and the Rain."*]

By a fortunate chance, I was conducted by a station porter, upon my arrival in Orléans, to the Hotel Terminus, situated near the station and within easy walking distance of the principal shops, the museums, and the great cathedral, where yearly in May, on the seventh and eighth days of the month, the great fête of Saint Jeanne D'Arc is celebrated, an occasion which brings thousands of pilgrims and visitors to this ancient city, and which will this year attract many Americans.

The hotel I found conducted by an amiable French woman, Madame Govry, who has for an assistant a young French woman who speaks English admirably. For twelve francs a day I was quartered in a large clean comfortable room with hot and cold water, steam heat, and a deep wide luxurious bed.

I came here at evening, in a train mixed of freight, and animals —I came with the animals—peasants from the North, a man and his two women. I smoked cigarettes all the time to kill the flat sharp rancid smell of their bodies—I gave them cigarettes. At Patay I had to change —the new compartment was cold and lit by a smoky lamp. Peasants again, men and women, who shouted humorous, but not good humoured, obscenities to the guards at each station—crying for more warmth.

There was a girl with them—the lamp made shadows on her face, but she had the loveliest eyes I have ever seen—she looked at me from the shadows and smiled at each new protest of the peasants. Presently two women entered, crowding us; the girl came and sat beside me shivering and putting her hands into the sleeves of her furry old coat—beneath it I could see she was dressed cleanly and freshly. We rode on at that crawling pace, over a dark flat plowed country: in a remote sky were multitudes of frosty stars. I didn't know whether I was going toward Orléans or not—earlier in another train I had heard the peasants talking about the Americain and the necessity for him to change somewhere for Orléans. I had got out and got in two or three times dumbly and silently like [*end of page*]

In the old parlour of the house on Woodfin street [2]—that musty old frame of the golden days, with its sweet cool narrow glade of orchard reaching far behind—I heard the sea for the first time. Below the marble-topped table, covered with the bible, the album, the stereoscope, and a glass-caged platter of waxen fruit, surrounded at every quarter by the horse-hair varnished sofas and chairs, enclosed by the four walls of sober brown, hung with the benign countenances of my whiskered ancestry—the first time, let me say, any of them had been hung—there were four great conch shells.

2. Wolfe was born and brought up in the house at 92 Woodfin Street which his father had built. This note is written on stationery marked Café Restaurant de la Rotonde, Place du Matroi, Orléans.

—and faint and far heard breakers pounding on the ends of earth.

I saw the sea first when I was twelve years old—a gangling boy, already just over six feet, who had hard work looking like a half-fare portion on the trains. At Miami, Florida, I came upon her first—a great blue rolling sheet under a blazing sun, tastefully serving as a background to the ladies' legs which decorated the beaches.

Write Monkeyville.
Write the "young" thing.
Write the idea of America.
Finish the Countess.
Write the University Divine.[3]

"Oh my youth, my youth; its glory that never was, its poetry, felt and written since, its pain, its pride, its loneliness, the children of my old imaginings. Give it back to me! Give back the thousand false and trivial discoveries of world old, world forgotten things; give back the great assaults on opened doors & breached walls; give back belief in the standing idols, in the day and in the moment; give back belief in remedies and young physicians; give back the prison of the years; the ignorant measurement of periods; the witless hoarding up of people in their centuries; the large contempt of everything forepast. Give back, my God, give back the lie and the emptiness; give back the treacherous ecstasy and the door that opened in my breast in Spring; and the vague mysterious pain which shot me in the month of May, big with deceitful promises of destiny and direction and an end. For I grow old enough to have my youth again, to know its use, and to steer it nobly; but it is done. Better a little smoke than a little dust . . . ."[4]

But we, who are determined to remain loyal to the religion of our fathers must be increasingly wary of the arguments of these people.[5] The devil, as is well known to any experienced demonologist, has power to assume many deceptive shapes. Hamlet knew this so well that he was at first committed to the impiety of doubting his father's

3. This series refers to a satire on William Jennings Bryan and the Scopes trial; a piece about the spirit of youth; a defense of America against British critics; a vignette about the "Countess of Caen," an old woman he met in Orléans; and a sketch that he later worked into "Passage to England" about the Dean of St. Ruperts.

4. The speaker is the Dean of St. Ruperts in "Passage to England."

5. This note and the next are material for an unfinished satire (modeled on Anatole France's *Penguin Island*), "The Isle of Quisay," about a holy man who cast out devils.

ghost. And yet, why should we condemn the young man for this perfectly natural suspicion? Who can declare with assurance today that the ghost of Hamlet's father was not the devil? Will you answer that, please?

Satanic conversions are innumerable. The fiend appeared first to Faust as a little black dog, who followed the learned doctor on his promenade with apparent innocence, weaving all the time circles of damnable sorcery about his steps.

The shapes in which he appeared to St. Anthony (the Copt) are manifold: the vulgar are familiar only with his embodiment as a young nude woman; but he came also as the Queen of Sheba, with four thousand Negro boys in retinue, and a caravan of gift-laden camels. Later, he impersonated learned doctors of all sects.

The Reverend Cotton Mather has recorded the appearance of the demon in his *Magnalia:* he often entered into the bodies of small children; and certain old crones of the Massachusetts settlement are known to have partaken of his spirit and to have communicated his powers.

The cathedral, too, was singularly favored with holy relics: under the altar there was enshrined the forefinger of St. Thomas the Doubter, still slightly hooked; in the sacristy were kept the elbow of St. Sebastian, three hairs from the bosom of Saint Bartholomew, and the right thumb-nail of Saint Catherine of Siena.

### CHORUS OF SAILORS FAR OFF

(Oh, the sailing men before were never found)
And if the earth is round, why were they never found?
Oh, tell me, Heraclitus, if you may,
Where are the ancient skippers
Of the quinquiremes and clippers
And the sailing men of Asia and Cathay?
And the Argive and the Norse
Who kept a level course
And who never came back to their places?
And though Swinburne speaks so plain of the vigil and the pain,
Where are the Thracian ships and all the faces?
And though it seems unsound to think the earth not round,
The ancient plan that flattened out the main

May not be dismissed; it must be, in truth, confessed
That this world is what we make it (Dr. Crane.)[6]
So perhaps the ancient seas ended at the Hebrides
And plunged through space in green eternity,
And the galleys of old wars go sailing round the stars
And the mariners see meadows in the sky.

"Look at them," he said with savage disgust, "look at them, will you. There's the Curse of Drink for you. Drinking water—day in, day out. Swilling it. Enslaved to it—"

"Wait, wait, Loop," said the other tolerantly. "You mustn't be so harsh. That's youthful intolerance. Oh, I know, my boy, I was an idealist too at your age. But you grow more tolerant to human frailities as you grow older. Why look here, Loop: we must be broad-minded about this. A little water for drinking purposes is an excellent thing. Any physician will tell you that. A small bracer, say, taken before meals. I know an old gentleman past eighty, as hale as an oak, and he swears he has taken a small glass of water every night before going to bed since he was twenty. And he believes it has improved his health—"

"I don't believe a word of it," said the other violently, it's merely an excuse to satisfy his craving, the damned old libertine . . . ."

. . . turned upwards on the neck, which dilated a little like a bird's, and in which a single pulse was beating slowly, slowly.[7]

This, then, that he felt, was the Life Force about which Bernard Shaw had spoken so frequently, about which so many other writers had spoken solemnly, balefully, portentously, but rarely gaily or exultantly; which penetrated so many religions, was adjudicated by so many customs and institutions, and was frowned upon at every convention of the Methodist Church, unless it was ecclesiastically tethered.

Ha, ha (for at this point he laughed to himself) ha, ha; one might as well tether a dragon with a leash of ribboned silk. He did not measure his emotion by ethical formuli; he did not interpret it under the radiance of painted windows, nor did he gauge it according to the infinite "would yous?" of all the mothers and sisters in this world, that ultimate & devastating test by which all conduct and all [*end of page*]

6. Dr. Frank Crane (1861–1928), Methodist clergyman whose pious, platitudinous essays were syndicated in the newspapers in the 1920's.

7. This fragment is the only place in Wolfe's writings in which he mentions Shaw's theory of the Life Force. The passage apparently refers to a vein in the narrator's neck.

Dr. S. Parkes Cadman[8] (getting up on a mossy rock and looking about with a gentle inquiring smile): Now are there any questions?

A Voice Over the Radio (somewhere in the Trees): I am a young man of 48 years, and I have just been appointed to a position of trust in the rubber department of a drug store. My parents were honest and God-fearing people, but I was kept in total ignorance of The Facts of Life. My rude awakening too late has almost unhinged my reason. My childhood faith, learned at my mother's knee, is slipping from my grasp. Like a drowning man, I clutch at every straw. I have read Freud, Ellis, and Krafft-Ebbing. The darkness deepens. Would Wolfe help? Save O save.

Dr. S. Parkes Cadman: Read Browning. Do not lose faith. Your problem is a common one, and is needlessly complicated by the shallow cynicism of the writers you mention.

[*The following notes come from a portion of a writing tablet that Wolfe used while he was in Italy in June, 1925.*]

Death hath run upon him and riven his life away.
Heard horns blown far off in a dark wood (forest).[9]

Genoa

Via Garibaldi—Palaces—The Museums[10]—Strozzi and the St. Thomas with the finger—cherubic face of Christ. Reni (Guido) and his Sybils—The ships of Columbus—the armour—the Venetian beds, chairs, mirrors. The Snyders and the taut lines of rushing boars and hounds—The Jenner and the child.

Murillo, Zurbaran, Teniers, Ruysdael.

Soaring city—Columbus' birthplace.

"I have been," he said, "where men have never been before. I have conquered the ether; established communications with the incommunicable."

He drew a large handkerchief from his pocket, and began to wipe away the blood which still flowed from his nose and ears. Then

8. The pastor of Brooklyn's Central Congregational Church and one of the earliest to use the radio as a medium for preaching.

9. Note the first use of this motif which Wolfe later developed in LHA.

10. In these entries Wolfe is referring to the Palazzo Rosso, which houses Bernardo Strozzi's "Doubting Thomas," and the Palazzo Bianco, which has such works as David Teniers' "Guard-room," Bartolomé Murillo's "St. Francis in Ecstasy," and Francisco Zurbaran's "SS. Ursala and Euphemia."

he set out slowly in the direction of the town. [*Sketch of a pair of wings.*]

He looked at the shattered wings which suggested that he had himself shed them; he looked at them without regret.

Leonardo da Vinci was in his day, a well known military and hydraulic engineer. In his leisure moments he amused himself by painting a little.

He was the tenth child of a family of ten, but probably was treated with no great amiability by his brothers, as his father had begotten him on a peasant woman without first making certain concessions to the church and state.

Upon a day when the sons of God had met, He wept.
And One said, "Why weepest thou, Lord."
And the Lord answered: "Because I have done a wrong."
And One said, "Lord, thou art infallible."

"Being a Person" (God continued) "I must always be Here; being omnipresent, I must also be there as well."

[*Scattered among Wolfe's papers are a number of notes and fragments which show that he was beginning to write about his childhood, his family, or his forebears. They probably come from the late part of his stay in Europe. The following notes constitute all that are extant of these materials dealing with home and family. The first long passage is a memory of his brother Ben, who died in his twenties in 1918.*]

Write fiercely for a month.

When the day opens
And the night ends.
Comrade and brother and friend.
There in the Lunch you sat smoking.

As I remember him now, sitting with his long legs crooked beneath him on one of the high revolving stools of the all-night lunch, holding a cup of coffee in one hand and a cigarette in the other, while the last copies of the morning edition fell from the roaring presses, audible a good block off in the silent streets, and while the route boys padded by, half bent beneath their heavy bags, folding papers as they went, and wondering if they could make their round by six o'clock; as I see him in this setting, so curiously cheerful and exciting in spite of the darkness, he seems to me to be a manifestation of permanence; an object of fixed reality in my life, on which I may place my hands at any moment. And he is gone.

And so you have gone in the night, Ben.
And the day opens without you.

Things For Which I Have Cared, Being Young:

Sounds (a train far off in Southern hills; a horse at night on a deserted street, particularly cobbles)

Odors

Tastes (Food; drink)

Sights (Places; Pictures)

Touch

Books and Music and Women

(Smell—of Horses and of Leather on a Summer's day. Of melons, bedded in straw in a farmer's wagon—particularly watermelons.)

The Smell of old books.

And the rain that falls from lean tall trees, and wets their bark; particularly from pines, which is the tiger and the king of trees. Thick dripping rain from heavy leaves I can't abide.

The smell of cool markets, caverned under ground; and the smell of earth and cobwebs in a cellar.

The smell of tar when it comes spongy in hot streets; and the smell of boiling tar.

The smell of wet black earth and of trees, and of the air, in summer after rain.

My father's hands: the sound of them on his face and neck when he washed in the morning.

The wind and the snow; the beauty and loneliness of Autumn in the Southern hills.

The York imperials stored in the cellar.

(Despise: Sunday cake and ice cream, of mid-afternoon, at a visit.

"Jew bread."

Scrambled Brains and Eggs with Fried Green Apples.)

The year was early: the young tender grass came out, and erased the frozen brown of the meadows; the cherry trees were blooming, and the scent of a prime April was upon the land. The mornings carried yet a bite; but it grew warm sooner, and young boys, for whom the Spring is fashioned, now came nimbly from their beds, and strained at the leash to be on their way to school. Tar grew spongy on the streets at noon, and gave forth a pleasant, pungent odor; children plucked it from the pavement and rolled it in balls; the boys put it in their mouths and chewed it. Among the tender grasses the dandelions were springing; they gave forth an unforgettable odor stored with memories of a million Spring-times; an odor fraught, impalpably and inarticulately, to young boys, with unspeakable magic, and with romance, and youth. Each gleaming morning kissed them in their beds, quickening their hearts with nameless anticipations, bringing with it inchoate promises of high adventure and of mighty deeds.

The lettuce, in the cool dark beds of earth, beneath the trees, came cleanly from the ground, still dotted here and there along its crisp white roots with clumps of wet, black loam. It was a joy to pull it in the morning, when the dew was on its leaves; it was a wonder and a happiness to pull the radishes from the earth; to cleave their acrid crispness with the teeth and to eat them with the earth still clinging to them.

There was adventure in the finding of the red, wet plums buried in the long grass below the trees:—some grew large and ripe and cracked with their own sweetness. The hearts of boys beat faster because of all these things; but they were transformed, they passed into disembodied and ecstatic contemplation when, at mid-day, or in the afternoon, a wind sported through the orchards and rained fragrant blossoms on them in blinding, dizzying [*end of page*].

And it was then, I believe, when I was sixteen, that I experienced for the first time the terrible and destructive maternalism of a woman's tenderness: that tenderness which can cry out in pity at a cut thumb: which can be moved to an ecstasy [*breaks off*].

Old Billy Woodsend—a hatter [11]—used "chamber lye" of entire family (i.e. its urine) in order to stiffen wool to felt—His son Sam follows the trade—"laziest man that ever lived."

Old Billy would appear coatless after a 50-mile jaunt from "over yonder" to visit one of his sons or daughters.

11. Wolfe's maternal great-grandfather, William Westall, was a hatter. These notes appear to be old family anecdotes. The one about the prediction of death Wolfe used in HB.

"I'm going to die tomorrow at ten minutes after six o'clock."

Will looked at him for a moment reflectively and curiously.

Will remembered a brother who had died of kidney trouble, his father's comment was: "Well, that's the best lye I ever did see."

Somewhere, like a great bell hidden in deep water.[12]

A fine smoky gold sun.

[*After his return to New York, Wolfe apparently continued to jot and scribble when he had time. Most of the following notes can be placed definitely in the period September, 1925, to June, 1926. The first batch are grouped together in a writing tablet.*]

—reeled in upon his winded Pegasus.

Necessity was always near to quell timidity.

He was a man of infinite innocence: He thrust his hand around the corner for his money, and got it back in an envelope.

It grows laughter in the lips of the fool.

If ignorance is bliss, why are not more of us blissful?

Old age: something we all detest and something we all hope to attain.

Yea: I would look at noses through a skull.

A most important meat-fly, big with destiny.

Indeed, there is a certain timelessness about the mob. It is faithful to superstition, although the shape and kinds of its superstitions vary.

There need be no great alarm concerning the destructive influence of the books of Charles Darwin upon the ancient faith of the citizenship of Tennessee. I venture to suggest (I could never remember figures!) that it will first be necessary for a considerable part of it to learn to read.

We are loyal to the destiny of waste and death. For in the idiot pattern of this dance of prophecy and ruin, this brute, blind [*breaks off*]

It was my great privilege to hear the Commoner [*William Jennings Bryan*] speak when I was twelve years old; he was at the height of his splendid powers which were entirely vocal. That man was a living voice; and when the voice grew old and died, as it did some years ago, the man died too.

12. The first appearance of Wolfe's metaphor for the faint memory of pre-existence, which he later developed for the baby Eugene in LHA.

The vitality of the town was enormous. It realized, vaguely at first, and then with increasing comprehension, that it had a destiny. The tide of the world was reaching strongly into these chosen hills: a tide that brought with it no poverty; a golden tide. The great average prosperity of the nation was reached and overpassed: in a few years Altamont became one of the wealthiest little towns in the land.

La Marquise de Bidraye [13] believed in the Church, the utterances of L'Action Française, and the triumphant return of His Royal Highness, the Duke of Orléans. History should be played by noble actors; without them it became chaotic and infamous gabble, unworthy the interest of devout and patriotic citizens. She had the intense loyalty and unquestioning belief of a stricken nobility: there is something terrific about these people.

The scene of Ralph and Eugene and Margaret should be rewritten—except the ending.

Second Act, Eugene expresses himself on the idealism of The Faithful Dog.[14]

Get off at Westall Lumber Co. and walk up hill.

Ask the Class for Discussion.

On Taste—The need of a certain measure of irreverence in Poetry. No absolute standard to taste. Is there any object in the world that people can agree on as beautiful? Kant and Hume.

See Arnold Bennett on "What Is a Classic?"

He was a drayman.[15] He drove his wagon, hauled by a wind-broken and spavined old horse, each day to the dray yards, a *square* of pavement just off the public square. Then, with his whip in his hand, he would go with the other draymen and sit upon the broad wooden steps that led up to my father's shop. They would sit there for hours at a time, chewing and spitting tobacco continuously, waiting for customers who seldom came, and passing the interval in horseplay.

I have not felt the world's imprisonment; I have wanted a key that would let me enter, not a key to set me loose.

13. The Marquise appears as a character in Wolfe's sketches about Orléans.

14. Notes for revision of *Mannerhouse*.

15. This is written on stationery of the Hotel Albert, New York, where Wolfe lived before and after his European trip.

Yet have I made propitiations for but one faultless moment: it is enough that the years be twisted if a day is straight; and if an hour is crowded, our lives have been long.[16] As for the rest, I shall possess my kingdom from afar, giving praise for things withheld. The old avowals drop away; only the old refusals stand. If we have inherited confusion, we have been spared the weariness of prescience. Our triumph and our glory lies, perhaps, in groping to things through the smoke.

—I saw a good show the other day.[17]

—What was that?

—Queen Victoria. Say, that's a good clean show. Of course, it's a box office flop but I enjoyed it. There's a woman in there who does some wonderful acting. Tells you a lot of stuff you never knew too. Historical, you know. The Queen falls in love with this German guy, and marries him, and, Oh Jesus, they were devoted to each other. Say, there's a fine scene in there with this guy Palmerston. The Queen hates him like poison, an' when he holds out on some important news, she comes in an' wants to know what the hell.

[*The following items are the earliest records of Wolfe's decision to write an autobiographical novel. The series of recollections set the pattern for the two notebooks full of memories, chronologically arranged from birth to age 23, which he used as a working outline for* Look Homeward, Angel.]

1–16—The Family<br>
—Society<br>
—Women

The Book shall have this unity—it shall represent the struggle of a man to stand alone and apart—such a man as would be forced to stand alone by his physical and spiritual structure—but who [*breaks off*].

Birth

First Recollections—the Sun—the Street—the Garden—the Shaded Porch—the Grape Vines—my sister going to school

St. Louis—Cincinnati—up the stairs—bicycles—house at S.L.—

16. This rhetorical flight is one which recurs in Wolfe's notes and drafts over the years. Edward Aswell finally used variations of it twice in Wolfe's posthumous books: YCGHA, p. 398, and HB, pp. 196–97.

17. This is the earliest example of Wolfe's jotting down an overheard conversation, a habit which he continued in order to master dialogue.

two little boys—Mabel—Grover—World's Fair—Grover's Death—Cooling Board—Return home—Grandfather's death—early years and recollections—Orange St. school—orchard—white wax—June apples—Playhouse—iron bar—cellar—pipes—bottles—Max Israel—Charley Perkinson [18]—the Fire Dep't we had—the thrill of going into musty old playhouse to read—the back room—my mother's room—closet with the curls tied with ribbon—the roof—hot tar—my father's room—the wardrobe—the gold-headed cane—.

18. These two neighborhood boys were Tom Wolfe's best friends up to the time he began attending the North State Fitting School.

# *Pocket Notebook 1*
## *September, 1926, to October, 1926*

*As soon as his teaching duties were over in June, 1926, Wolfe was able to begin work on his autobiographical novel,* Look Homeward, Angel. *He planned to spend the rest of the year in Europe. He had enough money to live for a while, and Mrs. Bernstein promised to provide the rest so that he would not have to return to the New York University classrooms in the fall. In July he traveled in France and England with Mrs. Bernstein while he completed a long detailed "outline" for his book. Actually it was a series of phrases recording his memories and impressions up to his last year at Harvard. He then bought several large accounting ledgers and settled down in London to fill them up with his large, penciled scrawl.*

*In order to have paper with him at all times, Wolfe took up the habit of carrying a little pocket notebook in which he could jot down ideas and phrases of the moment or draft passages for his book. Gradually he began to use it as a repository for his observations, especially during his travels. During the period covered by this first notebook, he was spending most of his time laboring hard at his writing, although he took a short excursion to Brussels, Bruges, and Antwerp in September. It was a lonely time during which he looked inward and lived in an unreal world of the past. Of the book he was writing, he was able to say, "It is a record of my secret life."* [1]

---

[*Wolfe describes his surroundings in a letter to Aline Bernstein, August 22, 1926.*]

I have two rooms (the whole first floor of a house in Wellington Square), the place is very clean and well furnished. . . . In this fine sitting room of mine I have shelves for books, already stocked with 75 or 100 volumes, a deep padded chair for reading, a large table for eating and writing, a cupboard for tea things: in my bedroom are more books and more cupboards. All I need now is someone to visit me . . . .

Well, I must spin out my entrails again—this time, I hope,

1. Letter to Aline Bernstein, September 11, 1926.

successfully—it is perhaps something of a beginning—or an ending—for me. My life grows sick and thwarted from lack of a bearing. But I shall not be too sick to heal myself.

[*The notebook begins with this entry:*]

*Wed.* Sept. 8:

In morning wrote American Express Company, St. Martin Lane, New Street, Covent Garden.

The Books—Andrew Lang on Oxford—The Union Politician Man—The Five hours a day man—The Chauffeur of Edw VII "yes, yes, yes, yes"—

The Folk Play—favorite words "belly-taut," "mush," "spindle-shanked."[2]

Marienbad—(Wiesbaden)—Brighton—The Front—The Burlington Arcade, St. James St.

Cut her in cubes.

The Puppet Players—The book is fictional biography—it must be lifted from fact—The puppet woman—Mrs. Glickstein.[3]

[*On September 13, Wolfe went to Brussels for ten days and continued work at the Hotel Bristol et Marine. He was writing episodes about Eugene Gant's years at Harvard—material that was later incorporated into* Of Time and the River.]

Teeth—Brussels, Sept. 23:

Eugene on going to bed—looked at his teeth—Horror of having teeth like Frank—of losing them by thirty five or forty.

When does a man get his second teeth, at ten years perhaps? Ten years and I've lost two—How many teeth has he? 28—with wisdom teeth, 32—Say, 32. I've lost one sixteenth of my teeth in ten years. Ah, but you've lost those two in the last two years. They're beginning to go. A tooth a year means that 12 will be gone at 30, at 40 you'll be practically toothless. He would peer intently at the teeth of all the people in the street noting which were false, which good.[4]

2. Wolfe remembers his days with the Carolina Playmakers, when Frederick Koch encouraged the students to write plays with a regional flavor.

3. Wolfe had an idea for a framework for his novel—like Thackeray's device in *Vanity Fair* where the narrator takes the puppets out of the box. Mrs. Bernstein was apparently to figure in it as Mrs. Glickstein.

4. This material was finally developed for LHA, p. 586.

[*About September 24, Wolfe traveled to Antwerp. The following entry in the notebook is an erotic fantasy that apparently had its origins in a visit to the Musée Royal des Beaux-Arts d'Anvers, for in a letter to Aline Bernstein, dated September 25, Wolfe uses the same phrase about Queen Helen:*

"From my father, I came by Dutch blood, and the love of opulence has always been in me—the pictures of Hondecoeter, tables groaning with fowl and fruit and fish; a butcher's shop hung with a dripping beef, the cows of Cuyp—and above all, the broad deep bellied goddesses of Rubens, and all the others, their blond hair wound about their head, a pearl in the ear.

"I want eternal life, eternal renewal, eternal love—the vitality of these immortal figures: I see myself sunk, a valiant wisp, between the mighty legs of Demeter, the earth Goddess, being wasted and filled eternally. I want life to ebb and flow in me in a mighty rhythm of oblivion and ecstasy. Upon a field in Thrace Queen Helen lay, her amber body spotted by the sun."]

"Upon a field in Thrace Queen Helen lay, her amber body spotted by the sun["]; the laurels bent to rotting lily pads; there were the feet of running girls in the groves. I lay upon the swelling cushion of her belly, locking her warm pillared legs around my neck from time to time, biting the thumb swell of her rosy palms, drinking, from her unmarked breasts, draughts of rich warm never-ending milk, renewed eternally in her embrace. Slowly I drank the thick sweet liquor of her tongue and throat. My blood grew rich as a slow wine; she bit cleanly through my shoulder muscle; below her arm I tore open mightily her silken breast, below the ligature of her arm. I drank her till I was drunken; we were ambrosial; our wounds were healed by kisses.

Eugene could not bear the defeat of a champion: it saddened him—Connected it with women—defeat and victory.[5]

The Sport news.

He read gluttonously the sporting news in five or six papers every day, particularly the accounts of prize fights and football games.

5. On September 23, Gene Tunney defeated Jack Dempsey for the heavyweight boxing championship. Wolfe explained his feeling about it in a letter to Mrs. Bernstein, September 27: "I have recovered from the pain of the man's defeat: the thing is a survival of Cambridge days, when I shared in every circumstance of a champion's humiliation. It was not he who was beaten, but myself: I saw myself beaten and battered to earth time after time by a rival, in front of my mistress." Wolfe was prompted to bring these attitudes into what he was writing about Eugene Gant at Harvard.

All the jargon of the sport writers—the senseless repetition of hackneyed argot—was embalmed in his memory. He became a fanatical partisan of contestants he had never seen: he never went to a baseball game, yet he knew exactly the progress of the Yankees, reading of their victories with sharp exultancy, of their defeats with a kind of sorrow.

[*When Wolfe visited the Musée Royal des Beaux-Arts, he wrote in a letter to Mrs. Bernstein, dated September 27:* "I soaked myself in Antwerp in the great cruel vulgar Dutch and Flemish pictures that I love so well." *The following entries indicate some of the paintings which drew his attention.*]

Antwerp:

Francken—the flaying of a man.[6]
The curling thin peel of a lemon.
The Dutch ship bounding on the boisterous inshore waves.[7]
De Vriendt—the fight of the fiends and angels. Beast-headed fiends with serpents, vipers, beaked vultures for privates.[8]
De Rigny—the Groaning Table, the rich warm belly of a mandolin covered with fruit and meat.[9]
Schut—The coloring of Greco—The unearthly light.[10]
Quentin Metsys—His anguished Christs.[11]
Brueghel, P. (de Jonge)—Child shitting—Man puking—religious ceremony—whoredom fighting.[12]
Brower and Teniers.[13]
The swarming composition of Rubens—too rich—the Italian coloring.
But Christ on a Cross against a black sky—
Great Picture of the Manger—and the rich robes of the kings—

6. "The Martyrdom of St. Crispian and St. Crispinianus," by Ambrosius Francken (1544–1618).

7. A reference to "View of Middelburg" by Bonaventura Peeters (1614–52).

8. "The Fall of the Angels" by Floris De Vriendt (1520–70).

9. "Fruits and Accessories" by Pierre De Rijny (1615–60).

10. Probably a reference to "Portiuncula" by Corneille Schut (1597–1655), Flemish painter of religious subjects.

11. An apt comment on the work of Quentin Metsys (Massys), the elder (1466–1530).

12. Details in Brueghel's "Flemish Village Fair."

13. Adriaen Brouwer (1605–38) and David Teniers, the younger (1610–90).

The fierce warriors—The buskined feet—the crimson togas —the strong black-bearded, war-like heads—
The strong Dutch head of Christ—His strong compositions.[14]
The Master of Frankfort [*Sketch of a building with three arches, suggesting the composition of his "Adoration of the Magi"*]

Eugene did not go home for about two years. At the end of his first year, as the summer vacation approached, he waited for some sign from his mother. None came. Summer had always been for her the time of money getting: correspondence, infrequent as it always was, ceased entirely during this period.

He enrolled at the Summer School, took a course in English history, read furiously in the sweltering heat, promising himself all along that he [*breaks off*].

Left:

—The Melrose affair.
—Rooms.
—All the Young Men.
—Home.
—The Last Year.[15]

Nothing would delight us more than to give to our readers some account here of the history of puppet plays and puppet players from remote antiquity to our present day, showing them, in a manner made popular by H. G. Wells, emerging from the primeval slime; belaboring one another about the heads with stone mallets in the days of Probably Arboreal.[16]

Meaty Whores.

14. The museum is rich in paintings by Rubens—religious, mythological, and secular. The references here single out "Christ Crucified" and "The Adoration of the Kings."

15. This refers to the "third part" of Wolfe's book (about Eugene at Harvard) as he was currently planning it: "There are five parts but one is an introduction that will be comparatively short. I have almost finished the third part; I am well on with the first." Letter to Aline Bernstein, October 14, 1926.

16. See LHA, pp. 35–36, for the elaborate fun-making that develops out of this note. The last words of the note can also be explained in this way: Wolfe had in mind a farce, set in the Stone Age, which he wrote at Harvard. The main character was named Probably Arboreal; he had a friend named Slightly Simian. The epigraph for the play quotes an "Eminent Scientist" as declaring, "Our earliest ancestor was probably arboreal." Wolfe had encountered the phrase in Matthew Arnold's essay "Literature and Science," where Arnold quotes Darwin's proposition that "our ancestor was a hairy quadruped furnished with a tail and pointed ears, probably arboreal in his habits."

The Last Book:

—New York—The Play.
—The Month at Home.
—Arrest and Capture.
—New York Again.
—Cambridge—The Widow—The Decision.
—The Year in New York.
—Voyage—The Boat—London—England—France—Paris—The Stolen Play—The Passionate Friends—The Widow—The World of Women—The Countess—The South and Madness—The two Women—The Puppet Players and Mrs. Glickstein.

Should the book end abroad or at home? [17]

[*The following is an early draft of material, based on Wolfe's uncle Henry Westall, that eventually went into "A Portrait of Bascom Hawke."*]

He went occasionally on Sunday to visit his Uncle Emerson and his Aunt Louise. Emerson Westall had been the scholar of his family—a man of powerful intelligence and disordered emotions, his eccentricities of dress, speech, walk had made him an object of ridicule to his Southern relatives, a ridicule streaked, however, with pride, since they accepted the extraordinary composite of his character as another proof they were an unusual family: "He's a Westall" they said, exultantly. "Queerer than any of us."

Emerson's youth, following the war between the states, had been embittered by biting poverty, the delinquencies of his father, the Major, who wrote bad poetry about a lady's hair, while his family went hungry, and by the multiplication of the Major's offspring.

"As each of them was ushered into the world" he declared later, his voice tremulous with passion, "I walked abroad in the woods, striking my head against the trees, and blaspheming God in my anger."

"Yes, sir," he continued, pursing his lips rapidly against his few loose upper teeth, and speaking with an exaggerated pedantry of enunciation, "I am not ashamed to confess that I did. For—we were living in conditions unworthy—I had almost said—the position of

17. At this point, Wolfe planned to carry his alter ego's adventures all the way through the first European trip. "I brood constantly," he wrote, "over the fourth and last [*book*]—the book lifts into a soaring fantasy of a Voyage; and I want to put my utmost, my most passionate into it." Letter to Aline Bernstein, October 28, 1926.

animals. And—What do you think?"—he declared, with a sudden shift in manner and tone, becoming, after his episcopal declaration, matter of fact and confidential—"Why—do you know, I had to take my own father aside, and point out to him we were living in no way becoming decent people"—here his voice sank to a whisper, and he tapped Eugene on the knee with his big stiff finger, grinning horribly and smacking his lips against his big dead teeth. It had smoked its way into his flesh—he had never forgotten.

He took what education he could find in a backwoods school, read everything he could, taught in a country school for two or three years and, at the age of 21, borrowing enough money for railway fare, had gone to Boston to enrol himself at Harvard.

Somehow—perhaps because the place has always had a certain submerged affection for fanatics—he had been admitted, secured employment doing various jobs, and lived in a room with two other starved wretches on $3.50 a week, cooking, eating, sleeping, washing, and studying in the one place.

At the end of seven years, he had gone through the college and the school of theology, performing brilliantly in Greek, Hebrew, and metaphysics.

Poverty, fanatical study, the sexual repression of his surroundings, had drunk copiously at his heart: at thirty he was a lean fanatic with sucked cheeks, grey bright eyes, and six feet two inches of gangling and ludicrous height, gesticulating madly before a grinning world.

He had married a young Southern woman of good family: her parents were both dead, she had lived for several years with an uncle in Portland, Maine, who had been constituted guardian of her estate amounting to $200,000.

The man had squandered part of her money: stolen the rest: but she was pretty, intelligent, had a good figure—Emerson was a cauldron of desire for her: he married her.

He got a church in the Middle-West: good pay, and a house. During the course of the following twenty-five years he was shifted from church to church—to Brooklyn, then back to the Middle West, to Jersey City, to Western Massachusetts, and finally back to the small towns surrounding Boston.

He preached magnificently, his gaunt face glaring from the pulpit, his voice husky with passion; his prayers were fierce solicitations of God, so mad with fervor that his audiences felt uncomfortably they were coming close to blasphemy. But, unhappily, on occasions Emerson's mad eloquence grew too much for him: his voice, always too near the heart of passion, would burst in splinters, and he would fall violently forward across his lectern, his face covered by his great gaunt fingers, sobbing horribly.

This, you will understand in the Middle West is not too well; but Emerson, who chose uncomfortable titles for his sermons, would be overcome wetly by his emotion on those occasions on which he talked on "The Breasts of Potiphar's Wife"—"Ruth: the Girl in the Corn."

[*Sedwick, in the following passage, is the earliest appearance of the character, based on Kenneth Raisbeck, who became Francis Starwick in* Of Time and the River.]

Sedwick lived almost entirely by historical precedent. He had been born in the Middle West, went to Chicago when he was 16 to study art, and like George Moore, failed as a painter; he had come to Harvard when he was 17, having submitted a play which showed evidence of imitation of Wilde, Dostoevsky, Moore, Frank Harris, the Restoration Dramatists, Tchekhov, and Tolstoi. It was a very remarkable play, but it would not act. The professor was convinced that he had found a man of genius: he took the boy under his closest wing. He guided him through the university, gave him employment at the most profitable salary he could arrange, as his assistant, and took him on a tour of Europe, introducing him to everyone who was resting on his laurels, as Jones, Pinero, Hauptmann, D'Annunzio, and Brieux. During the five months' visit Sedwick wrote scenic directions and invented a title for a new play: he believed, like Flaubert, that the artist should work slowly, for years if necessary.

Teeth.
Athletes.—The Antique Gods.
Uncle Henry—Aunt Laura.
The Melrose Girl.
The Death.
The Last Year.
Dramatis Personnae:
*Harvey*, *Jack*, *Clement*, *Albert*, *Billy*, *Hank*, Wayne, Day, Raisbeck, Daly, Carlton, Manley, Taylor, Levin, Gaston, Wallace, Withrow, Stevens, D. Sands, Oenschlager, Smyser, Goodnow, Brown.[18]

18. Names of Wolfe's friends and acquaintances at Harvard. Those which are italicized and whom he calls by their first names are all from the South. Those which are not italicized and whom he calls by their last names are all associated with Professor Baker's 47 Workshop. Of special interest are Kenneth Raisbeck, Donald Oenschlager, Dorothy Sands, and John Mason Brown.

Once, he broke, for the first time in five years, his isolation of residence; he had returned from Baltimore—the term had begun: he was without a room.

There were three young men from the South in the law school, who had acquired in less than two years a notorious reputation for riotousness. They lived in a small four-room apartment: they prevailed on him to join them, heartily insisting that everyone would have ample room, ample quiet—that each could join in or desist from the revels as he pleased. One of them was a young fellow of good family—strong in body, handsome, of dominant temperament: he was followed blindly by his two companions, one, Dick Henley, a young fellow with a white weak vicious face, easily taunted into any enterprise by Jim, whom he followed blindly. He, finally, found himself in difficulties with the authorities when he entered the class of a bearded professor in the Law School one morning, in a dinner coat stained completely with egg and whiskey, rising and declaring at intervals during the old man's lecture: "That's a good point, boys—a damn good point. Put *that* down."

The opening year of the twentieth century was not a happy one in the history of [*breaks off*].[19]

The Melrose Girl.
The Young Man.
Death.
The Last Year.

In the hall as he went out, he saw, hanging from an accordian hat rack, the absurd coat and hat which she had worn when he first met her: something gathered in his throat. He realized, for the first time, that they must be poorer than he thought. The woman, her white sullen little face, a trifle baffled and fearful, trotted down the hall, opening the door for him. There was in his heart a sad finality that burned through his flesh.[20]

Saturday [*October 2, 1926*]:

I'm back in London—I came back late Wednesday night from Bruges—I found a letter and a cable from you.

19. This is the first indication that Wolfe is beginning the narrative of Eugene Gant's birth. It is a draft of the opening sentence of LHA, Chapter III.

20. A draft about Eugene's parting from the Simpson family, which finally appeared in OT&R, pp. 208–209.

[*The following two unpublished passages are taken from the* Look Homeward, Angel *manuscript in order to illustrate what parts of Eugene's childhood Wolfe was working on in early October.*]

He saw that almost everything depended on communication, that communication was founded primarily in speech. But, even so, granted that children were thus imprisoned before they could talk, why had none of them described the horror, the futility, the revolting waste of the whole process, as soon as he had become articulate? The explanation came with electric horror. Eugene found that thought which was not built upon the sensuous images of speech was a house built on sand; he found, for example, on waking from a sound sleep, that what had been clear and sharp in his brain before he slept was now blurred, confused, inchoate, mixed with other thought and other time. For, without language, he saw that even the sense of time became confused.

Thus he was faced with the terror of watching the erasure, day by day, of all his mind had patiently and speechlessly elaborated. The stabbing truth came to him then at once that when his mind had learned to construct itself in speech images, it would be almost impossible to reconstruct its activity during the period when it had no speech.

All the feelers, the tender opening buds of taste and odor, were opening up in him, the cellular kernels of his powerful sensory organization, destined later to become almost incomparably hearty and exquisite, were expanding. He had the rare gift of enjoying the excellence of the common thing—of tasting to its final goodness the quality of a liberal slice of savory roast beef with creamed potatoes. He scented his food like an animal before tasting it: peaches and cream he gloated over sensually. He ate, when he could, on a bare table in the pantry: it was filled with musty spicy odors—the ghost of cinnamon, clove, new bread, vanilla flavoring. There one day, he met first the delights of toasted corn flakes. They came in a huge carton labelled *Force;* there was a picture of a comical, merry old man on the cover—as he remembered, an old man, with a hooked nose and chin, a Punchian and appetite-giving old man. For weeks he lived in hungry anticipation of toasted corn flakes, rich cream and sugar: the savory glutinous compound was the highest pleasure he had tasted.

---

[*The following three paragraphs are drafts of a letter to Aline Bernstein, October 14. The wobbly scrawl and misspellings indicate that Wolfe had been fortifying himself with beer.*]

I shall tell you how I feel. My life runs smoothly, without sorrow, through the day, I stay in my pajamas until one o'clock, writing. Then I dress and go to the Express. Four [*sic*] three or four hours I am heavy with lunch and beer, buying books in the Charing Cross Road or walking. At five or six I return and work to 8 or 9. Then I eat. I return at 11 or 12, and right [*sic*] to 1. The night hours from 7–9, until I have eaten and fortified myself with beer, are frightful. I am sunk in terror and desperation.

I warn you that I am lost to action: some day some leverage will compel me to go home—I will see I have to. But dogged as I am I can't escape from this enchantment. All this week I have said I would go to Oxford—I said I would go a week ago. I think I really shall go at the end of this one. Your letters are [burning?] and [*at*] present I cannot explain clearly—I have drunk a great deal—I remember you as if I am drowned at the bottom of the sea, but living still, thinking of you, knowing you are there, and not knowing how to get back ever. Or I should say I am the super Hamlet; my mind since my birth had been an enormous spider, now I am flattened under the weight of the spinning.

You remark that I do not really think I am a better person than you. "Let us say we are both equal." There is no equality and, curse you, I shall enjoy my humility. It is all the sweeter to me when I reflect how I have been tricked and fabled to.

My horse, with kingly hooves the grass sweet meadows wounds. He is lean and small in the head, broad rumped and shining:—a good male smell comes out of him; he breathes his sweet hot breath on me; and he laughs at me with his sensitive, flickering, comical, sensible mouth.

[*This is the first notation reflecting Wolfe's idea of a moment "caught" in time that lives "etched in memory"—like that of the "wisped-haired slattern" seen from the train in* Look Homeward, Angel, *Chapter XV.*]

Variations on a Theme:

A Bridge Swings up separating two people who have never met; or in the Subway they pass; or the ship sails; or on the platform she; or through a village in a car.

Eucharist.

Unus panis et unum corpus multi sensus, [*breaks off*].[21]

Paddington 4:10—Oxford 5:30.

21. The fragment can be translated freely, "Eucharist—one bread and one body of intense sensitivity."

## *Pocket Notebook 2*

## *October, 1926, to September, 1927*

*Since October 17, 1926, Wolfe had been in Oxford. By now he was living just outside of town in the lodging he later used as the setting for the sketch "The House of the Far and Lost." He described it in a letter to Aline Bernstein, October 20:* "Yesterday I found this place—it's called Hilltop Farm; it's 20 minutes walk from the centre of Oxford but like the country, up a noble avenue of trees, flanked by green playing fields. The house is a fine residence; I have a sitting room and bedroom—both magnificent places."

*During the next eleven months, Wolfe lived through the most important creative period of his life while he wrote the bulk of* Look Homeward, Angel. *At the outset he was alone in Europe, at first working himself into creative exhaustion, then roaming from England, to France, to Germany. He became so wrapped up in the world of memory that New York seemed unreal to him when he returned. He spent the next period "spinning out his entrails," as he called it, while living isolated in a dreary loft building on East Eighth Street. The notebooks reflect his fits of irascibility as the task went on. The love and care which Mrs. Bernstein gave him seem to matter little. In order to provide him with relief and change, she arranged for another trip to Europe in July and August, 1927. Although they traveled together and spent hours in museums and cafes, Wolfe allotted time for writing almost every day.*

*This pocket notebook carried during these months is one of the fullest that Wolfe kept. He was developing the habit of using it for diary passages, for the lists and catalogues he liked to set down, for storing away observations, whether on his mental travels or on a real journey. It is especially rich in reports of his visits to museums and galleries and in reflecting the cursory reading he carried on during his creative labors.*

---

[*The first notes are on loose pages because Wolfe tore them out, made some selection of notes, redated them "December, 1924," and published them in* Of Time and the River, *pp. 664–65, as excerpts from*

*Eugene Gant's notebook. He made very few revisions in the material, but he may have rearranged the order of the pages.*

*Most of the entries are phrases he set down while working on* Look Homeward, Angel, *Chapters VIII and IX, although some of the jottings ("plumdropping birdnotes," "the minute-winning flies") remained stored here until Chapters XIV and XV. Some of the phrases turn up in a passage about Judge Tayloe which was cut out of the book before publication. For example, the Judge meditates on time and appearance when a bird passes:* "Shadow and hawk, sound and the falling tree. Gone, which first?"

*It was this long series of entries that Wolfe especially had in mind when he reported:* "I lost my little fat notebook which I carry everywhere with me—Went to the bus company—They sent me to the Police Station—Found the sergeant reading it with a bewildered face—He treated me with all the courtesy one extends to the insane." [1]

Favorite soporifics—the poetical works of Gilbert Frankau.
"Shadow and hawk are gone."
Icarus lies drowned, God knows where.

Oxford in pursuit of a woman—one of the most dreary spectacles God hath given—Buol's in the afternoon.

Foolish question: why are the Tories so eager to say Democracy has failed?

Hair like a copper cloud—feather and flame come back again.
The gutted plums bee-burrowed.
The poisonous inch around the heart.
The cancerous inch.
The burning inch of tongue.
The hairy grass.
The long sea locks.
The hairy seas striped.

The other gate of ivory—Ida—Cadmus—blunt—drummed woodenly with blunt fingers—Sir Leoline the baron rich—thunder-cuffing Zeus—Erasmus fed on rotten eggs—What a breath—Has an angel local motion or [*breaks off*].

"The goose-soft snow."
Feathery snow—the feather-quilted snow.

1. Letter to Aline Bernstein, October 28, 1926.

Freckled eyes.

Wild Ceres through the wheat.

The slow dance of demons.

The bird swerves seaward like hope—September full of departing leaves.

A star I never saw before.

The latticed hearts of whores.

The windy bells across the snow.

The loosened scattered brain.

Heard windy bells across the sleeting snow.

The sun sets in the blinded eyes.

How through my jaundiced eyes the conspiratorial world—

"Burn off my rust."

"Batter against my heart."

Above the waters of Babylon.

Painter of ghostly woods Olympean.

He sat alone four thousand miles from home—the lonely death of seas at dawn.

The debauched swine.

His heart danced sadly to the Jazz.

This island of my life—the sun's wink.

Low muttering life goes up and down.

Our lives' last inch.

Bronchial horsecough.

The sounding gong—notes of a drum—the green lily depths.

The sunken mouth of toothless age.

The lake-washed wings of dipping birds.

Smooth bellied fish that glimmer in a pool—as one looks at a sleeping person, and will not waken her—because—because—

[*Draft for a cablegram to Mrs. Bernstein, sent October 26, 1926:*]

Comfortable lonely working monastic orders for Jew.

The decent and untainted eyes that look on spattered death—Eugene dreaming of old battles—For a child the spear goes cleanly through—The musical horses beyond the battle press—The phantasy of bloody death: the cloven brain pan—the one last second near enough to touch its brother life, but infinitely far—The windblown heights of the town.

Dream of Oct. 24–25 at Oxford:

At the house of D. H. Lawrence—The house at the foot of College Street where I toyed with McKenzie girl—Present Shorty Spruill, Nat Mobley, R. Wilson.[2] Shorty does not notice me—but I am in brilliant form—Nat amiable—Shorty reads from one of D. H. Lawrence's books. One of the characters says "Yes, sir"—immediately we all get up, begin snapping our fingers, D. H. included, and sing, "Yes, sir, that's my baby." I jump from one of D. H. L.'s bean rows to another—They all sit at table—I jest brilliantly—an old woman with a lewd whore's face comes for D. H. Lays upon the bed. I go out and play on Court House lawn—[*There is one more brief illegible statement about Shorty.*]

Gates of delight—Vergil's gates of sleep—one of silver—the other of polished horn—darkness and dumbness flawed with light. Slow fumes of the aerial structure of his inner life. Die, god, die. The rich waste of gardens—the reeking rotting weeds.

Napoleon (waving starwards), "Say what you please, gentlemen, someone made all that."

His soul stooped.
"a shrivelled pelt"—raw hide—fast rotting—"Miserable carcass" —papa.
A wandering flume through hell.
Gaseous ripstink.
Torn lips—the oiled rich glutinous womb—the gods that whistle in the dark.

By all that split fidelity be you paid,
For all the entertainment of your lust,
By the poxed property of your tainted blood.

Why, when you make a man, I'll make a God.
The sea-cold eyes.
Plum-dropping birdnotes—the young air full of.
A branch of stars.
Dry boughs stutter—stammer.
A hen and a pig—quills—frills—fringes—mired—feathers.
The vast low stammer of the night.
By the inn—the geese go waddling to the Fair.

2. Three of Wolfe's fraternity brothers from Chapel Hill days.

The minute-winning flies buzz home to death.

"Old England will muddle through, my lads"—She has muddled and she's through: but she's not through muddling.

Gull cry and gull are gone.

[*The group of loose pages ends.*]

The erogenous centre had not effected its boyhood transference from his mouth to his genitals; he was a staunch advocate of a larger navy.[3]

Darting, flirting, teasing, victorious in their momentary torture, the minute-winning flies buzz home to death.

In a hushed whisper: "The French are so much more *graceful* about it."

"The story goes false."

"a good chum."

Frankau's a Fool. His book on America[4]—his hatred of "highbrows"—anyone, that is, who is not a Tory. Still calls the Germans Swine—The bitter—praising half-and-half of Sinclair Lewis—thought Lewis a "highbrow"—Oh my God.

"25"—Apotheosis of Noel Coward—Masefield on the floor. "Be with me beauty for the fire is dying."[5] Dark Helen swimming in my blood. J. St. Loe Strachey's book on America[6]—Hands Across the Sea—The novelist with a pipe and a dog or a rabbit called Artaxerxes—Foch—Genevieve.

Moonwards the camels turn into Bythinia.
The little golden apples of delight.

Gray Rebecca, Gray Rebecca. In my Jewess-haunted blood.

3. This is Wolfe's crude joke at his own expense. When he was a schoolboy, he had upheld the affirmative in a debate on the proposition: "Resolved: That the U.S. Should Greatly Enlarge Its Navy."

4. "I picked up a volume which your kinsman Gilbert Frankau has written about America. It is called *My Unsentimental Journey:* It is bitter with the submerged jealousy of a small cheap man: it has in it something of the terrible and degrading bitterness and jealousy towards us which is gnawing the liver of England today." Letter to Aline Bernstein, November 8, 1926.

5. A line from Masefield's double sonnet on Beauty. Dean James Munn told Wolfe that this was one of his favorite poems and summed up his attitude toward life.

6. *American Soundings: Being Castings of the Lead in the Shorewaters of America, Social, Literary, and Philosophical,* 1926. Strachey was the editor of the *Spectator.*

Fri.–Sat. Morn:

A Dream—Riding with two young women in a cab or crowded car—opposite—their legs against mine—old fashioned style 1912 or so —Later on a hillside slope—often on a hill now I meet these women in dreams with the town immediate around as in an early Italian—"How old do you think I am?"—I am living in one time—they in another— What year is it?—1913—Are you sure? I turn the years up 15—There is a moment of astonishment, "Oh—I must be home." Then I turn them back and do what I will with them.

Death of Gant better at end of Third Book otherwise anticlimax.

Samson bound in green withes.
The Oxford Poets—all the sad young men.

Possible Titles:

The Building of a Wall.
Young Poseidon.
Poseidon's Harbor.
The Prison Wall.
Theseus.
The Hills Beyond Pentland.

Lean Death and Pale Pity
Went Out For To Take
A City! A City!
Awake!
Pale Death and Lean Pity
Went Out To A City,
Went Out To A City
To Take
These! These!
Way, way, if ye please,
To the thundering horse of my Symphonies [7]

*Thrasymachus or—the Future of Morals* [8]—Again the American broadside—"In America every one wants to be like every one else."

7. Wolfe never used this rhythmic chant in his published work, but the horseman Death and Pity ride through the night in OT&R, pp. 75–76.

8. A book by the British philosopher and educator C. E. M. Joad, 1925.

[*These are European cities he has visited. Those starred were first seen on this trip.*]

Paris
London
Bath
Bristol
Oxford*
Lincoln*
York*
Fountains [*Abbey*]*
Ripon*
Leeds*
Ilkley*
Edinburgh*
Glasgow*
Ambleside
Windemere
Keswick*
Grasmere
Brussels*
Antwerp*
Bruges*
Chartres
Tours
Orleans
Lyons
Avignon
Marseilles
St. Raphael
Cannes
Nice
Monte Carlo
Genoa
Milan
Venice
Montreux
St. Germain
Versailles
Chateau Thierry
Rheims
Soissons
Brighton*
Torquay
Exeter

[*These are cities he plans to visit after he leaves Oxford:*]

Plymouth*
Paris*
Strasbourg*
[*Cologne crossed out*]
[*Nuremberg crossed out*]
Munich*
Stuttgart*
Zurich

(Coppard's Book of Stories, *Clorinda Walks in Heaven*—The Spaniard drops nuts into the country woman's breast) The full white breasts of country women—calico legs in the sweet hay.[9]

9. This phrase recurs in Wolfe's notes. It is associated with the erotic image of Queen Helen on a field in Thrace. Note that both phrases are juxtaposed in LHA, Chapter 15.

Another Book on America by two English—Bitter, Grudging, Jealous (Under the Eagle's Feathers.)

Garnett's Books In Large Type—*The Lady Into Fox—The Man In the Cage.*[10]

Bloody awful i should think.

[*Scattered here and there among other entries in the next few pages are trial passages and phrases (like "the nettle-rash") for a poem Wolfe was composing to send to Mrs. Bernstein. Although the piece is no longer extant, he told her this much about it in a letter, November 13:* "The other night I wrote something for you which I am sending to you. It is called 'Super Flumen Babylonis,' which means 'By the Waters of Babylon.' The name is not mine; it is the title of a poem of Swinburne's, which I read long ago, but I believe it comes originally from the Latin Bible. What I have written is not a poem—You know, I believe poetry lives now silently in the hearts of poets who are too loyal to speak at a time when only the small cad, who has never written poetry, is called one. America is full of them. I wrote the thing because it is about you and me." *Here are some samples of his working with the stanzas:*]

SUPER FLUMEN BABYLONIS

So many years, so many days have passed.
Sunward the city melts into the sun.
Come, let us give our love its last
Hours by the waters of Babylon.

For when our walls are rusted by the river,
By the dark Medes
Captived our old gods forever,
Burnt book and creeds,
Your wall and your god will persever.

My Gods with bird cries in the sun,
Jewelled of eye,
The multiform Gods of Babylon,
Hang in the sky

10. Short novels by David Garnett.

Guarding the night with one
Beast and bird cry.
Here where the mined sands run
My Gods shall die.

Nor all the Gods of now and then
With all their art
Unbury the dead king again,
Unsilt his heart,
Unwind the river from his brain,
Make his dust restart;
Nor stir the city's dust to life,
Prevent her fall.

"Done, for a ducat." [11]

I am still an American—I cannot feel at home in any place but America—and not even there.

[*Wolfe was reaching the point of exhaustion in his day-to-day routine of writing. By November 8, he wrote to Mrs. Bernstein:* "I shall stay here two weeks longer and try to get as much of the Second Book on paper as I can. The first is done, the third almost done. I shall finish the last one in New York."]

I have not courage to face boredom.

The dream last night of the negroes. I had thought of the yellow bodies of their women for days—Now at a cabaret—murder and nastiness—Food slimey with filth and grease—Tailor shop in cabaret—They were making me a suit.

[*While Wolfe was writing about Eugene's boyhood reading and his imagined heroics in Chapter IX, he was moved to make the following statement in a letter to Mrs. Bernstein on November 10. He puts a mythological construction on his attraction to older women:* "I am going to tell you how I have felt since you left. When I was ten years old, I read myself blind and dizzy in all romantic legendry:—the Iliad and the Odyssey at the same time as the Algers, the Hentys, the Optics, and hundreds of the popular English and American writers of the time—Louis Tracy, Chambers, Phillips, Davis, Locke, Farnol,

11. Cf. *Romeo and Juliet,* III, 4.

Churchill, McCutcheon, Major, Hope—scores of others. Sometimes I was the valiant young minister of the fashionable church, arrayed in warfare against my wealthy congregation in my fight against the slum conditions, and aided by the millionaire's daughter, other times I was the bronzed young Yank, ex-captain of the Yale crew, fullback of the team, the wonder of the world, adventurously adrift across Europe, Asia, South America—the vanquisher of Dago armies, the leaper over garden walls, the climber of moonlit balconies. I was always 25, and she 22 or so. And the trees were always green.

"But I was born my dear with an autumnal heart. With me since I was twenty, ripeness has been almost all. I began then by endowing my princess of 22 with all the golden wealth of 35. But for two years I have been unable to think of the running maenads without boredom. I think only of Helen and Demeter moving their rich bodies in the ripening fields. Or of Peer Gynt's wife. And, in this grey English autumn, I think of my childhood autumns at home—the pain, the desire that was so much deeper, so much more nameless than spring, the sharp knife—the maple's burning red, the smell of ripening persimmons, the tired rich smell of the earth. Once, when I was reading Homer—I was 16—I asked the Greek professor if Helen was not very old when Troy was taken: it had worried me so much that I had figured it out, and knew she must be more than 50. And that old man, who had lived so long among this ageless and unwasting beauty, flayed me with his bitter tongue. I am no longer that bronzed young giant who was impeccably handsome, and always victorious. Too much water and blood has gone under the bridge since I was 10. The young man bores me, as does his doll-faced queen. And like God, I see myself always beaten, forever lost, forever hunted, forever driven by the furies. I am beginning to get a jowl, a bit of a paunch—I swing heavily along now with a man's stride—the racing thin boy who leaped into the air is gone; but through all of this gathering flesh, this growing heaviness, I exult to see the faun's face shining yet—the ancient eternal morning madness that grows wilder, younger, as my body ages. I sat with the young men in a college room the other day: all of the young men talked to me like clever boys, I talked plainly, simply, and I realized suddenly that three years ago I should have wanted to talk like a clever boy, and write like one. . . . and suddenly I knew that I no longer cared to shine in that way—I seemed somehow to be sitting on a good-humored but unpatronizing rock, laughing deeply, caring for nought but to have the eleven boys amuse me, enjoying myself. And I think most often of your hair flawed with grey, but not in the way you think. It seems to me that this great pageant of my life, beginning in cheap legendry, in which all was victory, faultless perfection, has led my dark soul across perilous seas, scarring me here, taking a tooth or an ear, putting its splendid blemish on until now I come to my autumn home, the streaked hairs, the rich widehipped body, the brief repose which lasts forever because it is founded on sorrow and the skirts of winter—beyond youth, beyond life, beyond death. You live timelessly like Helen, like deep-breasted Demeter, like Holveig."]

Saturday, Nov. 13:

Drunk—went to the pub—fell in with poacher—two electricians—Terrible beerdrunk—Tried to ride elec. bicycle—Fell all over Cowley Road—Finally can—Skinned hand—wrenched leg.

Monday, Nov. 15:

Two letters from A. Must get home by Jan. 1 now. Finish Book then. Grey weather, heavy food—depression of spirits. Can't work.

The Catalogs in Rabelais.

I am depressed and weary—want no more of England for a long time—I'll see if the Germans are better.

[*These manuscripts were on exhibition at the Bodleian Library:*]

Benedictine missals (Via Sancta Catholica).
Psalter—English Illuminated—1st Half 14th Century.
Bestiary—Moralized Natural History.
Caedmon—Old English Meter—Paraphrases of Genesis, etc.

The Magnolia Gardens.
The Chapel and Dining Halls—Depression at Oxford.

Sat. Nov. 20:

Went to the Pub at Night—all of us very drunk.

St Cecilia's Day [*November 22*] at Exeter Cathedral.

Wednesday, Nov. 24, 1926:

London again. Found cable and money from my Jew—How shall the years pass, Jew?

Introduction:

Throughout the Michaelmas Term of the year 1794 at Oxford the rain fell coldly and steadily, the river valley steamed with heavy weather, and certain hundreds of the more sensitive undergraduates at the ancient university fell victim to the formidable depression that follows a considerable period of bad food, cold lodging, and atmospheric clamminess and heaviness.[12]

George Moore's *Eloise and Ebelard* [*sic*] and the "Ah, Gods! Ah Gods" every few feet.

The Book on America written in 1902—with the apologetic preface by the author for the good things he said about us.

I can not work—The weather has *drugged* me—not depressed me.

The Nat'l Gallery again to-day.
The old women copying Turners.

"Here I sit, broken-hearted
Paid my nickel, and only farted."
"Here I sit, in silent bliss
And listen to the falling piss,
Now and then a fart is heard
That signifies a coming turd." [13]

[*The following notes record Wolfe's visit to the Wallace Collection, which includes painting, sculpture, furniture, and other objects of art and craftsmanship.*]

The Wallace Collection in Manchester Square.

Remember two years ago—The Bayonets (Italian)—The Armour—The Horse Spead-Headed.

The Doorknockers, Italian Genius astride a Sea Beast.

Lancret, Boucher, Greuze, Fragonard.

The houses are 5 stories tall on Nov. 26 at 4 o'clock. The place was steeped in a drizzling yellow mist. Street lamp burned milkily—Tea here at this time?

12. An attempt at the introductory section of LHA. At this stage Wolfe thought to begin with the maternal ancestor, whom he called Charles Westall, who was a student at Oxford. Volume XVI of the LHA manuscript has about twenty pages of this material.

13. These folk verses from the latrine were probably set down while Wolfe was at work on Chapter VIII, which includes Eugene's introduction to the schoolhouse obscenities.

Sat. Nov. 27:

Last night in London—Ate at Simpson's—Went to see *And So To Bed*—the Pepys play, and found it very amusing [14]—Later, watched the dance below in the hotel—How horrible and lean and awkward the girls looked in their cheap "evening dresses." How vulgar the young men. How much more comely, physically beautiful—how much more grace and gaiety have the Americans.

Chain mail—Peacock and Aldous Huxley—The Pope who lunches on wine and olives—A rich piece of marble.

America is the best country in the world at present for the libertine who would find employment.

Sir Henry Newbolt—that he had found only 700 poets from the beginning in English lit. up to present—but that there must be 1500 at present.

A man who has been de-Freuded.

South London—Going to France from Victoria—the winter trees—the playing fields—Denmark Hill—Houses like this [*drawing*] Peckham Rye.

I arrive in Paris—Il faut vous mettre dedans—written at Vetzel's —10:10—an hour after my arrival.

How many times have I come and returned to Paris?

1924—From London.
1925—From Tours.
1925—From Switzerland.
1926—From America.
1926—From London.

Tuesday, Nov. 30:

Again—The Dome—the Rotonde—I return the bad 25 centime piece given me last summer to waiter—Mais ca c'est paste.

Harry's New York Bar.

Spendable lendable unendable commendable money.

14. A comedy about Samuel Pepys by James Bernard Fagan, 1926.

The Historical Gallery in London—Sargent's picture of the generals—The head of Phil May.[15]

Brasserie Universelle—The old man's mistress who flirted with me.

Lipp's in Saint Germain—Choucroute Garni.

The linen fold of Cathedral work.

Dec. 2:

My heart beat 81 to the minute at 5:20 Taverne Royale—By the clock.

[*Additional passages for the "Introduction" to his book:*]

The first Westall who came to America in 1796 from England, was a Cambridge man:—he had been a year in Italy, he dabbled in paints, and did bad pictures after Romney—there are some still of Americans in Baltimore. The soul of this young man was blind—he saw nothing but he felt everything; he was something under the sea, groping without eyes, but with a thousand feelers. He saw nothing, and he felt everything. He was one of the most complete romantics that ever lived. Wordsworth and Coleridge *knew*, or thought they knew, what the Revolution was about—they wrote poems about it: this young man *knew* nothing, but lying on the hills in the Lakes he saw clouds float across the checkered field below, heard a dog baying, and the sea far off upon the island cliffs: at this moment he thought someone is being stabbed in France. He heard the guns and saw the peasant women in the level fields of Touraine their calico sunny legs widened in the sweet hay. I will stretch them open but I will not stick my nose into it but certainly not my tongue. If only sweetly it might come from bodies washed through and through, each drop of blood filtered in some enchanted medicinal water in a forest heart but the field sweat and salt and the tiny glutinous deposits of a thousand peasant pricks before me. But if from ambrosial flesh the white sweet dew distilled itself rushing to a milky core the gathered strength of [*breaks off*].

He had a scorbutic hand; on the back of his left hand there was a scaled corruption at which he tore constantly with his stubby fingers; it did not come at all upon my great grandfather, but my grandfather

15. A reference to the National Portrait Gallery, to John Singer Sargent's painting "Twenty-two Generals of the English Army," and to May, the nineteenth-century cartoonist for *Punch*.

had it on his thigh; my mother has it on the back of her left hand, my uncle on the back of his right, at which he tears continually with a queer itching smile of delight on his face, finally paring his nails with a bunt knife, and scraping the blade across the flaky scales: I have it on the nape of my neck.

Paris, Thurs. Dec. 2—

Ate at the Nigger Morgan's—Fried Chicken—near the Tower—The Taverne Royale in the Rue Royale—a certain richness—The middle aged florid Frenchman and his young mistress—cock-spent intelligence.

A strong young hard riding Horse-Cock woman.

[*The following references are apparently to the statutary in the Salle de Prisonniers Barbares and the Salle de l'Hermaphrodite de Velletri.*]

The Louvre:

Young Bacchus and The Grapes.
O Artemidorus Farewell.
The Spear of Wisdom (Minerva).
Apollo—Hermaphrodite.
Jupiter with a Chancred Prick.

[*Several sketches follow—of figures, heads, legs. One is labeled with the phrase "The Bull-thewed legs," another with the statement "Early Apollo at the Louvre."* [16]]

The Middle Sauce-Glass-Napkin-etc. stand in a room in Prunier's [*a detailed sketch*].

When you find you are loved a little more you love the lover a little less.

Paris—the city of superficial observation.

The Rhodes scholar at Oxford speaking of nearly everything said "superficial."

Saturday [*December 4*]:

I feel like work again—a letter from the Jew today—lunching at Régence again.

16. Probably one of the sixth-century Apollos in the Salle Grecque.

Goethe about the Irish—Like hounds upon a noble stag—Anderson's book of *Tar*—the jaundiced *Theatre Arts* "I will now say a few words about Woman."

These new towns since I came this time:

| | |
|---|---|
| Strasbourg | Ilkley |
| Torquay | Leeds |
| Edinburgh | Glasgow |
| Keswick | [*The*] Trossachs |
| Oxford | Exeter |
| Brighton | Stuttgart |
| Brussels | Munich |
| Antwerp | Zurich |
| Bruges | |
| Lincoln | |
| York | |

Grosser Preisabschlag (Because of the Falling Franc)

The Restaurant Valentin Sorg—The best in Strasbourg—Rue de Vieux-Marché-aux-Vins.

A man with blonde hair—came over with the Vikings—One darker with the Mayflower.

Dreamed last night before I slept what often as a child—gathering speed down a hill—the triumph of speed until one leaves the hillside for the air, sloping down to earth once in a while to bound airward again.

Nous sommes d'accord.
The moderns in France today:
Valéry Larbaud, Pierre MacOrlan, Jean Cocteau, Paul Morand, Drieu La Rochelle.

The rose pearl apple spray in the nacred dawn.

(To the *Dial*):
"Pardon, monsieur—vous êtes écrivain?"
"No, monsieur—Américain."

Strasbourg, Dec. 6:

Today I left Paris at 11:40—Got cable from my Jew before—Gare de L'Est—My baggage has not come yet—Darkness at Nancy—The Valley of The Marne—We passed again by Chateau Thierry—The low commanding hills behind the Marne.

The desire to escape of imprisoned toes.
A fibrous pulpy toenail.

Strasbourg—The maid at the hotel—The Teutonism of all—The vast beer place where I now sit—The curtained windows—called "Grande Brasserie De la Paix"—(Schutzenberger—Père et Fils).

Gloria In Excelsis—My Baggage came.

Strasbourg, Tues. Dec. (7?)

About in the town—Cable from my Jew at Exprinters—The gabled toyland roofs—The vast Brasseries.

The language one hears in Strasbourg is mainly German. The French they speak is abominable.

"Inoculation, heavenly maid."

Beer-Bulged eyes.

I am a iolly IERMAN In My Harte

Strasbourg, Tues. Dec. 7:

Tonight—at the old House—Dinner—Sluttish landlady—Pâté de Foie Gras and the Omelette—Pancake burnt below kirsch—"Come back to-morrow," fit elle.

Wed.

Sorg's—Ah God, ah God, the Food.

The Alsacian Museum—The vast wood carvings—the great masks—the grinning faces for the "moulin."

Early primitives—[*Drawing of a mustache*]—a pair of Strasbourg moustaches being wiped away from beer.

[*Sketch of a man's head*]: Back of Hun-neck.

[*Sketch of a man with apron*]: Concierge.

The third-rate Americans fall into Europe more easily than the first-rate ones, for the same reason that one man makes a better waiter than another.

A Hun's shaved skull above his neck seems to have been sawed off and fitted on because of the ridged folds of fat.

Ratskeller, Stuttgart: Ach Gott! The neck. The neck.

Sing sunk gesank in a new country—Who can do this so well as I?

Stuttgart, Thursday night [*December 9*]:

Kaffee—Restaurant Königen Olga Bau.

As I went over the Rhine today from Strasbourg—another country added—The evening in my camp I gloated, "Aha, you bastards you can't take this from me." [17] The flat land reeling infinitely away in the blurred dim woods.

The hun-head—small compact above a full large face—seems to be something to batter to smash to drive with.

Stuttgart:

*Frau Warren's Gewerbe* von Bernhard Shaw.

The Book Shops here contain editions of British and American authors—Galsworthy's *Forsyte Saga*, Shaw, Chesterton, Cooper, Mark Twain, Wilde.

Heute! Heute!

Das Grosse und Kleine Schauspielhaus.

Stuttgart hill—broad, winking with bright pearled hill lights in the evening—The town plain—The market place, Rathaus and the [*picture of a gable*] gabled overhanging bright colored toyland houses.

A valley that flows like a river among the hills.

Cannstatt—A suburb of Stuttgart.

The trip from Stuttgart: Friedrichshafen, Augsburg, Ulm—In the first part of the journey the romantic scenery—the steep close hills

17. To Mrs. Bernstein he reported his strange behavior while crossing the Rhine: "I went nearly crazy with excitement and exultancy, rushing from one side of the compartment to the other to look down at the river, and crying out, 'I have fooled you, you swine!' because I get these obsessions that I am being hunted, thwarted, checked." Unmailed letter, December 10, 1926.

—the laboring horse—slow winding engine—Towards dark the fields —the strips of grass and ploughed earth—duller, I think than France.

The old German in the carriage with me. The closed compartment—We both go to sleep drugged under the heat—The conductor with the upturned uniform.

Munich—flash by outer stations—local and electrics waiting—Similarities of all big towns everywhere under industrialism—the station—the trestle.

Through the gates I wait outside in a mounting frenzy. While he goes off with the Gepäckschein [*baggage ticket*] to the Gepäckaufgabe [*baggage office*].

The old man with the cart—the sarcastic comments through the crowded Weinachts streets—Hotel Vier Jahreszeit.

Later—the Hofbrau Haus—Lower middle classes—The magnificent beer, dark dark dark—The place sloppy and powerful with beer and smoke and the great cheerful dynamic vitality of their 1200 voices.

[*Sketch of a beer stein*]—The Hun chauffeur or doorman opposite me. The red ruby beer-wet lips dribbling with belched beer. The hat angle [*sketch*]—The waitresses in their black dresses—toothless bad cheerful faces—keys at waist—sinew and butt-bone walk—young blond man in Alpine costume—Old man scrapes bread across the beer slop before eating it—Marvellous tramp with beard who lights great pipe [*sketch of a long, curving pipe*]—Bows to people at next table ceremonious but daffey.

Drunken jolly voices rising above the noise outside—corner wet with piss—Teniers[18]—Tomorrow Sunday, but everything open, last two before Christmas.

[*The following notes record Wolfe's visit to the Alte Pinakothek, Munich's greatest art museum.*]

Stillleben.

Hals—"Fischermädchen."

Rubens' picture of the Rape of The daughters of Leukippos.

Rubens—"Meleager and Atalanta."

L. Cranach's picture of Lucretia's killing herself—The blond magnificent body.[19]

18. "A choir of drunken voices sang beyond the doors—Women and men —ugly and hearty, swung toward each other in a thousand natural powerful mug-lifted postures as they do in Teniers." Letter to Aline Bernstein, December 13, 1926.

19. A nude holding a dagger in a stylized suicide pose.

Christ's Body in "Die Beweinung Christi" of Dürer [*The Lamentation for Christ*].[20]

Rembrandt's "Holy Family."

Weenich and Cuijp and Raphael.[21]

Frans Hals.

The El Greco of a young woman in the Munich Gallery—Face of a corpse [*sketch of a face*] [22]

Interesting small canvas of Rubens—"Landschaft mit dem Regenbogen" [*Landscape with Rainbow*].

Rubens' rich Dutch Beauty—Helene Fourment.

Nicholas Poussin's picture of Bacchus and Midas [*sketch*].

Tintoretto's great battle pictures—Philip the II coming into Mantua.

Perugino.

Sandro Botticelli's picture of Dead Christ [*sketch*].

Deutsche Museum [23]—Vast fascinating—The little German boys who were allowed to play with the machines—Leibnitz, Ohm, Röntgen—Wärme [*heat*]—the energy—the picture of the air pump and its demonstration in Magdeburg—Horses could not apart pull.

But ah, the aeroplanes—I understood them because they were first conceived by mad men—men like myself of no science.

Sunday Night, [*December 12*]:

*Der Zug noch Westen* Deutsches Theater—A revue like most other revues—French and American—The little tables in the balcony where I sat—The childlike delight of the audience in the American women dancer—The fat German blond comedienne—She was funny —they all ate and drank in the intermission—

After—The Wiener Restaurant—Wien goulash—Why are cigarettes so expensive in Germany?

This morning Welt Reisen—Two letters from the Jew.

Glyptothek [24]—The finest Apollo I have ever seen [*sketch below*].

Ein gut weiss wein—Deidesheimer Leinhöhle

20. A magnificent grouping around the body of Christ just taken down from the cross. In the background is the sea and a city on the hillside.

21. Jan Baptist Weenix (Weenich), Dutch painter (1621–63), and Aelbert Cuijp (Cuyp), Dutch painter (1620–91).

22. The sorrowful face of St. Veronica, holding the cloth.

23. A huge museum of science and industry.

24. The great sculpture gallery in Munich.

Karlplatz—Ein dunkeles bier.
Dunkeles gibt es nicht—gibt es weiss bier.

The books on America and England in the windows.

The students with the cheek wounds after the theater in the München Café—One with inch long cheekwound just healing was—The movement of men in the street—This moment gone and caught forever.

The dear the inestimable side of boys is their eagerness. The boys in France and Germany who would write me in New York.

Tuesday—Rose late—German waiter laughed to see me snooze so. Went to the Amtliches Bayerisches Reisebureau—No cable—Went through the great Frauen-Kirche [*Sketch*]—Like two Stiff Pricks The Towers Are.

In the Dark and Frozen Maximilianeum[25] I have my foot gespraint. It hurts now. How the Dark River Ran—Concrete—Cascaded around an island—the wood chips stuck in it.

[*Sketch of a head with descriptive phrases:*] Hun-head—sword cut—the neck-line.

What does the world do farther on?

Tonight—Shaw's *Mensch und Uebermensch*—Done with Teutonic thoroughness—The Interlude in Hell—How they loved it! God—what setting—and how unpleasant to look at some of the people were—But nice the women.

[*Sketch*] Hunhelmet.

*Das Rheingold* tonight magnificently done—I was in the fifth and last gallery, wedged on the side with frauleins kicking holes in my kidneys. But terrific—The enormous bulk of the giants—The murk, the great horns blowing through the murk—the flaming red bank, like terror of Evil—the rapier in the gigantesque murk.

[*Two drafts of a cablegram to Aline Bernstein, December 16, 1926.*]

BEEN ILL GOING PARIS FRIDAY DEAREST. TOM.

EXHAUSTED PARIS FRIDAY STEADFAST DEAREST. TOM.

25. A nineteenth-century school for royal pages, which houses an extensive collection of historical paintings. Wolfe wanted to visit it when it was closed and fell down the stairs in the dark.

Went again to the Alte Pinakothek—Holbein's great pictures of the apostles [26]

Dürer's naked Lucretia and Cranach's lovely one—The Herr Doktor Professor who was lecturing on Raphael—The old German Masters and the religious pictures at the entry.

Rubens' legs sitting with his wife [27] [*sketch of fat crossed legs*].

The villainous mugs of the saints in Early religious picture high-boned—small eyed—bluelipped.

Sent another cable to the Jew this afternoon.

Neue Staats Museum [28]—Horrible, horrible pictures by the Victorian Germans but two interesting rooms with Cezannes, Van Goghs, Matisses, Renoirs, and Manets.

The thousands of German students who belong to duelling corps—The sword cuts on their faces—cheekbone, generally—[*sketch*] nose scar.

A man with a broken nose. But a sword cut not as bad as the cut the years give.

Either when a man is your host or your guest do not discuss his work with him, unless a basis of friendly understanding rests under you.

It is the work of the small cad—generally Yankee—to hunt out an opportunity for scathing criticism. Strike him in the face.

If one of these scar-faced boys challenges you answer his challenge by smashing his head in with a bottle or his face with your fist—They are used to the knife, proud of the scar—Let's see how they like knuckle work.

The art of Hatred—It is so rare, so great an art that it may be successfully practiced only by people of great soul.

Part of our joy in the German defeat was legitimate—It is pleasant to see the man who lives in prospect of a fight, trains himself to belligerence, beaten.

26. He is mistakenly referring to Dürer's two panels of the Four Apostles done for the Nuremberg town hall. The faces of Paul and Mark are those he characterizes below as having "villainous mugs."

27. A self-portrait, in which he is seen sitting with his first wife, Isabella Brant.

28. A gallery of European painting since 1870.

The American as soldier—We were as soldiers children—The temperament that starts a bar or bawdy house fight and delights in a four minute rough and tumble is different from the temperament which can wheel march shoot obey and drive on for four years.

For and against a subsidized theatre—The great German Schauspielhaus—Like a government building—Concrete halls and stairs.

Platzl. The Bavarian Vaudeville—Perhaps the most interesting thing I saw in München.

Wiener Cafe—Orlando di Lasso—This is where I met the duelling students—sitting at their table unwittingly.

Saturday—On The Train Again—In Alsace Lorraine. I came yesterday from Munich, to Zürich—Got there last night—Began to snow in Munich in the morning—Down through Bavaria—in the hill country—flurring snow—Ground white—The consumptive who rode with me in the carriage—His rather young and handsome wife at Munich.[29]

Zürich a German city—Everyone speaks German—Zürich to Basle—Pretty spoiled little German girl, feeding constantly; her devoted mother—They keep the door closed constantly—Thoughtless of other people—The French want to be left alone—have their country to themselves—the Germans are the immigrants, the colonists—they *can't* leave things alone.

The Comedy in the railway carriage today—immediately after we got into France (Alsace Lorraine) the immense difference in the temperaments of the people—the gaiety, the fluidity, the humour of the French—quick to see the ridiculous—The man with the dog—the young wife—the baby. "C'est un expédition"—The young man who wanted his place—if you weren't with a woman I'd move you.

The infinite wrangling with French dishonesty—the taxi men, and all the others.

Monday, Dec. 20:

Comédie-Française tonight *Les Plaideurs*—and Phèdre—Respect for play grew and for actors diminished and went on—The French applauded loudly when Madame Weber ended a long declamation on a

29. Wolfe later developed these brief notes into the short story "Dark in the Forest, Strange as Time," published in FDTM.

screech. Later to Regence and Harry's—Bought some books at Brentano's—Saw Mrs. W. H.—story of how she had been robbed—The picture galleries and antique shops of Rue des Saint Pères.

What I must do tomorrow:

Rise at 9.
Buy steamship passage and railway fare.
Buy neckties and another shirt.
Buy books and postal cards.
Buy a fitting present—but something useless for my Jew.
Go along Rue de Rivoli and over on Left Bank.
Take remainder of money in francs and in dollars.

[*Cablegram, December 22, 1926:* Majestic Westward Ho. Tom.]

The Boat began to move away from off Cherbourg at 10:45 Wed. night, Dec. 22, 1926. Here ends my second trip abroad. Here began it. America I come—you are a strong drink. Cutting hail blew across the deck almost as soon as we got under weigh.

Her funnels smoking straight across into France on the left.

Lights on the coast blinking, the circling lights of Cherbourg—the winking beacon lights of red. I thought we were out—but they have done this for a harbor.

At 11:03 she had a good pitch on.—Aha, thot I.

I went to bed as she went down by France—Slept drunkenly in fatigue.

The green water walls.
The water forest.
By God I kept the faith.[30]

The last night in Paris—Savoir gave a party—Benoist and Duvernoir, their wives and mistresses were there.

I went to the Dome—Filled this time with Germans and Jews—Jew-German, German-Jews.

The young so-called artist—Who drew pictures of the Dome "types"—The habitués kissed habitually the habituated whore's hand—She was French—dark and had a slight mustache.

30. This statement, plus such phrases as "Monastic orders" and "Steadfast" in his cablegrams, indicate that Wolfe remained faithful to Mrs. Bernstein throughout his stay in Europe.

The cold fresh air of Paris at three in the morning—Like the place better then—Down from the clustered cafes of Montparnasse—Boulevard Raspail—the shuttered windows—the Classic book shop—Mon coeur au Roberta—Works of Platon, Cicéron, etc.—The theological book and art shop—Bleeding hearts—saintly tracts on the pronunciation of Latin—Rue de Lille French imports for 1926—The Quais—works of Buffon, Flammarion, [*sketch of book*] bound edition like that.

The row at the Palace revue in Faubourg Montmartre—36 francs for two fines and a citronnade—How they hated me—The three naive conspirators—I paid 20 finally.

The antiquaire in Latin quarter—The place big with glittering chandeliers—Rue des Saints Pères—The wine shops—Bronzes, shepherds, shepherdesses, silhouettes, miniatures, cheap Napoleons.

Marrons Glacés, Nougat—The last night walk up the Boulevards—Garters in the little shop in Faubourg Montmartre—The row at the Palace with the barman and the whore—What children they are—all their devices are cheap and obvious—Dislike French hotels—the servile insolence of the service—the room with the stupid wallpaper—Border of old houses behind—[*sketch of*] stairs down which I saw the ladies' legs—The round-up at Capucines and Duphot three in the morning by the bicycle cops and plain clothes men—Searched.

The brightness of the Dome.

The young Jewess in the Dome who surveyed the crowd through lorgnon.

On the Boat: "And if *she* didn't, some one else would, so why not let *her* have it."

Americans next to me at table tonight talked about W. J. Bryan, "Died for truth"—They said.

Bring money boat. Tom.

Sat. Dec. 25:

4:05—Have waited all day for some form of Christmas greeting from the Jew—Nothing nothing nothing—I spent half my remaining money last night sending her one—Why does she forget a holy day? I have tormenting fears for her safety—anger because of her neglect—She got me on this boat.

The Polish and Russian Jews aboard are filthy. They vomit where they sit and refuse to move—The stewards are frantic.

Monday, Dec. 27:

2:45—one half hour ahead of New York time—Land tomorrow morning. Bright day with freezing wind. Sea exploding in clouds of smoke—Beautiful. Got radio from Jew yesterday—Christmas greetings one day late—young Englishman from Roumania on boat.

I shall land with perhaps $1.00 tomorrow after tipping stewards. Will the Jew meet me? The Christmas and sadness of this trip—I am carrying one continent into another—The Old Welshman (Denis) at the table—Violently patriotic for England—The Swedish Girl—The American dry goods traveller and his wife next to me—The Book of original drawings for Goethe shown me in Munich—The novel in woodcuts[31]—How the hotel people of Vier Jahreszeiten gathered about.

The solid Greekness of German museums and municipal theaters.

What rut of life with the Jew now? Is this a new beginning or a final ending? Get the book done.

The Italian brick layer—no English—Speaks French—In America 14 years—lost his wife "a fine big woman" bled to death from bowel hemorrhage—5 months ago—Going back now—he had trouble saying hemorrhage—His sad burdened face—The Spanish chef—criticism of all the Americans—Likes the "French spirit"—but he's coming back where the dollars grow—The slack cheap mouths of some American girls—the beauty of others.

The mid-western college professor—the nasty old man—leads tourist parties abroad but not astray—psed, psed, psed about women at Foliés Bergère, French whores, etc.—Professor of "psychology." Germany and the middle west—goes around with books by Freud and Anatole France on women. Afraid of me now.

The loud and heavy Jew who "has been everywhere"—Arguments with the loud light Englishman as to who has travelled most—"from Yucatan to Portland Maine," etc. etc.

Monday Night 10:15:

Got a radio from her at 9:30 Tomorrow. Tomorrow (But not to-morrow). The passionate Welshman—The English flapper and her retinue—I hate cheap queens—Long deck walk with the Spanish cook again. The Welshman and the Jew—The piano quarrel. What a princely lot of cut-throats and second-raters this boat has.

31. Probably one of Frans Masereel's works.

[*Sketch of man with cigar*] Welsh—fiery red.

[*Sketch of man with beard*] The Rabbi.

A clear night pricked with blazing stars. Running down the American coast now.

The little boy from third class who was thrust back behind the barrier.

Tuesday morning, Dec. 28, 10:25:

We are off Staten Island—The doctors just came on board—We have been here since seven o'clock this morning.

An oyster is a good thing to joke about.

Harvard Club, Thurs. Evening 8:00:

Came to the dock at 8:00 o'clock yesterday morning, after day's delay in New York Harbor fog—She was standing at end of wharf and she danced up and down when she saw me—Strange day—I talked with difficulty—Like a dream—Getting back to reality today—Air of New York like a cold wine.

January First, Six o'clock in the morning:

Write it up before you retire.

5:52—went to toilet to pee when I wrote above—it was then about 5:35—Met Jew at 11 o'clock—waited until after New Year's in Eighth Street[32]—Went then to Webster Hall—11th Street—Fine Arts Ball—Danced with her—Floor Crowded—Nearly Everybody drunk—Met young man Stuart—Went upstairs to Neighborhood Playhouse box. Carrol there[33]—young men and women came in—Young man drunk—Gives me drink—Tells me he likes me—Later puts arms around Her—Speaks of her daughter—I ask her if she minds—He questions me challengingly about that—I throw him back in his seat—Excitement and disorder—Presently he says if I want physical satisfaction (altho he likes me) he will give it to me—I will give you all you want I said—I get up and face him, and they all surround me—She insists that I come below to dance—when we get there, says we must go—we walk to Eighth Street very sad—She weeps for an hour and says my attack was unnecessary—that he was "just a kid" and "loved Edla very much"—I am cut to the heart—she says no heroics—but I

32. The loft that Wolfe and Mrs. Bernstein had rented for Wolfe to live in at 13 East 8th Street.

33. Albert Carroll, comedian and female impersonator with the Neighborhood Playhouse.

talk to her plainly—I say I have acted badly but like myself—I am no better than I was tonight—I do not want them to put their hands on her—I told the young man so—I did what I felt like doing at the moment—I am no better—no worse—and I am not a belligerent person —She says we must never go out among people again.

I am terribly sad. "I'm sorry, but you mustn't put your hands on her," I said.

The plum tree, black and brittle, waves stiffly in the winter wind. In the Spring, loaded with fruits and blossoms, she will grow young again. Red plums will ripen will drop bursted on the wet warm earth. And when the wind blows, the air will be full of dropping plums and the trees with warm-throated birds who will fill the air also with plum-dropping birdnotes.[34]

The dogs will run if you let them.

Harvard Club—Wednesday Night, Jan. 5—

8:40—Letter from Mama tonight—50$^{00}$. Uncle Henry married —She has leased half of Market Street for ten years at $2500 a year plus building at end. Greetings from Fred [*Wolfe*]—I moved into Eighth street Monday—Slept at Carlton's [35] Monday night—8th street last night—Very nervous Trying to work—Offer from N.Y.U.—Anxious for me—Want to write—but nervous. Must decide what. Must finish book.

I am weary of the old forms—the old language—It has come to me quite simply these last three days that we must mine deeper—find language again in its primitive sinews—like the young man, Conrad—Joyce gets it at times in *Ulysses*—it is quite simple, but terrific. Build the book brick by brick.

The whitefaced fairies of New York.

Why do I become so angry when people stare at me?
Ripe-fleshed blondes.
Eingang an der Ecke [*entrance on the corner*].

34. A draft of the opening paragraph of LHA, Chapter XIV, which shows that Wolfe is beginning the next "book" of his novel.

35. Henry Fisk Carlton, a Harvard friend from the days at the 47 Workshop, who lived at Croton-on-Hudson near Harmon.

Fear—Fear—like a cold oil around my heart. Of what I do not know.—Always carry in your heart the war on fear, fear, fear.

When a man wearing glasses watches you, you are not always sure—How certain are the French in France. Ah, certitude, certitude.

"—nothing common or mean in the hour of danger."

Damned bad port, Master of Balliol. "Where, Arthur, Oh where, is Lancelot?"

In a world of men you have not been afraid. In a world of men and women—yes.

Hatred of loudness and emotion with a woman present.

America began to come back to reality again today—Yet, I am still frightened.

Spring—the spinning presses. Night—a cool bowl of darkness, pearl radiant at the rim.

Spring lay strewn lightly on the earth like a soft veil.

Sunday, Jan. 9:

Returning from Harmon to New York—Visit to Henry's. Second trip out—The cruel harsh beautiful frozen earth—Hudson in distance—the brown leafed rugged woods—Walking trip with Henry, Mac, the two wives—Argument with No-Trespassing Warden—Women shouting insults—Men more circumspect—Mabel Carlton below by several vultures—Henry's quiescence—Slipping into the arms of necessity—occasional smouldering hurt over the play.[36] The bright-winking cold gemmed Hudson River lights.

[*The following notes were developed into the lunchroom scene in* Look Homeward, Angel, *Chapter XIV.*]

A Lunch Room next to an Undertaker's—Did you ever see that?

In The Lunch Room:

Dr. Glynn (drunk).

Dr. Colby.

Later Dr. Meriwether (coming from country club).

36. The production of Carlton's play, "Up the Line," in November, 1926, had not been a success.

Ben.
Harry Brigman.
Bearded Joe Cathey.
Horseface Hines—the Undertaker (midnight embalming).

"Be good to Colby, Hines—he's always been a friend of yours"

"Going into training for the bughouse, Gene," said he.

"I never take anything out that I don't put back. Anyway, I always leave them something to go on with."

"Literature, literature—Dick—It's been the ruin of many a good surgeon. If you read too much Dick, you know too much. The letter killeth. Me—I'm a carpenter, Dick, I'm an interior decorator, I'm a mechanic, a plumber, an electrician, a butcher, a tailor, a jeweler. Dick, I'm a jewel, a gem, a diamond in the rough. I take out their works, spit upon them, trim off the dirty edges, and send them on their way again. I economize, Dick. I throw away everything I can't use. We're filled up with useless machinery. Efficiency! Economy! Power! Have You A Little Fairy In Your Home? You Haven't? Then let the Gold Dust Twins do the work—Ask Ben—he knows."

"Oh, my God," laughed Ben thinking, "listen to that won't you."

The floors have no doors; the floors have cuspidors.
The ceiling has no feeling.
The chairs have no stairs, hairs.
The bottle has no throttle.
The walls have no balls.[37]

The pisswet pocket chewing plug.

[*The following notes show that Wolfe was at work on Gant's interior monologue after the old man's return from California. Although this episode now appears in* Look Homeward, Angel *as Chapter VII, it was originally part of Chapter XIV.*]

Gant's musings—Bowman—Santa Catalina islands—Rich man some day—Merciful God, the ships again.

A gracious friend from us is fled.
Gray's Elegy.
But two months dead.

37. Wolfe later used this silly word play for the joking between George Webber and Esther Jack in W&R.

Fat root that rots itself on Lethe's wharf—This fearful awful and damnable climate.

Lillo—the dramatist.

Golden horses chomp the hay.

Great buttered seasteaks in Frisco—must go someday.

I am the tail that wags the dog.

Open for me the gates of delight.

[*A list of actresses and plays that Gant might have seen.*]

Fay Templeton.
Eva Tanguay.
*Hazel Kirke.*
*East Lynne.*
*Shore Acres.*
*Virginius.*
*Rip Van Winkle.*
*Robin Hood.*
*The Merry Widow.*
*Mary.*

Mrs. Osborne[38]—a summer's morning—with a parasol—Her great processional.

*Potemkin*—Battleship.[39]
Exciting picture—dull ending.

Depravity of word-power within me too.

Jew Book Shop—Works by Trotsky, Upton Sinclair, Robert Ingersoll, Lenin and other fearless thinkers.

Fulton W. 46—B. Lillie.
*Pirates of Penzance*—Plymouth W. 45.
*Broadway*  Broadhurst W. 44.
Clark and McCullough  Lyric W. 42.

Sheeps Head Bay Sunday, Jan. 16:

Very cold—Snow and Ice of Last Night. Frozen—one month ago tomorrow.

38. The first mention of the character who appears as Mrs. Selborne in LHA.

39. A reference to Eisenstein's famous film.

Read—Jules Renard—Long Island City—*Poil de Carotte*—Good play—Terrible story of a woman's hate for her son.[40]

[Arcturus?] Adventure.
sea-cucumbers—*heptocephalus.*
Deep Sea Medusae—silvery hatched—everywhere.
Sea squirts.
Phantom eels.
Tubular nostrils.
black seadevils.
Boobies, Gulls, Terns.
Hawkmoth.
Eater of Stars.
Lantern Fish.[41]

[*The following entries reflect Wolfe's work on the characterization of Judge Webster Tayloe, whom he fashioned after Webster Sondley, a wealthy, learned, eccentric Asheville citizen who later willed his extensive library of North Carolina history to the Asheville Library. He appears in* Look Homeward, Angel, *pp. 181–83, but a good deal of Wolfe's material has been cut out, including Judge Tayloe's drawings of various concepts of God and his theory of the defeated God:*

"Do beaten troops follow a victorious general? And are we not always beaten? Which do you remember oftenest—Austerlitz or Waterloo? Aye—and where are the old gods now? Beaten, beaten, beaten. And *what* are they now? Demons and devils. (With reverent incantation, he spoke the great names of Ashtaroth and Baal, of Moloch, of Amaimon, Barbazon, and Zuminar, of Dionysos, and of riverhaunting Pan.)

"But to follow a God who is forever beaten—to endure hunger, exhaustion, battle and death for one great leader, as we go bleeding backward over dark plains, to stand at length against the final cliffs and hear his horn—and go again to death—how fine a thing would that be! Yes, and in later years, adrift in the great banishment, to meet some veteran comrade of the wars, and to speak again of the Battle of the Cliffs. What genius he showed that day! What courage! What strategy! We would have won if only—

"If only Beelzebub had not arrived with the reserves. Yes! and

40. Wolfe's copy of the play is in the Wisdom Collection.

41. Probably notes that were not developed for an account of Eugene's trip to Florida with his mother.

waiting his return, to speak again of our great leader, guarded, caged upon his prison rock, but come again some day to lead us back into defeat, for whom our love, our life—how fine a thing would that be!"]

Work on the myth.

He looked with pleasure at one of his mulatto sons.

(Building a wall) Webster Sondley—His pictures of God—they were only rough sketches—Dedalus and Icarus—Ceres in the kitchen.[42]

Finish list of demon-books [43]—Also His theory of God—Belief in Myth—The Great Work—God By His Own Side.

[*The following notes point to other characterizations which Wolfe developed for the awakening-in-Altamont scene. They were cut out before publication. One recognizes with interest that four of these figures had made an earlier appearance in Wolfe's play "Welcome to Our City": Rutledge and Dr. Johnson, the Negro physician, were the principal antagonists; Bailey and Sorrel were the chief boosters of Altamont's climate and location.*]

In Niggertown—Johnson awaked on top of the hill.

Fried Mush and Scrapple with molasses.

Rutledge in the town.

Joseph Bailey—club foot—Board of Trade.

Henry Sorrel—Real Estate.

Sinclair the Dentist adjusts his false—

Julia in clouds of string at Dixieland [44]—sweet Smell of glycerine, Vicks Pneumonia Cure and Mentholatum.

Unlighted Grove.

42. While the Judge is musing about the gods, he is also reflecting on the attractive Negress, the mother of his two mulatto sons, who is cooking breakfast for him. At one point his thoughts take this form: "Young Icarus lies sunken, God knows where. But winedark yet the sea. The food smell reached him again. Ceres in the kitchen." LHA MS, Vol. VIII.

43. Another passage, cut before publication, describes the Judge opening a package of books. Obviously Wolfe drew great delight from compiling a learned and varied list of books on demonology, a subject with which he had become acquainted in a seminar under John Livingston Lowes. In the list he also included a volume entitled "*Selected Studies in Neo-Platonist Demonology*, translated from the writings of Jamblichus, Porphyry, Michael Psellus, and Proclus, with annotations, a glossary, and an introductory monograph by Thomas Clayton Wolfe, Ph.D. (L.L.D. Oxon; Camb; Harv; Sweet Briar; Bryn Mawr; Zurich; Centre College; Valparaiso; and Allegheny College), and Stoke Poges Professor of North American Folk Lore at the University of Chickamauga."

44. Wolfe used his mother's real name, Julia, throughout the manuscript.

"this loathsome and leprous confluence of robbery, adultery, murder and cowardly nonsense."

"a superfetation of blasphemy upon nonsense"—Critique on Bartram.

"hypocritical over-much"—Macbeth.

A great passionate discussion of the writings of Thomas Wolfe in part III.

Tuesday, Jan. 24 or 25:

Good day's work—McKee [45] came in with his divorce case. Got me very nervous—Went to see them at 6 o'clock.

hawks
toady
broodmare
clotheshorse
Scavenging (scavenger)
tangled
saffron

The awful sanctity of the persons of policemen and school-teachers.

[*The following note is an indicator that Wolfe was at work on Chapter XV, which includes the description of Eugene's memory and his experience of a transcendental moment fixed in "no-time." In the* Look Homeward, Angel *manuscript at this point he has these jottings:* "His enormous grip on detail—station at dawn, things seen from train window, a road untaken, a woman in doorway."]

Friday, Jan. 28.

Unreality of things seen in motion—from a train (The striving and dividing sea is very deep).

[*The following stanzas are drafts for a poem that Wolfe intended to place near the end of* Look Homeward, Angel, *in the scene in which Eugene visits the grave of his brother Ben. At length the poem was written and appears in the manuscript. However, Wolfe was persuaded to revise it, to make it into a series of prose phrases. See* Look Homeward, Angel, *p. 582.*]

45. David McKee, a friend from Asheville.

A light swings over the hill,
A star shines over the town.
The earth is dear and very still
I shall go down.

Over the hill, a light,
Over your mouth the earth,
Over us all the night,
And then dawn's birth.

Over the dawn a lark,
And wind and music far,
Over the door the dark,
Over the town a star.

Over us all the hill,
A light and a star, but not
An Eye in the dark—a Will
Over the darkness, what?

You have taken the half of my breath.

The Arabian style: "Know O King"—The Ablution of Defilement (after Sexual intercourse)—

"Thou art the vein (apple) of our eye."

Oh inevitable, beautiful and unswerving chance, when we have faltered, you have willed it, when we have wasted you have measured out.

You have guided our blind feet into destruction, you have saved our desparate lives from battle, and you have brought the king news of his enemies in the belly of a fish.

Chance makes of each of us the focal point in life.[46]

Sunday, Jan. 30—

Simonds article in *Review of Reviews* on Europe's hate of us.[47]

Late at night—Geo. Moore's *Evelyn Innes*—convent, slow fume

46. The draft of a passage, part of which was cut before publication, for Chapter XV, in which the narrator develops an apostrophe to Chance. The conclusion appears in LHA, p. 193, the passage beginning, "The seed of our destruction will blossom in the desert . . . ."

47. "America and the European Picture," by F. H. Simonds, March, 1926.

of prayer for Mankind—Bach Sonata—Nuns at matins—Sinus Pacis—Bay of Peace.

R. H. Davis, Susan Lenox, Her grey blue eyes—Marriage scene with mountaineer good—propaganda book.[48]

French Riviera—Vence—Nice—Mistral blowing (in brain)—lateen-rigged craft—Fréjus—Riviera Dreams.

Eating at Moore's—Monday, Jan. 31: When you go back, put in bit you forgot about holding breath while you count 4, repeating prayer 16 times, etc.[49]—Hold yourself in, son. Hold your courage—and your temper.

[*The following entry appears on some blank pages in the* Look Homeward, Angel *manuscript at about the place Wolfe was working at this time. It invites comparison with the final apostrophe in the book, in which Eugene recognizes that the journey of search into himself is the most important one of his life. It is not clear whether the first paragraph of this material is separate from or preliminary to the rest of the passage, as it is on a page by itself.*

"O flower of our soul, O great dark flower of evil and of good, unfold, to us, the pitiful, the proud, the sea-wild comrades of Odysseus, the eaters of new lands. Our insatiate eyes are fed with men and cities, the hunger in our blood is quenched with weariness, over all the enormous and sterile variety of this earth, life reveals itself with idiot repetition. The winedark seas are smeared with oil and offal. The ships come home at 20 knots with Ginsberg and the models. And Europe, like a bitter whore, waits for the clink of the eagle.

"We have haunted ourself across the desert, we have looked for ourself among the crowd, we have fled from that which we sought and now, weary of all other voyages, we face the only one that matters. We stand on the terrible shores of that dark sunken sea, hearing only its mighty and secret whisper, the terrible and insistent evil of its music beating, below the little sugar bank of our defenses, the awful rhythm that unites us to eternity. The sad family of this world is damned all together, and joined, from its birth in an unspoken and grievous kinship: in the incestuous loves of sons and mothers; in Lesbic hungers

48. *Susan Lenox: Her Rise and Fall* is a novel by David Graham Phillips, 1917. Her forced marriage to an ignorant farmer is a widely known episode. Why Wolfe gives R. H. Davis as the author is not clear.

49. Wolfe did not put it in, but years later it appeared as part of George Webber's boyhood rituals and superstitions in W&R, p. 84.

and parricidal hatreds; in the terrible shames of sons and fathers, and the uneasy shifting of their eyes; in the insatiate sexuality of infancy, in our wild hunger for ourself, the dear love of our excrement, the great obsession of Narcissus, and in the strange first love of every boy which is for a man.

"And as we stand in the crowd, lonely, silent, and abashed before the mockery of the fool or the threat of the coward, which of us has not felt hard shame because of his silence? Which of us has not felt a secret unspeakable joy at the thought of this voyage into a newer stranger land than Magellan dreamed of, a world more golden than Columbus thought to find? We stand upon the shore of the magic world, unable yet to see it save for the bare appalling flashes that the great wizard of Vienna has thrown upon it. But he has spoken a century too soon: we need tougher sinews, greater hearts.—We will fight desperately yet awhile to save our fudge, we will dilute terror and beauty with milk and water, and as long as we can we will proclaim the idiot health of the animal, and deny the epic disease that makes us men. So, until daybreak, long live Tom Sawyer! Long live Penrod and the Rollo Boys. God's in his heaven and the wicked shall be punished."]

1909—Prohibition in N.C.
1907—(70 out of 97 counties).

Lister—the carotid artery of a horse—work on the ligature.
Fichte—Thesis antithesis synthesis.[50]

Lamentations.
Open for me the gates of delight.[51]
Next time, Gene.

*'Εντεῦθεν ἐξελαυνει σταθμοὺς τρεῖς παρασάγγας πεντεκαίδεκα ἐπὶ τὸν Εὐφράτην ποταμόν.*[52]

Sunday, Feb. 6:

Harv. Club—Saw *Chicago* last night—A Vicious Cheap Play but interesting at the beginning—Some good lines.

50. Wolfe first became acquainted with Fichte in his philosophy classes at the University of North Carolina under Professor Horace Williams, who was a Hegelian.

51. Used as a comic reference to Eugene's attraction to Bessie Barnes, LHA, p. 205.

52. "And then they advanced three stadia and fifteen parsangs to the Euphrates River." This passage in Greek, which Wolfe placed at the opening of LHA, Chapter XXIII, is from Xenophon's *Anabasis*.

Darius and Parysatis had two sons, the older, Artaxerxes, the younger Cyrus.[53]

Tissaphernes—Satrap.

Tues. Feb. 8—2:25 A.M. (Wed. morn):

Met Geo. Wallace [54] at 6 o'clock went with him to girl's room—man named Hess there—gin—Later his room—gin—Go-getter 38 or 40—Later Barroom across street—Domineering insulting voice—squeezed my arm—British lot of four-flushers "We won the war"—Argument with barman over drinks—I lost—paid—Hess got more and more violent—Talk with manager—Called him Canadian—Settled that other night said manager—Forget it—I went out to piss—Came back—Geo. Wallace doing ju-jitsu—Geo. said Hess was talking of what he'd do to me—I took him by coat collar and sat him down on floor—lifting him up again—Furiously angry but afraid of "big gorilla" as he called me—Geo. and I left—George hugely delighted at what I had done—Barman told us outside he had put him out time or two—I didn't hurt the man.

The Body is not capable of much evil—That's why the French are fools.

Wed. Feb. 16:

I have worked very hard this week—5 hours again to-day—Where shall book end—End of *Third,* I think—Get it on paper by April.

The trouble with people with faultless taste—perfection, subtlety, but the great thing missing.

After Frank—Mabel, Fred, Ben—his loves—The loves of Ben—autumn.

*The Road to the Temple*—Susan Glaspell.[55]

53. The opening sentence of Xenophon's *Anabasis*.
54. A friend whom Wolfe had known at Harvard.
55. A biography of George Cram Cook, the director of the Provincetown Players.

*The House of Quiet*—Benson—Lane End.[56]

The Veinnous legs of women after 40—men's not—why?

Trouble with taste—too much of it—Every great poet has bad taste.

The 48th part of an ass.
Twittering—appetizingly.
Flameflowers.
Sailor—Every man his own picture gallery.
Snakes—Housepet in Philippines—peeps out of man's coat.

WHORE'S EPITAPH

She went away in beauty's bloom
When life was young and fair. Before her life was spent.

She went away in beauty's flower
Before her youth was spent
Ere life and love had lived its hour
God called her—and she went.

Yet whispers faith upon the wind!
No gríef to hér was gíven
She left your love and went to find
A gréater ońe in heáven.[57]

Feb. 24:

8:40—Wrote 3 hours—Read Westermarck, *Goodness of Gods.* —Look over A. Bennett and Somerset Maugham (*Of Human Bondage*) tonight at Harvard Club.

[*Wolfe jotted the following notes while reading a book on psychoanalysis:*]

56. An autobiographical work by A. C. Benson, Master of Magdelene College, Cambridge University. Chapter 4 includes a reverie on the search for beauty and mystery, which the author especially associates with following a lane to "the home of incommunicable dreams." At the lane end is Grately Mill, a scene surrounded by "a magical charm." Note that later in this notebook Wolfe uses the symbol of the lane when he writes a draft of the rhythmic proem "a stone, a leaf, a door . . . ."

57. Drafts for the tombstone inscription, LHA, p. 268.

Male genital—Trinity of persons.

Female—landscape with a chapel, hill and forest.

Drawer of her writing table to see if anyone has been through it.

Deep hole in the vineyard which she knows was made by pulling out a tree.

Officer with a red cap follows her up stairs—She slams back door (It can be safely done openly).

Two friends of sisters (her breasts).

She strikes low hanging chandelier so that her head bleeds.

Often I think of the beautiful town
With its mill wheel and the mill
And the winding stairs that go up and down
And the steeple on the hill.
I see thy rocks and rills—
Dear Buncombe [58] tis of thee,
Sweet Land of Liberty
    Of thee I sing
I love thy ways and [*breaks off*].

They played the pornograph.

11:40 at Dinty Moore's—Eating there—Steak coming—Stayed at 8th St. until 11:10 oclock. A Big Fat Go-getter at next table—Bald, red—An affected Englishman—a gorged American—George McManus the cartoonist and a woman (with Go-getter).

An Englishman and an American correcting each other on accent.

The way the party turned toward McManus.

Dream:

A ship—didn't get off in time—Make 7 trips over instead of one —See Mrs. Roberts and J. M.[59] in dining saloon—She is looking around for me.

Sunday, Feb. 27:

Eating at Charles'—Fantasy of meeting Rebecca West—going

58. Asheville is in Buncombe County, North Carolina.

59. Mrs. Roberts was Wolfe's English teacher and "the mother of his spirit" at the North State Fitting School. J. M. Roberts taught him Latin and Greek. The couple appear as Mr. and Mrs. Leonard in LHA.

to Eng. with book of questions and trying it out on literati in Hampstead Heath. From that an English *Ask Me Another.*[60]

The Americans are children—Yes, But children are tyrranous if they are in power.

Come into the garden, Maud,
With one clear call for me,
For the woodbine spices are wafted abroad,
The best is yet to be.
I said to the lily "There Is But One."

Brotherhood of ghosts.

[*In early March Wolfe took a trip to Boston to visit friends and to get his books, which he had left with his uncle Henry Westall.*]

Providence—Tiered windows of a cotton factory in opaque light—How I have thought with nausea of the Party at [*Philip*] Moeller's the other night.[61]

[*The phrases in the following entry are from the "Bronze by gold" passage in Joyce's* Ulysses.]

Boston—Sunday [*March 6*]—After wine at Italian's:
chips—rocky thumbnail.
and gold flushed more.
Idolores—Musician.
Jingle—Jingle—Jaunted—Jingling.
Tympanum.
Moonlit nightcall—spiked and winding.
gouty fingers nakkering.
jogjaunty—warmseated.
ardentbold—grampus.

60. A popular American book of questions and answers, like *Information, Please.*

61. "Went to one terrible studio party where I met a man named [Carl] Van Vechten, a novelist, and horrible woman named Elinor Wylie, who is all the go now—she writes novels and poetry—and her husband Will Benet—I hated them so that I managed to insult them all." *Letters,* p. 121. Here is the origin of Chapter 30 of W&R. Moeller, who was associated with the Theatre Guild, had been a friend of Aline Bernstein's since childhood.

Monday, March 7.

Leaving Concord—George Wallace—Dinner at Colonial Inn—Old woman like those at Eng. hotels—Hawthorne's House—The Tower—Drew up ladder behind him—overheated cars of Boston and Maine's Smoking Cars—Black Leather seats smooth—Railroad smells.

Thursday—Returned last night from Boston—Went to see her, stayed till 3 o'clock—came home—night of damnable nightmares—Dreamed of her and another man who ran a carnival show—we went down the river on a river boat—a Negro with thin legs and enormous feet—the other acrobat with thin undeveloped legs and arms but great strength—her sexual relations with older man who runs the show—He is a mixture of evil and wisdom. I discover. I destroy my book tearing it to pieces and feeding it to the fire—I fall senseless—.

[*A group of loose pages follows. Wolfe had torn them out to use the notes to represent Eugene Gant's literary opinions for* Of Time and the River, *pp. 661–62.*]

. . . Love's bitter mystery—Into the dream scenes of riotous living—a café like a small French one—Neighborhood Playhouse people upstairs —Young men from home within—Perry Tomlin, Jim Rickard—Jim Daly [62] and the old closed hotel—Begging friuts about the town.

Monday, M'ch 14:

Worked over 5 hours up to present (9:40) Cigarettes and coffee —very tired.

Tuesday:

Worked 4 hours yesterday—Very tired today—only an hour—more tonight—McKee came up, stayed afternoon.

Wed. March 23:

Good week's work last week—Four or five hours *actual* writing every day—I may succeed ultimately because I'm not content with what I do.

I was born in 1900—I am now 26 years old. During that period I think the best writing in English has been done by James Joyce in *Ulysses.*

62. A young poet whom Wolfe knew in the 47 Workshop at Harvard.

I think the best writing in the ballad has been done by G. K. Chesterton in "Lepanto."

The best writing in sustained narrative verse by John Masefield, particularly in the *Dauber*, *The River*, and *The Widow in the Bye Street.*

The best writer of satirical epigram in verse—Humbert Wolfe. The writer best able to touch a simple sentence with indefinable magic —Sir James Barrie.

The greatest and most various talent for fiction—H. G. Wells.

The most careful workman of writers who produce copiously —Arnold Bennett.

The best practioner of the Essay—Belloc.

The most gigantically thorough realist—Theodore Dreiser.

The most sparing, selective and unfailingly competent—Galsworthy.

The best play for poetry—*The Playboy of the Western World.*

The best play for fantasy—*Magic* by G. K. Chesterton.

The best play for wit and wisdom—*Major Barbara.*

The Best Playwright—Shaw.

The Most Disappointing playwright and novelist in view of his gifts—Somerset Maugham.

The Best Shortstory Writers—Sherwood Anderson and A. E. Coppard.

The Best Journalist—Sinclair Lewis.

The young writer with the highest potentiality—Aldous Huxley.

The critic with the greatest subtlety—T. S. Eliot.

The critic with the greatest range and humor—H. L. Mencken.

The best woman writer—May Sinclair.

The next best—Virginia Woolf.

The next best—Willa Cather.

The best woman poet—"H.D."

Quadrupedante putrem sonitu quatit ungula campum.[63]

[*End of loose pages.*]

63. This line from Virgil may be loosely translated, "With the sound of galloping hoofs beating the loose soil." Wolfe used it with mock-heroic reference to Pap Reinhart's horse in LHA, p. 326. But the onomatopoetic sound of the line continued to fascinate him. Later, in OT&R he played with the words in rhythmic rearrangements, p. 76. They represent the pounding hoofs of the horses ridden by Lean Death and Pale Pity, keeping time with the railroad train rushing through Virginia.

Reading in Coleridge—The god suspected in the line. Only 50 pages of gold ore, but I'll match them against any other 50 in the world.

Rime of the Ancient Mariner—15
(with first edition variations —3 or 4)
Christabel —10
Kubla Khan — 3
The Knights Tomb — .5
Dejection —10
France (certain pass.)
Youth and Age — 1.5
Hymn Before Sunrise — 5
Metrical Experiments,
Translations, etc. —20

S. T. C. called Donne "wit's press and screw."

Cataract.
Ships leave their lair.
Read over "Dejection" when you go home.

O what sad comfort when in foreign fields.

This is my own, my native land.
I'd rather write than be president.

[*Cut from the manuscript of* Look Homeward, Angel *before publication is a sequence about Eugene's trip to Washington, D.C., with his mother. This material at the end of Chapter XVII contains Eugene's first sense of national awareness, together with Wolfe's characteristic shifts back and forth between dream and reality.*

*Eugene visits the capitol at night and sees the lights play upon the great dome:* "Eugene was touched with the glory of Rome. The stars burnt cold deathless flames above the new land. The sharp tonic excitement of the air shot through his exultant limbs. There was the wail of a train in Virginia, and the great dome—absolute, enduring, tranquil, and imperial—brooded above him."

*When the time came for him to go home:* "Eugene thought of the South with a sense of desolation. He was as far North as he had ever been. He wanted to pierce farther on into the opening Spring. As they went back across Virginia, the vision of the undiscovered land at whose door he had knocked made a great wound in him. He stared moodily out of the window at the raw bleak windy land. The little illusion of his power was gone. He felt the poverty, the imprisonment of his life. Suddenly he dared phrase within him his disapproval of the discomfort and ugliness in which people lived.

"The great shaft of light swung through his brain again: the enduring beauty and strength of the dome burnt in his memory. Something in him was touched by the breadth, the depth, the wild romantic strength of the American landscape, but something called out desperately for fences, for beauty, for Arcadian perfection. He wanted a land that was rich, near, and forever green. He was frightened and depressed by this sweeping panorama of powerful frozen fields, red clay railway cuts, gouged out crudely for the passage of trains, seared and blasted gulleys, rough massed woodlands tangled with thick undergrowth and rotting fallen trees. He shivered clammily as the train passed the cheap inadequate houses of the upper South—thrown together with plaster and clapboarding, flimsy barriers against the raw indecisive weather. He experienced a composite physical discomfort as he looked at them, drawn from numberless memories of draughty halls, damp sheets, entering gusts of cold air, toasted skins and frozen spines, catarrhal eyes and noses, raw phlegmy throats, and the boiling sudsy wash.

" 'I hope the pipes haven't frozen in this coldsnap,' said Julia . . . .

"It was the last journey he ever made with her. Spring blossomed in the hills again. His heart turned north. There were new lands."]

Saturday Night:

11:40—McAllister's—The Arty Eate Shoppe—Left her just now—Night of Grand Annunciation to Neighborhooders[64]—In all day with Jew—Work all tonight.

Spring here—a clear cool day—Crystal—with touch of chill in it—Nerves better last few days—must finish by June.

I think of Italy—I want to go back—Capri or Amalfi?

64. Probably the first time that Wolfe allowed Mrs. Bernstein to tell her Neighborhood Playhouse friends that he was writing a novel.

Sunday, April 9—

Went with Smith[65] to his Sister's—Jewess married to Christian—Both musicians—Played for me—piano, violin—Other Sister and husband and kid—Millineress New York type—Jazz, emaciated, nervous sullen whiskey-bibbing—Diamond bracelets, etc.

Harvard Club later—Clear Crisp night—blazing moon and starlight—Fifth Avenue—Saw Thompson upstairs and the Lewd Librarian—Last night the great annunciation to the Neighborhood Playhousers—permanent company—Tonight George Antheil, the modern Composer.

Read May Sinclair's *Mary Olivier*—Enormous Skill—Small cruel terribly competent brain.

Reading Stanley Unwin's Publisher Book [*The Truth about Publishing*]—Powys *Dark Laughter* (B-lood! B-lood!)

[*The following group of notes comes from Wolfe's reading of Summers' book, probably to prepare for Judge Tayloe's interest in demonology.*]

Montague Summers—Hist. of Witch. and Demonology:
"Departure for Sabbat"—Teniers.[66]
*Démonomanie des Sorciers*—Jean Bodin.
Albertus Magnus.
Matthew Hopkins—witchfinder (The Discovery of Witches).
The Brocken.
Incubi and succubi.
Pus of St John of the Cross—scent of lilies.
The Fragrance of the Saints.
Thomas Aquinas—male frankincense.
Saint Pachomius—the cenobite—stench of heretics.
"Har, Har, Hon, Hon danse ici" [67]

[*The following notes, mostly brief quotations from well-known poems, were made in preparation for Eugene's saunter home from*

65. Abe Smith, the former student of Wolfe's and now a devoted friend, who typed the manuscript of LHA.

66. A painting by David Teniers, which was used for the frontispiece of the book.

67. The traditional chorus sung at a Witches' Sabbath when held on the island of Guernsey (according to Margaret Murray).

*school with George Graves in Chapter XXIV, where the lines of verse are used for ironic commentary on the townspeople of Altamont.*] [68]

Lap me in soft Lydian airs.

Drear and naked shingles of the world.

Fat root that rots itself by Lethe's wharf.

She took me to her elfin grot.

A snake's small eye blinks dull and shy.

The army of unalterable law.

And as he rode his answer sang.

Ancestral voices prophesying war.

The wandering airs they faint.

Cupid and my Campaspe played.

O fountain Arethuse, and thou honoured flood,
Smooth-sliding Mincius,
That can sing both high and low.

Kings in Armour—Morris Dancers.
Cynewulf—Aelfred.

Falconer—I gaze, adore, and die.

68. The lines and phrases which the editors have been able to identify are these: (Lap me) Milton's "L'Allegro," (Drear) Arnold's "Dover Beach," (Fat root) Shakespeare's *Hamlet,* (She took me) Keats's "La Belle Dame Sans Merci," (The army) Meredith's "Lucifer in Starlight," (Ancestral voices) Coleridge's "Kubla Khan," (The wandering airs) Shelley's "The Indian Serenade," (Cupid) Lyly's Song from *Endymion,* (O Fountain) Milton's "Lycidas," (Bleat, bleat) parody of Tennyson's "Break, Break, Break," (Fielding, etc.) phrases from *Tom Jones,* (His fingers) Adelaide Proctor's "A Lost Chord." For a full discussion of Wolfe's use of poetic tags in this scene, see Floyd C. Watkins, "Thomas Wolfe's High Sinfulness of Poetry," *Modern Fiction Studies,* II (Winter 1956–57), 197–206. A rather strained and dubious treatment is Mark D. Hawthorne, "Thomas Wolfe's Use of the Poetic Fragment," *Modern Fiction Studies,* XI (Autumn 1965), 234–44.

The vocal incense.

Sadly social with my lay
The winds in concert weep.

Bleat, Bleat, Bleat
To thy cold grey flock, McKay.

Impertinent mixture of busy and idle.

FIELDING

Strongly limbed.
Some loss of blood and hair, and of lawn and muslin.
"proceeded to discharge half a dozen whores at the lady up stairs."
"as two handed a wench as any."
Chastity of temple of Vesta.
"Ulysses—best stomach in that eating poem of the Odyssey."
"Say then, ye graces, you that inhabit."
Embracing a whore his hellish design.

His fingers wandered idly over the noisy keys.

With fire on his lips.

Mabel: Oh Decidedly! Decidedly!
(Woman in Steve's)—"This is decidedly a Spring Dress." Dominant woman in Steve's—I was very self-conscious.

Sat. May 21:
Lindbergh reached Paris.
At Carlton's for past week.

[*The following passage, scribbled when Wolfe had been drinking heavily, is not always coherent.*]

Wed. May 23:
She at lunch—Worked a little—Gamzue [69]—Rum Punch—A Pint—Neigh-Playh-house—Got drunk—Long Talk—Dot. Sands—Al-

69. Boris Gamzue, one of Wolfe's colleagues in the Department of English at New York University.

ice Beer [70]—My Dear—Long Talk—Our Relation—Amazing Declarations—She said that Alice Lewisohn told Agnes Morgan [71] (these as near as I can be *our* words) that I was a very arrogant young man—the most arrogant young man she had ever known—that this was the only reason she didn't do my play [72]—we had it out—I said essentially she hated me!—She accused me of wanting to leave her—I spoke of her suicide threat when I was away—Once, said she, only! *Twice* or *thrice*, said I—I said she was strange—Hostile scene—Coming in taxi—suddenly —casually—I asked if her daughter was [*a*] whore—She spoke later —gathering strength—Don't you *ever* say that again—Too good for you to talk about—etc. Don't you ever—I said [*it*] because I wanted to hurt her—So,—(By the way—she said I had the dirtiest lowest mind she had ever known etc.) ask her why—when I have been so deeply moved over the treatment I had from Miss L.—and she has heard me talk of it so much and talked to me of it so much she has never told me that Miss L. said I was most arrogant young man she ever knew—Ask her if there are not a great many other things she has held from me? Because I have always felt this:—her halving in two worlds—one thing there—one here!

This is how I have felt all the time—The secret of half my passions:—she has lied, because she has withheld and been silent (Besides—where last night was her daughter?—Dorothy—the Hoochy dancer—The other dancer—Where the daughter?)—Morgan always hostile to me—(What Geo. Wallace told me—What the Jew always denied)—Ask her why Morgan told her—in what spirit why?—Morgan seemed hostile last night why?—The young effeminate man with Morgan as I passed—Long hair—rimmed eyes—muttered an insult for me to hear as I passed (I had never said she known anyone as good as her family).

[*There are no more entries for about six weeks, although the margins and blank pages of the* Look Homeward, Angel *manuscript have a number of jottings for this period—including a map of Asheville. Prominent among the notes are words and phrases which indicate that Wolfe was rereading* Ulysses. *The most curious of these is a list of*

70. Dorothy Sands, whom Wolfe had known through the 47 Workshop at Harvard, was now a featured player in the *Grand Street Follies* every year. Alice Beer was an old friend of Mrs. Bernstein's and sister of Thomas Beer, the biographer of Stephen Crane.

71. Both were members of the Board of Directors of the Neighborhood Playhouse.

72. Wolfe had submitted *Mannerhouse* to the Neighborhood Playhouse in January, 1926.

*scenes in* Ulysses. *But the fourteen scenes set down are placed in reverse order, so that the list actually runs as follows:*

Before Dialog:

1 Prose—Drunken discussion.
2 Gerty and Bloom.
3 Conversation—Bloom and the Citizen.
4 Bronze by Gold.
5 Father Conmee—Simon Dedalus.
6 Stephen and Shakespeare.
7 Bloom promenades.
8 Newspaper Headlines.
9 Dignam's Funeral.
10 Bloom's early morning walk.
11 Bloom rises eats and shits.
12 Stephen on the beach.
13 Schoolroom scene.
14 Introduction—Tower and Sea.

*By July, Wolfe was well into the last section of his novel and was ready for a change of pace. He arranged to meet Mrs. Bernstein in Europe for a two-months' tour of Paris, Prague, Munich, and Vienna.*]

Sunday, July 17—

Left New York Tuesday—Sweltering hot—Don McRae with me all last day—Boat trip calm thus far—People dull and common—The Captain—a Common and insolent boaster—adventurous life: how little it means—The old Scotchman: most interesting man I've met on the boat—all over the world—engineer for sugar cane industry—ship's concert to-morrow night—A radio last night from Paris—from my dear Jew: I have not been able to answer yet—The hum of the engines under me—a slight bounding vibration—rattles the window at present moment in the smoke room—The little Nicaraguan on this boat—dirty little fellow, insolence and servility—Show off—Captain's voice not loud—but vulgar and dominant.

The birth of the child stays with me yet.[73] Phosphorus in the water—Little minute patches.

The little German girl at our table—with the flaxen hair—And Mrs. Siegel—who doesn't know what she wants—The Jew Consum-

73. On July 9, Wolfe's college classmate, Dr. Donald MacRae, had brought Wolfe into the delivery room of the Manhattan Maternity Hospital to witness the birth of a baby.

mate—The Jewish Rabbi who wants to win all the deck games—at the table playing poker—the Captain, the old man from Miami, the Lithuanian artesian well driller, the Belgian Jew, the young German-American real estater from Chicago.

Last night a strange thing: Just after I got my dear Jew's telegram—O thank God for that! said I; went to the radio—when I came back everyone on boat knew about it—Giggled among themselves and were afraid—I thought they were "down" on me—but I frighten them and seem strange to them. Looking back at people—trying to out-stare them—Foolish and common.

[*There are no more entries until the end of the summer. Wolfe continued to write and carried his narrative well into Eugene's college years. Among the few scattered notations in the manuscript, he encouraged himself:* "Get up to Ben's death before going to New York." *He was also looking toward the conclusion. He noted:* "Possible ending. We, my brother, are alone." *Later he planned this sequence:*

"1) Summer in Norfolk.
2) Ben's Death.
3) Remainder of Year in Pulpit Hill (Plays and Greenlaw).
4) Summer after (Scene in Graveyard).
5) Last year at Pulpit Hill (Williams).
6) Summer at home—Dissolution—Parting.
7) Final scene with Ben upon the porch shop in moonlight."]

Nürnberg, Aug. 24—Wednesday:

This morning to German Museum.[74] Magnificent Wohlgemuth—His pictures and carvings. Pleydenwurff—the Virgin and child—Exquisite clarity. Cranach's great Lucretia and Dürer's two kings—one Charlemagne.

Aug. 25 Thurs. 12M:

At Bar Across from hotel. Back to Paris tonight at 7:25—Must send card to Fritz Day and George Wallace—Bring record of this trip to date—from now on. Food in Nürmberg wonderful—Gansbraten—(Leipziger Allerlei splendid) Lovely white wine (Riesling)

The costume books the old man with the lewd silly giggle

74. The Germanisches Nationalmuseum, which houses collections representing the history of German art and civilization. Among the early German painters Wolfe mentions, two are Nuremberg artists: Hans Pleydenwurff (mid-fifteenth century) and Michel Wohlgemuth (1434–1519).

showed me in the bookstore this afternoon—Some by Rops,[75] some by Rowlandson—some simply Parisian, München, and Wiener photographs. Picture of Mary Magdalen—Naked woman writhing on ground before a crucified prick—Rowlandson's picture, of women with open legs and vast genitals—Rops, of gentlemen feeling ladies' teats at opera (stealthy Gallic gesture)—18th century pictures of beaux entering bedrooms—elegant sofa scenes—phalluses carved from wood and symbolic pictures—two eggs and a sausage—Italian one of womans legs sticking above the wheat (Two eggs and sausage—still life)

Sept. 2:

At Brasserie Universelle—Ave. de l'Opra—my Jew gone two days. A Book of Manuel Schwabs this morning along the Seine—Still bewildered by the junk—Must buy many books. Got suit of clothes yesterday. Fitting today—The woman at the hotel—Saleswoman—35 —Intrigante.

Costumes on Revolution for Rolland play.

[*Wolfe apparently saw an exhibition of French Impressionist painters at the Musée du Luxembourg and made these notations about reproductions:*]

Luxembourg—Buy These:

"La Guinguette"—V. Gogh
"Angéline"—Manet
"Réunion de famille"—Bazille
"Le Moulin de la Galette"—Renoir
"L'Estaque"—Cezanne
"Femme"—Suèda
"L'Etude"—Zingg
"Chambre Bleu"—Valadon
"La Femme au Lit"—Puy
"Femmes"—Gauguin
"Danseuse"—Legrand
"L'Etude"—Charlot
"Le Balcon"—Manet
"Au Jardin"—Monet
"Restaurant de la Sirène"—Van Gogh
"Atelier de L'Artiste"—Bazille

75. Félicien Rops (1833–98), French painter and sketcher noted for the licentiousness of his work.

"Un Café"—Degas
"Danseuse"—Degas
"Portrait"—Couture
"Le Cercle"—Béraud.

Sunday, Sept 4.

Along the quais of the Seine this afternoon—Book shops—Quantities of junk—made me sick to have to leave them—the pornographic books—*Lovely Lisette, Journal of a Masseuse, Sadie Blackeyes,* etc.—the pictures—I bought a few—Knights in armour.

Les Petites Annonces: In Paris this time news was Flight of Levine—the Princess who flew and was lost—the attempt of the French—all about flights.[76]

Fontainebleau—the great forest—The Chateau—Hall of Francis the first—The Great Library—The steps. The Hotel de France et D'Angleterre—the little boy who waited on us—the Americans—the pause in the woods—pirate's den.

Statue of De Musset with his directive genius—Comédie Française—above, Voltaire and the [buskins?] of Rachel[77]—Within, the dead convention of the acting.

Last night *Knock*[78]—Tomorrow buy some books and pictures—make a schedule.

Our fight in Vienna—she was going through the streets weeping—My terrible embarrassment—Waiting in room—not knowing where we were going—The night man at the hotel—smooth-shaven and grave and the old men who looked like Franz Joseph—the two maids—The beautiful women at Vienna Cafe 1st day we came.

Paris—She was buying clothes—Stayed 4 days—Went to *Maya*[79]—Nasty Little Theatre place—Sat in Loge with Frenchwoman

76. The colorful American avaitor Charles A. Levine was planning a transatlantic flight, first with Maurice Drouhin and later with Clarence Chamberlin. Rival French fliers were hurrying to get a French plane ready for a Paris-to-New York flight. British flier Leslie Hamilton and his passenger Princess Lowenstein-Wertheim were lost on a flight from Ireland to New York.

77. The foyer of the Théâtre Français contains the famous statue of the seated Voltaire, and in the vestibule is the statue of "Tragedy" (the actress Rachel in the role of Phèdre).

78. A comedy by Jules Romains.

79. A play by Simon Goutillon, 1924. *Maya* is the story of a prostitute who is the mythic embodiment of the Eternal Female. Mrs. Bernstein especially wished to see the play because the Neighborhood Playhouse group was planning

and her daughter—Maya beautifully acted—woman who played Maya—Where do you come from? The sea. Where do you go? Back to the sea. The dressmakers place we visited Rue (Ave?) Montaigne—Tall elegant blonde "Hostess"—Reading English letters with pretty assistant—Casino de Paris—Dolly Sisters (Foul!)—Hal Sherman—Good—Beautiful dancer.

Strasbourg—Hotel Hanung—Old German Porter at station—Hotel—Baths—Sharp and delicate old woman who ran it—Old man at Alsatian Museum—Nasty young man (said he was American) who explained things to me—Other museum [80]—Josephine's bed—View of Cathedral—The Alsacian cap she bought for daughter—They tried to cheat—Lace work Cathedral—The clocks and engines in Museum—Costumes belonged to House of Rohan—Pictures—I forget—other (City) Museum—City of Strasbourg in relief [81]—Flat country with many rivers.

Valentin Sorg's—she cried—Americans who looked—That night to Germany—Soldiers who saw us kiss and laughed at station—People who looked in window at station during night—Karlsruhe—Stuttgart—Morning, flat country around Munich—*Munich* (place she loved).

Monday Sept. 5:

Eating at Monteverdi's—Italian Rest.—Talk with Saleswoman at hotel—French, married American—has lived in Philippines and all over (Mrs. Sterling—probably a great stock in trade)—Last night at Dome—The college boys in evening clothes—making themselves unpleasant as usual—U. of N.C. glee club—[*J. Paul*] Weaver [*the director of the glee club*] embarrassed me when he saw me—he told them about me—Young Americans at next table who sang (Hi Ho le dairyo ce n'est pas gentil).

To the Louvre now—at Monteverdi's—table of five—3 women, 2 very handsome—2 Frenchmen—bald, not fat, Gallic, hard—American and young Frenchwoman at Monteverdi's—He felt her tits—She submits—veiled disgust.

Tuesday [*September 6*]:

A La Pomme de Pin—71 Rue des Petites-Champs.

Boeuf à la Mode—8, Rue de Valois.

---

a production for the following year. When the play did open in New York in February, 1928, it was closed by the District Attorney after fifteen performances for "tending to corrupt the morals of youth."

80. The Municipal Museum of Art in the old Episcopal Palace.

81. In the Reading Room of the Museum of Industrial Art, which is also in the Palace.

Day's Schedule—

(1) Buy book container.
(2) Lunch.
(3) See about steamer.
(4) Go to Louvre.
(5) Go to Tailor.
(6) Buy Books—Go to University Press.

Saw *Trois jeunes filles nues* last night—They all looked at me—all dressed up—The handsome and clean looking girl in the play—Charming, tender, and clean—Later along the Boulevards—the closing news kiosk—the cops with furtive hard suspicious eyes—The guides "always something new in Paris"—The two old beggars collecting trash and papers in front of Weber's—I ate at Régence—onion soup—cold chicken in jelly—Discontent of the waiters—I came late—Finally American and his wife out of money—were staying out of town—Had Express checks—Took them to Harry's.

At the hotel—at night—People in salon—Amer. woman strange teeth—queer mouth—very voluptuous—Young man—the effeminate American type—Very sure and blasé about everything—woman with flat Mid-western accent—Young man New York—Old boy from Chicago with Fairy lisp.

Books I saw today: Josephine Baker's Memoirs—Y'vette Guilbert's—Dekobra—You'll be a courtesan and all the others. The little Art Books—Goya—Henner (?)—*Le Fleuve de Feu*—Mauriac. *Génétrix*—Mauriac. *Le Baiser au Lépreux*—Mauriac.

[*Wolfe listed the following reproductions that he wished to buy. Although he did not supply the full title of the work or the name of the painter in every entry, they are given here.*]

At the Louvre:

1007 Clouet, "Francis I."
126 Clouet, "Francis I."

Le Sueur (Terrible) But get 588, "Plan of the Ancient Chatreuse."

737 Poussin, "Ruth and Boaz: Harvest."
745 Rigaud, "Portrait of Louis XIV."
899 Van Loo, "The Halt out Hunting."
664 Octavien, "The Fair at Bezons."
3092 Gillot, "Scene of Two Carriages."

670 Oudry, "The Farm with Toy Animals."
982 Watteau, "The Embarkation for Cytherea."
689 Pater, "Outdoor Fete."
28 Boilly, "The Coach."
526 Le Brun, "Portrait of Madame Molé Raymond."
3075 Ducreux, "Portrait of the Artist."
1312 Giotto, "St. Francis Receiving the Stigmata."
1273 Uccello, "Battle."
1322 Ghirlandaio, "Portrait of a Young Florentine."
1260 Cimabue, "The Virgin with Angels."
Manet, "Portrait of Emile Zola."
Gericault, "Race Horses."
Daumier, "Scapin and Crispin."
1729c El Greco, "St. Louis, King of France, Accompanied by a Pope."
1747 [*unidentifiable*].
1704 Goya, "Portrait of Guillemardet."

At the Louvre—I felt sick before I went because of last night in Montmartre—but sicker as I went along. It is the greatest junk heap in the world—with a few great things that no one looks at—Awful Salle Vandyck and Salle Rubens—But a great Greco (two or 3), the magnificent Cimabue, the Giotto, and Uccello, the Goyas, Ingres portraits, the Manet, the Corot, the five Clouets and early French ones. Boucher a sugar tit, 4 rooms full of a terrible fellow named Le Sueur—The Henner—naked girl with hair lying on her belly reading [82]—Napoleon's advance on Waterloo,[83] Mona Lisa—this is what they look at.

Prague—our troubles there—how sick we were of Baroque. The scene we had with waiters who tried to cheat us in the outdoor garden. She took up for me against little waiter; he was fingering my lapel "nicht berühren" [*don't touch*]. Mr. Bondy [84] on the train—a charming man with a foul breath—a collector—The museum in Prague [85] with all the Bondys—Czech interiors, colored Bohemian glass —something nasty about it all—a few good pictures in picture gal-

82. "The Reader" by Jean-Jacques Henner (1829–1905).
83. Perhaps he is referring to a panoramic painting of Napoleon at the Battle of Eylau by Antoine Jean Gros (1771–1835).
84. Walter Bondy, an expert on Chinese Art, especially ceramics.
85. The National Museum devoted to Bohemian history and culture.

lery[86]—The Cranach: woman embracing lewd old man and filching from his purse[87]—Church of the Loretto—Baroque—The beautiful Bohemian towers with little flanking spires—The castle and cathedral and the Belvedere. Below Prague the good but somewhat indecent food —tripe soup—a smell of decay in the back alleys—like Augsburg.

Many Spaniards at Hotel Pont Royal, a few French, the rest Americans.

Bavarian Museum in Munich[88]—Enormous and magnificent place—the Gothic madonnas—The crazy German youth who trailed us—The miles of junk in the GlasPalast[89]—Pictures of Americans on boulevard funny and savage—The Apollo in the Glyptothek—Awful pictures in New Pinakothek—one or two fair ones by Lenbach.[90] But great ones in old Pinakothek.

Berchtesgaden—Beautiful country, foul people—we began to get very tired of Hun-heads and triple necks—Hotel where we stayed —Scrubbed floors—Bavarian lads and lasses climbing mountain all night singing drunken songs. I was touchy, on edge by this time.

[*Paris*] Sept. 8—Thurs.

This morning to Place des Vosges—Victor Hugo's Place—and Carnavalet[91]—Carnavalet much bigger than I remembered—Magnificent rooms—Articles of revolution interesting—Portraits bad.

Carnavalet:

Drawings of Clouet painting—"Guinguette sous Francis Ier."
In the Library—*Histoire Universelle de France.*
*Hommes Illustres* (Demachy).
The Drawings of Raguenet of old Paris.

[*The following entries are again on loose pages which Wolfe had torn out to use for Eugene Gant's Parisian journal. After some*

86. The upper floor of the Künstlerhaus contained the Picture Gallery at the time Wolfe visited Prague.
87. "The Amorous Old Man," one of a pair in the collection, the other being "The Foolish Old Man."
88. The Bavarian National Museum devoted to German art and civilization.
89. A building something like the old Crystal Palace of London in the Victorian Era. It was used for annual art exhibitions and other displays.
90. Franz-Seraph von Lenbach (1836–1904), a Munich portrait painter.
91. The museum devoted to the history of Paris, especially during the Revolution.

*alteration and selection they appeared in* Of Time and the River, *pp. 665–66, 673–74.*]

Sam's: The man from San Francisco with the lewd dark debauched face. We had ham and eggs for lunch across at "Ciro's Annex" —The two barkeepers in Harrys: "Chip" and Bob—Names like dogs and horses.

Velasquez in the Louvre.

Vetzel's again 12:30 apéritif (X365). The arch of the Opera I have never seen before. Things sit like this [*sketch*].

Remember Faust at the Opera—the Promenoirs—The vast stage —click-clack of feet in the music.

I awoke this morning in a crucifixion of fear and nervousness— What if she hadn't written? What? What? What? My agony as I approached the place—My distrust of Paris in peril—City of light disloyalties. Sun never shines more than two days (for me) here— Went to White Star—Harry's Bar—The men at Veztel's eating—Rue Caumartin off Capucines—the waiters at luncheon (Regence).

In Prunier's I saw this: (and 1000 places elsewhere) the French are not bad but children—Old men too wise and kind for hatred—but French French French and suspicious.

How beautiful the Fratellini are!—How fine a thing is a French circus. Their enormous interest in children. The lion-taming act—by far the best and fiercest I have ever seen—and I felt sorry for the lions —Savoir is right in this.

Sunday night:

The Fratellini Brothers—How in his rich robe I saw him—the younger brother—waiting for the act—Looking us all over—The burlesque musical act—they were great, sad, and epic—what clowns should be.

"Réveillon de Noël."

The Jazz Orchestra in Sam's.

The Louvre again today: *Salle Rubens* with all the meat—all the people clustered about dull Mona ugly Lisa—"The Virgin with Saint Anne"—a great picture—Guido Reni [92]—the sainted and sugared faces. The Italians—Veronese—*The Cana*—The gigantic three-story canvases —The Murillos—"Immaculata" [93]—Zurberan—Goya and the Grey

92. An Italian painter of religious subjects (1575–1642).
93. Murillo's imaginative canvas of the Immaculate Conception.

—Picture of Gentlemen—Cuyp and the men on horseback [94]—Nicolas Maes—Rembrandt's picture of his brother—Some of the drawings magnificent—the costumes—the more modern collection—Sardou [95] in his study—Decorations of French academy—the Clouet drawings fine.

When I open my casual mind to people I spill out looted ore as if I tore open a sack fat with golddust.

Tuesday:

Got my ticket and my suit of clothes from tailor's—Have been buying books since—Flammarion (Blvd. Haussmann), Les Presses Universitaires, Odéon, Shakespeare and Co., and the Quais—Enormous number of books on science, chemistry, etc.—also on Psychology—Junk on the Siene—the old books—Bréviaires—Wonders of Nature, Universal Histories, etc.—also the near-pornographic books—the little stalls selling china and gimcracks.

Audreé Tusy at Concert Mayol—She was near 50—magnificent teeth—so good they made me uneasy—those things in her head—But how? They keep them so. This comes to me—that they spend lifetime seeing about them.

[*Wolfe has at this point a long, rather illegible list of wines that he has tried.*]

Thurs–Fri. Le 8–9:

On the Boulevards—3:20 du matin—reading the *Sourire* for Whore House Items—I want to find now a Ballon of Champagne—First of all—the preservatif—right to my left around corner Rue Faubourg de Montmarte in Front [*is all night pharmacy*].[96]

For the Morning if I get home late (or early as I will):

The Bookstalls on Seine.
The Odéon.
St. Germain.
The Louvre.
The Battle of Montmartre.

94. Probably "Riding Party" by Aelbert Cuyp.
95. Victorien Sardou (1831–1908), playwright and painter.
96. Wolfe added this explanatory phrase in his revision for OT&R.

[*Friday*] 7:30:

Café at corner of Faubourg Montmartre—I have just come from a whore house—In over two years first time I've betrayed her—Took preservatif—hope it works—Drinking beer at present to urinate—Paris is waking up—Almost broad daylight—At this point it never stops.

It was between 6:30 and 6:45 (a little later perhaps) it was 7:10 when I left—at 7:35 I peed and used the preservatif a 2nd time—On way to the heights of Montmartre.[97]

Along the quais again this afternoon to the bookstalls—Made afraid by the junk—Bought a dozen books or so, but no "prints" or "etchings"—Countless old fashioned prints, pictures of Versailles, the Palais Royal, the Revolution—Sentimental and cheap pictures—Florid ones *La Courtisane Passionée*, etc. Stage coach pictures, etc.—works of Eugene Scribe—the little books bound or tied, so you can't look—nothing in them—*Vie à La Campagne*—countless cheap books—Ah, I have a little of it all!

[*In writing* Look Homeward, Angel *Wolfe had already made use of the symbols of the stone, the leaf, the door. But the following entry is his note for the proem which opens the novel:*]

Of men, of the forgotten faces, of a stone, a leaf, an unfound door, the lane end into heaven.

O lost, and by the wind grieved, ghost, return.

The leaf it will wither and rot.

The binding [*breaks off*].

97. In his revision Wolfe added here, from an earlier part of the notebook, "My heart beat 81 to the minute at 7:42 by the clock."

## *Pocket Notebook 3*
## *Fall, 1927, to September, 1928*

*Wolfe returned to teaching at New York University in September, 1927. During the college year he somehow managed to finish his novel. Unable to place it with a publisher, he doggedly went ahead with plans for a new and hopefully more salable book, "The River People," a love story about a wealthy young painter and an Austrian girl whom his family scorns because of her humble background. But the rather conventional plot Wolfe had conceived did not hold his interest. When he went off to Europe in June, he roamed through galleries, museums, and bookstores, and when he jotted notes for his book, another character (again autobiographical) captured his attention. The difficulty of starting a new book was complicated by emotional upset when he determined to alter his relationship with Mrs. Bernstein, and during his aimless peregrinations he wrote her long letters full of his torment.*

*Only a few entries in this notebook come from the period of college teaching. Most of them were made from June to September, 1927, many of them records of the random interest provoked by museums or by the windows of European bookstores. It was characteristic of this time of uncertainty that he wrote to Mrs. Bernstein from Paris, on July 19, 1928:* "I spend hours looking at the thousands of books, unable it seems to buy a single one. . . . But I'm going to see some more books and pictures. I've got to make up my mind during the next day or so where I'm going. I want to get to work now." *He really did not know yet what work he wanted to do.*

---

[*The notebook begins with a number of drafts and notes which show that Wolfe was writing the final chapters of* Look Homeward, Angel. *The first entry is for Chapter XXXVIII.*]

Nobody said: I know you.

Nobody said: I am here.

In nakedness and loneliness of soul he paced along the streets. Nobody said: I know you. Nobody said: I am here. The vast wheel of earth, of which he was the hub, spun 'round.

Most of us think that we are hell, thought Eugene. I do. I think that I am hell. Then, in the dark campus path, he heard the young men talking in their rooms and he gouged at his face bloodily with a snarl of hate against himself.

I think I am hell! And they say I stink because I have not had a bath. Bruce-Eugene! Marshal Gant, the savior of his country. Ace Gant, the hawk of the sky, the man who brought Richtofen down! Senator Gant, Governor Gant, President Gant, the restorer and uniter of a broken nation, retiring quietly to humble life in spite of the weeping protest of one hundred million people, until like Arthur or Barbarossa, he shall hear again the drums of need and peril.

Jesus-of-Nazareth Gant, mocked, reviled, spat upon, and imprisoned for the sins of others, but nobly silent, preferring death rather than cause pain to the woman he loves. Gant, the unknown soldier, the Martyred President, the Slain God of Harvest, the bringer of good crops, Duke Gant of Westmoreland, Viscount Pondicherry, Twelfth Lord Runnimede, who hunts for love and truth incognito in Devon and ripe grain, and learns the joy of calico white legs embedded in sweet hay.

I was with a man over there—a good substantial man with a Texas Oil Company.

He was sittin' across the table from me—just like you.

You'd do it again tomorrow wouldn't you?

(Vicious woman—gold digger—flaccid chin—whining ironic voice when she wants to be nice)—Well, honey, can I speak now, etc.

You're a fighter, honey, I want to see a fight—etc.

All this happened at Cavanaugh's between a middle aged gold digger and her lover—A crowd of loud Jews came in for supper—During over an hour in here I heard nothing pleasant, lovely, kind or good—nothing that indicates why these people should be allowed to live any longer.

After "Think I'm hell scene"—three teachers—after that last night on campus—Graduation—Departure—Old Man at window—Bell ringing—Last summer at home—dentist's wife—squabbles over property—Eugene signs release—Gant lost and indifferent—Final Scene.

The American city temper is cowardly, vicious, and cruel—servile and cringing when it is powerless; arrogant and overbearing when it holds the reins. Never put a uniform on an American—not even for running an elevator. He can't stand it.

From the slow beating of the drums, and cries oppressed.

The beech leaves quiver.

Stilicho and Alaric—Romulus—Cyrus—Hapsburg face—Velasquez pictures of Infanta—the Moors—Pepin—Charles the Hammer—Vercingetorix—the Goths, the Vandals, the Franks, the Visigoths, the Gauls—the Saracens, the Steppes of Tartary, Hengist and Hertha, Cnut, Ivan, Peter, Catherine, Ming, Chung.[1]

Fat John Harvey.[2]

"Someone was telling me about you the other day, Gene," he began.

"Yes," said Eugene. "One of God's spies. What do they know about me?" he went on nervously and eagerly.

He will know; he has been put here for that purpose—his destiny, his life it is; to track my hidden life.

1. Dances—Gym—Y.M.C.A.
2. Vergil Weldon.
3. Playwriting.
4. English.
5. Graduation.

You bastard.

Don't you call me a bastard. You take that back. Don't you call me a bastard. I'll slap you in the face.

Well what the hell are you. We'll select another name.

My father and mother were the most wonderful people in the world with a flag over their shoulder.

You just came to see me. I'll wait another year till I get a hard on and then I'll see you.

You dirty cad! You were never on my side until you saw I was on the winning side.

You dirty hypocrite.

You're a Roman Catholic. That's what you are. I'm glad I found you out. You never slept with me and you told it all over the country.

I have slept with you and I've told it nowhere.

I'll come over there and tear all the clothes off your back, you dirty Roman Catholic.

Liar. Liar and hypocrite.

1. Probably a list Wolfe was preparing for the parade of civilizations that marches through Eugene's vision in the final chapter. The passage was cut out before publication.

2. A character based on Wolfe's friend John Terry. This material was also cut before publication. Wolfe later developed the character as Jerry Alsop in W&R.

Finish the drama.
Greenlaw.
Finish Vergil Weldon.

"My husband: she said, stopping Eugene in a campus path, "is a Great Man. His name is Vergil Weldon. We have plumbing in our house now; it was put in only last week. It's so white and lovely. Later on we're going to have electric lights. My husband is a Philosopher. He's never believed in these things. You must take his courses."

Then, peering with mad intenseness into his face, she said: "Never marry a girl with thin lips, young man. They are not to be trusted."

Eugene would go away from Pulpit Hill by night, by day, when April was a young blur, and when the Spring was deep and ripe. He liked best to go away by night, rushing across a cool spring countryside, under a great beach of moonlight, barred by long ribbed clouds.

He would go to Exeter or Sydney: sometimes he would go to the little towns he had never before visited. He would register at hotels as Robert Herrick, John Dunn, George Peele, Robert Blake, and John Milton. No one ever said anything to him about it. Once he registered at a hotel in a small Piedmont town as Ben Jonson. The clerk spun the book critically. "Isn't there an *h* in that name?" he said. "No," said Eugene. "That's another branch of the family. I have an uncle, Samuel, who spells his name that way."

Sometimes, at hotels of ill repute, he would register with secret glee as Robert Browning, Alfred Tennyson, and William Wordsworth. Once he registered as Henry W. Longfellow. "You can't fool me," said the clerk, with a hard grin of cynical disbelief. "That's the name of a writer."

Schedule for Eng. 36

Spring Term Thomas Wolfe

Feb. 1–March 1. Romantic Poetry.

Wordsworth—Coleridge—Lyrical Ballads. Preface to Lyrical Ballads—Chap. XIII–XIV Biog. Literaria—Lamb: Christ's Hospital Five and Thirty Years Ago—Lowes—The Road to Xanadu—*Byron.*

March 1–15. Victorian Poetry—Tennyson and Browning.

March 15–April 1. Modern English and American Poetry—Poetry of the War—The Literature of Disenchantment: Sassoon, Gibson.

Dear Professor Watt: [3]

I am writing you this letter before I speak to you because I feel you might like a formal record for your files.

After long consideration I have decided not to accept a teaching appointment at the university for next year. I think the time has come when I must make a bold venture with my life: in some way—not, I am afraid, very clearly defined yet—I want to get the energy of my life directed toward the thing it desires most. In short, I am going to try to support myself by writing—by hack writing of any sort, if necessary, and if I can—stories, advertising, articles—but *writing.* I know that this is a gamble, but it occurs to me that we can afford to gamble once or twice in an effort to get at the heart of our desire. The most reckless people, I believe, are those who never gamble at all.

During the last few days, in the tragic misfortune of Mr. Powell, I have seen again the splendid generosity which shows that New York University is not simply a group of buildings with elevators.

Magazine—Adventure, Popular Sea Stories, Asia and India, Western Stories, Mexican Stories, Stories of Am. mining interests everywhere—War and Marine stories.

TERM PAPER

*Short Story*

Kath. Mansfield's *Garden Party.* As beginning, write on *Social Protest in English and American S.S.*

A study of prose-poetry in the work of DeQuincey, Walter Savage Landor, and Ruskin.

*Drama*

Compare the use of suspense, irony, and fate in *Riders to the Sea* with the use of them in the *The Agamemnon* of Aeschylus, *Oedipus the King* of Sophocles, or *The Trojan Women* of Euripides.

3. Homer Watt was the Chairman of the Department of English at New York University. This is a draft of Wolfe's letter of April 1, 1928, *Letters,* pp. 132–34. The last paragraph refers to Desmond Powell, an instructor in English who was stricken with tuberculosis. New York University continued to pay his salary while he recovered. Arrangements were also made for his move to Colorado, where he could live and teach in a climate better suited to his lungs. His fellow instructors suspected that Dean James B. Munn had paid for Powell's move to the West out of his own pocket.

Stories for Writing:

Sea Story

Scene: A Crack Atlantic Liner—New York to Cherbourg.

People: A Beautiful American girl, a handsome and rich young American man, a third woman—beautiful but intriguing—An international jewel thief for whom the police of two continents are searching; a humorous cockney steward, who turns out to be Inspector Fortescue of Scotland Yard.

*Story* (I confess)

Girl in a Southern town—prominent socially—daughter of a Judge—Mother loves—Mother dies (?) Judge wants her to marry young rake, son of his deceased partner, distinguished man (formerly Governor of State). But she loves honest young fellow—stigma over his name—no great social prestige. Finally gives in to her father.

Start story with short paragraph or with single sentences.

Forgive—its a little word
To forget, make out, let live.
As if you hadn't heard
It's a little word—forgive.

A boy about 14 years old went into Perry's blacksmith shop to collect for the morning paper.

"Paper boy," he said, "Come to collect."

"Hello, son" said Mr. Perry. "How's your corporosity sagatation?"

"Pretty good," said the paper boy. "How's yours?" [4]

THE RIVER PEOPLE

Persons—Grosbeak.
His sister—Ducks.
John comes through Vienna on way to India.
Next-to-Last Chapter—Lili's death at hands of John.
Last Chapter—Party of friends.

4. Wolfe began a story called "Paperboy," which he never finished. A few pages are to be found in the LHA manuscript, Vol. XIII.

THE RIVER PEOPLE

Chap. I—Harvard
Chap. II—New York—Hotel—Summer
Chap. III—The River People—The Hudson
Chap. IV—Europe
Chap. V—New York—Autumn—The River
Chap. VI—The Winter—The Garret
Chap. VII—The Spring—The Lodge—The House
Chap. VIII—The Picnic and Lawn Party—*John* (a cousin)
Chap. IX—Fourth of July at Astor's
Chap. IX—Vienna again—They live together there
Chap. X—Winter—New York—He is now away from them completely —living with her
Chap. XI—New York again
Chap. XII—The River—Reunion—The girl—Cousin John—Mother —Pups
Chap. XIII.

Tues. May 15:

Left this book at Italian Rest. Friday night—found it here tonight—Saw J. Walter Thompson Company today—offered job [5]—don't know what I shall do.

Call the Old Man Vater.

Olin Dows. Joel (Joly) Pierce.[6]

Portrait of Fraulein L. Picture he painted of her—one great picture—touched with love and madness—the monkeys at boys club on East side—mad, too.

Last scene—"I have no passions. I cannot let myself go (as you can) I have only a small talent—I shall make the most of it."

Synoposis

Chap. I—Evening in Spring—Eugene (?) striding across Harvard yard towards Widener Library—Two young men standing there

5. Mrs. Bernstein had shown Wolfe's novel to Mrs. Helen Resor of the J. Walter Thompson advertising company. She made him an offer of a job writing advertising copy. Wolfe considered it reluctantly for the remainder of the year.

6. Olin Dows, a friend from Harvard, was the model for Joel Pierce, the young hero of "The River People." Wolfe had dinner with him later: "Told him I was going to write a book about him as he ought to be—always grand, noble, and romantic. Seemed interested and amused." Letter to Aline Bernstein, June 28, 1928.

watch his approach—Grosbeak[7] and Joel Pierce. "He's marvellous! Simply marvellous! Do you suppose I could get him to sit for me?"

(Get planted here the Man-Mountain attitude) Joel Pierce goes away leaving Grosbeak and Eugene.

"He's a Great Swell, you know—a Very Great Swell."

"He has a hole in his trousers."

Old Joly—Joel's grandfather—Grand old man, a little baroque, *only one arm*—His wife—Mrs. Joel—Scene at old Joly's house— "Why, sir, I should have to conclude then that he was a Scoundrel."

"Ah! Ixx-ac-ly," murmured Vater. His eye fell tenderly upon the smooth curves of the serving maid.

Have Joel paint portrait of Lili (Greta)[8]—one *great* (?) picture? of what kind? Touched with struggle—(*Madness*(?))

It had come—the hard moment of parting.

The two young men stood in painful silence, staring awkwardly at each other.

Then, as he looked at that fine lean head—that head of Eastern agony and repose—charged with a passion that would never again break forth, the enormous pageantry of the life they had known together—that rich swell of pain and love and death—surged over Eugene its enormous beauty. His head swam, his throat contracted, his heart was glutted with pain and wonder. For a moment he was blind and dizzy.

Then, swept forward on the tide of indefinable impulse; unable to check himself, unable to reason, he plunged towards his friend at his terrible stride.

His long arms were stretched out in a gesture of agony and supplication, his long arms were hooked like claws.

"Joly," he cried. "My dear Joly!"

Joel stepped back quickly, with the old startled gesture. It was as if he had suddenly lifted a shield before his face.

"Yes," he said quickly, "Yes." But that fatal word meant *No*.

Eugene stopped abruptly. His arms fell slowly to his sides.

In a moment he extended one hand quietly. The other young man grasped it and shook it briefly. "Goodbye," they both said.

7. A character based on Kenneth Raisbeck.

8. Apparently Wolfe planned to base the character Lili on Greta Hilb, an Austrian girl whom he had met on the ship returning from Europe. She was married to Emil Hilb, a violinist who came to the United States to play in an American orchestra.

Then Eugene got into the car and was driven swiftly away towards the river.

THE END

[*On June 2, 1928, Mrs. Bernstein went abroad for a European vacation with Theresa Helburn, one of the directors of the Theatre Guild. She and Wolfe had had a series of stormy scenes during the spring, when Wolfe was attempting to shake loose from his relationship with her. Now he wrote to her contritely about their distressful hours:*

"Since you have gone, I have thought more clearly about you. I think of you with pain and with love, and I think I always shall. And it is very bitter for me to know that I have acted meanly and badly toward you. But the snake-headed furies that drive us on to despair and madness are inside of us: how to unroot them from the structure of our soul is a problem that gets me sick with horror. What I mean to say more plainly is that, no matter what you did or are about to do, I acted badly. That is as far as I can truthfully go now. I wish that I had the strength to be finer, but I felt like an animal, who had to endure mockery and torture until it got out of its cage, and it made me crazy . . . .

"I don't want to talk wise, or to try to appear detached. I am still stupid and numb over what has happened to me. But I have lost my ugliness and bitterness, and I can not deny, Aline, that I love you more than anyone in the world. This is as honest a record as I can make at the present time—Tom"]

Penn Station—Asheville train—K19 at 1:05 standard and 2:05 City time.

He rode through the rich (lush) Virginias.

Sat. June 10, 1928—

On this day I left New York for a few days in North Carolina, where I was born.

Eugene gets Joel and Li an apartment in Vienna—*Detail* here.

Shows I Have Seen This Year:

Shannons of B'way, Volpone, Show Boat, Rosalie, G'd. St. Follies, Joe Cook, Manhattan Mary, Maya, If, Good News, The Love Nest, The First Stone, Improvisations in June, Keep Shufflin', Plough and the Stars, Taming of the Shrew, The Royal Family, Black Birds, Diamond Lil (midnight show).

Went to Hoboken Thurs. [*June 28*] to see ship—ate at Hofbrau Haus—very good—beer excellent—waterfront—U.S. lines, Manson line, Holland-Amerikan.

Thurs.—[*June 28*]:

Get Suitcase Fixed—Buy shirts and underwear—Write Elaine [9] and Robert Bunn [10]—Write J. Walter Thompson Co.—Write Mrs. Boyd [11]—Get Envelopes at Harvard Club—Leave mailing instructions there—See Greenleaf about Rent—Phone Miss Stott [12]—Make out J.W.T. application blank—Get toilet articles—Buy mss. book—get French Visa—Phone A. Smith about typewriter.

*Books to be taken—*

French and German Dictionaries
English Dict.
A few French books.
MSS of book.
MSS of plays (?) Yes.

Friday, June 29:

Morning—Buy shirts and underwear—Macy's (see about suspenders and tie also) get valise—See Greenleaf—pack—see dentist—Pack—write Mrs. Resor—other letters?—see A. Smith about typewriter.

Paris—6:47 from Boulogne 2½ hrs. to Paris.

The great liners—Les Transatlantiques.

Monday, July 9, 1928:

Landed at Boulogne—stayed here the night—watched boat trains go by the bridge on way to Paris—wrote postals—Investigated town—finished letter to Aline.

9. Elaine Westall Gould, Wolfe's cousin in Boston.

10. A friend and former neighbor in Asheville.

11. Madeleine Boyd, wife of Ernest Boyd, the literary critic, was Wolfe's agent for the sale of his novel.

12. Margaret Stott, Mrs. Bernstein's old nurse, who was to look after his apartment in his absence.

Tomorrow—up early—go to Wimereux—Climb up to old town —go to Amiens in afternoon.

Use Dictionary—words—bottes, air, soulier [*bunches, garlic, shoe*].

What are French words for wooden shoes—cobble stones? The café tonight—three French women and queer dark little man who spoke nothing but Eng. but badly. Woman said dog was her youngest daughter, and hard to bear—they spoke of cats and litter of kittens. Quel Ménage! (elle dit).

July 9, 1928:

Last day in Boulogne—Rose late (10 o'clock) took walk through town—up the hill through old city and Quartier des Mains—interesting but dirty and filthy—Rue St. Pol—Madame Louise—Filthiest street in town—Marriage at church in Basse Ville—ate at Brasserie Liégeoise—food good—Moules Mariniere—Ris de Veau—Bordeaux—nothing like Fr. cooking—Wimereux this afternoon—going to Amiens later.

Wimereux—up the coast from Boulogne about 4 or 5 miles. Bathing resort, with promenade, and miles of new painty, glaring, plastery, fancy hotels, villas, and pensions. Hotel Belle Vue. Pension Gai Sejour, etc.—pretty French women in bathing suits—big wet butts, pot bellied men.

Amiens *Hotel de L'Univers*

RESERVEZ UN CHAMBRE POUR UN SEUL PERSONNE A PARTIR DE MERCREDI SOIR.

Wed. July 11:

Amiens—all day seeing city—Ready to depart by 5:52 pour Paris. Hotel people said I had lost key. Terrific row. They called the police. At height of battle they found key—I missed train—Profuse apologies, free drinks (Beer 250—free tel. call to Paris?) I missed train, lost two hours, but saved 40 francs (and a little pride)—on way to Paris now.

Thursday, July 12:

Got up to Paris last night—Met Mrs. K.—T.L.N.—Affair at Amiens—Got her up at two o'clock today—bathed.

*[Here begins a series of loose pages that Wolfe ripped from this notebook, redated 1924, and drew on for Eugene Gant's Paris diary. See* Of Time and the River, *pp. 666–67.]*

Friday, July 13—

Night—streets of Paris full of people dancing—tomorrow national holiday—I feel rotten.

July 14:

Sweltering heat—but interesting day—took river boat up to Suresnes—Got off and ate at Hermitage—Bois du Boulogne—all the French middle class on outing—Sprawled on grass with shoes off—suspenders down—paper and egg-shells everywhere.

Tonight—walk along boulevards—terrific crowds dancing in streets—a million concessionaries—Porte St. Denis—I did not feel gay, but [*breaks off*]

Things in Paris I should like to see—*Père Lachaise*[13]—Also investigate old quarter again around Place des Vosges—go *there* first thing tomorrow—go to Cluny Musée[14] again—and up and down Rue de la Seine—also Île St. Louis.

Thursday, July 19, 1928:

I am getting a new sense of control—millions of books don't worry me so much—went along the Seine today after Louvre—most of it worthless old rubbish—I must begin to put up my fences now—I can't take the world nor this city with me.

Books I want—

Julien Benda
New one by Soupault (?)
Charles Derennes—*L'Education Sexuelle*
Read one of the Vautel things.

Get for inspection—and at random: Le Petit Livre, Mon Livre Favori, Bibl. Nationale, Livre Epatant.

Go into Court of Palais Royale—investigate there.

13. Wolfe probably wished to visit this cemetery to see the tomb of Balzac, whose work he admired greatly.

14. The Musée de Cluny is noted for its great collection of medieval arts and crafts. It is also the oldest inhabited building in Paris.

Louvre today—Mantegna's picture of St. Sebastian (?) grey marble flesh. Giotto's great picture of St. Francis D'Assisi receiving stigmata from Christ—[*sketch*].

Gros—pictures of Napoleon at war—the one of the leper's house at Jaffa a good one—Huge naked leper held in kneeling position —weight of body. [*sketch*]

Books I want—

1. Go to bookstalls on Seine for books on Paris twenty or thirty years ago, with naughty illustrations.
2. Buy one or two old bindings—get one or two books of Les Grands Seducteurs.
3. Get best books of Maurras and Benda—Bought Bordeaux [*La peur de vivre*]. René Bazin, René Boylesve, Octave Mirbeau, Marcel Prévost, Claude Farrère, Marcel Boulenger, [*Francis*] Carco, [*François*] Mauriac, Willy (Colette), Les Marguerittes, André Salmon, Marcelle Tinayre, (*Ma Route*—Vioux), Henri Lavedan, Henri Bataille, Alfred Capus.

Saturday [*July 21*]:

Shave, Guaranty Trust Co., Am. Ex. Co., finish letter to Aline —Louvre—Cluny—Pantheon—Books—Dentist (?) where?

Tomorrow—Monday:

Dentist, Sainte Chapelle—the Cité Universitaire.<br>
Bookshops on Boul. St. Germain—and Rue du Seine.<br>
Great medical book shop on B. St. Germ.<br>
Great law " " near Pantheon.<br>
Try to get into Bibliothèque Nationale for look around.<br>
Antiquités—Ameublements—Where do they all come from?<br>
Get book on Julien Benda.

Went to Panthéon today—Coolest place in Paris—crypt—cool off with V. Hugo, Zola, Voltaire, and J. J. Rousseau. Rabble staring in curiously at tomb of Voltaire.

Murals—some by Puvis [*de Chavannes*]—legend of St. Genevieve of Paris.

Buy Vigny's *Confession.*

No matter what I have ever thought or believed about you,[15] the feeling has become very clear in my mind that I do not deserve you and that it has been a very great thing for me to have known you. This is not to say that I think of myself as "a lucky fellow." I picture your friends as saying contemptuously that I am a lucky fellow, but it is not luck to sweat blood. And I do not know what it may mean for my life to have known you. I wish I could believe that it might mean some sort of triumph or success, some such deposit that would add to my value and my power. But I neither believe nor disbelieve this—the whole engine of my life and soul mounted to its greatest drive and expenditure, but whether on this account it will hereafter be a better engine I can not say. But my dear Aline, I believe there is a truth beyond belief and beyond reason. When I have been most bitter about you, my bitterness has always been below my conviction about you—that you were burning in all of heaven like my great star, and you have always burned above my life like that great star—all that I have believed or known have been like little noises below my grand and everlasting star.

Tuesday, July 24:

Along Seine again—Looked at thousands of books and bought one—a critique on Julien Benda [16]—miles and miles of books—but, also miles and miles of repetitions—the pictures—cavaliers seducing pretty ladies; one of woman half naked embracing pillow—called "Le Rêve" —People in old French stage coaches—then 1000's of La Chimie, La Physique, La Géologie, L'Algèbre, Le Géometrie.

Letters—Morceaux Choisis of XVIII S. All the authors I have never heard of—but *that* is the same at home.

Wednesday, July 25:

Today bought books—little book shop on Rue St. Honoré—Stock's—bought Benda there—along the river—Tons of trash—*L'Univers—The Miracle of France—4 mos. in the United States,* etc., etc.—Les Cicéron, Ovide, Sénèque, etc.—Bought *Confessions of Alfred de Musset*—stall at Mont Neuf with dirty books—*Journal d'une Masseuse, Sadie Blackeyes, Lovers of the Whip, The Pleasures of Married Life*—the Galleries of the Palais Royal where the dirty bookshops are—whole series edited by Guillaume Apollinaire.

Pictures, stamps, coins—Daumier-like picture of man having

15. Draft of a letter to Aline Bernstein, June 22, 1928.

16. "It is about a man named Julien Benda and his philosophy and writings: he spits on Bergson and is one of the great moderns." Letter to Aline Bernstein, July 25, 1928.

tooth pulled—the near dainty ones of ladies with silver wigs—silhouette-like—then the near XVIII century ones.

Old books—seem to be millions of this too—*Essais of L'Abbé Chose Sur La Morale*, etc.

[*Here end the loose pages. For Eugene Gant's diary Wolfe added the comment,* "The Faustian hell again!"]

*The French*—they are literally unconscious of the rest of the world. They know nothing of its extent, of the 16,000 miles of sea, of its grandeur, its diversity, its immensity. They are completely contained within themselves—this certitude comes from the rigid and narrow limit of their life, which does not seem rigid and narrow to them. This came to me one night as I watched them throng past on Boul. De Sébastopol; saw them ogle their girls; heard them talk behind and around me at café tables. For this reason Americans who play the monkey to them are fools. For even the dullest American has the sea in his mind, and the immensity of his own country.

[*The following entries were recorded in Brussels when Wolfe visited the Musée Royal des Beaux-Arts Belgique.*]

51—Van Aken [17]—"Adoration des Bergers."
66—Bouts—brutal but good—"L'Épreuve du Feu" [18]
785—[*Master of*] Flémalle—"L'Annunciation."
389—Rubens—"Negro Heads."
242—Jordaens—"Le Roi Boit!" [19]

The museum is limited but some of the Dutch and Flemish things are very good—Early Dutch primitives good—Memling: [20] Dieric Bouts.

The element of French imitation everywhere.

Revue—Bruxelles Aux Nues—Song between man and woman—Chose-uh-Rose-uh-Repose-uh—More stupid than the tooth ache—there is a heaviness about the women that is not French—some very

17. Jerome Van Aken, usually called Hieronymus Bosch.

18. A reference to one of Dieric Bouts's two panels on the legend of Otho. The Emperor Otho is ordering his treacherous wife to undergo the test of the hot irons in order to prove her innocence. She holds in her hands the head of the innocent man whom she had accused and caused to be executed.

19. There are two versions of this roistering scene. Wolfe bought reproductions of both.

20. Wolfe was especially attracted to Hans Memling's "Portrait of Barbara Vlanderbergh."

good looking but a little thick—The Ring Sellers here also in front of the cafés—and the peanut vendors.

Brussels—one of the most luxurious and elegant cities in the world—they call it the Little Paris, but it is really a far more voluptuous place than Paris. The elegance is on top of the hill—the great Boulevard de Waterloo with its cafés and restaurants—avenue two hundred feet wide with four traffic lanes, separated by avenues of trees.

The wine shops—the beginnings of the Dutch interiorness—a touch of elegance in the cafés even.

To Aline: [21]

In your letter I think you talk a great deal more of your love than I do in mine. I feel that I am always bringing in other things—what I have observed, or felt, or thought, or what has interested me in a great many ways. And when I read the letters over later—I am sorry for this; I wish I had talked to you about love more, for I feel somehow that as regards me you are interested in that alone. You know so many people with greater talents and better intelligence than mine; and I know that I can say very little about anything that will be interesting and original to you. Your own feeling towards things is usually subtler and finer than mine. Yet I bring all these things into my letters, because I used always to dream of a life with you in which all of this would figure, and even now I am always a little ashamed when I have said again and again how much I love you. You can say it, and it is always interesting and new, for you have the power to say it in a thousand ways. But I lack that power. I used to feel that love was part of my life or rather that my life and all those thousand things that swarmed through my mind was part of love; I have never been able to cut them apart, as you have—your life, your many activities, and your feelings for me. And I think a great deal of our trouble has come from that.

Check made out New York July 9, 1928, $316.66.

Salary for July and August signed by Leroy E. Kimball [*and*] W. H. Hendershot.

281 [*Nicolas*] Maes—"Portrait [*de Laurent de Rasière*"].
79 P. Brueghel ["*La chute des anges rebelles*"].
680 P. Breughel ["*Le dénombrement de Bethléem*"].
778 P. Breughel ["*L'adoration des Mages*"].
768 [*Pieter*] Huys ["*Le jugement dernier*"].

21. Draft of a letter, July 27, 1928.

50 Bosch [*"La tentation de Saint Antoine"*].
255 [*Bartholomeus de*] Bruyn—"Portrait de Femme."
122 L. Cranach [*"Portrait du Dr. J. Scheuring"*].
65 Bouts, [*"Le supplice de l'Innocent"—the other panel from the legend of Otho*].
780 Lucas de Leyde [*"La tentation de Saint Antoine"*].
300 [*Quentin*] Metsys [*"La Vierge des sept douleurs"*].
292 [*Hans*] Memling [*"Portrait de Guillaume Morcel"*].
545 Maitre Brugeois [*de la Legende de Sainte Lucie—"La Vierge avec Madeleine et les vierges"*].

Dear Mrs. Resor:

Thanks for your very kind letter which was sent on to me and which I got just before I left Paris. It gives me confidence and hope to know that I still have a chance with J. Walter Thompson when I come back to America. I must find some sort of place for myself at home: I belong to my country and am always a little homesick elsewhere.

The charming lady who wants culture also interests me. I have a little culture and no money. I am willing to sell my goods at very moderate rates. But I am afraid it would not be as painless as a course in Mysticism under Yogi Yam, the Yama. She would have to work, and perhaps to write me a paper once a week.

I stayed in Paris two or three weeks and came on to Brussels a few days ago. This is one of the most elegant and luxurious cities in Europe—it out-Parises Paris in many ways. The people are very gay, there are solid blocks of cafes, and a splendid prohibition law which forbids your ordering anything but all sorts of wines, beer, and champagne. If you want anything stronger, you must go to a store and buy at least two quarts at a time. That's the right idea, Isn't it?

The girl—Greta—Mrs. Weinberg—Husband Viennese Jew—Her history after the war; married to him when she was 16; he comes to America—job in orchestra here—Vater.

Sunday, July 29 (?)—

The modern museum [22] with the old Belgo-American—old man a little cracked but good at heart. His face marked by America—mouth mixture of tenacity and sullen petulance because of struggle during his early years. His strange jargon and the strain of listening and

22. The Musée de Peinture Moderne, which houses mostly nineteenth-century work.

understanding—it got on my nerves at last—Pictures in Modern Museum very bad—Huge historical paintings of Lepanto. Revolt of Belgium in 1830 with noble peasants waving flags. Bloodstained but otherwise spotlessly white shirts, romantic young patriots with little moustaches and willing torsos giving up the ghost in the arms of pure faced and weeping virgins—old Belgian liked all this.

A few pictures by Matisse and Gauguin—rather bad—a good nude in the very modern manner by a Russian [*Lacovleff*]; and a great many bad attempts by bad moderns.

The Book

(Hugh, Philip, Stephen, Eugene, John, Bill)—needs money more than Joel—understands it better, is more of the sensualist and epicure.

The place of Europe in an American's life—what is the centre of Europe's leisure and culture—it comes very close to being beer—the café—the greatest effort of European civilization towards the enjoyment of its leisure after 2000 years—It is much better than anything we have evolved, but if we come to a better life I hope we do something better than that.

Some Conclusions about the good life: The only happiness comes in finding the work you want to do, and to do it without obstruction.

Modern life ought to be more severe in its moderation than ancient life: "Fullness of life" may be achieved only through strenuous selection—working within narrow limits.

The position of women—occasionally on the bed, often in the kitchen.

Simplicity without affectation.

When he went by the pastry shops on the Rue St. Honoré he lusted to eat everything in the windows—the fat little paté-pies, the flaky tarts, the thin dainty wafers, the rich cakes studded with candied fruits—so with the books.

He began to get back on his large useful feet again.

European Scenes:

Eugene with the mountainous Dutchmen—Antwerp and Brussels.

Eugene with the Countess at Orleans and Blois.

Eugene with the women of Paris—the Negress (I stuck tongue in tooth here—ache—stopped writing—1:25 a.m.)

Monday, July 30, 1928:

Went with old Belgian-Amer. (Warney?) to Hotel de Ville and he got man to take picture of us [23]—then to the upper town again—another picture in the park—we had heated argument about imperialism—he felt it Christian duty of Christian nations to rob, pillage, and "civilize" non-Christian races—the lowly Chinese and Indians.

Wednesday, Aug. 1—

Today wrote Aline again to Vienna: wrote Elaine [*Westall Gould*]; explored the lower part of city to suburbs—walked away from Bourse until I came to open country. Streets filled with thousands of small shops. How do they keep alive? There seems to be a butcher, delicatessen, taverne or brasserie, bakery, etc. for almost every family—the big square (of the Duke of Brahant, I believe) where there was a drug store in the modern style of architecture.

Story: From first time in Paris on—woman at hotel is Greta Weinberg—Falls sick there after friend and two women depart—She nurses him—feeds him—keeps him (make her very poor—little apartment on Rue Lepic—They go there to live.)—Then he breaks away—she digs him out of dirty holes—the beggars' lodging near the markets—then he starts out over the country—Orléans—The Countess—Tours—Broke—Return to Paris—Brussels—the North—then South—Lyons—Avignon—*Marseilles*—St. Raphael—Nice—Writes her to Paris—Half crazy—goes to Italy—Finds letter for him at Venice—Come to Vienna—He goes to Vienna—Six weeks in Vienna—Vater—Munich—Germany—Home again.

New York—Joel—the Boys Club—Parting—up the River—The University—Arrival of Greta—The hotel—Late in the spring, Joel meets her—Vater—the trip up the river—Weinberg—Scene at Rhinebeck—John—Summer passes. Hugh goes abroad again—Four months pass—Cable from Joel—in Munich—Meet them in Vienna. He meets them there—gets apartment for them—Arrival of John on way to India—Arrival of Margaret & Mother—Agreement to divorce and marriage. Weinberg paid off—Eugene to act as witness (with John?)

23. Three snapshots of Wolfe and Pierre Varney are in the Wisdom Collection.

Back to New York again—the garret—divorce proceedings—Final papers—up the river—the last scene.

Character of Greta: Lightness and gayety and sensual quality over everything else—but great profundity and sorrow beneath.

What does she do—something very clever, with her hands—something light, trivial and lovely—Vater her nemesis—like old man of the sea—make her only *half-Jew*—Vater a Christian.

Vienna: Take notes carefully—make picture of life there as seductive and appealing as possible.

"Do you like painting?" Joel asked.

"No," said Hugh. "I know very little about it. My taste is very bad."

"His taste is goot" said Greta. "It is vot you call—superp, I tink he could not like a bat painting if he try."

"I like only pictures that tell a story," Hugh said. "I do not understand any other kind. And that is bad, isn't it? There are not over a dozen painters that I know about and care for."

"Whom do you like?" Joel asked.

"Pieter Breughel," said Hugh, "is the greatest painter that ever lived."

"Hugh!" said Joel. Then shaking his head with an incredulous smile, he said, "Good Lord!" and gave it up as if hopeless.

Why he likes Breughel—all the world resolved there—richness without triviality and waste—Used to dream of a book on the stalls of the Seine that would have all the other books in it.

Thursday, Aug. 2—

Today—again to see the pictures—there are some very lovely old ones there—Van der Weyden too—the XVth century was one of the great centuries of history.

After museum a very long walk up the Avenue Louise and into the great Bois—the Bois is one of the most beautiful forests I have ever seen. It surpasses by far the Bois de Boulogne—Cafés hidden in the trees—places for middle class folk with a dance floor and a very bad orchestre—Les Jeunes Filles Belges— dancing together.

The wealth—the immense display of wealth along Avenue Louise—the rich houses, and the expensive cars—with my brief case beside me I felt like a pauper.

Bookshops—Little series with André Salmon, Julien Green, J. Lacretelle, Pierre Mac-Orlan.

What are *Les Provinciales* de Giraudoux? Investigate.

Many translations of J. O. Curwood and Jack London—they like to read about great open spaces.

The dislike and mistrust of foreigners among these people touches me much less than it did two years ago.

Who are the authors of modern France worth reading? Cocteau, Mac-Orlan, J. Benda, Soupault, Giraudoux, Mauriac, Mme. Colette.

"Are you going to remain a man without a country?" Joel asked.

"We are all men without a country," Hugh answered. "We have been born in exile, and as exiles we must continue to live. There is no man on earth who is not a stranger. In her dark womb we did not know our mother's face."

Time: Spring of 1924 to Spring of 1927.

Beginning:—1923—Yard at Harvard—Year following New York—N.Y.U.—then trip abroad—Paris and abroad 1924–25—1926 New York again—1926 Europe again—1927—End of story.

Friday, [*August 3*]

Sent letter to Hendershot[24]—Took walk through town—was told table was reserved at Central Hotel (?) Restaurant after head waiter had put me there—I went to another restaurant without comment.

Saturday [*August 4*]—

Telegram from Vienna—Aline—Shave—lunch—Modern Museum again—a few good pictures—"L'Attrapoire" [*The Trap*]—of [*Félicien*] Rops—[*Eugène*] Laermans' Dutch pictures[25]—Picture called "Dimanche"—Three Priests—a fellow and his girl rowing—and a fat bourgeois, his wife, and child, out walking. Alfred Stevens—Pict. of Salomé—Bookshop.

24. A financial officer at New York University who was responsible for sending Wolfe his paychecks.

25. Actually he was a Belgian. Wolfe was attracted to his realistic paintings of peasant groups. He bought reproductions of "Le retour des champs," "Le chemin du repos," and "Le mort."

The stamps of P. Brueghel—the Louvre in XIV and XV centuries—articles in paper on censorship in Belgium—Restaurants with the libraries—Do not see the dirty books you see in France—Most Catholic country—Notices in Notre Dame des Victories to read no books or papers that do not tend to "bonnes moeurs."

The pictures of [*Albert*] Servaes [26] in Modern Museum—Horrible.

Tomorrow—Go to Laeken—Visit the Musée de Cinquantenaire—buy some books (?)—what?—Lacretelle, Giraudoux—*Les Innocents*—*J'Adore*—*Le Bétail Humain* (?) Look over recent editions of N.R.F.—Monday go to Malines, and from there on to Antwerp. Write Mrs. Roberts before leaving Brussels.

Street women of France and Belgium all say the same things—it's stupid—Venez chez moi, chéri; Ecoute, mon petit bonbon, vous vous ennuyez tout seul comme ça.

Ah mais tu es avare—she said.[27]

Sunday, Aug. 5—

Saw a monster parade of the Socialists—conservative papers give it as little space as possible—but there must have been between 50,000 and 100,000 in the parade, and 100,000 more watching—Parade brought up the rear with thousands of magnificent red flags—banners—of workmen's organizations—gymnastic societies etc. A forest of huge red banners recreating the pageantry of chivalry, of the Crusades, among these working people.

The people of Belgium are small like the country—there is little in the country that touches or moves me profoundly. Today when the working men began to walk past something gathered in my throat; then I grew weary of them.

They dislike us—but surlily and obviously. They lack the perfect metallic finish—the impregnability of the French.

There is something heavy and dull in the country—Latin civilization bores me enormously after a while—there is an enormous monotony below it all.

26. A twentieth-century Flemish painter.

27. "Come to my place, dearie; Listen, my little sweetie, you get bored all alone like that."

"Ah, but you are stingy," she said.

[*Sketches of houses and of a "very elegant café—near Palais de Justice.*"]

Tomorrow—Monday [*August 6*]—must be last day in Brussels —get up—go to Am. Ex. Co.—wire Aline—get bill—send post cards —pack—go to Antwerp.

Tower at Malines [*Sketch of tower*].

Antwerp (station) 12:30 a.m.—very difficult but interesting day —Left Brussels at 4:50 this afternoon—Have spent most of time since trying to get room in Antwerp—I have walked many many miles—not a hotel in Antwerp has a room—Great Congress of Esperantists having meeting here—It is fantastic weird unreal—Now at dead of night I am going back to the little country town of Malines in an effort to find room for the night—It is fifteen or twenty minutes away. Antwerp is a strange place—the whole district around the station and main parts of town is almost solid with little cafés, wine shops, and closed-in "taverns" which are whore houses—Gigantic dance halls where you pay one franc to get in and where thousands of middle class people—soldiers with their girls and so on—are dancing—Walked the whole way to the harbor, and back through old twisting Dutch streets. These too filled with little taverns, multitudinous shops, people dancing to automatic pianos, accordians, etc.

Where in God's name do all the goods—sausages, pastries, cheeses, wines, beers, laces, pottery, books, engravings, etc., come from? Who buys them?

Wednesday, Aug. 8, Köln:

Got here last night after weird experiences over Northern Belgium trying to find room. Malines—where I slept among thieves—Antwerp—the amazing spectacle of that town—the innumerable cafés—and little closed "taverns" and wine shops—Walk through old town in search of room—To come always like this at dark to a town—But old streets with innumerable little dirty joints not very attractive—along the docks—Canadian-Pacific boats tied up lengthwise.

But the halters of earth are broken,
The feet of the wind are shod,
And we that were dumb have spoken
And we that were lame have trod
On the perilous seas—and awoken
The flame and the [lark?] and the sod.

But the halters of earth are broken,
The feet of the wind are shod,
All the words that you hear not are spoken,
All the sundering seas are trod.

Thursday [*August 9*]:

Up at 10—had dainty German breakfast of Tea, Marmalade, Rye Bread, sausage, beef, ham, and tongue. Spent rest of the morning writing to Aline—Then laundry and Hofbrau Haus for Beer and Haus-Platte—Then [*Wallraf-Richartz*] Museum for Pictures—Some very beautiful Early German Primitives—Meister Von Mariens Lebens—Pictures of Christ crucified among the thieves—Early Kölnisch paintings showing Christ with little loin cloth but no manly organs—Two thieves wear large well-filled codpieces—idea of Eunuch God thus an old one not merely a Y.M.C.A. notion. Big Della Robbia of Virgin—Modern paintings—impressionist and post impressionist schools: most of them very bad—but magnificent Picasso—A Spanish Family, and fine Van Gogh ["*The Draw Bridge*"], and good Renoir ["*The Sisley Family*"]. Must go back.

After that to German Koffee Haus—After that for shave—most elegant place—pretty young German girls as manicurists—after that to Bookshop—again I notice [*breaks off*]

Here in Germany, as the time for her going home approaches—it begins again—not the great desire to see her, but the memory still aching and bitter, of the pain and shame I endured.

Köln. But Oh! the comfort of being in a country where things are done well—where (generally) one price is charged; where there are not countless attempts to cheat and haggle. The Germans may be the thieves and traitors their enemies say they are when it comes to treaties, contracts, and national promises; but when it comes to hotel bills, standard prices, tips, etc., they are more honest than the French have ever been.

Köln—"Presse"—they have built the most tremendous Exhibition Buildings I have ever seen—all in the modern manner and *very very good!* There is a decision and powerful energy about everything they do that shows their inconceivable will to "come back." They say, room by room, completely and exhaustively everything about newspapers that can be said. And the magnificent book exhibition—many editions by the French—Carco, Morand, Cocteau, Larbaud, etc. LaFontaine—Voltaire—LaBruyère.

Germans—Hauptmann, Schiller's und Goethe's Gedichte, Count Luckner, Rilke, Rathenau, Wasserman, Schnitzler.

Many first pages of the Bible magnificently typed and in several languages—Edition of Hamlet in German ed. by Hauptmann, with Latin and French sources at the side.

The effect of the "exposition" is overwhelming. As usual, the Germans have done things with absolute thoroughness—the mind sinks before the tons of newsprint exhibited here.

Saturday morning [*August 11*]—

Breakfast—then to Cook's where telegram from Aline in Berlin—then to bookshop where I bought a book on "Kleine Plastik" of the Renaissance—and a little guide to Cologne—then looked over books—Count Luckner's description of good will voyages to America—Many editions of Ludwig—Sinclair Lewis in German—*Volk Ohne Raum*—new one by Wassermann [*Der Fall Mauritius*].

Book—novel—called *Er* [*by Hans Bartsch*]—book—novel—called *Amerika* [*by Franz Kafka*]—a large enough title—Insel Verlag—*With Stanley in Africa*—Ossendowski—Who is Titaijna? [28]—Isadora Duncan's Memoirs—Hendrick Van Loon's *Story of Mankind*—Briand—*France and Germany*.

Passed three students in Corps uniform—they were in taxis, and carried big naked swords—fat unhealthy looking pigs but impressive in all their plumage—fine feathers make fine birds—they arouse my hostility and make me want to fight them—who wrote *Der Grüne Heinrich?* [29]

In this world whether there is room for all kinds or not—we must make room, if necessary, we must not give way unjustly. We must observe and forbear to waste ourselves in futile antagonisms, jealousies, and hostilities. I am becoming more and more adjusted to my place in the world—what it may finally be I do not know but I must build up out of chaos a strong sufficient inner life; otherwise I will be torn to pieces in the whirlpool of the world. It is not for me to say now "Am I better than this, or worse than this?" but "Am I making use of myself to the best of my capacity?"—I do not know whether such an idea belongs to any school of philosophy now outworn—or not. It

28. The pseudonym of a popular French novelist.
29. A novel by Gottfried Keller.

does not matter. I must do this for myself—in this, at present, is my chiefest hope.

The conversation between Eugene and La Belle Negre was as follows:

Of what country are you? he said.

I am of Martinique, she answered.

Have you habited there long times? he asked.

Since four years, she answered, And you?

Since certain days, he said. But I have been here several times, and I rested here over for certain months.[30]

Cologne, Saturday, [*August*] 11th:

Books again—books on animals, voyages in Ost Afrika—one called *Yankee Land*—One on the occupation of the Rhineland, with the American flag on its cover.

Lint Gasse—an old narrow lane, cobbled, between ancient overhanging houses—foul blousy looking whores stand in the door ways and they try to pull you in.

Saturday [*August 11*]—Kunstgewerbe Museum [*Museum for Crafts and Applied Arts*]:

Two or three magnificent wood crucifixes of Christ from 11th and 12th centuries—beautiful surplices inlaid with gold and rich colors—and Christ upon wooden donkey with wheels—A wooden Christ covered with terrible wounds—flesh torn open in thousand places—pictures of martyrs being thrown off cliff on to sharp spikes—Bloody—one saint having guts unwound around an iron spit—many pictures of Saint Ursula and her maidens.

Aug. 11, 1928

Dear Aline:

I want to send this letter tomorrow morning so that it will surely reach your ship before she sails. I got your telegram in answer to

30. Wolfe revised this entry later. He changed all the "he's" to "I's"; he characterized the conversation as "very genteel"; and he added the following material: "When I picked her out from all the others in the Hall of the Thousand Mirrors, or whatever they call it, the other whores looked at one another significantly and a low and humming murmur passed between them. 'Ah-h,' said they, 'il préfère les noirs.'

'Mais non, mademoiselles. C'est seulement la literature.' "

A full development of the scene appears in W&R, Chapter 45.

my letter this morning; and I was glad to know my long letter had reached you.

What can I say to you before you sail? This is a time when I wish more than I have ever wished to be one of the great lords of language; to make one word open the heart as a thousand others couldn't; to get into a hundred words all the terrible fulness of my soul.

Dear Aline, Can't you see, can't you understand by now how terribly you have hurt me? Don't you realize what you have done?

[*The passages above give some indication of the anguish that Wolfe's wrenching himself away from Mrs. Bernstein was costing him. Only a week earlier he had refused to go to Berlin to see her; but now that she was sailing back to America he grieved over her going. The following excerpts from the letter he sent her, August 11–12, 1928, reflect not only his present troubled spirit but also something of their tempestuous difficulties the previous spring, when he was finishing his book:*

". . . it is not now that I am losing you—that happened a number of months ago. I saw it and knew it when it happened—I was obsessed with the work I was doing, driven on desperately to finish it, and unable to stop and try to save us both at the same time. I was like a man engaged in some violent effort, who is yet conscious of all the sounds and movements around him. I think you must have seen and understood something of the agony of those months—my job to do, the horrible pain lengthening out day by day, and no escape—until I roamed the streets of New York by night cursing like a madman, bolstering myself to face them with doses of raw gin, and so far losing myself as to call your house at unexpected times, day and night, in an effort to keep track of you. When I remember all this now I almost go blind with the pain of it, and can hardly see to write. . . . I am not very hopeful, Aline, about the future of my life, of our life—of anything, at present. Love made me mad, and brought me down to the level of the beasts. I have a smouldering faith which will not down that somehow or other it may also have power to heal and restore.

". . . I grieve for you as I do for myself, and this world's wrong. I see you caught up in the ugly web of life, stained and spattered as we all are by its million evil lusts—worn and jaded and devoured by it, thirsting for a satisfaction we never get. I have thought of you these last few days more and more, and as some moment in the past comes back and burns a hole in my brain, I have caught at my throat with my hand, twisted with a cry in the streets, covered my face and eyes until all the people have stopped to look at me. I will pray for you as I have prayed for myself if it is to nothing but the unliving silence; and I have a sombre but undying faith that we may yet be saved."]

Soviet exhibition at *Presse*—

The books: thousands of books and pamphlets—mostly small ones, in several languages—Georgian, Lett, White Russian, Ukranian and Great Russian—Many for children—I examined some—Pictures—Many with pictures of capitalists—fat swine, half-plunged in gold. Book of pictures showing men horribly mutilated—was it a picture of war time? I expect so. Many picture books for children. Translations—Mark Twain, Harry Domela, Francis Carco, A. Dumas, A. France, T. Mann, etc. Thousands of pamphlets and trade journals. On walls thousand composite photographs—Lenin in a hundred poses, working people, revolutionaries, mothers, etc.

Went to Rathaus today—great Hansa Hall—very magnificent—Tower and court—Rococo room with scenes from Austrian history—Also the Natural History museum—Beasts beautifully mounted but it was noticeable how often helpless beasts—deer—were shown being devoured by wolves, etc.

Press Exhibition again—Room with all the German papers in it—where is Breslau? Houses like this [*sketch of pointed roofs*] and a theater like this [*sketch of many-columned building*]. A million papers all speaking simultaneously of the Kellogg pact, Catholic clergy in Magdeburg, etc.

American exhibit very disappointing.

Who are the German writers today?

Novelists and Playwrights: Thomas Mann, Wassermann, Schnitzler, Werfel, Hauptmann, Zweig, Von Hofmannsthal, Kaiser, Ernst Toller, Heinrich Mann, Neumann, Bruno Frank, Feuchtwanger.

Who were? Goethe, Schiller, Heine.

How many cities in Europe are bigger than Köln—Berlin, Hamburg, London; Glasgow, Liverpool; Milan; Naples, Paris, Vienna, Amsterdam (?)

Of same size, Manchester, Leeds, Brussels, Lyon, Marseilles, München, Copenhagen.

[Forlausch?] Wein Stube [*detailed sketch of bar with bottles and glasses*].

"My mind is open to receive all truth," said Dr. Pangloss.
"Mine is not," said Eugene. "That is too far open."

A wild and wintry place where love the ever-warm would keep us.

It has been almost three years since we met.[31] I have crossed the ocean five or six times during that time, a thousand scenes have passed before me—it seems very long. How long it must seem to you, who have carried it along with fifty other things, I do not know. We all mint life into our individual coin. Everything I have said or seen during the past three years have been radiated by you, or have streamed in toward you. You are past any sort of recovering my great illusion. To see you as you are I cannot. My glorious and beautiful Aline who are one immutable youth to me. I love you, I love you. My tender and golden love, my other loneliness, we were forsaken and lost in ninety countries among the eighteen hundred million people of this earth. My dear, my darling, we were the only lights in this enormous dark.

Last letter missed boat God bless you dearest Tom.

Tuesday [*August 14*]—

Been here a week—wrote final and very long letter to Aline today, only to find that her boat had gone today instead of tomorrow. Got it back from post office and changed address to New York—Went again to Press Exhibition—this time, history of printing and communications from earliest times down to the present—The Roman Signals; Caesar's code, sending messages in slave's hair or sandal. Then the story of printing—the hand-written books and incunabula—the first printed books—the Gutenbergs, and the press—then the books of the 16th century—the broadside sheets—the first newspapers, Martin Luther's pamphlets—Catholic and Royal Proclamations—The sea of print begins to accumulate—Early newspapers and pamphleteers—the time of Frederick the Great, the French Revolution, Napoleonic time—the English caricatures with balloons coming from the mouths of the people. The French ones—Venom of these—one shows King Louis

31. Draft of part of a letter to Aline Bernstein, postmarked August 14, 1928.

removing mask of his face revealing a wine jug where his head should be—another a picture of the devil vomiting at the death of royalty; another of royalty upon a fat, pregnant sow, entitled "Two of a Kind."

Revolution time again—proclamations to Strassburger in two languages—"Strassburgers come and join us since your hearts are French."

When I came to books or papers written in French today, I had a sense of great ease and pleasure. Among that giant wilderness of Gothic print, the French seemed more familiar to me than my own tongue—there is something dark, like the Gothic past, Unfamiliar and Barbaric, in German print. I always feel a little, at present, as if I were translating Chinese—Towns where many of these books came from—Mainz, Bonn, and Wien—all, I suppose, great medieval towns.

[*Wolfe returned to the Wallraf-Richartz Museum, which is especially rich in religious paintings by early masters who are usually identified by the name of their best-known work. Wolfe described his impressions in a letter to Aline Bernstein, August 14, 1928:* "The picture gallery has some fine things: early German pictures, mostly by unknown people, that are beautiful. Those Germans of the 14th century never painted a bad picture. . . . There are some pictures of surpassing beauty by the man who called himself The Master of the Life of Mary." *The following items are a selection of the entries he made at the Museum.*]

Jan Steen—"Die Gefangennahme Simson" [*The Betrayal of Samson*]—man being mocked by his captors while another man fumbles the breasts of his whore. One with long needle in his hands points to his eyes to blind him.

Cornelis de Vos—"Familien Bild"—A Dutch family—Delft faces—man with Van Dyck—several children.

Great many paintings by Unbekannter Meister [*Unknown Master*].

"Golgatha"—Unbekannter Kölner Meister—Christ between the Thieves.

Der Kölner Passionmeister—"Altar Der Heiligen Sippe" [*Holy Kindred*].

Der Meister Des Kölner Stadt Bildnis—Acht Stehende Heilige —8 Saints Standing—4 men and 4 women.

Unbekannter Meister Nach Der Mitte Des 15 Jahrhunderts—"Engel der Verkündigung" [*Angel of Annunciation*].

Stephan Lochner—"Weltgericht" [*Judgment Day*].

Meister Des Marienlebens—"Erzengle Gabriel and Maria"—altarflügel.

Meister Der Heiligen Sippe—"Christus Am Kreuz"—interesting face of Christ—beardless—like young peasant.

Meister von St. Severin—"S. Franziskus Empfangt Die Stigmate" [*St. Francis Receiving the Stigmata*]—This man a great painter.

Bartholomäus Bruyn, der Alte—"Weltgericht."

Hieronymus Bosch—"Heilige Nacht"—Original or copy in Brussels.

What is a "Kreisblatt?" [*county newspaper*].

Wednesday [*August 15*]:

At the exhibition again—the College, High School, and Student Exhibition—thousands of school publications—another ocean of print —pictures of students duelling societies on walls.

Villa Kroll (?)—the student jail at Heidelberg—pictures on the walls by imprisoned students.

The Hochschule—thousands of publications.

The Social Hygiene Room—thousands of pamphlets against Tuberculosis, Syphilis, Childrens Diseases, etc.—Pictures of Great Scientists, mainly Germans, on wall.

Köln—Aug. 15—2 a.m. Cafe Bauer—next to me—the terrible hogs—the Germans at their most unpleasant—the greasy woman with glasses who laughed earnestly all the time at the jokes of a huge fat man without a collar wearing a loud necktie.

Köln—on Rhine Boat—for Bonn—first part of trip not exciting —River wide but muddy—Banks flat and sandy—country green and flat covered with factories, ugly new-looking houses, boat clubs, etc. [*Sketch of steeples and a great building:* "Going up River From Köln to Bonn."]

Friday, Aug. (16 or 17?):

Bonn—My little hotel seems clean and good and costs only 3.50 for room and breakfast—got up, bathed, had breakfast and read *Right Off the Map* [*by C. E. Montague*]. Then for walk through town—took street car to Godesberg, ate at big hotel overlooking Rhine, then crossed up to Königswinter, the Rhine hill scenery begins after Bonn. There is nothing yet to compare with the Hudson, but the charm of the place comes from its legendary antiquity and from the comfort of eating and dining arrangements—returned to Bonn by big steamer, mailed post cards and got thoroughly lost trying to find hotel again—walked around, about, and through city. Much bigger than I thought —100000—Passed enormous book shop.

[*Sketch of palatial villas entitled* "Near Bonn"]

The size and grandeur of the villas in the inter circles and shoulders of these German towns. How do they do it? Rooms in great places like this [*sketch*] in Nero-tal advertised for 2.50–3.00 a day.

Tell a story—oh yes! always tell a story!

"Come in!" said Joel Pierce. "Look out for your head!" he whispered quickly, but it was too late. Hugh had already cracked his head against the door.

"God damn it!" he yelled, and struck the door with his fist.

"You are very tall, aren't you?" Joel murmured politely.[32]

Francis

Joel Pierce

Oliver, Hugh, Edward, George, Harry, Fred, Tom, Will, Bill, Jim, Jack, Henry, Philip, Ralph, Albert, Herbert, Harold.

I A Meeting at Twilight
II Portrait of the Artist
III Meanwhile
IV The River People
V A Passage to England
VI The Three Close Friends
VII
? The Inner Music

Books in the Windows—Bonner Buch Stube:

*Rebellen*—Alfred Neumann.
*Zwei Menschen*—Rich. Voss.
*Die Agonie de Christentum*—Miguel de Unamuno.
*Geheimnis Eines Menschen*—Werfel.
*Volk Ohne Raum*—Greiner.

32. The opening lines of "The River People," Chapter II, "Portrait of the Artist."

*Die Aufzeichnungen des Malte Laurids Brigge*—Rilke.
*Materialismus und Idealismus*—Brunner.
*Wir Junge Männer*—Hans Wegende.
*Geschwanen* [*sic*] *Sang*—Galsworthy.

"We young men must stand together," said Oliver.

Go upstairs and write, write, write!!!!

[*The first pages of a large accounting ledger contain the opening Chapter of "The River People," dated "Friday-Sat. Aug. 17–18—Bonn, Germany 1:10 A.M." A sample of the chapter follows:*]

CHAPTER I

*Meeting at Twilight*

In America, people who are in a hurry do not often attract marked attention, even in so unhurried a place as the Harvard Yard at twilight of a day in Spring. But nature had contrived that the young man who strode across one of the paths of that pleasant enclosure one evening in June, 1923, should not enjoy this desirable obscurity. He was a gigantic scarecrow almost six and a half feet tall and as he rushed across the quiet Yard two young men, who were standing at the foot of the great stone steps that led up to the Widener Library, were watching his approach with intent interest.

It was the end of the college year, the examinations were on. The Yard and the buildings were steeped in relaxation; there was a brooding rather mournful quietness everywhere, broken by far sounds. A few students loitered across the paths, a few went briskly in and out of the library, someone was playing a piano in one of the dormitories. The whole place was drenched in soft, beautiful dusk: there was sadness and peace and the sense of departure in the air.

But the young man who came striding so fiercely across to the library carried with him a sense of struggle and torment. He was obviously in a tremendous hurry to get Nowhere. He was being pursued and he could not escape, because he did not know from what he fled, or where he could find peace.

As he drove himself forward at a high bouncing stride, muttering savagely to himself, and using his long arms like pistons, two or three students who were loafing across the Yard together turned to stare after him. One of them spoke to the others, and they all laughed: he turned upon them, snarling like a wild animal into the lax astonishment of their faces. For a still moment he seemed ready to leap upon them; then he half lifted his arms above his head clawing at the air with his long hooked hands, in an arrested gesture that was full of torment and frustration, and turning he came on again, cursing hoarsely and bitterly.

The two young men at the foot of the library steps watched all this quietly and without laughing: their faces were bent forward eagerly and they watched every movement he made with the rapt attention people give to a strange and interesting animal at the zoo.

"Frank, he is marvellous! Simply marvellous!" one of them said in a whisper full of eager curiosity and good breeding. "Do you suppose he'd let me paint him?"

---

Bonn, Sunday, Aug. 19:

Walked through city—ate out on terrace of big cafe—(Kaiserplatz). Walked past the university through beautiful grounds into Stadt-Garten overlooking Rhine and Siebengebirge—had two glasses of Rhine Wine and listened to the music—Wagner and Waldteufel.

"I should like to be one of those cultured magnificents that you are always meeting in books," said Oliver. "These Cyrils and Hilarys and Maitlands and Napiers, who divide their lives between London and Paris and Vienna and Rome, and speak twelve languages beautifully and without effort. These bastards were born superior to all the agony and weariness of life. They were cut from their mothers umbilicus rattling epigrams in French."

Joel Pierce.

Francis Haddock, Chedwick, Strudwick.

Oliver Crane, Weaver, Webster, Gudger, Hazzard, Westall, Bruce, Gordon, Randolph, Harris, Rollins, Wright, Lindsey, Aldrich, Bryson.

Books in the window.

[*A list of twenty-four assorted books follows.*]

John—had studied at Bonn a year after the war. Here bring in the Buddhistical books. Get their names.

[*A list of books on Buddhism here.*]

In book windows—enormous number of guides (Fuhrers) and maps—Germans like statistics—Baedeker's—Rheine—Rheineland—Ober-Bayern—Schweiz, etc.—Many books on America and "Amerikanismus"

Freytag, Keller, Schiller, Kant, Storm, Goethe, Hebbel, Heine.

Enormous number of books on Renaissance (Burckhardt) painting and sculpture, and painters and sculptors of all time, and all schools —the little yellow books—Feuer, etc. the cheap chief reading.

In *Kunst-Antiquariat* Buch Handlung behind university—Lousy selection of English and French books—tremendous number of German—Koptic—Egyptian readers.

Mittwoch, Aug. 22:

Today walked down broad Poppelsdorfer (?) Allee—between rows of enormous solid luxurious and rather ugly houses. Schloss Poppelsdorfer at end—Low yellow building—big circular court inside —all closed—walked around and behind up street to outskirts—Cigar shop—how many and rich they seem—sausage shops—grocery shops —fruit shops with big luscious grapes, peaches, and bottles of Malaga wine. Came back and walked through University—tried to get into Bibliothek but it was closed—also Akademisches Kunst Museum was closed. It seemed small and stupid.

Examine their culture and civilization as minutely and carefully as you can—Kaffee Haus on Kaiserplatz—Remember great lovely blonde with coarse stockings, deep breasts, and beret—saw her before in beer house.

Thursday, [*August*] 23:

Left Bonn this morning—view on Rhine boat—nothing extraordinary yet—Freiheit Bund Proletarischer Freidenker [*Association of Proletarian Freethinkers*]—little boat loaded with them—singing in their coarse blonde voices, as we passed.

Like the enormous big barges—strings of them that we pass. Came away from hotel with key and lamp screw—mutilated and destroyed a few articles in room as they cheated me a little.

Mainz, Friday [*August*] 24:

The trip up the Rhine was lovely and magnificent. It was somewhat disappointing up to Koblentz; after that it became unreal and magical—the landscape is really magical—it has a faery quality—

and the vineyards that take up every inch of the great piles of rock which form the Rhine Bergs—the vineyards which are one marvellous network of elaborate terraces, and the great castles sometimes a ruin—a wall, an arch, a door that leans above the cliff—completes the atmosphere of magic—And the boats, the pleasure boats that swim by under this breathtaking loveliness filled with huge gross people all eating and drinking, drinking the glorious wine and peering through the glass at magic, sustains the strangeness of it. The wonderful part is only 30 or 40 miles long—but you get the impression that you have been through the measureless realm of Elfland.

Matthias Grünewald—Great Picture of St. Erasmus and St. Mauritius (a black man garlanded with jewels, in armor) in Alte Pinakothek, München—very bad copy in Mainz.[33]

*Wiesbaden,* Saturday, Aug. 25—

Left Mainz today—boiling sunshine—low Rhineland simmering moist sticky heat—no hope for Wiesbaden—tired of traveling—Wiesbaden seems lively—Beginning of the Rhine hills—great solid-looking houses—Germanic city manner—outer ring with huge solid-looking houses—but something charming in city—I have lovely room in beautiful hotel for 6 marks a day (with breakfast) Mineral water baths—Town has something of the desirable cosmopolitanism of a resort town—occupied by English.

Sunday [*August 26*]:

Up. Read the papers. Took walk, sat in little garden and had beer. Saw English woman run over by automobile—Looked bad and turned me sick for a moment, but I don't think she was badly hurt—Crowds greatly excited—taking of names witnesses—A Sunday flavor over town—people out walking but most everything has a "closed" appearance—started 2nd chapter of book last night—must work at least 4 hours a day from now on—last night went to Kursaal—thousands of people behind in the gardens watching the fire works—they were magnificent—the whole night burst out into glory—two great pieces—one a horseman on horseback trotting across through the night, another a Rhine riverboat with spinning paddles—But I liked the great rockets better—Read in paper that [*Michael*] Arlen and [*A. E.*] Coppard and Beatrice Lillie were at Antibes—etc., etc., etc.

In windows—a double window that seems crowded with books—most of them strange—really has only 300 in it—counted them. I

33. In the Municipal Picture Gallery in the Electoral Palace.

think the English here may annoy the Germans more than the French in Mainz; but the German feeling against the French is probably stronger.

[*A list of nineteen books follows.*]

Sunday, Aug. 26:

Wiesbaden at night—at Bols Liköre Stube—Englishman here who pretended to be an American, and then began to run America and Americans down—Spoke with American accent overlaid on his English voice—Had probably lived in America for several years. Hatred of America showed in every word—Boiling with hatred also of Italians and Jews, and suspecting me of being both and a Catholic. I agreed, and also said I was a Russian spy—one of the most unpleasant people I have met on this journey.

The English unhappily hate us—we are young, strong, and powerful. They are thinking of a war with us to get on top again, at the same time suspect us of damnable cleverness and Machiavellian machinations against them.

## CHAPTER III

### "*Meanwhile*"

But Oliver was not able to stay until the picture was finished. The day after the second sitting he received a telegram from home that his father was dying. He left Cambridge on forty minutes notice in spurting rain and arrived home thirty six hours later. His father had died ten hours before; as he ate breakfast in the dining car, a morning paper was given to him in which he read of his father's death. The train wound slowly into the great fortress of the hills but the strange and enormous mystery of death seemed to rest upon them. They were enchanted by the presence of his father's strange wild life which now had gone out among them.

Before the train stopped he saw his family lined upon the station platform, four broken phantoms, pale with grief and weeping.

Within four days after the funeral they were fighting like savages over the estate. The oldest brother, an alcoholic and drug eater for years, got vilely drunk and screamed at Oliver and the other brother that they were trying to cheat him out of his inheritance in the estate.

He followed Oliver through the house, screaming abuse at him and plucking at his arm with his yellow fingers. Oliver ran away but could not escape and finally he struck the yellow pustulate face away from him. Oliver sick with regret and nausea went out on the porch and vomited.

While they were still howling curses and accusations at one another he ran away to New York with his play, which he was convinced would be produced by the Art Guild in the autumn. He lived for several weeks with some young men who were employed by the National City Bank and had an apartment on the edge of Harlem. Meanwhile, he worked sporadically on his play, revising it, and getting it retyped. Early in September he sent it to the Art Guild: his money was gone, he went home again.

For a month longer he watched the mail feverishly, waiting each morning for the letter that would tell him of the acceptance of his play and his advent to fame and fortune.

Wiesbaden-Museum—New Paintings—Feininger—Cubist drawing of a room—geometrical design—light and shade—quite good.

Wiesbaden, Tuesday night [*August 28*]—

Sat up late last night writing Aline a long letter. Finished it this afternoon and sent it off—went to the Kochbrunnen for hot water and to the museum where I looked over the Roman, Stone and Bronze Age antiquities—went to a book store and looked over stock—came home and wrote until 10 o'clock in the evening—read novel of Robert Hichens.

Consider making Oliver deaf towards end of book—came from writing letter to Aline about Beethoven and herself—the lovely listening look on the faces of deaf people.

[*Wolfe was especially interested in deafness because Mrs. Bernstein was already partially deaf when they met. In Bonn he had visited Beethoven's birth place and felt a deep pang of sympathy upon seeing the large ear horns. He described his idea about making Oliver deaf in a letter to Aline Bernstein, September 1–7, 1928:* "Do you know that for one whole day this week I wandered about with my ears stuffed with cotton? I wanted to see what the world seemed like to Beethoven and yourself, and what that strange music on your face is like. It was wonderful. Do you know that I think about it by hours—deafness—since I left Bonn, and that I have written thousands of words in my book of a person who finally comes into his place in life, and is suddenly and beautifully released from the useless toil and weariness, after an illness has left him partially deaf. It may sound foolish, but it has turned into something exciting and interesting—the whole terrible effort of a person to get close to his own spirit, to find himself among the jargon and roar of modern life, is suddenly resolved; and while people are feeling sorry for him because of his 'affliction' his heart is really swelling with a secret and profound joy, because he knows he has found himself at last. On his face that was once so full of torture and struggle, there comes that strange eager listening look that deaf people have . . . ."]

His book was being published in October, a few weeks after his twenty-eighth birthday. He read the publisher's letter of acceptance—a brief business-like note—he read with none of the elevation of spirit that he had always anticipated. Almost bitterly he reflected that even this bit of magic had been taken from him—too much water and too much blood had gone below the bridge since first he began to put patterns of words upon a paper. He had only the feeling he had had as a boy of twelve. He closed his eyes in pain as his brain swept over the ironic hunger of the past years—the belief in the enchantment of print, the going to heaven by means of the press, that he had visioned. He thought of the millions of books that he had seen—the two-mile stretch of book stalls along the Seine in Paris laden with the work of the innumerable obscure—the weariness, the horror, the infinite commonness of print.

Wiesbaden (Thursday or Friday, Aug. 30 or 31):

I have lost track of time—dining tonight at Loesch's Weinstube, 11:20—Have worked hard and rapidly all day—Idea of deafness came last night—went to see Brasilean Review thinking of it. Review better than I had hoped—far better than such affairs in small Belgian and French towns—the star—Madame (?)—"The Indian Princess" a very beautiful and voluptuous woman—Later to several places in search of food—Schnittchen of bread and cheese in one—Tartar Beefsteak with egg in other—Rhine wine in both. Later upon streets a woman—brought her back with me—Porter unwilling—Greased his palm—the whore was nice but faded terribly as all do under the light—she wore thickly padded drawers because she had rheumatism she told me.

One of the most remarkable changes that his deafness had brought was a sudden and overpowering hunger for music.[34] Although he had always liked music, his interest in it had been desultory and

34. A draft for a chapter of "The River People" entitled "The Inner Music."

sporadic, and could never at any time have been compared to his interest in poetry. Now he went constantly to the symphonic concerts in which New York is far richer than any other city in the world. Joel and Li went with him but he was more often accompanied by Li alone. They got good seats far up towards the front; as the clatter of talk all over the place sank to a buzz, and the lights darkened, and the director lifted his arms and looked over the silent company before him, Oliver's long body bent forward from the waist and on his face there came the look of a man who listens to a far horn wound among the hills. And this far listening expression of his face would continue not only during the music, but unchanged after the music had stopped, during the tempest of applause. Indeed, there was a strange suggestion that he was not listening to this music at all, and when once or twice Joel had bent eagerly towards him, and said "That was lovely, wasn't it?" he had replied vaguely and indifferently, seeming to recall himself with an effort.

The sense of strife and bitterness which he had carried almost every foot of the way through life seemed almost entirely to have vanished. He very seldom burst out against the world, but when he did it was inexplicably against musicians and the people who attend concerts. He scowled malevolently at the orchestra as it filed in from opposite doors in the great stage and took its seat. He looked at its members—Austrians, Slavs, Germans, Jews, Americans, fat bald-headed men in cut-away coats—the whole unhandsome personnel of a great orchestra—with an expression that was close to nausea and that persisted during all the period of buzzing, and scraping and tuning.

Sometimes he would mutter loudly between clenched teeth. "Filthy swine!" and Joel would turn to stare wide eyed at him, breathe "Lord!" and begin to laugh softly and incredulously to Li.

In fact, the fear of places and of people gathered together in crowds which had been almost constantly with him before, now manifested itself only when he went to one of these concerts, it was obvious that the business of tickets, and getting through the lobby and down the aisles was an ordeal to him: he kept darting his eyes about quickly and furtively in the old attitude of suspicion and fear; he struck at the air with his clawed hand and twisted his neck about convulsively. Once in his seat he would glower around fiercely at the people behind and about him, staring with open ferocity at the adepts and professionals—Jews with their ironic faces, twinkling eyeglasses, thick hair and little silky moustaches, who chattered excitedly with rapid hands.

"Curs! Lice!" he would mutter.

"Feel them! Can you feel them?" he would whisper hoarsely to

Joel. "Is there anything in the world lower and more venomous than a musician!"

"Oll!" Joel protested softly.

"Can you feel them flow over you and down your back?" he said exactly, "Oi-i-i-lee Gree-ee-see! Poi-i-sonous vi-perz! Waiting their chance to his-ss and sting in the dark." And he shuddered convulsively in his seat as if at that moment he felt a musician wriggling its way down his back bone.

And those peculiar insurrections which spring up constantly in a musical audience and come and go like wind freshets across a lake—the stealthy whisperings, the low ironical laughter, the hiss of disapproval which comes somewhere out of the great dark pool of faces and which may not be traced—all these he sensed and sometimes heard, and they filled him with choking fury. Once when the orchestra had played the locomotive piece by Honegger, to which he had been completely indifferent, he heard, when the partisan battle of cheers and hootings had died down, a loud long hiss behind him. He rose instantly from his seat, with a convulsed face, and turning in the direction from which the sound had come, he snarled fiercely: "Snake! Snake!"

[*Sketch of "Loesch—Wiesbaden window and fountain."*]

Beethoven's House in the Bonn-Gasse

Great cities of Europe I haven't visited: Berlin, Moscow, Madrid, Rome.

Cities I have: Paris, London, Vienna, Brussels, Milan.

Powerful Philosophic Heads of Germans—Freud Smoking Cigar—German who came to restaurant of Hansa Hotel to meet friend, smoking cigar—masculine wardrobe—iron grey hair—thin—Professor, strong-cigar, good-glass-of-wine type.

Wiesbaden, Friday, Aug. 31:

Up late (11:30) breakfast—Next to booksellers—bought Grieben's Guide to Wiesbaden und Umgebung—Looked at several books —Dom [*cathedral*].

The man began to rock back and forth coldly and nervously tapping his fingers together.

"Of course, Mr. Crane,"[35] he said, "Your work still shows traces of the influence of Zola."

35. In his "River People" ledger, Wolfe has written a long scene about the impending publication of Oliver's book and his conversations with his publishers Gilbert and Erskine Hoyt.

Oliver winced for a moment. He has been saying Zola to every other poor devil who has sat here during the past twenty years, he thought.

"No doubt it does" he agreed easily. "I read a piece about him once in the New York Times Literary Review," he added maliciously. Instantly he regretted it.

"Oh, of course!" Mr. Hoyt said hastily, turning his pornographic eyebrows quickly and furiously towards his victim. "There's the Sherwood Anderson influence too, that's very evident."

"O Jesus!" Oliver thought. But aloud he said very cordially: "Yes, I agree with you there. I've read both *Babbitt* and *Main Street*."

Mr. Hoyt glanced quickly and rather suspiciously at him, started to speak, and then said nothing.

"But of course the two men I have studied constantly for several years and have deliberately tried to imitate in my writing are ______"

Mr. Hoyt waited expectantly.

"Voltaire and Dickens," Oliver said with a level earnest stare. Mr. Hoyt did not bat an eyelash.

"Oh, of course, I could see that," he agreed easily. "The note of cynicism! Ha, Ha."

"Yes. Just as you find it in *Candide* and *Richard Feverel*," Oliver said smoothly.

Wiesbaden—Neroberg—Friday Aug. 31 (?):

Looking at Grieben's Little Guide which I bought in bookshop this morning—Almost bewildering variety of *Bad's Kurhaus* (*en*), *u.s.w.*

I came up to the Neroberg a little too late to get good view of city—it was 7 o'clock (about). It is now dark—I am sitting among the trees in front of the hotel—carefully planted small trees—[*sketch*]—umbrella-shaped, in avenues—looking out over city—the air is cool and sharp—Wiesbaden miles below me with a thousand lovely lights—shimmering diamond winking—Hotel—great L-shaped verandah giving immediately on gravelled terrace and trees.

[*Sketches of furniture in his hotel room.*]

Sat., Sept. 1—

Last day here—Walk through town—Begin to weary of it—incessant terraces—Kaiser Friedrich Bvd. Book Stores—"Vater Goriot."

Books I may buy—look at large illustrated book called *Deutschland Volk Ohne Raum*, something of Hermann Hesse, *Grüne Heinrich*.

(Charles Baudouin—book with the quack spiritual looking face.)

Wiesbaden, Saturday, Sept. 1:

After lunch went to Kochbrunnen—English people there laughing at idea of drinking water—I drank much today—Weintrauben Kur begins—little tables out—what is it?—Bought post cards of town—back to hotel, packed—paid bill—ready to go to Frankfurt.

Frankfurt—Saturday night Sept. 1:

[*A list of the largest cities in the U.S. and in Europe*]

A woman in the cafe and Konditorei [*confectionery*] here on Bahnhofs Platz rather old looking—masses of beautiful red hair—red nose—looks as if she hits it up—and delicate features—Beautiful dainty legs and slim lovely hands—Looks a little like Miss Alice Beer—she is with a German and a big black dog—he met her here—she has rich voice, carries on incessant conversation, pats his hand.

6 or 7 hours from here to München—Richness and solidity of life in Germany—building and energy—The town has miles of rich shops—cafés—great boulevards—Where does it come from? What's here?

Frankfurt, A.M. Sunday, Sept. 2:

Wrote part of letter to Aline last night—today up late for coffee—fine cool sunny day—sparkle of early autumn in the air—this is a fine city—all the German cities are—eating in beautiful garden under the broad leaves of the trees (?)—already beginning to turn yellow.

Go to picture museum this afternoon.

Bookwindows again—books looking familiar—who is Herman Löns (?), Sinclair Lewis, Galsworthy, Zweig (The Fight with the Spirit (or Demon))—Studies of Kleist and two others.

Great Schauspielhaus—with Goethe's and Schiller's bust. *Die Dollar Prinzessin* on at operetta theater.

Sunday afternoon—7 o'clock at hotel—Took long walk through city and came back along other side of river—Museum closed—Hundreds of young people boating—had their boat clubs at foot of bridge and ran races methodically and punctually in machine like order. Taking their sport very seriously, but they were a lithe healthy looking lot—saw another big "Red" parade—nothing to equal the one in Brussels but very impressive—Walked up through old section of town—bewildering windings of streets—wonderful old houses.

Sunday night—Went to the Revue here—it is infinitely better than the things you see in France and Belgium—but all are dull—bad costumes mostly—great machines for the chorus—one representing the various buildings of Vienna, etc.[36] But some of the girls were lovely—brown-blonde dark Viennese with lovely slim legs—bubbling with gaiety—what a difference between them and Germans—Remember the blonde girl sculling with young man at boat club today—she was German—very handsome but lacking the Viennese slenderness—No one eating at restaurant called Falstaff—very elegant and very deserted—don't know what food will be like—Falstaff 1921er Niersteiner Burgundy.

[*Wolfe noted the following pictures on his visit to the Städel Art Institute in Frankfurt:*]

1102 David Vinckeboons—"Kirchweihfest" [*Church Consecration Festival*].

Hans Holbein der Ältere (1460–1524)—"Hochaltar aus Frankfurter Dominikaner Kloster." [37]

Hans Baldung [*Grien*]—"Altar des Hl. Johannes."

Jerg Ratgeb—"Bildnis der Margaretha Stalburgerin."

MODERN GALLERY

Peter Rasmussen—"Selbstbildnis." [*Self-portrait*].

E. Heckel—"Blick auf die Strasse" [*A Glance in the Street*].

E. Heckel—"Paar" [*Couple*].

E. L. Kirchner—"Selbstbildnis"—Picture in blue uniform—with bloody wrist-stump of one arm—In the war probably.

E. Heckel—"Belgische Familie."

Fritz Pollak—"Droschke" [*Cab*].

36. "The Revue claimed to be Viennese: and there was a scene in which one girl walked out dressed like the Stephanskirche, and another like Schönbrunn, and another like the Rathaus and so on. You may not believe it, but it was there, windows, steeples, and all." Letter to Aline Bernstein, September 1–7, 1928.

37. Holbein's altarpiece of the Passion came from the former Dominican Cloister in Frankfurt.

Hans Feibusch—"Pierrot am Fenster" [*Pierrot at the Window*] —not bad.

Beckmann—Picture of figures on beach[38]—man standing on head—naked woman under parasol with man feeling her cunt—American flags upside down stuck in sand.

Karl Hofer—"Zwei Freunde"—Two naked fairies together, one of them fingering other's guts.

Cezanne—"Mannes Kopf."

Picasso—"Frauenkopf."

Kokoschka—"Monte Carlo."

OLD PICTURES

A German named H. Thoma—Draws like Daubigny and Coste —good.[39]

Trübner—"Starnberger See."

Lieberman[40] and Trübner.

Zuloaga—"Zigeunerin and Andalusierin." [*Gypsy and Andalusian*].

Khnopff, F.—"Der Jagdaufscher" [*The Gamekeeper*]—good.

Max Klinger—"Bildnis Einer Dame Aug Dem Dach Eines Romischen Hauses" [*Picture of a Woman on the Roof of a Roman House*].

Auguste Renoir—"Le Déjeuner"—good.

OLD PICTURES

Primitives 807—Barnaba da Modena—"Madonna."

Spanischer Meister—"Maira als Himmelkönigin" [*Mary as the Queen of Heaven*].

Two good primitives by Hals—one of a cavalier; one of a woman—

A picture by a Dutchman called "The Donor of the Rats."

The Brueghel Followers—Hans Bol, Lucas Van Valkenborgh, Adriaan Van Stalbemt.

38. Max Beckmann's "Der Strand" [*The Beach*].

39. Wolfe is probably referring to Hans Thoma's "Am Waldesrand" [At the Edge of the Woods], the catalogue number of which he has placed on a list.

40. Wolfe was perhaps attracted to Max Lieberman's "Simson and Dalila."

# *PART TWO~*

# *EUROPEAN WANDERING*

## *Pocket Notebook 4*
### *September 4, 1928, to October 24, 1928*

*During the next two months, Wolfe continued his dreamlike wandering. He explored Frankfurt, he steeped himself in the drowsy autumn of Munich, he got into a fight at the Oktoberfest and wound up in the hospital; at length he headed for Vienna after a brief stopover in Salzburg. During this time he continued to frequent museums, attend plays, jot down impressions of German life, and work sporadically on "The River People." His obsession with books, which began at Cologne, increased. He spent hours combing bookstores—or merely staring at their window displays—jotting down titles and authors of German, French, and English books. Many pages of this notebook are filled with such indiscriminate lists, only a sampling of which we have included. This automatic setting down of words reflects a number of things: Wolfe's dissatisfaction with his project "The River People," his loneliness in being cut off from Mrs. Bernstein, and, in general, his concern with multiplicity.*

---

Wiesbaden [1]—Tues. Sep. 4—

Today on Rundfahrt [*circular tour*] of city—Sat next to Mr. James Joyce again [2]—His ghost haunts me through Europe—The ride intensely interesting—Went through old quarter of city—Stopped at Römer [*the old town hall*] and Goethe's Haus—Had a short talk with Joyce at Goethe's house—He wanted to be friendly, and I was awed before him—He remarked that Goethe's house "was a fine old house" —I agreed—Stupidly—Then we parted in an indecisive manner—both going back towards Altstadt—I went to wonderful old house where one gets Apfelwein and Frankfurters—both very good.

Tonight to Operetten Theater—perhaps the simplest, most

1. Wolfe wrote Wiesbaden unintentionally for Frankfurt, even though he had been in Frankfurt three days when he began this notebook. Perhaps his excitement at seeing Joyce again caused the slip.

2. In September, 1926, Wolfe had made a tour of Waterloo on the same bus with Joyce. See *Letters*, pp. 114–15.

modern, and *most beautiful* theater I have ever seen—The play was terrible—a Music Revue called *Die Dollar Prinzessin.*

Eating tonight at Restaurant Zum Jung—on the Zeil—Had a steak casserole—veal and beef—with potatoes, carrots, beans—excellent —Also a Swedish Hors D'Oeuvre—Schwedisch Gabelbissen.

Books To Be Bought: *Grüne Heinrich, Deutschland, We Forget Because We Must.*

In the new Tauchnitz editions just published there is a novel by W. B. Maxwell called *We Forget Because We Must.* It is one of the most beautiful titles I have ever read.

Franz Bey, Auffarth—Buchhandlung—Frankfurt. Very Big Shop. These are some of the books in window—bewildering number of small pamphlets. [*Followed by a list of titles.*]

Bigger than Frankfurt: (1) Berlin; (2) Breslau; (3) Dresden; (4) Hamburg; (5) Köln; (6) Leipzig; (7) München.

Frankfurt—Wed. Night—

Völker Museum—First—the tribes—Bismarck Island, etc.—spears—teeth necklaces—shields—skulls as trophies—tatooed women.

Sumatra; Java; China; Japan; Abyssinia.

American and South American collections not so good.

Liberian Rider—In Armor and Shield.

Arab Powder Horns—Chinese, African, and Ukrainian music instruments.

Wednesday Night—

Eating late (10 o'clock) in garden next to Schauspielhaus—Went to Völker Museum today—Fine collection of Asiatic, African, Malaysian objects.

Sumatra—great wrought robes of gold brocade.

Java—The Dance Dolls—Like *Grand Street Follies*—One of them looked very much like Trueman girl.[3]

3. *The Grand Street Follies* was produced annually from 1922 to 1929 by the Neighborhood Playhouse in New York. Beginning in 1924, both the costumes and the sets were designed by Aline Bernstein. One of the leading performers was Paula Trueman.

Kaiserstrasse 60.

T. W. and S. P. W. M. W. T. h. an. M. d. T. H. I. S. F. G. an. T. F.[4]

Frankfurt—Thursday—

Up till 5 o'clock this morning—investigation of Frankfurt's night life—Kabarett [Close?]—Fledermaus, u.s.w.—heavy and dull and vicious.

The Römerberg under moonlight—old house with electric lamps and wine on table outside—very lovely.

Today—City Historical Museum—and if time is left—museums across the river.

Today—

I went to the City Historical Museum and to the Old Houses open For Exhibition—They were unforgettably beautiful—there is an enormous amount to be seen here—Then went to Neumann's book shop in the Goethe Strasse here and bought book on Matthias Grünewald—It was getting dark—dropped in at elegant little tea shop for tea—very tired from night before—Went home and after writing a little more to Aline went to sleep and slept from 8:30–11:00.

In Lichtenstein house—fine old house with memorials of great families there—particularly De Neville family—Books on heraldry, etc. But the Haus der Goldene Wage (?) is beautiful, lovely—Went up story by [*breaks off*]

*Kang-Hsi*—Walter Bondy.[5]

Last summer—Paris, Strasbourg, Munich, Salzburg, Vienna, Prague, Nürnberg.

This summer—Paris, Brussels, Cologne, Bonn, Mainz, Wiesbaden, Frankfurt, Munich.

Aline—this summer—Paris, Rapallo, Karlsbad, Vienna, Berlin, (Nürnberg? Munich? Dresden?).

4. Perhaps a parody of "the heavy wooden table . . . scarred with the names and initials of a thousand students who had sat there before him," that Wolfe had seen in a Bonn beer hall and about which he later wrote, or the Joycean collection of initials in *Ulysses*.

5. A book on Chinese pottery by Bondy: *Kang-hsi, Eine Blüte-Epoche der chinesischen Porzellankunst* (München, 1923). Wolfe and Mrs. Bernstein had met Bondy on a train en route to Prague in 1927.

Plays Announced: Shakespeare's *Othello* and *Twelfth Night*, *Der Prozess Mary Dugan*, *The Royal Family*, Kaiser's *Oktobertag*, Sascha Guitry (?), Schiller's *Don Karlos*, Somerset Maugham's (?).

The big Bier Keller on Bahnhof Platz—Pschorr Brau—Bavarian—or supposedly Bav.—orchestra in costume—The Bavarian all over Germany is supposed to be witty fellow—Antics of orchestra leader—Drinks up beer leavings all over restaurant—Yells loudly—Crowd roars with laughter—Band makes terrific noise—all of it loud—thick with smoke—terribly heavy—This is in their blood—a characteristic exhibition—and I don't like it—That's why I get tired of them.

Band plays Ein Prosit, Ein Prosit—When someone buys leader a liter of beer—He holds it up and everyone lifts his glass—Don't they ever get tired of it?

Friday—

Up and to the Kunstgewerbe Museum—Two beautiful rooms—One magnificent guest chamber from old Frankfurt House—Another Swiss house interior of 17th century—Then to Hamburg-American Line—No automobile service to Munich—Then to bookshop—Saw Mr. Walter Bondy's book on Chinese Pottery in window—Asked for book on Frankfurt—They had none as good as one I've got.

### STÄDEL ART INSTITUTE

Max Klinger—Picture of a woman on roof of a Roman house.

Zuloaga—"Zigeunerin und Andalusierin"

1350—Alfred Sisley—"Seine Ufer im Herbst" [*Bank of the Seine*].

Vincent Van Gogh—"La Chaumière" [*The Cottage*].

1444—Daubigny—"Obstgarten zur Erntezeit" [*Orchard at Harvest Time*].

Peter Rasmussen—"Selbstbildnis."

Cezanne—"Mannerkopf."

Picasso—"Frauenkopf."

Süddeutscher Meister.

Hans Baldung—"Zwei Hexen" [*Two Witches*].

Lucas Cranach Der Ältere—"Venus."

Hans Holbein Der Jüngere—"Sir George of Cornwall."

Januarius Zick—what a name.

Joh. Dav. Passavant—"Heilige Familie."

Pforr<br>Koch } Bad.<br>Richter

L. Giordano—"Kampf der Tugenden und Laster"—[*Battle of Virtues and Vices*]—Bad.

Veronese—"Mars und Venus."

Botticelli's "Mädchenbildnis."

766—Massys—"Männliches Bildnis."

[*Three pages of Wolfe's sketches follow, mostly of men's heads.*]

Go to a good book store and buy small Goethe Book as "Errinnerung."

Saturday [*September 8*]—

Book Store last morning here—Bought post cards—Looked over stock—Looked over several books on Frankfurt—Had seen them all—Looked over books—Hedwig Courths-Mahler—Harold Bell Wright of Germany—Jack London and Edgar Wallace—Wassermann and Walter Rathenau—Thomas Mann—Tragödie Ein(er?) Kaiserin.

[*Sketch of a bar.*]

Art Gallery here—2nd Visit—Best Pictures—Renoir—Man & Two Women dining out of doors—Monet—Le Déjeuner—Daubigny—An Orchard—Renoir—A Young Girl—Degas—Orchestra musicians—a good picture—Portrait of a Man by Vincent [*Van Gogh*]—Then side rooms—the Rathenau collection—Picture of woman on Roman roof—Selbstbildnis of Rathenau—good—Room with pictures of [*Johann*] Grambs, Thoma, and ?—who painted himself on horseback—Side rooms not interesting—Filled with bad pictures—Zuloaga—A gipsy woman & an Andalusian—both corridor rooms leading back—very bad—Filled with work of Frankfurter 18 & 19 century artists—Frankfurter families, Rhine landscapes, etc.—Portrait of Goethe interesting because of nobility of the sitter—Cabinets with medieval figures interesting—also great chest with women bent backwards over the edges—and chairs with naked whiskered men with women's breasts.

Coming down from Frankfurt over Würzburg—Fine but rather hot day—Würzburg small—did not look interesting—Some of the country beautiful—gets flat around Munich—Forest of tall pines (?) —their light straight trunks stood like magic.

Ingolstadt—München—Moon not up—Many stars—Stood in corridor of rocking train—Head cast enormous shadow upon opposite track—Rushed across Bavaria at 50 miles an hour with his head darkening the landscape.

Munich—Sunday Night [*September 9*]—

In Bar at Rathaus Place—Today Very Hot—Ate at Neue Börse —it is still good—Walked to Alte and Neue Pinakothek—Both closed Sun. aft.—Glyptothek and Stadt Gal. also—Went to Glas Palast again —Miles and miles of mediocre pictures—Girl and girls there—Went back and had tea in garden of Regina Palast [*Hotel*]—Tonight late dinner at Pschorr Brau—where they have the good Paprika Schnitzel —The weight, the heaviness, the heaviness—and yet the grandeur— This is a noble city—Books in window—In Book shop near Karolinen (Obelisk) Platz—A Series of the [Heyn?] books of which I saw *one* in Wiesbaden—*Kunst Der 19 Jahrhundert*—Go back and ask prices—A window filled with 1 mark bargains—of which I recognized only one or two—Wassermann and Stern.

Munich Monday Night—

Went to Deutsches Theater tonight—Revue—Better than most of the French ones but stupid—Had the Benvenuto Cellini scene from Folies Bergère, and the girl dancing with balloon scene from somewhere else, and so on—Paid 3 marks for ticket—Some of the finales and chorus work very good.

Went to the [*Amtliches Bayerische*] Reisebüro this morning— Found over 40 letters & post cards for me—nearly ½ from Aline— Terribly excited—Took me 2½ hours to get through them.

Went through Residenz [*Museum*] this afternoon—Thing vast, bewildering, and almost nauseating—Miles and miles of gilt—of the heaviest baroque—On Hofgarten side some lovely rooms—Later had tea in very elegant shop—Went to bookshop, and bought Maxwell's novel with the fine name: *We Forget Because We Must.*[6]

Munich—Tuesday—

Had Malaga Apértif at Bodega—Got Draft ok'd at Reisebüro— Ate at Böttner's "Kurier Stör"—Food very good, but expensive—Got

6. William Babington Maxwell, *We Forget Because We Must* (London, 1928). Wolfe probably purchased the Tauchnitz edition, but his copy is not in the Wisdom Collection. Maxwell took his title from a line of Matthew Arnold's "Absence."

addresses of Pensions, Hotel, and an Apartment—Looking for room today—Read up history of Ludwig (Mad King) of Bavaria—*Grüne Heinrich* written by Keller about Munich life—Went to Haupt Bahnhof—paid 3 marks for privilege of hunting up apartment tomorrow—Pretty Italian waitress in Kaiserhof (?)—Good looking women at hotel—Laundry came—Tonight wandering about—ate at Viktoria Cafe—Wrote—Went back to Hotel by Odeonsplatz—Wrote—Came to cafe for beer—Wrote.

[*We have seen that one of Wolfe's most moving experiences in Europe was his visit to Beethoven's birthplace. In the following passages, which he intended for "The River People," he describes Oliver Weston's stopover in Bonn—an emotionally heightened parallel to his own experience.*]

CHAPTER (?)

*The Island Universe*

About forty minutes away by train from the city of Cologne upon the right bank of the fabulous Rhine is a town called Bonn. It is a quiet place of perhaps 80,000 inhabitants and is marked by very few distinctions that, in the words of Baedeker, "need detain the tourist." There is a university there, housed in an old chateau, and during the term there are several thousand students with shaven heads, and sword cuts on their faces, and gorgeous dueling corps regalia, and favorite beer houses where they go, and talk and shout and sing and clash their mugs together, and drink liters and liters of beer. Perhaps there are also times when they read some of the 36,000 books that Germany prints every year, but this cannot be found out. At any rate, they have a great time, and in the manner of college boys, are quite proud of themselves and consider themselves tremendous fellows.

Oliver went up the narrow crooked stairs without excitement. Above him in one of the rooms he heard the fat rapid voice of a guide full of gutteral spittle, and the creaking of old boards like the creak of leather, as the ponderous feet of German tourists tramped up and down. He waited a moment on the stairs until the noise grew fainter and moved away from him. Then he mounted to the top.

In a little dark room at the end of the hall so low he had to stoop to enter, all the music and all the glory had been born. There was little furniture—a bust of Beethoven with a faded wreath at its base; a glass case with a few scraps of yellowed paper in it. He moved on into the other rooms filled with all the memorials, some cheap and tawdry, others fine, of the composer. There were birthrecords, little notices of early concerts in tattered old newspapers, an organ on which he had played, various musical instruments.

And in one cabinet there were several enormous earhorns of brass—great clumsy devices of the early eighteenth century. Oliver looked for a moment, remembering suddenly what he had forgotten—that all this magic which had enchanted the ears of the world had fallen on its own deaf ones. Something like a hand was clenched around his heart; his eyes were blind for a moment. He moved on.

He began to look at the paintings and drawings of the composer which covered the walls. Few of them had great artistic worth—the greatest men on earth have not often had great artists to picture them. He came to the death mask—on that wasted shell of struggle and weariness was still written the fierce tumult of music that had stormed within him. Oliver went slowly about the room from one picture to another staring for minutes at that wild and stormy face in which music was blowing like a wind. And always there was that sense of listening, of seclusion within the fortress of one's self that he had come to notice on the faces of the deaf. There was one picture in which Beethoven came stamping across uneven ground, with a great wrack of cloud behind him, and his wild hair blown in the wind, and a tempest gathered in his stormy face. And it was Evident from this picture that this man was a world complete unto himself—the earth around him did not matter, the storm behind him did not matter, nothing human or divine or earthly could touch him—a storm wilder than any in heaven was gathering within him; in him were all the elements of creation. And again there was a picture showing him seated before the window of his apartment in Vienna: behind him one could see the roofs of the Old Town and the magic spire of the Stefanskirche—a rug was thrown over Beethoven's knees, several great portfolios of music were scattered about on the floor, and behind him on a marble shelf there was a single thick book. And again Oliver felt as he looked at that terrible face bent above the universe of its own creation that there was nothing beyond him and around him which could add to this man's sum; the single book on the shelf became in itself a universe of knowledge—it stood for and included, and said all that the million other books might say.

Oliver moved on—the rooms were deserted; below there was a faint noisiness from descending and departing tourists. Oliver moved on, again and again around the room, with the thousand shapes of that immortal face before him. And presently he too had forgotten the world, and the million sounds of life; he had felt the all-inclusive power of that great face; he was entrenched within the ramparts of his own soul, and he felt the elements of a world within him. Presently he stood again before the case where the ear horns were, and as he looked at their great clumsy shapes a gate swung open suddenly in his heart, his senses seemed to drown, and a smothering flood of passion and of joy rose up and smote him in the throat. His eyes went blind, and he began suddenly to weep. Great hoarse cries were wrenched from him, great tearless sobs that filled that house of music with their harsh pain, but which he neither heard nor was conscious of. The house was alive with his harsh broken cries, and yet he did not know he wept; he only knew that a gate had opened in his heart and he had found release.

But presently he grew aware of someone near him, and turning he saw vaguely the fat distressed face of the short attendant, and felt that the man was plucking at his arm.

"Bitte—der Herr . . . . Bitte! Bitte!"

[*The following is a draft of a letter to Mrs. Bernstein. The first paragraph relates to Wolfe's proposed meeting with her during the summer just past, when she was traveling with Theresa Helburn. Initially Wolfe had wanted to meet Mrs. Bernstein somewhere in Europe, but she had opposed the plan. At length she changed her mind, and on August 4 she sent a telegram to Wolfe in Brussels to meet her in Berlin on August 10. This was the final opportunity for them to meet, as Mrs. Bernstein was to sail for home aboard the S.S.* Reliance *from Hamburg on August 15.*

*Wolfe declined to come to Berlin and gave his reasons in a letter written from Cologne, postmarked August 9:*

"I earnestly wanted to see you this summer, but your plans as you described them before leaving Carlsbad did not permit it, and I knew you were right in saying this was no time for us to see each other again. I have thought about Berlin a great deal, and I have decided not to go there. To see you for three days in a new and strange place before you sailed would be too bad and too unsatisfactory. Its effect on me would be explosive—I am at length achieving a kind of peace and certainty, and I have faith and confidence in a day when we can meet again in terms of loving friendship."

*The second paragraph of the draft concerns a visit to New York by Wolfe's Asheville friends and former teachers Mr. and Mrs. J. M. Roberts. He had invited them to stay in his Eleventh Street apartment in his absence. Mrs. Bernstein, who had her workshop there, objected. Mrs. Bernstein later wrote Wolfe that the Roberts did not come.*]

I can find little of real love and certainly no tenderness in many of your letters. The last one I have from you is postmarked New York Aug. 28, and in it you say that my letter to you was "most beautiful"; but that is about all the mercy I get. You say you are sorry if you have said "mean things" to me in some of your letters—which you certainly did—but that your letters did not begin to show how furious you were with me for not coming to Berlin. I do not complain if you have said "mean things" to me—I know I deserve all I get, and that I have said far meaner things to you. But in the letters I had from you before you went to Berlin you gave no sign of wanting to see me; you said we had come to a strange time in our relation and that it was best that we keep apart; and in one of your letters after you left Karlsbad you said you would like to see me, but that it was for such a short time that it would be harder to see each other than not to see each other, which is about what I said to you in my letter.

I was not seriously concerned about the Roberts visit—on the whole, I preferred that they should not come to Eleventh Street, although in an over-impetuous moment at home I mentioned it to them. But your reply to me is certainly violent—*why* have you become so excited at the suggestion—it was nothing more than that? Are you really afraid that they will pay a visit to Eleventh Street and discover the *present* occupant?

Oliver went into a book shop behind the University.[7] The place covered the entire upperhalf of a block; its windows looked out on two corners and contained hundreds of works on Buddhism, modern architecture, painting, economics, religion, and fiction. He recognized the Roman profile of Mr. John Galsworthy in several places and going in, demanded a copy of *Bitter End* which, he told the solicitous attendant, was the latest work of the master, and must surely have appeared in the Tauchnitz Edition. The distressed salesman came back after a fruitless search and explained that at the moment the book was not in stock, but could be ordered.

"And yet," said Oliver, glancing around at the towering shelves, "this is a big store."

"There are so many books," said the salesman apologetically. "Even a store like this can not keep up with them all. We do not know what to order," he continued with a hopeless gesticulation. "In Germany alone last year we printed over 36,000 books."

"That's a great many, isn't it?" said Oliver calmly.

7. This passage reflects what Wolfe occasionally did as a perverse joke—ask an obsequious and obliging German clerk for a nonexistent book.

"Have you any nice postal cards?" He selected a half dozen views of the city and the Rhine, lighted a strong German cigar, and walked out into the street.

Now what, he said to himself thoughtfully, should a man do in a case like this? I have it! This is Germany. I think, he said slowly, I think that I will drink some beer.

He went into a large dark place, with gloomy arched vistas and walnut panelling all around. He sat down at a heavy wooden table; its round leaf was scrubbed white, and the surface was scarred with the names and initials of a thousand students who had sat there before him.

The waiter came up with that cheerful and businesslike gusto that German waiters have.

"Guten Tag; was wünscht der Herr?"

"Do you have beer here?" Oliver asked.

"Jawohl!" and the waiter began to laugh hoarsely.

"Ein helles!" [*A glass of light ale.*]

"Yes," said Oliver, "a liter of helles."

And he began [*breaks off*]

[*Three pages of boarding houses with addresses and rates.*]

Mrs. Samuel Richards, c/o Anton Lang, Oberammergau.[8]

CHAPTER

One of the very few places on earth which lives up to its legend—which grows in beauty and charm as one comes to know it—is the

8. Wolfe met Mrs. Richards in Munich, and a description of her, though she is not named, appears in a letter to Mrs. Roberts (*Letters*, p. 166). She was the widow of a painter who had studied at the Royal Academy of Munich, and she had spent a large part of her life in Germany. She developed a consuming interest in the Oberammergau Passion Players from the time she first saw them perform in 1890, and her interest had become an obsession. Her book, Louise Parks-Richards, *Oberammergau—Its Passion Play and Players: A 20th Century Pilgrimage to a Modern Jerusalem and a New Gethsemane* (Piloty & Loehle, Munich, 1910), is an account in English of the Passion Play, with many personal reminiscences of the actors and actresses as well as pictures of them. In 1922 Mrs. Richards published a third edition, revised and enlarged. At the time Wolfe met her she was working on another book about the Oberammergauers—apparently to have ready for the Passion Play season in 1930—and she sought Wolfe's aid on the book and tried to extract a promise that he would complete it in the event of her death. After his release from the hospital, Wolfe did visit Oberammergau with her on October 7 and 8 and met some of the leading actors, but there is no evidence that he seriously considered becoming involved in Mrs. Richards' project.

city of Munich in Bavaria. It is not easy to find a reason for the city's seductive power. There is little that is quaint or particular, like the canals of Venice, or the Old Town in Frankfurt.[9]

Sunday—Sept. 16—

This last week I have spent in going about Munich chiefly in search of a suitable room for the next three weeks. Now I am at this Pension—I hope my room when it is ready will be comfortable and quiet and that I can break this lethargy, which has kept me from doing much writing—If I can write 50,000 words—2,500 a day—for the 3 weeks I shall stay here, I shall consider my stay not useless.[10]

Room—with breakfast 4:80—mit Halb-Pens 6:50—mit Ganz 7:50.

The next day they moved to the flat in the Rue Lepic. The day had been bright and cold; they completed their moving in the afternoon and they saw Paris down below them gold in the cold bright sun —it was unforgettable. Then a frosty dark came on—it was clear and full of stars. Oliver took Li down to Wepler's at the Place de Clichy, where they ate—onion soup, sole marinière, Chateaubriand garni, Camembert, Nuits St. Georges. He was terribly excited.

320—Head of a Roman [*in the Glyptothek Museum*].

The heads of the Romans are really the heads of Harvard Club Americans—the boys who have the rocks, and not much [uneasiness?] about them—shrewd faces, big straight nose with bony ridge, faces lean and creased, with wrinkles half-hard, half humorous under the eyes—big ears, thin hair at the sides—lean, mercenary, shrewd and humorous.

### MUNICH

In a few days he became weary of the hotel. The military servility of the hired people, the gaudy lobby, and the heavy lounge, in

9. Wolfe copied this passage into the "River People" ledger (p. 165) and expanded it (pp. 165–68). Later he tore these two sheets from the ledger, and the expanded passage, in revised form, became the beginning of Chapter 46, "The Pension in Munich," of W&R, p. 650.

10. The pension referred to was Pension Bürger, Luisen Str. 50. At this point Wolfe later added the following note: "Vienna—Monday Night—Oct. 24 (?)—On reading the above: I really wrote about 25,000—and got my head and nose broken, and wasted a great deal of time, and saw a great deal, and lost some quarts of blood—and perhaps—learned something."

which large German women and fat men with shaven heads were interminably drinking tea or coffee, or eating cakes, became a leaden drag upon his spirits. He had been travelling for two and a half months; he had been alone and seen much, but this interminable conversation with himself, his almost entire isolation during this time began to rest heavily upon him. He realized how necessary a place he could call his own was to him—he shrank as he entered the hotel because it brought to him all the restless impermanence of travel; he would have liked it better if he had had to pay for his bed day by day before he slept in it—this heavy mask of commercial hospitality sickened him—beneath it all he saw constantly the outstretched and insistent palm.

He realized suddenly that he did not "enjoy" travel—it was a spiritual necessity to him; in some measure it fulfilled a deep hunger in him for knowledge and change, and it awoke him from the lethargy into which he fell after he had been for too long in one place.

But if it renewed him, it brought with it also incessant struggle, incessant tumult and disorder.

Monday—Sept. 17—

Worked until 3:30 this morning—up at 10—10:30—off for mail —Then, buy paper, coffee, get books.

Tuesday Night—Sept. 18—

Working now and doing very little sightseeing—weather cold, raw, and grey—Very heavy and dismal—Bought *Der Grüne Heinrich*[11] in 2 vols. this morning at Buchhandlung in Salvator Platz —Must write at least 2,000 words a day from now on—Have done 1,000 so far today—Writing this after late dinner in Ratskeller—Sitting now in Augustiner Bier House in Neuhauser Str.

Munich—Arches—Bier halls—Arches—Körper Kunst [*flesh "art"*]—*Figaro*—naked girls with their pussy hair showing.

Oliver Weston, Joel Pierce, Francis Strudwick, Li Weinberg, Vater (Graf Rudolf Von Ling), Pups, Mrs. Pierce, Lula (Laura).

He boarded his ship—a 12,000 ton cruiser—in the river off 79th street three hours after the *Gargantua* had left the dock. Ten minutes later, the grim grey sides of the cruiser were slipping swiftly through a startled tangle of river shipping, which scattered like geese as he bore

11. Gottfried Keller, *Der Grüne Heinrich* (Stuttgart, 1921), 2 vols., is in the Wisdom Collection.

down on the Battery. She went out across the harbor unrolling from her funnels a thick black ribbon of oily smoke, and as she entered the Narrows the cloven waters stood in a stiff white sheet across her bows.

He caught the *Gargantua* ninety miles off Sandy Hook and bore up across her wash at thirty knots an hour. She hove to starboard and came to a dead stop, as he came up under her counter.

[*The following passage is the draft of a portion of a chapter of "The River People" entitled "Why Joel Whispered." Wolfe expanded this chapter and later had part of it put into a typescript that comprises twenty-two pages of elite type. The chapter gives the family history of Joel Pierce. Samuel Pierce, the founder of the family fortune, is pictured as an archetype of the nineteenth-century Robber Baron.*]

Under these circumstances Joel's father had been conceived, during one of the intervals of the season at which Society may devote itself to procreation, and he spent the prenatal period very fashionably in Newport and Wiesbaden, and only escaped getting born very elegantly in Paris. But Mr. Samuel Pierce, who had never interfered in his son's family business, spoke with the ripsaw snarl that had lashed 3,000 men across a desert.

"Tell the bitch," he said, "that the boy is to be born an American and in America. She's got to come back at once." And everyone knew that he was to be obeyed.

He had always referred to his coming heir as "the boy," and it had never occurred to anyone to debate the matter with him.

So the lady took the largest and fastest vessel home—the ocean greyhound raced back in thirteen days, and four days later a grandson was born to Samuel Pierce.

This was Joel's father. His mother left him almost immediately after his birth, and he saw her thereafter only when he caught her on her travels, or visited with her in Paris. The boy grew up a complete Transatlantic—his summers he spent in America on the estate his father had built on the Hudson. From his eighth to his sixteenth year he was sent to the English public school at Harrow; he spent the next two years on the continent with his mother, and he came back to enter Harvard when he was eighteen years old.

This was in 1895, the year after the death of Mr. Samuel Pierce. The estate had been very capably managed for fifteen years now by Hugh Pierce—he had done little but tend his garden, but he had done that very well. In the spring of 1898, however, when Hugh Pierce, Jr.

was in his third year at Harvard, his father died very suddenly on one of his visits to Paris. Hugh Pierce, Jr. just before his twenty-second year found himself possessed of fifty million dollars and no desire to do anything in particular.

Old Mr. Joel came slowly across the lawn accompanied by Vater.

Dr. E. F. Du Bois, Pension Isabella, Teng Str. 31.[12]

Schlafanzug [*pajamas*] 2, Hemd [*shirt*] 1, Kragen [*collars*] 3, Taschentücher [*handkerchiefs*] 2. [13]

"She is not a Jew," said Oliver. "She married one. That's all."

"But why?" said Mrs. Pierce patiently, as if trying to find circumstances that might extenuate the crime. "Why did she marry one?" [14]

(Oliver and Mrs. Pierce)

She slowly and elegantly fastened a cigarette in an amber holder eight inches long. He struck a match and held it for her somewhat nervously.

But although the central trunk of the Pierce family was admirably sober in the conduct of its life, other members of the outlying branches had learned to display some of those amusing eccentricities which are the privileges of wealth and royalty.[15]

Slowly, but with implacable disgust, they began to wash their hands of Trade.

There was growing up in America a new race of millionaires with strange and forbidding names—Schultes, and Gimbels, and Fleischmans, and Kahns, a race whose thousand millions made the hundreds of the Pierces and the Goulds and the Astors look paltry.

12. The American doctor who assisted Wolfe after he had been injured in the Oktoberfest fight. See *Letters*, pp. 146–47.

13. This list is written in another hand, apparently while Wolfe was in the hospital.

14. The "she" under discussion is Li Weinberg.

15. Joel's aunt, for example, was interested in Oriental cults, wore sandals and a long white robe, and "existed exclusively upon a diet of barley soup, green cabbage leaves, and hot water." Typescript of "Why Joel Whispered," p. 19.

With quiet dignity the older millionaires began to entrench themselves in their traditions. They might be poor but they were not vulgar.

Oktoberfest—Today is Wed. Sept. 26 (?)—I have made few or no entries here for a week or two—I have been soaking in the true life of this place—Last night again to the Wiese—Oktoberfest—I am trying to recover today from this nightmare that has paralyzed me.

Coningsby Dawson, Compton McKenzie, Cosmo Hamilton.

"Are they all the same person?" Oliver asked. "I have always felt they were. Probably there is a difference," he said after a moment, "but it's not important."

Monday—Sept. 24 (?)—

In the little cabaret late at night—Somewhat garish—The waitresses stinking with Cunt and Trickery—The drunken [cuckolded?] men—The fat whorish women—Tonight with old Mrs. Churchill—The horror of verschiedene [*sundry*] life.

Oktoberfest: A fear greater than any he had ever known rose up and inundated his heart. He was terribly and desperately afraid—he was surrounded and beset by them, he was drowning among them, he was cut off from all hope of succor.

Tuesday Evening—Sept. 26 [*25*]

I have made few entries since coming to Munich—I have been completely possessed and drowned in the life of this place until I have almost lost the power of writing.

Yesterday in Englischer Garten with Herr Steinbauer [16]—Last night with him again to Oktoberfest.

The peasant woman drained the remainder of the great stone mug with a single gulp. She rose suddenly to her feet with a scream that rose high above the smashing blare of the orchestra, and held the mug for a moment high above her head. Then suddenly, she swept down upon Oliver from the side and back, bearing him back in his chair as if he had been a child. She seized his chin and head between her strong brown arms and planted terrible kisses upon his face and mouth. He was drowning in her embrace; he was caught fast in the gripe of her mighty legs.

16. The brother of Wolfe's landlady at the Pension. For a fictional description see W&R, pp. 654–55.

GERN [17]

Distributed among the innumerable smaller buildings of the Fair like lions crouched among a rabble of smaller beasts there rose about them now the great beer halls erected there by the famous breweries. And as thick as the crowd had been in the lanes before the shows and booths, it seemed small compared to the crowd that filled these vast buildings—enormous sheds that each held several thousand people.

Jan (Kossak?) [*Gossaert, also called Mabuse*] Münchener 14th cent.[18] Brutal pictures of the crucifixion.

Brussels—Cartoon in front of—Bruxelles Aux Nues—Englishman's girl—You Are A Beeg Peeg.

Max Josef Platz at night—Restaurant opposite Hof Theater—Maximilian Strasse—Pension off.—"Walkure"—I went there for rooms—Toothless Zimmermädchen [*housemaid*] and agent on prop. who wanted 10 marks down—Then the other scene in Max. Str.—Girl—dark Ital. looking—probably Bayerischer [*Bavarian*]—wrote down address of one farther up above Vierjahreszeiten.

Tonight—Scene in Marseilles—End of "Why Joel Whispered."

"You're hitting them up, aren't you, son?" the Captain said.

"All I can," Oliver answered.

"Good!" said the Captain approvingly. "But what are you drinking there? Cognac! And you call yourself a man! That's a drink for high school girls!"

"If you know anything better," said Oliver with dignity, "I should be grateful for advice."

"How do you want to feel?" said the Captain professionally, "Drunk or crazy?"

"I can't get drunk," said Oliver pathetically. "I've tried and it

17. Gern is a German adverb meaning willingly or gladly; it is also the name of a section of Munich on the Nymphenburger Kanal. Here Wolfe probably intended the adverbial meaning as a title for the following passage describing the beer halls of the Oktoberfest.

18. Mabuse (1484?–1532) was actually a Flemish painter.

doesn't work. I keep drinking and drinking these little things but nothing comes of it. Nothing happens to me! I've had nine already—that should be enough for something, shouldn't it? But nothing comes of it." He stared for a moment at the milky greenish stuff in the Captain's glass.

"I have lost track of time," he said. "I think I have been here only three or four days, but at the same time I know that I have been here over three weeks. The hotel people told me so today."

"Where are you staying?" the Captain asked.

"It is a little joint around the corner here," said Oliver. I pay fifty cents a day for my room. It is on the street and the streetcars come by all night long. I hear the earth and the buildings begin to rattle away to the end of Marseilles; if I am in bed I lurch and wiggle there like a hooked fish until they come by. When they come by it is like an earthquake. Then when they have gone, the other end of Marseilles begins to rattle and shake again. "Nothing looks right," he went on in a discontented voice. "All the people look funny and so do the buildings."

"In what way?" said the Captain. "How do you mean?"

"Why," said Oliver, "the buildings are not straight—some of them lean out at you; some of them lean back; and the people are the same way—their faces seem to be carved out of a block of wood, part is light and part is shadow, and the eyes and noses are set at funny angles. It is all like a painting by What's-His-Name. I think I must be a little off my base."

"I think you are," the Captain agreed. "You're a little nutty, son. How long have you been like this?"

"Not over a month," said Oliver. "Before that I did not feel good but I could see straight. It began in Avignon. I was up there in a garden by the Pope's Palace looking at some kids playing, and it all began there. I began to see things funny. When I went home to the hotel where I was staying the stone flags on the floor looked crooked. That night I looked down a little crooked street and I saw light coming out in one place and heard music. I went down there; a woman was standing under an arch. She reached out and pulled me in. We went through a courtyard; the arch looked crooked, and the courtyard looked crooked. We went up some stairs and down a corridor. We passed some rooms with open doors. In one of them I saw a man and a woman sitting at a table."

"Did they look crooked too?" said the Captain.

"Yes," said Oliver. "They looked crooked too. I heard them laughing at me after I had gone past."

Tuesday afternoon—4 o'clock—

Tea at American Library with German friend from Electric Exhibition.

Food—3:60; Beer—4:00; Bread—0:20.

[*On Sunday night, September 30, while attending the Oktoberfest, Wolfe had his celebrated fight with a group of German revelers. The following day he entered a hospital and remained there until Thursday, October 4—thus spending his twenty-eighth birthday as a patient—during which time he was treated by Geheimrat Lexer, a famous German surgeon.*

*Wolfe immediately determined to make literary capital of his misfortune and while still a patient wrote the following passages about his hospital experiences. Since he was working on "The River People" at the time of his hospitalization, he here calls his autobiographical protagonist Oliver, and apparently he intended to include this new and unexpected development in "The River People." After his release he continued to work on the hospital scenes, portions of which, after many shiftings, finally appeared a decade later as Chapter 48 of* The Web and the Rock.]

Herr Geheimrat looked: "Dies ist gut," he said gutturally, "aber dies ist besser." Having delivered himself of this astonishing profundity, he strode unperturbedly from the room followed by the gaze of his dazzled following.

What a man this is! Oliver thought, who has only to look and see that this is good, but that is better.

And he congratulated himself on having secured this eminent scientist as his physician.

During the night, however, his head began to throb and hurt like forty devils. It is the wound, Oliver thought, the wound that is healing. Herr Geheimrat, in his great wisdom, foresaw all this, but he wisely said nothing to me about it.

But in the morning when he spoke of the matter and pointed, the interne discovered another wound one and one-half inches long which the penetrating eyes of the great man had passed over entirely.

"Ach!" said the interne reproachfully, "Why didn't you speak?"

This time when they cleaned the wound it hurt. And they completed the shaving of his head until it was covered only with the black stubble of his hair. But this time Herr Geheimrat did not make any mistakes. He came in from the lecture room while his assistant was looking at the wound, squeezed and pressed it with his heavy fingers, and delivered instructions rapidly in his guttural voice. Then he went out again.

Oliver was now considered so far advanced towards recovery that he was told he could leave the hospital the next day. His nose was mending rapidly, and seemed to be resuming its former shape, although it was still thick and swollen between the eyes. The left side of his head contained several raw ugly-looking scars, his eyes were wildly black, and his nose and face bore numerous scratches from the lady's fingernails.

Oliver looked at the plain face of the American doctor for a moment.[19] It had, he saw now, below its prim precision, and the cold twinkle of the eyeglasses, much humor and kindliness. And although this man had come here only as a student of the burly German doctors, was here to take notes, to listen, to defer to the great ones, Oliver began to see now a quality in him that dignified and ennobled his prim figure. But he was still suspicious and alert with that mistrust which is the unhappy acquisition of an American travelling in Europe. His mind was asking Why? What does he expect to get from me? How much is this going to cost me?

He said rudely, "How much do I owe you for your services?"

"Nothing," said the American doctor primly. "Ahem! I was glad to be of service."

"But I owe you something," Oliver insisted. "How much? You paid those taxi fares the other day. How much did it come to?"

"Oh no," said the American doctor, "wouldn't think of it, really. I enjoyed the ride with you."

And after this palpable absurdity, he looked somewhat confused and upset, and moved with hasty indecision towards the door.

"I do not understand this," Oliver said thickly. "People do not often do things like this." He was silent a moment, while a final conviction swept over him and pierced his heart. Then he said, "I think you are a great person. I have not often heard of anything so enormously decent as this." And, his bloody swollen eyes suddenly wet with tears, he stepped forward on the man with his hands outstretched.

The doctor moved hastily away, startled and shocked, his lean Yankee face burning a still deeper hue.

19. A fictional sketch of Dr. Du Bois, who refused to accept any remuneration for his services to Wolfe.

"Not at all, not at all," he protested. "Glad to—" Then suddenly he paused and said in his prim dry voice: "I have a son about as tall as you are. He's in school at a military academy back home." Then he added after yet another pause, "Fellow countrymen, you know. Ought to stick together—"

His eyeglasses seemed for a moment to twinkle with dew, and he went out very quietly.

Thursday, Oct. 4th.

Came from hospital this afternoon a little after two o'clock. People at Pension seemed genuinely concerned and glad to see me. Went out for hat and mail. Bought a kind of loose skull cap to cover my bald scarred dome—such as the Korps studenten wear. Found letter from Greta [*Hilb*] and a cable from Aline. My wounds seem to be healing rapidly. Can't say yet about nose—But it looks as if I may get out without any permanent disfigurement.

Oliver was pacing up and down the floor when suddenly Herr Geheimrat and the young assistant came into the room.

"Wie geht's," grunted Herr Geheimrat, "Gut?"

"Rotten," Oliver snarled, ripping the bandage savagely from his head. He pointed angrily to the wound among the luxuriant fringe of hair that had been left to him. "See that? You never saw it before, did you?"

Herr Geheimrat looked, probing at the place with his heavy fingers. "You'll have to get your whole head shaved," he muttered, and left the room rapidly.

Oh, yes, Oliver thought bitterly. The great surgeon. The great Herr Geheimrat. The greatest head surgeon in Germany—Nay! he croaked bitterly—In all the world. This is good, but that is better! The eagle eye that misses nothing—only occasionally slips over inch long wounds.

While he was pursuing these reflections, Johann came limping in with razor and clippers.

They all limp, Oliver thought again, as if this were the crowning infamy. They all limp! And they are all blind in one eye.

He was drowning in oceans of mud, choking, smothering.[20] He felt the heavy bodies on top of him, snarling, grunting, smashing at his face and body. He rose, as if coming from some terrible quicksand, but

20. An account of the actual fight. For a published version see *Letters*, p. 145.

he slipped and sank again into the bottomless mud. He felt the mud beneath him, but what was really blinding and choking him was the torrent of blood that streamed from four gashes in his head; he did not know he bled.

Somehow finally he was on his feet again, moving towards the dark forms that swept in towards him. He struck the smaller figure full with his fist and saw it dive into the mud as if hurled there by some giant's hand. Then as he turned toward the larger figure, he saw the heavy fist whiz towards him. It struck him full on the nose and he was turned half around, feeling at the moment the numb crunch of broken cartilage. Then he struck at the figure and missed, moved forward, struck again, and sent it to the earth. It rose; they struggled, swaying drunkenly in the slime. The blood from his wounds was drowning him. With a final effort he threw the figure over and plunged upon it. He could not see, but he fastened his fingers on the eyes and face below him determined to hold on until he drowned in that ocean of mud, or until that grasp on his throat should loosen, until he felt no life there in the mud below him. And at length the grasp was loosened, but still he held on. Someone was beating him over the head and shoulders, someone was on his back tugging, pulling, clawing at his eyes and face. Still he held on. Someone was screaming loudly—a woman's voice. But still he held on, until hands seized him from behind and pulled him off.

Saturday, Oct. 6—

Up early—police detective wakened me—he promised me it is now all over, but I've half a notion to clear out—Tomorrow I am going to Oberammergau, I think—got letter from Mrs. Richards today—also hospital bill—Went to Nymphenburg this afternoon and through the various palaces—Grounds beautiful with the autumn tints—American people I met there—Fat old woman who knew it all—girl nice—young fellow a typical natty Amer. stiff—Tonight to Theater am Gärtnerplatz—Another bad show—operetta—but with somewhat original ending—Three Poor Little Mädchens.

Munich—Monday night—Oct. 8th (?)—

Came from Oberammergau tonight—Went down yesterday morning—I was terribly depressed—Full reaction against the affair of a week before had set in—physically very tired—Met interesting old German on train and he took me to hotel where Mrs. Richards was staying—Old woman busy on her book—My head was hurting on top where wound had broken open—We got Dr. Anton Lang—Pilate—to dress it—Evening to theater to see Garmisch-Partenkirchen players do

*Schuldig*[21]—Then back to hotel where late over beer and schnapps with old German who had been in Africa—and village Hauptlehrer [*senior schoolmaster*]—great red faced man who smoked long pipe.

For Tuesday—Get ready to go to Vienna—Get Austrian Visa—Pay hospital bill—Go to German Museum—See about books—finish letter to Aline.

Tuesday night [*October 9*]—

Wrote some more of letter to Aline in Pension—Went to theater—*Die Schule Von Uznach*[22]—Horrible disgusting exhibition—Play itself cheap and vulgar—but not good enough to be evil—People—all the German slime and evil came out—wet.

Wednesday night [*October 10*]—

Today for last time to doctors—Did not see the great Lexer. Young doctor grew ecstatic over my appearance—"Ach! Wie Schön! Wunderbar!"—Partly ironic—This afternoon I went to the German Museum and went through 140 rooms and got as far as the airplanes—It is magnificent and bewildering—When I came out at closing time I was exhausted—Worse even than first day at Oberammergau—Came back through the Thal—a part of München I knew nothing about—But it is swarming with heavy Teutonic life—a place of beer and sausage and food and fruit and cheap merchandise—a feeling almost of horror—I am weighed down under it—Tonight weak as a cat—Went to Sendlinger Tor movie—*Unterwelt*—When I came out tried to eat—A heavy steak, cooked with onions—I got down most of it and then had to rush to the Abort [*toilet*] to vomit—I must finish the German Museum—or get finished by it—and go to the National Museum and Alte Pinakothek again—Also for ride into Isar-Thal if possible—Try to go to Salzburg Sunday—Stay there day or two and then to Wien.

ALTE PINAKOTHEK

894—P. Brueghel—"Das Schlaraffenland" [*Land of Cockaigne*].[23]

21. The title means "guilty." In an unpublished portion of his two-part Oktoberfest letter to Mrs. Bernstein, Wolfe wrote: "I had expected to see a folk play, but this was a modern or semi-modern thing—a kind of German Galsworthy about a man who has been imprisoned for 20 years for a crime of which he is innocent." To see this play was one of the main reasons Wolfe had gone to Oberammergau.

22. Carl Sternheim, *Die Schule von Uznach; oder Neue Sachlichkeit* [*reality*]; *ein Lustspiel in vier Aufzugen.*

23. Wolfe later mentions this picture by name and describes it in his portrayal of Munich as "an enchanted land of Cockaigne." W&R, p. 658.

El Greco—"Die Heilige Jungfrau."

Room Full of Tintoretto—Battle Scenes.

Botticelli—"Die Beweinung Christe" [*Lamentation for Christ*]—with the uneven stone circle.

A Room Full of Rubens.

Bern. Strigel—"Die Acht Kinder und Konrad Rehlingen."

H. Holbein—"Ecce Homo."

Meister des Marienlebens—"Maria Geburt" [*Nativity of the Virgin*].

Mich. Wolgemut—"Auferstehung Christus" [*Resurrection*].

M. Pacher—"Kirchenväteraltar" [*Altar of the Church Fathers*].

M. Pacher—"Verkündigung Maria" [*Annunciation*].

Friday night—

After Pinakothek today went to Büro—no mail—Then to book store—bought *Ägyptische Helena*—Von Strauss und Hofmannsthal—and *Gyges* [*und sein Ring*] von Hebbel—before at bookstore near Obelisk—Wedekind's *Kammersänger* [*Chamber singer*] [24]—Went to Bodega—Promenadeplatz—Waiter said old man & girl had come there yesterday asking for me—The whole damned place is getting too thick—Then to see old woman [*Mrs. Richards*]—She has gone quite crazy—Kept saying "O what *am* I thinking about? Was it yesterday or today?"—Swore they had broadcasted me on radio last night—as a criminal—Amerikaner Verbrecher [*criminal*] etc.—Left her—Went to Pension left packages—then to *Ägyptische Helena*—Found it very dull and unmusical—but had standing room under a light and could follow text beautifully—Later—and now—in Hoftheater [*Restaurant*] opposite.

To Buy: Something by Kleist, Good life of Ludwig II—Vienna Dove!

Let no day pass from now on when you do not seek out something new and good.

When I saw Germans picking their teeth with one hand carefully raised above [*the*] mouth, I thought: How disgusting and how sneaking! But they do it for courtesy!

24. Paperback copies of Richard Strauss and Hugo von Hofmannsthal, *Die Ägyptische Helena* (Berlin, 1928); Friedrich Hebbel, *Gyges und sein Ring: Ein Tragödie in fünf Akten* (Leipzig, n.d.); and Frank Wedekind, *Der Kammersänger* (München, 1920) are in the Wisdom Collection. There is no writing or marking in any of them, and *Der Kammersänger* has only about half the pages cut.

*S. S. Stuttgart*, Boulogne, Sailing Nov. 2, 1928.

Sunday—Oct. 14 or 15 [*14*]—

This afternoon to the Deutsches Museum again—Think I have seen it all now—Went through Physics, mechanics, chemics, telephonics, radio, music—God knows what else—Ended at room 220 (of 400)—Great crowds around submarine and torpedoes in ship department—Day is slate grey, heavy, cold, dark, raw—Must go tomorrow.

German Museum: Here Faraday, and Ohm, and Gauss, and Agricola, and Leonardo, and Galileo—here in other times an entire life of the mind from which I am forbidden.

I have really seen so much—too much—despite my present feeling—I regret my inability to read German rapidly—but when I have translated something—What—What do I find?

I am overpowered by number—not by quality.

Boulogne, Amiens, Paris, Brussels, Antwerp, Malines, Cologne, Bonn, Mainz, Wiesbaden, Frankfurt, Munich, Oberammergau. Vienna.[25]

Sunday night—

Eating for last time at Neue Börse—A sharp head cold has caught me—almost within a week it came on—Weather outside is murderous—I have so much beyond enough of Germany this time that I draw every breath almost with effort—Went to Volks Theater tonight—Show called *Arme Ritter* [*Penniless Knight*]—It was execrable—far worse than Gärtnerplatz—I am smothering in the great heavy people all around me—They have become visibly hoggish—They bump and thump against each other everywhere—In a crowd you can feel the great beer bodies bumping and thumping against you.

What I Must Do Monday Morning:

1. Get up—See that all bags are ready.
2. Old Pinakothek—Buy pictures.
3. Travel Büro—Money, Ticket, Mailing Address.
4. Post cards—Souvenirs.
5. Books—Dr. Du Bois' Book—Go to Art Store as well.

If possible, Theater Museum.

25. Wolfe's itinerary on his current trip. Vienna is his next destination.

Bauwesen and Bergbrau—What are they? Hütte? [*foundries*]

Monday Evening—[*October 15*]—7:30—

Eating in Traube Hotel—Salzburg—Have a bad cold, but that is not sufficient to kill my joy at getting here—I think as usual that life is going to be different and more beautiful now—and I believe it will be —It seems to me—I am certain—the people here are different—true Austrians—Even though they are only over the border—Ride down beautiful—At first great flat land—cold and bright in the sun—with München's raw wet (sometimes bright) cold—People plowing the fields that stretched away level and vast from the train—Then rolling land—beautiful sweeps of rolling fields—the dark German forests—Then in the distance The Magic Mountains—lying cold, golden, white, magnificent with snow—Below me a town nestled in a valley—with the gabled houses—the German church—a team of great slow-footed horses coming down a road of tall trees—the trees of Germany yellowing in the autumn—Color lovely but not beautiful as our American ones—A German station—how to describe it—dull—Reichbahn freight cars in the yard—Stairs going down under tracks—large sign marked Ausgang—A Funktionär with a military hat [*sketch of hat*]—Freight train slid past with Funktionär clinging from side—papers in hand—Shouted something to someone on our train—Great shaven-headed swine on opposite seat from mine.

Old lady came to see me this morning just as I was packing—Insisted on kissing me good bye—"like a mother," she said.[26]

[*Wolfe reached Vienna on Friday, October 19.*]

Geselligkeit [*good fellowship*].

Hotel Höller—Burggasse—5 or 6 schillings.[27]

26. This actual account of Mrs. Richards' farewell to Wolfe on his departure from Munich is quite different from other accounts he gave. Wolfe wrote Mrs. Bernstein about his experiences with Mrs. Richards and said, "The old woman is dead." He then proceeded to give an account of Mrs. Richards' death while she was listening avidly to the reports of the Graf Zeppelin on its trip to America, and how her Oberammergau friends came to Munich and took her body back to Oberammergau for burial. He also wrote a similar account to Mrs. Roberts (*Letters*, p. 167). Mrs. Bernstein questioned the story of Mrs. Richards' death, and he later admitted that is was his own invention. He apparently wanted to test his fictional technique on two people who knew him well. He later questioned Mrs. Bernstein as to how she knew the death account was a fabrication.

27. Wolfe's letter to Mrs. Bernstein postmarked October 26 is on the stationery of the Hotel Höller.

Sunday [*October 21*]—

Theater in Evening—*Sie Werden Lachen* (But I Didn't)—*Neues Wiener Journal*—Columns of advertisement from courtesans—massage salons—pretty widow wishes honorable connections—etc.

Vienna—Monday Night [*October 22*]—

Coffee House on Kärntner Ring—Today took 3½ hour bus ride through city to Grinzing and Kobenzl—The Wiener Wald was beautiful and yellow—Vienna lay out in a great misty plain below me—Visibility poor—Donau and side canals wandered like a still frozen smoke through it—Came back through the more grimy section and by the heuriger wine places—Then into the bewilderment of the city—Schubert's birth house—Then old city again—Judengasse—old University—a bewilderment of crooked streets—small crowded shops—book and hat stores—with momentary glimpse of Bourse—etc.

Bought guide that is filled with Everything and a copy of Schiller's *Don Carlos*[28]—I am bewildered and sick—Perhaps I can make some order out of it.

Young Rumanian who spoke French with me and was unpleasantly curious—An overdressed mannikin with a mannikin's handsomeness—Second rateness of second rate nations—Went home and had long hot bath—Too tired for theatre—Then out to eat—Met the Czech (or so-called) woman on the street—Very handsome, save for small deformed teeth and protuberant ridge of bloodless gums—Took her into small Gasthof and bought her a drink—Drank a heuriger[29] myself.

Stopped off at Hofburg today—interesting—Rooms not terribly overloaded with baroque as are Residenz rooms in Munich—Many of them very beautiful and delicate Rokoko.

Vienna—Tuesday [*October 23*]—

Up late again—out to lunch—Ate at Gasthof near Akademie [*Theater*]—Went to Wiener Bank-Verein—Thence to Cook's—Went through Stephans Kirche—Beautiful—but confusing—It is too dark inside—a single stop in the organ emitted one high piercing sound—Never before seen such devotion as the women before little picture of Virgin—all lighted with candles—I have rarely in my life seen what I thought was the religious feeling—but I saw it here amid sin and poverty—Several of the women were young prostitutes—they held

28. Wolfe's copy of Friedrich Schiller, *Don Carlos* (Leipzig, 19??), in the inexpensive Reclams Universal Bibliothek, is in the Wisdom Collection.

29. Heuriger is new wine on draft, the product of the last pressing.

their hands and gazed adoringly and entreatingly at the picture, and one kept pleading gently: "O Mary, help me"—Then to be shaved—Then for bit along Stephans Platz and in the Graben, and in the street of elegant small shops—Kohlmarkt—One of the most elegant and expensive streets I have ever seen.

Deutsches Volks Theater—*Perlenkomodie*—Bruno Frank.

Der Frauenarzt.

Wednesday—

Today—up late again—Dressed—out to Bank—as usual was shunted around—told to come back—ate nearby—Went to Cook's—found letter from Stott—explored Old City—looked at books with sick heart—went to cafe—came back to bank again—got checks o.k.'d—said come tomorrow—Went to National Library—investigated reading room—bought pamphlet—went to bookshops—to cafe—tried to find American Consulate—went to get shaved—conversation with barber about my wounds—from there to cafe—from cafe to restaurant—from there to theater—*Nord Express 133*—an English mystery play—from there to Beer cellar—other side of ring—and from beer cellar to Restaurant Hopfner—Müde [*exhausted*].

Thursday [*October 24*]—

Up somewhat earlier—Two beers—Then to bank where at length got drafts transferred to checks—Bought note book in Graben—Eating at Graben restaurant—and later on tour of city from T. Cook's.

At Restaurant—under ground, but quite elegant (and not cheap)—Geflügel risotto mit Parmesan (4:80)—¼ Wein (140).

## *Pocket Notebook 5*
## *October 25, 1928, to November 15, 1928*

*This notebook covers Wolfe's long stay in Vienna and a two-week visit to Hungary. He was charmed by Vienna and intrigued by Budapest, and his notebook entries reveal his effort to capture the quality of each of these cities. There is very little additional work on "The River People." But his stay in the hospital had in no way subdued his compulsive fascination with bookstores and their display windows. He seemed almost to feel that he was searching for the secret of how to be a published author whose books would be exhibited by the bookstores of European cities. The notebook is again filled with lists. In fact, the inside of the front cover has a scribbled list of authors of several nationalities and the front end paper contains a list of representative Hungarian proper names and miscellaneous Hungarian book titles. Once again, we have deleted most of these lists.*

*Wolfe described his bewildering behavior in a letter to Mrs. Bernstein October 25, the day he began this notebook:*

"I circle the maze of the Old Town here like a maniac, taking down the names of hundreds of books in the windows trying to dig out of all the nightmare horror of dust and forgetfulness and junk with which Europe is weighted down, something that may have a little beauty, a little wisdom for me. This terrible vomit of print that covers the earth has paralyzed me with its stench of hopelessness. I can not lift my head above the waves of futility and dulness. I have no hope, no confidence, no belief in my ability to rise above the level of even the worst of it. Impulse is killed in me, hope is dead—for I am sure so much of this—most of it!—was begun hopefully, was thought good by its perpetrators, fond praisers. And to think that this world is full of people who say this and that confidently, who write criticisms, and talk confidently of literature and art, who peck around in the huge mess with a feeling of complacency and pleasure—I cannot follow them, understand them."

---

Bought this book Thursday Oct. 24 (25?) in Graben, Vienna.

Thursday Night [*October 25*].

Vienna. Went on another Rundfahrt this afternoon through city, Prater, and Schönbrunn. Beautiful day. American Jew from Baltimore who sat next to me. Met him at restaurant behind opera later. He is staying at Bristol—as are most of the Americans. Ate with him, killed most of evening on his account, and at length found woman for him. Like a fool told him my Munich Story. (Woman I found for him the one I bought glass of wine for the other evening.)

*Simplicissimus.* Cabaret-Revue in the Wollzeile. Musty steins and corridors below, old decayed smell.

Schönbrunn today, the royal apartments. Some of the rooms very grand, simple and lovely. Delicate Rokoko. Other American-German-Jewish family. Father quite elegant, had an English drawl, but was a German Jew.

The great park at Schönbrunn yellow and beautiful in the autumn. The paths and lawns leading to the carriage houses covered with pallid yellow of leaves. A misty smell of autumn in the air, and in the late pearly sun, already the ghost of the moon big over Vienna. That is Vienna today, the dropping yellow leaves.

Maria Theresa and her 16 children. Pictures of her wedding. The one showing the rich coaches and the elegant people winding to the ceremonial church. Then the other showing the feasting, the banquetting, the concerting. Desk where Emp. Franz Josef I wrote, worked, "and had his food served to him." The 139 kitchens. The great upward sweep of the forest and lawns behind Schönbrunn to the fancy French columns and arches, with chariots and prancing horses, of the Gloriette.

In Vienna, attached to most of the larger cafés, "Beer and Rummy Stube." [1] They come here at night, whole families, to play.

Ring café. Lower. Had omelette, read *Le Matin* and *The Times.* The enormous amount of little advertisement in the *Times,* the huge pages, the small print. The tremendous amount of wealth still left in England. The wills that had been filed, that are filed daily, one for £600,000, others for 200,000 [*and*] 100,000, etc. Then the sale of estates, great number of houses of 12, 14, 20, 30 bedrooms. Estates up to 3,000 acres, etc.

Friday:

1. Go to station and get books—First Thing.
2. Go to Kunst Historisches Museum [*marked out*].

1. The term is Wolfe's. Card rooms were provided by the cafes, but, though rummy was played, bridge was the common game and coffee the usual drink.

3. Go to City Historical Museum.
4. Evening: Go to Grinzing or to theatre.
   Hungary Visa? See Cook's.

In Germany and Austria Today:

| | | |
|---|---|---|
| T. Mann | Bruno Frank | Kaiser |
| Wassermann | Feuchtwanger | Spengler |
| Schnitzler | Sternheim | Werfel |
| Hofmannsthal | Toller | Klabund |
| Hauptmann | Hasenclever | Eulenberg |
| R. Neumann | H. Mann | |

Their Own Dead:

| | |
|---|---|
| Goethe | Heine |
| Schiller | Lessing |
| Kleist | Wieland |
| Hebbel | Herder |
| Körner | Chamisso |
| Uhland | Storm |
| Keller | Freytag |
| Hoffmann | Fontane |
| Klopstock | Wedekind |
| Grillparzer | Kant |
| Nietzsche | |

The German word *Erotik* and Schönheitspflege [*beauty culture*].

Foreign Writers Living and Dead Most Often Seen in German Book Stores (In German Translation):

*Living*

| | |
|---|---|
| Galsworthy | Gorki |
| Shaw | Dreiser |
| Sigrid Undset | Edgar Wallace |
| Selma Lagerloef | Knut Hamsun |
| Romain Rolland | Gunnar Gunnarson |

***Dead***

| | |
|---|---|
| Strindberg | Dostoievsky |
| A. Dumas | Ibsen |
| Dickens | Shakespeare |
| Wilde | Tolstoi |
| Bjoernson | Manzoni |
| Flaubert | Baudelaire |
| Jack London | A. France |

Scene: drunken young lovers, child with clay pipe in its mouth, dog eating pie, etc.

After visiting the gallery [*Art History Museum*] today ate lunch. Then went to National Library and found collections closed. Then to book shop, bought two beautiful pictures by Michael Pacher, and a book about Vienna. Then to Cook's, no mail, and to American Consulate for doctor's and dentist's addresses.

The multitudinous advertisements in newspapers are governed by certain laws of sameness. The scenes of life are millionfold, but governed by monotony. The hardest thing in the world is to find an original action, an original situation, an original life.

Tonight—Friday [*October 26*]—

Wandered into new section of Vienna—up the Wienzeile (VI) —across to Margareten Str. and now in Wiedner Hauptstrasse—Eating at Restaurant Rotes Klössel (in Favoriten Strasse)—The great number of shops—the small loaded shops with their wearisome suggestions of life—sausage shops, shirt shops, kitchen pots and pans shops, flower shops, furniture shops, barber shops, tobacco shops (with copies of the naked cult papers), etc.

Café Parsifal—Walfischgasse—old place just off Opera and Kärntner Strasse—where respectable mistresses and their sugar boys come—play cards.

Here is a modern Europo-American type—man with thinning hair brushed back in a slick blackish pompadour—grey trousers—black coat—pouched eyes—somewhat thin cynical face—a bow tie and open collar—Elegant cigarette smoker—and always with good looking woman to whom he talks (and she) with weary sophistication.

For Saturday—Art museum again—or Rathaus—afternoon—Albertina—Hotel—Books—Hungarian visa.

[*Wolfe's notes on his visits to the gallery consist mainly of lists of catalogue numbers and names of painters. The following three entries are a sample and include those which offer some kind of comment.*]

There are small portrait figures of Tintoretto that suggest [*Hugo van der*] Goes.

Bad room with Annibale Carracci 1560–1609, Guido Reni 1575–1642, Ciro Ferri 1634–1689, [*Mattia*] Preti, [*Domenico*] Feti, [*Lodovico*] Carracci, [*Pietro*] Cortana, [*Giulio Cesare*] Procaccini. And then in the next one, O Jesus! [2]

Hans Muelich (1516–1573)—He's in the room [*VII*] that has the wonderful pictures—the Cranachs—the Baldung [*Griens*]—Lucas Cranach (There were two—the younger and the older)—L.C.d.a. [*der älter*] was probably greater painter.

*Soll und Haben*—by Freytag—Begins "The City Hall clock was striking (12?) in the great industrial city of M . . . . ." [3]

Saturday in bookstore—Bought play by Korngold and Burckhardt's Italian Renaissance—Looked at many others.[4]

Saturday Night [*October 27*]—

Saw fire engines going to a fire tonight—Equipment good—but wagons lumbered past slowly (This was near Graben in Old City) blowing a set of deep New Years' horns that had an up-and-down sound.

Akademie Theater—*Ein Besserer Herr*—2 Akten—Walter Hasenclever.

The door opened and Dr. Le Roy came in quickly at his soft rapid tread. He put two books on the table beside the bed and and gave

2. A room devoted to Italian schools of the seventeenth century.

3. Wolfe is mistaken. Gustav Freytag's famous novel *Debit and Credit* begins, "Ostrau is a small town near the Oder, celebrated even as far as Poland for its gymnasium and its gingerbread . . . ." Wolfe did not buy his own copy of *Soll und Haben*, a handsomely bound German edition now in the Wisdom Collection, until October 31.

4. A paperback copy of *Das Wunder der Heliane* (Mainz, 1927) is now in the Wisdom Collection. The "play" is actually an opera; the libretto was written by Hans Müller and is based on the play by Hans Kaltneker. The music was composed by Erich Wolfgang Korngold, an Austrian composer. A copy of Jacob Burckhardt, *Die Kultur Der Renaissance In Italien* (Berlin, 1928) is also in the Wisdom Collection.

Oliver two or three letters and a cable. Oliver's heart began to pump rapidly with excitement as it always did when he got a telegram or a cable. His mind leaped to a dozen terrible surmises—sudden death, mutilation, or execution on himself of some retribution for unsuspected crimes. But he did not want to open the cable while Dr. Leroy [*sic*] was there: he wanted to face the worst—whatever it was—alone.

He thanked the doctor for the books, grinning faintly as he saw the titles. One was Conrad's *The Secret Agent,* he had never read, and the other was Mark Twain's *The Innocents Abroad,* in the Tauchnitz edition. He held it up in his hand:

"Was this deliberate?" he asked, "—or just a happy stroke?"

The doctor stared primly and carefully at the title for a moment, then he laughed suddenly and loudly—he was delighted and went over the matter again and again in his mind.

"Why—haw, haw—no, I hadn't intended—but it does—" and so on.

Then he looked politely into Oliver's bloody eyes and at his swollen nose, and at the wounds on his head and said, "Oh, yes. Everything is clearing up nicely."

Then after asking if there was anything more he could do, he went out softly.

When he had gone, Oliver opened the cable feverishly. The message was from Gilbert Hoyt, the publisher. It read:

"Book has begun to sell. Letter following. Have photographs made and send immediately."

Oliver stared at the little scrap of paper for a moment, then collapsed suddenly into the mountain of pillows, laughing hoarsely and uncontrollably as he had never laughed before. He laughed so hard that he blew the bloody wadding out of his nose: the laughter that welled up in him was harsh and broken, as is the speech of a man who has lived alone in the wilderness—his heart was filled with a terrible merriment, and this harsh noise broke from his lips and filled the quiet room with savage echoes. The noise brought the Little Sister on the run; her startled face looked at him from the door—he was bleeding from the nose, and roaring with laughter, and all the time he kept waving the cablegram at her. She disappeared like a startled cat and in a moment returned with the young assistant and Herr Geheimrat, who came pounding in at his heavy limp, slowly like a puzzled grumpy child.

"Was ist?" he growled quickly.

"O funny! Funny!" gasped Oliver, waving the cable at him. "Funny, Herr Geheimrat, but you couldn't see it."

Herr Geheimrat, after a quick glance at his bloody nose, began a hasty examination of his skull, pressing down heavily with his fingers. Oliver found this too very amusing and began to laugh again.[5]

Today, Saturday. First I went to the Natural History Museum, then to see the pictures. The Natural History Museum has a huge collection of fishes, reptiles, birds, animals, etc.—but so have we. This is not what one comes abroad for—to see stuffed crocodiles from Florida, butterflies from New Guinea, and beautiful parakeets from South America. Here is a huge palace, a duplicate of the Kunsthistorisches, given over to withered reptiles in bottles, etc. Incongruous.

After looking at thousands of books, I find that there is hardly one in a thousand that I want to buy. Certainly one does not come from New York to Vienna to buy Theodore Dreiser's *Der Titan* in 3 volumes, or John Galsworthy's *Schwan Sang* or Upton Sinclair's *Petroleum*. But there are some books—mostly art books—that I should like, but they are all very expensive.

Saturday. Tonight again the marvellous milk-soft moon. I walked through the old deserted streets of the Old City, through some of the streets and narrow little "gasses" [*alleys*] that lead away from The Graben. The great tall houses, shuttered below—delicate yet massive—in the delicate Baroque style. The great dark windows in the upper stories with the deep recessed walls. Within—what?

Oliver thought:

When travelling abroad it is always good for me to remember Dr. Johnson's remark to one of his hostesses at dinner—that she was a better cook than he was, but that he knew more about food, since he had eaten at a great variety of tables. When I sink into a swamp of despair because of my ignorance of the language, of many of the books I see, at my inability to cope with the enormous vomit of print that inundates the earth, I must remember that no other man is able to cope

5. This passage, intended for "The River People," not only shows Wolfe incorporating his recent experience into his fiction, but also reveals how that experience is reshaped by his imagination. His artist-protagonist Oliver learns of the publication of his book in America by cable while he is recuperating in the hospital. This episode is apparently spun from whole cloth, since Wolfe had not yet learned that Scribner's was even interested in his manuscript "O Lost." Mrs. Bernstein, after a telephone conversation with Madeleine Boyd, cabled Wolfe about Scribner's interest on October 17, but had sent the cable to Munich. It was returned the following day with the message: "Addressee has left. A copy has been forwarded by mail."

with these things either. And although I am ignorant of many things that most Viennese know, so are they ignorant of many things that I know.

Bookstore—Vienna Buch Adelgesellschaft—Bargains in Art Books.

Things I remember from Munich: The sweet-faced Nuns at the Krankenhaus [*hospital*]—The wooden Christ above my door—The gardens outside the Krankenhaus, leaves growing yellow—The interne Johann, who limped—The other, big fellow with moustache—The police inspector: "Perhaps," he very carefully suggested, "it was in the Löwenbrau"—Herr Geheimrat—The young interne.

The people at the Pension—Little old lady who was always so "elegant"—The old German and his wife—The two Steinbauer men —The young Italian surgeon from Tunis—Studied at Bologna—how we would go to Café Innsbruck for terrible coffee and talk French— The book shops—the technical bookshops in the Theresien Strasse— one across from the Pension—Another further down towards the Ludwig Strasse—Still lower—a university book shop with quantities of old obscure books in the windows—And the sense of weariness and despair I used to get when I went by the bookshop near the Lenbach place which handled law and judicial literature. Who buys them? Who reads them?

[*The next six paragraphs are on loose pages which Wolfe tore out to use for Eugene's notebook in* Of Time and the River, *pp. 677–78.*]

Sunday Night—

I feel low—dispirited by the Mass of Things again tonight—I must make some decisive action—The new web of streets behind the dome has depressed me.

The mind grows weary with such a problem as mine by constantly retracing its steps, by constantly feeling around the same cylinder from which there seems *at present* to be no escape.

The European temper is one that has learned control—that is it has learned indifference—Each man writes his own book without worrying very much about what the other has written—he reads little, or if he reads much, it is only a trifle—a spoonful of the ocean of print that inundates everything—Picture Anatole France—with a reputation for omniscience—picking daintily here and there among the bookstalls of the Seine—To go by them afflicts me with horror and weariness—as it does Paul Valéry—but I lack his power to resist—I must go by them—and I do again and again whenever I go to Paris.

More and more I am convinced that to be a great writer a man must be something of an ass—I read of Tolstoi that he read no newspapers, that he went away and lived among peasants for 7 years at a time, and that for six years he read nothing except the novels of A. Dumas—Yet such a man could write great books—I almost think it is because of this that he did.

Bernard Shaw, one of our great [6] prophets at the present time, is worshiped past idolatry by many people who consider that he knows everything or practically everything.

From what I have been able to discover of his reading from his writing, I can be sure that he has read Shakespeare—not very carefully—Ibsen very carefully—a book by Karl Marx which made a deep impression on him—the tracts of the Fabian Society—and the writings of Mr. and Mrs. Sidney Webb.

[*End of passage*]

Books to be bought: Buy one or two of Göschen Sammlung; buy one or two of Körper und Kultur Books.[7]

Tonight from café on Rotenturm Str. through Wollzeile—To café on Ring—across from Prückel—Then along ring past Urania—across bridge to Prater side—back—up along Quais (with the closed bathing houses—A wind had come up and was blowing winterishly)—then into Rotenturm Str. again—and big back street around into Graben—Writing this from Graben café—bright and new—all red—and silver plaques—and bright lights and loud orchestra.

Book shops to visit—Three or four in the Wollzeile—Big one in lower Rotenturmstrasse—Two in the Opern Ring—Several in the Graben and near by—Two in the Mariahilfer Str.—Perhaps buy Schnitzler's *Therese.*

What do the little signs say on some of the big dark buildings—Perhaps to find Vater or Li, I must go into one of these streets—Spiegelgasse or Dorotheengasse—and climb up two flights to consult Herr Goldman? But what—Tapeten [*wallpaper*]? [8]

6. The word "great" is heavily marked out and does not appear in the printed version.

7. The first refers to a popular, inexpensive, reprint series; the second to "physical culture" books.

8. A note for "The River People." The names are of actual streets in Vienna.

Walk I must take—From Urania back—not along the Ring but between Ring and river—See if it circles around to Schwarzenberg Place and takes in fashionable residential district.

Burg Theater—*Faust*
Akademie—*Sommer*—Thad Rittner
*Komtesse Mizzi*—Schnitzler

For Sunday:

Either to (1) Albertina
not seen before } (2) Modern & Barok Galleries
(3) Vienna Historical Museum
Buy *Till Eulenspiegel.*

Sunday [*October 28*]—

Up late & to symphony concert—Then to elegant Cafe Vindobona behind Schwarzenberg Place—then through the City Park, along canal, where young lovers sat on benches against the wall—Then across park to Ring and into Inner City by new street (Singer Strasse) —Music I heard was Wagner overtures from most of the great operas —orchestra only fair—and singers—large faded woman (who shrieked and sometimes made no sound at all) and man—somewhat better, but made terrible faces with a constant rolling of r's—were bad.

Gösser Bier is the best bier here.

A beautiful blonde-dusky color some of these Viennese women have—A kind of *gypsy*-blonde it is.

Prater Strasse at night—Somewhat deserted—Large light café with phallic lights and Jewish families playing cards.

Monday: Go to City Historical Museum, Albertina, Library, New Gallery.

Magnificent Rooms of the Albertina. Large and grand with a few good drawings on the wall. This is the way things should be arranged.

The reason our life fails after a time is because of the faults in me.[9] I have an ideal world which I demand but which does not

9. Draft of a letter to Mrs. Bernstein.

exist—which can not, has never existed. I think my ideal world is a perverse world—I am not sure even that it is beautiful and good, although I think it would be better than the one we have. But of course every one's world is better than the one we have. That is the astounding thing about it—I think I have never known a person who did not—or could not—imagine a better world. Why haven't we got it then?

Aline, I have usually told you the truth—(outside of the innumerable lies I told you from perverseness or curiosity—but you always knew or were told they were lies)—the towers of New York again will give me, I think, a great thrill. And after a time I will no doubt come to hate them and everything in them again. But I must control this, if I can. And I do not know whether it is the spires of New York so much as the knowledge that somewhere among them is moving your marvelous flesh, that your strange flower face is blooming among them. You are almost entirely the inhabitation of this earth to me. You are almost entirely the only person in the world for me. I am not saying you are the whole world for me. I have a whole world—a whole vast swarming world of things and people that drives me mad, that exhausts me, that occasionally gives me something—and then I have you. If only my picture of life, my will to work and my knowledge of what I should take and do were as certain as my desire for you. As far as love can go I want nothing but you—the world is shut out, it dulls and afflicts me. As far as the other part of me is concerned I am banged about through chaos blind and dizzy.

Monday [*October 29*]—Tonight—

I bought two or three more books—I went to the Albertina—the great high noble rooms—So delicate and dainty—with only a few small things on the wall—but those things [*are*] the greatest things in the world—the original drawings of Dürer—Then into the large hall—with bad statues of the muses—Clio, Apollo, etc. around but you don't mind that—then I called for Pacher, and Baldung, and Grünewald. I had originals by Baldung and Grünewald and bought book on Baldung.

Get book on Hildesheimer?

[*Wolfe received his first information about Scribner's interest in "O Lost" when Mrs. Bernstein's cable finally reached him on Monday, October 29. Rather surprisingly, he refused to be elated by the news and casually continued his preparations to go to Budapest. His reaction to this new ripple of interest in his manuscript is expressed in a letter he wrote that same night to Mrs. Bernstein.*

"I got two more of your blessed letters tonight and a cable about Scribners. In my present state Scribners does not make even a dull echo in me. I have seen so much print that I feel it is criminal to add to it. Perhaps you can help me to get back a little vanity, a little self-belief, a little boastfulness. God knows we all ought to have some, and all my egoism has plunged downward and left me stuck in the mud."]

Tuesday [*October 30*]—

Today I went to the Hungarian Consulate and got a visa—Met there a woman who helped me—gave me address of a hotel in Budapest —and told me her story—She is an Austrian—a Viennese—she married a Hungarian (in Luxembourg, I believe) and they lived here and in other parts of Europe for six years before going to Budapest—But the Hungarians refused to recognize their marriage although they had lived together for six years, and they had to get the ceremony performed all over again.

Lunched—then went to Belvedere—not the Baroque Museum but the Upper Belvedere—Pictures not good—there was an interesting nude by Renoir, and a great many bad ones by the multitudinous obscure from Everywhere—But the look out from the windows is magnificent—below you sweeps the great circled terrace, with geometrical patterns of lawn, and hedge, and little tree plants stretching down to the Lower Belvedere—and then beyond Vienna with its spires and roofs and domes, all magical for a moment in a glint of sun that came through.

Walked up on an exploration tour to the East and South Railway stations—They are on the "Girdle"—Then took cab back to Stephans Place where found letter from Mrs. Boyd which I answered at once [10]—Then for a walk along the crowded Kärntnerstrasse with its splendid shops, and on the Graben—then quickly into two of the

10. Madeleine Boyd wrote Wolfe on October 15, but, since she did not have his current address, her letter reached him on October 30. She wrote: "This is what has happened, Covici-Friede read the book, and although struck by the excellence of some passages would not undertake publication. Mr. Maxwell Perkins was next, he is very much interested, would like to see you to talk things over, now where I am [*sic*] to get you?" As this was the second time in two days he had heard about Scribner's interest, and here more specifically, Wolfe replied promptly, writing to Mrs. Boyd from Cook's office, but he did not change his Budapest plans. Neither did Perkins' name register with him. He reported to Mrs. Bernstein: "Today I got a letter from Mrs. Boyd—on her way to Paris—saying a Mr. So-and-so was interested in my book."

"massage" places in the Spiegelgasse—The evil woman that stood there in the big dark room and refused the "manicure" but offered the "massage" at 15 schillings.

Goldegg Gasse—Near Belvedere—Large and rather splendid looking apartment houses—Perhaps here?

Perhaps Li's marriage had been arranged by Vater through an advertisement in the paper.

Wednesday [*October 31*]—

Bought Grieben's Guide to Budapest—Grimmelshausen's *Simplicissimus*—Freytag's *Soll und Haben*—Bought ticket to Budapest—bought Maderno and a little book because of the name—Bought ticket to Orska—One act plays tonight.[11]

Bookstores visited—Big one near Kai in Rotenturm Str.—None of them so big when you get inside—Mayer's in Singer Str.—Little one near Albertina and Bibliothek.

Engel—Short and Long History of German Lit.[12]

Christ, Tolstoi—The Gelehrte [*scholar*] who mentions them together.

The leaves are yellow in the Wiener Wald.

Buy at Ring Book Store—Herder—*Von Deutscher Art und Kunst.*

Thursday [*November 1*]—

Volks Theater—*Perlenkomödie* [*Bubbling Comedy*]—by Bruno Frank—It seemed to me to be a very good sharp comedy—of the real comic stuff—witty seriousness the base and body.[13]

To go from Edinboro to Russia—What is [*Ent*]fernung [*distance*]?

11. Actress Marie Orska appeared at Die Wiener Kammerspiele on October 31, 1928, in Strindberg's "Die Stärkere," Molnar's "Stilleben," and Barrie's "Die Medaillen der alten Frau." The Reclam edition of Hans Jacob Christoffel von Grimmelshausen, *Der abenteuerliche Simplicissimus* is in the Wisdom Collection. The volume is unmarked, but all except the last two pages have been cut.

12. Wolfe chose the short one: Eduard Engel, *Kurzgefasste deutsche Literaturgeschichte* (Wein, 1919). His copy is in the Wisdom Collection.

13. *Perlenkomödie* had its premier at Vienna on October 13, but it was not just because it was a new play that Wolfe went to see it the day after he had attended Maria Orska's three one-act plays. The usually anti-theatre Wolfe became an inveterate theater-goer in Vienna because, he wrote Mrs. Bernstein, "In my torment the theater here is cake and pudding to me."

| | |
|---|---|
| Edinboro—London | 400m |
| London—Paris | 250 |
| Paris—Vienna | 900 |
| Vienna—Moscow | 1,000 |
| | 2,550 |

It will need 4–5 days. America in ship 5–6 days.

A Typical German Newspaper. [*Followed by a list of items in the paper.*]

The Germans think the student stuff is swell. When they came into the Hofkeller, Vienna, single file, singing, and the people all smiled.

Foolish and Un-Foolish Titles:

Forest Conservation in Northern Denmark

The Classical and Renaissance Influences on the Character of "*Seraphina*" in the Prose Romances of Robert Greene.[14]

Decline of the Herring Industry in Norway in the years 1914–1917 (Publication of the U.S. Dept. of Commerce)

The Eucalyptus Worm in the Forest of Eastern Alabama

What They Made (A short history of the bees)

Carved by Successful Artists during the 19th and 20th centuries

Novels:

Monsieur Desired a Negro Virgin

Monsieur A Desiré Une Vierge Nègre

The Journal of Monsieur Frederic, A Masseur

Yvonne Maubergeau

The Truffle Hunter

Gold Stand Propaganda

In China During the Revolution of 1916

I Loathe You: Romance by M. Albert Gédic

Death by Starlight—Gerald Hendershot

Thursday—

Today—Lunch on Ring in cellar next and under the Café Sacher—Pantherbräu—Consulted my map—hailed a taxi at the Opera and drove to the Sport Palace—driver did not know where it was—he had

14. While Wolfe was a student at Harvard, he wrote a term paper for his course in comparative literature entitled "Italian Influences in the Prose and Dramatic Writings of Robert Greene." One of the best student papers he wrote, it received a grade of "A–" from Professor John Livingston Lowes.

to consult map—I went up to the outer rim of the great Vienna circle —to the foothills of Wiener Wald—We swung into Mariahilfer Strasse —turned into Girdle by Bahnhof—went past—and turned up towards Sport Palace—Then I went on foot—Came back by Ottakringer and Thalia Strasse—outskirts of a great city—Cobbles here—mud there—a meaningless little pattern of cobbles in the dirt—down a dirt bank to cross a cobble street—then a bumpy road again—scattered buildings of all shapes—ragged little gardens, with multitudinous tiny garden (?) houses—and in the distance the gentle hills of the Wiener Wald—In the smoke haze along the circle—edges smoke stacks—Around the great field new apartment houses of the Vienna government—on the outskirts suburbery—American houses all alike.

From my own point of view the most artistic people of modern times (painting) are the Dutch—also one of the thriftiest and most commercial peoples.

[*On Friday night, November 2, Wolfe arrived in Budapest. Before he left Vienna he wrote Mrs. Bernstein about his projected trip:*

"I am going to Budapest tomorrow or Friday and shall stay there four or five days. Then I am coming back here and going to Italy where I shall get a ship for New York. It is the farthest away from home I have ever been; I think of the Hungarians as being a strange—almost Oriental—race. But I am quite excited about the city, and what I shall find there. Everyone who has ever been there has spoken about its beauty. I wonder if there are good pictures there, and if I can get along with German there. I hate to lead the life of the hotel tourist, who is nursed along certain main highways like a child, and is told everything by a guide with a memorized spiel in English or French. But I will never succumb to this."]

[*Grand Hotel*] Hungaria—Room 479—Fraulein Heilprin.[15]

[*At this point Wolfe visited the Museum of Fine Arts and made notations, without comment, of a number of artists' names and catalogue numbers. Among them are several of his favorites: Brueghel, Cranach, Baldung, Metsys, El Greco, and Goya.*]

15. Though Wolfe employs the German term, as was the custom there, Miss Frances Heilprin was an interior decorator from New York who was also traveling in Europe. Through her Wolfe met an Australian family staying at the same hotel and two young Hungarian women whom Miss Heilprin had met on the train coming from Vienna. Wolfe did some of his early sightseeing in Budapest with one or several of this group, but he later struck out on his own. While he was in Budapest he occupied room 473 at the Hotel Hungaria.

| | |
|---|---|
| Budapest | 10th largest city of Europe |
| London | 1 |
| Berlin | 2 |
| Paris | 3 |
| Vienna | 4 |
| Moscow | 5 |
| Hamburg | 6 |
| Glasgow | 7 |
| Liverpool | 8 |

Naples, Milan, Bucharest, Warsaw, Budapest.

The works of Jókai in 110 volumes.[16]
The Old Nut Tree.[17]
Szabó, Dezsó.[18]

The newspaper offices of *Az Est* [*The Evening*]—with the crowds outside reading dispatches—Borah Szenator [19]—The books in the windows.

Beyond Vienna the East begins.

Budapest—Wednesday—Nov. 6 or 7 (?) [7]:
Curia ut, Étterem [*restaurant*] Kovács.
3 Csillagos (stars) Kávé [*coffee*].

Names of Actors:
Delly Ferenc
Harlty Hanna
Rákosi Pal

Vis-a-vis—National Museum—the swarming bookshops.

16. Maurus Jókai (1825–1904), Hungarian novelist, editor, and politician, whose enormous literary production made him his country's most prolific and widely read writer. His work runs the whole of the literary spectrum.

17. This restaurant became one of Wolfe's favorites. While its name in Hungarian was Öreg Diófa, he usually calls it by its German name (Alter Nussbaum) or, as he does here, the English translation. It was located in Buda on Pálya Utca and was famous for its fried chicken and shakely goulash.

18. Szabó was a Hungarian novelist and short story writer (1879–1945) who had gained great popularity with his three-volume novel *Az égesz látóhotár* (1919). Wolfe became intrigued with the Hungarian custom of writing the surname first and the given name last, and played with this form in his own writing while he was in Budapest. See *Letters*, p. 157.

19. William E. Borah, U.S. Senator from Idaho, 1907 to 1940, was then the very vocal chairman of the Senate Foreign Relations Committee and was widely quoted in the European press.

Hungarian Book Windows
Writers
Ady Endre
Gárdonyi Géza
Rákosi Jenó
Herczeg Ferenc
Somlejo Zoltán
Babits Mihály

[*Wolfe's initial reaction to Budapest is clearly set forth in a letter to Mrs. Bernstein, November 8, 1928:*

"I have just come in after walking miles and miles through this city. You must come here—you must come here in the summer. Then I think you will get all its splendor. It is one of the ugliest places I have ever seen—and also one of the most beautiful. The buildings are very, very ugly, with rare exceptions. They look as if they had been built by French architects with German blood in their veins. They are big solid ugly buildings from 1880 or so down to the present. They have meaningless bumps and balconies and protuberances—they are of grey plastery looking stone or dull brick. But at night along the river it is a magic sight. The Danube is a grand stream, like the Hudson, and it sweeps between Buda and Pest with a grand curve. I am living in Pest, which is by far the greatest part of the place. But Buda is by far the most beautiful. Buda is on a series of lovely hills which begins just across the river."]

Signore Mussolini burning the bonds.[20]

The Tone of English Papers
The Tone of French Papers
The Tone of German Papers

In another month perhaps I may be able to get my hand in my hair.

New York Café [21]—Budapest—11:20—The—shall we say gaiety—lasts all night here, I am told. The place is indescribable—therefore I

20. On October 27, the eve of the sixth anniversary of the march on Rome, Premier Mussolini with great fanfare burned 140 million lire (about $7,364,000) in public debt certificates contributed by citizens all over the country. The ceremony, which took place on the steps of the Victor Emmanuel monument, was designed to dramatize the resurgence of Italy's financial condition under Fascist dictatorship.

21. A favorite haunt of Budapest intellectuals at that time.

shall try to describe it. We will begin with "barbaric." Yes, it is barbaric—but not pretty. It is as if rich barbarians with jewelled nose rings had learned of Europe about 1890, hired German architects from Munich who had studied in Paris in the 80's, and then added suggestions of their own. The dining room is in a great long well, or court, roughly in the middle of this place. One descends thereto by red carpets. The chairs are backed and I suppose seated with red plush, there are onynx columns straight and gnarled—there is heavy darkish gilded wood bursting into scrolls and excrescences every inch of the way. There are great mirrors and marble floors, and red plush coverings over the railings, and balconies above with elaborate glass work—and dark browny gilty ceiling with flowers and fruits and naked boys—there is a chaos of unlovely and disorderly detail. It is barbaric and it is not pretty.

TRIUMPHS OF MODERN EUROPEAN CIVILIZATION [22]

Le Louvre.
The Residenz in Munich.
The Folies Bergère.
Café New York in Budapest.
Harry's New York Bar.
The Dome.
The Rotonde.
The Paintings of Salvator Rosa.
Baroque Architecture.
The German "Schönheit" Magazines.
The paintings of Lenbach, Kaulbach, Schwind, Stuck, Böcklin in Munich.
The Modern Picture Gallery in Brussels, and especially the

22. After compiling this satirical list, Wolfe wished to test his criticism against Mrs. Bernstein's taste. He wrote her as follows on November 15, the day before he left Budapest: "My dear, I believe in this: I believe that I shall see you once more and hear your voice. Here is what I want you to do: In a blank book write down under this heading 'A List of The Things That are Good'—all the good things that you can remember. I will do the same, although I have begun badly under the Ironic Title of Triumphs of European Culture; a list which starts, I believe, with the Residenz in Munich, and goes all the way through the paintings of Salvator Rosa to the Place Pigalle, Paintings of the Modern Hungarian School, Excursions on The Rhine, The Confessions of Alfred The Masseur (To Be Had Along The Seine), Manchester and Leeds, The Daily Mail and The London Times, and The Café New York in Budapest. This is only a small part of the whole. . . . Perhaps there is a little gold in the mud in which I'm covered. We'll see."

pictures showing the struggle for Belgian independence in 1830.

The Crazy Museum in Budapest (New York made wrong).

The Works of M. Maurice Dekobra.

The Personal Advertisements of Manicure and Massage Salon in Vienna Newspapers.

The Schwanthaler Sculpture Museum in Munich.

The Paintings of Peter Paul Rubens.

The Paintings of Paola Veronese.

The Place Pigalle and surrounding districts.

The Museum of The Louvre.

Modern French Architecture.

Modern German Architecture.

Modern European Architecture.

Paintings of the Modern Hungarian School, especially those who depicted the Fight For Freedom.

The Daily Mail.

The Daily Express.

The London Times.

German University Students.

The Church of Sacré Coeur in Paris.

The Works of M. Félicien Champsaur.

The Plays of Herr Karl Von Sternheim.

The 36,000 books that are published in Germany every year.

The fashionable residential sections in Cologne or any other German cities, including the residences of the manufacturer of Stollwerck chocolates and Herr Oppenheimer the banker.

Rue Faubourg du Montmartre.

The Boulevard des Italiens.

The French Middle Class on Sunday in the Bois de Boulogne.

Excursions on the Rhine.

The German Haircut.

German Bath Resorts.

The Houses of Parliament in Budapest.

The Works of M. Paul Bourget.

The Riviera.

Photographs of members of the English Aristocracy at The Shoot.

Italian Grand Opera.

The Novels of Signore Pitigrilli (*Kokain*, etc.) [23]

23. Pitigrilli is the pseudonym of Dino Segre (1893——), whose novel *Cocaina* was published in 1921.

English Industrial Cities—Manchester, Leeds, Birmingham, Stoke, Glasgow, etc.
Louise of Tours, 13 Rue Rochechouart.
The stores in the Arcades of the Palais Royal.
The Paris edition of the New York Herald, particularly its correspondence department.
Americans Who Live In Paris.
Americans who live in Munich.
Americans who live in Europe.
The French Riviera.
The Germans in my Pension in Munich.
The Confessions of Alfred, A Masseur—To be secured in the Bookquays of The Seine.

The Bookquays of The Seine with all Their *Wonderful Treasures: Die Üppige Weib* [*The Voluptuous Woman*] (anywhere in Vienna), *Wie Bist Du Weib, Figaro, Bühne.*[24]
The Lintgasse in Cologne
The Quartier des Marins in Boulogne
English Cooking
Oberammergau
The beautiful Viennese Operettas of Herr Lehar
Femina, Vienna
The Works of the Great German Writer, Thomas Mann
The Works of the Great German Writer, Heinrich Mann
The Works of the Great German Writer, Jacob Wassermann
The Works of the Great German Dramatist, Gerhart Hauptmann
The Works of the Great German Dramtist, Franz Werfel
The Works of the Great German Historian, Emil Ludwig
The Works of the Great German Sociologist, John Galsworthy
The Works of the Great German Writers: Tolstoi, Strindberg, Dostoievsky, Dickens, Rolland, Shakespeare, Shaw, Wilde, Hamson, Lagerloef, Gunnarson, Undset, Bojer, France, Tchekov, Ibsen, Björnson, Jack London, Upton Sinclair, Theodore Dreiser, Curwood, Zane Grey, Edgar Wallace.

"It takes kwat a bit of doin' to live clev-ah-ly, you know what I mean," said one of the English ladies.

24. The article should be Das instead of Die. *Wie Bist Du Weib* is a book by Bernhard Bauer (Wien, 1928) that was new at this time. *Figaro* and *Bühne* were magazines.

Why, God-damn it all to hell, Oliver reflected, This is Perfectly Damn Charming, etc.

Tokaji [*Tokay wine*]—(1904!).

Moi, Je suis un gourmet! A cause de cela, je m'ennuie beaucoup, depuis le fermeture des meilleurs Cafés du monde et le r'ouverture de petits buffets commerçants.

Lisette est grande blonde demeurant 12, Rue des Batignolles.

Voici, Mon poule!

Ah, songeat-il tant mieux! Il faut le fils.

Dame! Un echec! fit elle.

Le matin d'execution de jugement de la tribune etait arrivée. Vers cinq heures Charles se leva et allant a la fenetre ou le jeune soleil etait dejà imprimée en flocons d'or, il se mit au travail de sa fuite.

C'est votre interet, il dit, qu'il s'agit.

Moi non plus, fit elle.[25]

Thursday Night [*November 8*]—

Today for long walk along the river below Elizabeth bridge—Through the market district past grain elevator to edge of town—Huge piles of stuff in market stalls—Hundreds of baskets and trays of apples—but scrawny and poor looking compared to ours at home—The section I passed through dismal looking—dull heavy buildings of indefinite architecture—Then the dirty streets—little poor shops—and the slums.

Friday [*November 9*]—

Budapest—Rainy—thick grey day—To the bookshop of *Az Est* on the Great Boulevard where I bought the beautiful costume and decoration book—Believe the foreign books there outnumbered the Hungarian—Large selection from Tauchnitz—Large Reclam—and

25. This passage, apparently written without a dictionary, is poor French. Translated it reads:

Me, I am a gourmet. That's why I get so put out between the closing of the world's best cafés and the opening of little stand-up bars for tradesmen.

Lizette is a big blonde who lives at 12 Rue des Batignolles.

That's my broad.

Ah, he thought so much the better. We must have the son.

Damn it! Stymied! she said.

The morning when the court's judgment was executed had arrived. About five o'clock Charles got up and going to the window where the morning sun was shining in golden flakes, he started to work on his escape.

It's a question of your interest, he said.

Nor I, she said.

then the German and French "Nouveautés"—In Hungarian new books by Wells, Mark Twain, Claude Farrère, Dostoievsky, etc.

A Scene: Midnight—on the northern outskirt of Pest—rainy night—muddy roads—open fields (of the flat Pestian plain)—Small poor looking houses of yellow-brownish plaster.

A Scene—The southern part of Pest—road near the river—slimy with mud—lamplighter coming along to light gas lamps—long one story building of yellow brownish plaster—little filthy shop rooms—one looks in through thick archway at large filthy court behind—slum buildings.

Oliver opened the letter and read: [26]

Dear Mr. Weston:

I am enclosing herewith several critical reviews of your book which we released on September 16. As you will see, the majority of the reviewers, including those in the *Times*, the *Nation*, the *Springfield Republican*, and the *Boston Transcript*, have not been very favorable. I am very pleased, however, to enclose a most generous, if not enthusiastic, review from the reviewer of the *Christian Science Monitor* who seems unfortunately not to have understood the purport of certain scenes. Most of the critics, although they find certain passages of excellent quality, are united in declaring the book too long and as the critic in the *Transcript* has it "of a somewhat strained bizarrerie."

Thus far, I regret to say, only 237 copies have been sold, and unless some extraordinary and unforeseen circumstance occurs to boost the sale, I am afraid we must reckon on a total sale of not more than 300 copies.

I am sorry about all this, but you must understand that it is our loss as well as yours, and that for the present, at any rate, our loss is the more material. I want to add, however, that we have not lost faith in you and that we will always be glad to see any of your future work. We feel that with the coming of years and greater experience, you may also acquire the saving balance and sanity of outlook which a significant writer must have, and which, I am happy to believe, is not

26. This passage, written for "The River People" shows how Oliver Weston, then in Europe, learned of the reception of his first novel. Wolfe had earlier written of Oliver: "His book, which had been refused by two or three of the advanced publishing houses, was being brought out by one of the oldest and most conservative firms, which did a thriving business in the works of Victorian novelists, memoirs of Woodrow Wilson written by ex-cabinet ministers, and in the confessions of aged and respectable actresses and politicans. Of the old House of Hoyt, Marshall and Company, the two brothers Hoyt, of the second generation remained in charge" ("River People" ledger, pp. 413–14).

altogether lacking in your book. My brother joins with me in wishes for your present welfare and future success.

Cordially yours,
GILBERT HOYT

To this was scrawled in ink across the bottom of the page in a small nervous hand:

Let the donkey bray!
And
Better luck next time! I feel about the book exactly as I always have.

BENJAMIN HOYT

Terribly Rainy Evening—Bahnhof near Park Hotel in Budapest—slimy night—Street cars loaded with people going in all directions—67, 71, 75, 6 etc.—"To what strange port"—at railway bookstall H. G. Wells, Arnold Bennett, P. G. Wodehouse in Hungarian.

Kávéház [*coffee house*]—always, immer, toujours—There are many poor in Budapest—and in the rain they look very poor and wretched—Woman I passed on Great Boulevard last night—She was barefooted—and pushed me by the arm to keep me from treading on her feet.

Miss Heilprin—the Alter Nussbaum—the Tunnel—Margaretensinsel—her two friends—etc.[27]

Some of the writers (still living) who seem to be most widely read in Europe today:

| | |
|---|---|
| Claude Farrère | Claude Anet |
| Maurice Dekobra | Mme. Colette |
| Theodore Dreiser | Margueritte |
| John Galsworthy | Pitigrilli |
| Bernard Shaw | Wassermann |
| H. G. Wells | Thomas Mann |
| Knut Hamsun | Emil Ludwig |
| Selma Lagerloef | Molnar Ferenc |
| Arnold Bennett | Schnitzler |
| P. G. Wodehouse | Edgar Wallace |
| Sigrid Undset | Stefan Zweig (?) |

27. The Tunnel is a Budapest landmark. Nearly 400 yards long, it runs through the hill on which the castle is situated and connects the South Station with the Széchenyi Bridge. It undoubtedly reminded Wolfe of the recently completed tunnel through Beaucatcher mountain at Asheville. St. Margaret's Island in the Danube is an amusement park with a bathing beach, a spa, and a number of fine restaurants—a Hungarian version of Central Park, Newport, and Coney Island all on one river isle.

Authors Well Known in Their Own Country—But Not Specially Disseminated:

Germany

Walter Von Molo
Alice Berend
Bernard Kellermann
Fritz Von Unruh
Heinrich Mann
Agnes Gunther
Julia Von Stochhauser
Hermann Eulenberg
Klabund
H. Courths-Mahler

The Sausage Shops of Budapest—the long strong garlicy looking sausages—the big chunks of hot meat and pork steaming, and the man who fingers them over getting a suitable piece for a customer.

The mistake of growing ecstatic over mere strangeness—Oh, how musical is their speech, etc.—People do not cease to be dull because they are Hungarian.

If I should travel again what new places would I see? Dresden, Berlin, Rothenburg, Rouen, Madrid, Seville, Stockholm, Bologna.

It takes about 6 trips to Europe to get a comprehensive idea of the most visited parts.

Budapest—Saturday [*November 10*]:

After reading an English newspaper—40 hours away, or more, is London—with the bookshops in the Charing Cross Road, the vast library of the British Museum, and so on. The world is too large for mastication and digestion.

The problem of modern culture is to extract from the enormous ocean of impermanent things some of those things which will endure beyond the moment. But what?

The amazing thing about so many distinguished people is their enormous satisfaction and confidence—For example, Arnold Bennett, Mencken, H. G. Wells, Bernard Shaw. They come down hard with settled opinions on a thousand difficult things; and of many of these things they can have no very exact knowledge.

For example, a man will come flatly into print with some such statement as this: "*The Bridge of San Luis Rey* is one of the three or four important books of the year." Perhaps it is. But how far does his knowledge of the books published in a year's time go? In Germany alone over 30,000 books are published every year. How many of us in America read even 1,000 of those books? That would be only 20 a week. In Europe and America together there must be not less that 100,000 books published every year. We are told that we need critics —that we must have good critics. But spacious criticism, comprehensive criticism is becoming rapidly impossible. No man living can cope successfully with even three of the extensive modern literatures—I mean English and American, French, and German. There are men who do not hesitate to write books called Studies in Five, Ten, or Fifteen Literatures, but these pretensions are backed up with more pugnacity and brass than knowledge. We can not set ourselves up for critics in the German literature, for example, because we have read *Faust*, parts I and II, Dr. Spengler's *Decline of the West*, and two or three volumes by Von Molo, Von Unruh, Rilke, or some other figure as yet not very familiar to the American reading public.

[*Two names and Budapest addresses not in Wolfe's hand.*[28]]

Aquincum—Roman Soldier's Stone? [29]

IMP CAESARI

TIT AELI O

HADRIANO

ANTOINO

AUG PIO P P

COS III

LEG II ADI P F

POSUIT

The oil tanks and a railway embankment nearby.

Museums, Etc. This Time
Boulogne—Old City, Churches, etc.

28. Two women's names and addresses are written in separate feminine hands at this point. The first is Margaret Surányi, a well-known Hungarian writer whom Wolfe apparently met—probably in a bookshop. The second is Irma A. Apor, who operated a shop on Turr Istvan Street specializing in Hungarian needlework. Her business card, printed in four languages, is still in the notebook.

29. Wolfe visited the ruins of the Roman Colony of Aquincum near Budapest. The inscription reads: "The Second Legion Adiutrix, ever loyal, has erected this in honor of the Emperor-Caesar Titus Aelius Hadrianus Antionus Pius, Father of his Country, in his third consulship." Legion II Adiutrix had its headquarters in Aquincum, and the inscription dates from 140 to 145 A.D.

Amiens—Cathedral, Picture Gallery.
Paris—Carnavalet, Louvre, Luxembourg, Notre Dame, Cluny.
Brussels—Old Picture Gallery, New Picture Gallery, Hotel De Ville, Cinquantenaire Gallery, Edith Cavell Barracks, Louvain, Churches, etc.
Antwerp, Malines.
Cologne—Picture Gallery, Press Exhibition, Natural History Museum, Asian Museum, Cathedral.
Frankfurt—Old Houses, City Historical Museum, Picture Gallery, Sculpture Gallery, Arts and Decoration Gallery, Town Hall, Old City, Dom, Goethe's House, African and Tribal Museum, etc.
Mainz—Picture Gallery and Roman Antiquities Gallery.
Wiesbaden—Picture Gallery and Roman Antiquities Gallery, Newberg.
Bonn—Beethoven's Birth house, Poppelsdorfer Castle, Church, etc.
Munich—Alt Pinakothek, New Pinakothek, Schwanthaler, German Museum, Glyptothek, Staatsgalerie, Gabelsberger, Mus. and Library, Nymphenburg, Bavarian Museum, Schack Gallery, Opera House, Residenz, Nat'l Theater, etc.
Oberammergau—Church, [Freskomalerei?], Lang's Baroque Museum and Woodworks, etc.
Vienna—Kunsthistorisches Mus., Stefanskirche, Natural Hist. Mus., Hofburg, Upper Belvedere, Schönbrunn, and Carriage houses.
Budapest—Picture Gallery, Agricultural Mus., Royal Castle, Coronation Church, Aquincum, Houses of Parliament, Ethnographical Museum, Trip to Mezökövesd.

The Ethnographical Museum in Budapest is the most interesting thing I have seen there.[30]

30. Part of his enthusiasm for the Ethnographical Museum was due to his interest in costumes, which had been whetted by Mrs. Bernstein's activities as a designer. He wrote her enthusiastically about the museum. "This is the second fine thing I have found here—for it is so good that it would be worth *you* coming across Europe to see it. It is a place that has been divinely created for you—I was at once enormously excited and terribly disappointed because you could not be here. . . . It is first of all the most magnificent costume museum I have ever seen. . . . There were a few very beautiful Chinese and Indian things, but what interested me most were the costumes of the Baltic and near-Asiatic peoples. You can almost follow the trail of the East beginning in Hungary . . . ." Unpublished part of his letter of November 13.

How I Murdered The Old Woman In The Antiquariat.[31]

The Ulloi Ut, Andrassy Ut, Museum Ut.
Stenmer ódon, Gróf Tisza István Utca.[32]

The above is a book antiquariat—Some magnificent old books and prints displayed in the windows—Many of them English. [*Followed by a long list of titles.*]

WIEN—Bookshops I can remember:
2 in The Mariahilfer Str
2 on Ring above Opera
1 on Ring below Opera
3 on Kohlmarkt
3 on Wollzeile
1 on Singerstrasse
2 on Rotenturmstrasse
1 on Kärntnerstrasse
3 on Graben
2 or three near Graben
1 near Albertina
1 (art store) near Albertina
1 on Wiedner Hauptstrasse
1 on Schottengasse
1 on Schottenbastei.

Sunday [*November 11*]—

Before I forget—Five minutes after leaving Mezökövesd—[33] Just passing next village—great haystacks—vast plowed fields black and

31. This is apparently another story, like the one about the death of Mrs. Richards, which Wolfe wished to try out on his friends to see if they could discern the difference between truth and fiction. The gist of the rather Dostoievskian tale is this: in the darkness of an old bookstore in Budapest, Wolfe choked the proprietress to death because she was a cruel, vicious old woman who had made a whore out of her daughter. The setting was drawn from the "book antiquariat" on Ulloi St. in Budapest.

Wolfe told the story to one person, at least, who believed it—John Terry. For years after Wolfe's death, Terry circulated the rumor that Wolfe had committed a murder. Richard Kennedy first heard the story in 1943, when Terry asked him to check the police records in Budapest, should the tides of war carry him there.

32. Ut and Utca are the Hungarian words for street.

33. Mezökövesd is a Hungarian village which was well known for its needlework. It had become a tourist attraction, and visiting celebrities were often taken there. When the Duke of Windsor, for example, visited Hungary as Prince of Wales he was shown Mezökövesd. For Wolfe's account of his own trip, see *Letters*, pp. 150–57.

green—Then the village with the small white houses and the strawed pigsties and barns—Great plain and vast fields all around me—but to the right low hills—The vast melancholy of this earth with the grey leaden skies. In scenery how? This one of the most astonishing sights I have ever seen—The thing that will remain is the square before the church at 2 o'clock—Blocks and battallions of young men and women each by each—The blinding color of those costumes—the great neck-pieces—first part seemingly delicately embroidered silk with a great thick fringe of yellow, crimson, or red—The aprons of men and women alike—The pleated skirts—the thick ruffled folds kicked up in a billow by the feet—the enormous variety and color of the skirts—the head pieces—rather several covered by elaborate scarfs—of dark blue or black for older women—bright for the girls—Young men with their brilliant aprons, boots, derby hats (with green or yellow bands) perched on top of their head.

The great coat of the old men—A solid stiff sheet of white wool or velvet with elaborate trimings at wrist, along shoulders, etc.—One of the most dignified garments I have ever seen.

Monday morning—

Slept 12 or 14 hours after returning from Mezökövesd yesterday —Today magnificent bright day glittery with sunlight—Day at Mezökövesd one of the most remarkable I have spent in Europe—Man at hotel tells me that the drummers in uniform after church are reading out official announcements—names of people delinquent for taxes, etc.

[*To a long list of European cities and a population list of cities in England, Wolfe appends the question:*] But what do most Europeans know of Europe?

The trip back from Mezökövesd—greater part the vast wet dreary plain—with now and then a village—Enormous steppes of plowed and fallow land running straight away to the horizon. The great wooden farming implements.

Magyar [Apaszerep?]—This is the name of the great white coats embroidered so magnificently.

Magyar Kanász (shepherd?) [*swineherd*]—The saddles and bridles black leather—The shepherd's sticks—The great horn and spoons of horn.

1,000 VOLUMES

| | |
|---|---|
| Works of Jokai | 100 |
| Works of Balzac | 100 |
| Works of Karl May | 100 (or 150) |
| Works of H. G. Wells | 100 |
| Works of Goethe | 100 |
| Works of Voltaire | 100 |
| Works of Dumas | 250 |
| Works of W. Scott | 100 |
| Works of B. Lytton | 100 |
| | 1,050 |
| Works of Shakespeare | 2,000 |
| Works of Lope De Vega | 500 |
| Works of Grote | 50 |
| Works of Moliere | 1,000 |
| Works of Rousseau | 500 |
| Works of Liberty Boys | 1,000 |
| Works of Nick Carter | 1,000 |
| Works of H. B. Wright | 100 |
| " " Curwood | 100 |
| " " Zane Grey | 100 |
| Works of Edgar Wallace | 1,000 |
| Works of Jack London | 100 |
| Works of Bennett | 100 |
| Works of Paul V. Margueritte | 100 |

From the Daily Mail:

New York, Nov. 7, 1928: Herbert Clark Hoover, 56 years old, who made a fortune of $8,000,000 from mining industries in Russia, China, Australia, Peru, and Arizona, before he left business to enter politics fifteen years ago, was today elected thirty-first President of the United States by a popular vote of 7,000,000 and an electoral majority of 446 to 87—the most overwhelming victory in the history of American politics.

The new President of the United States is remarkable for the vitality of an ox, the precision of an electric clock, the mathematical exactness of a yearbook, and the colossal dulness that one might expect from the union of all these qualities.[34]

34. Wolfe, a warm supporter of Al Smith, was greatly disappointed at Hoover's victory. For his comments on the election see *Letters,* p. 150.

But what is good?

In the bookshops visited today—The fine vols. of costume books I was shown everywhere—Then Jokai—Then a Hungarian series corresponding to Reklam—Then the Tauchnitz editions—The innumerable books on technical subjects, medicine—hundreds of depressing looking pamphlets.

[*A list of the major languages and numbers of people who speak them.*]

An Inquiry Into the State of My Culture:

I know a good deal about
- Amer. Lit.
- Eng. Lit.
- The Theatre.

I know considerable about
- French Lit.
- German Lit.

I know some of the Best of
- Latin Lit.
- Greek Lit.

As to those people writing in South America, I confess my total ignorance. There are forty or fifty nations there, and I am sure each is publishing thousands of books a year. The only one I remember is a gentleman who came to New York last year with his wife and ten or 16 children. He was taking them around the world on the prize money from a novel.

A Library for a Young Man of Today:

*Phaedo*—Plato
*Voyage to Italy*—Goethe
*The Idiot*—Dostoievski
Histories of Herodotus
*Penthesilea*—Kleist
Stories—Poe
*Peer Gynt*—Ibsen
*Germinal*—Zola
Poems—T. Hardy

*Hamlet*—Shakespeare
*Ulysses*—James Joyce
*The Wild Ass' Skin*—Balzac
*Faust*—Goethe
*Queen Victoria*—Strachey
*Poems and Ballads*—Swinburne
*The Father*—Strindberg
*Jean Christophe*—Rolland
*History of Gargantua*—Rabelais
*Penguin Island*—A. France
*The Cloister and the Hearth*—Reade
*Don Juan*—Byron
*The Man of Property*—Galsworthy
*The Death of Nick Carter*—Philippe Soupault
*The Decline of the West*—Oswald Spengler
Lyrics of Heine
Grimm's Fairy Tales
*Buddenbrooks*—Thomas Mann
*Hunger*—Knut Hamsun
*Oktobertag*—Georg Kaiser

But I am tired—the desire for it *All* comes from an evil gluttony in me—a weakness—a lack of belief.

Armistice day in the English and American papers and all the twaddle printed about it—Striking of noble attitudes, fine speeches, etc. It is to vomit!

In America, the Election—In Germany, Zeppelin flight—In Austria, Revolution—In France, Kellogg Pact—Geneva, secret agreements, etc.—In England, Naval Dispute, Unemployment, etc.

Men selling books who come into restaurants and coffeehouses in Budapest. (Can you make something out of this?)

Foyles in the Charing Cross Road—London (1,000,000 books).

I should like to see: Her Face—All wreathed in flowerlike smiles and loveliness.

Tuesday [*November 13*]—

Today to the book store of the Franklin Society—Probably the largest one here—Spent the afternoon looking over books there—I bought: Eng. Hungarian Dictionary, a Book by Jean Paul, *Hamlet* in

Hungarian—[35] Books on sale there: Jos. Conrad, Jack London, Galsworthy, etc. in Hungarian—They brought me a book profusely illustrated with horrors called *A Septulis*—which they said they had published—Also works of Molnar Ferenc in 20 vols.

German Travel Books fill several shelves—When the Germans travel apparently they try to get a book out of it.

How many letters have I written Aline?
1—From New York
1—From Boulogne
3—From Paris
2—From Brussels
3—From Cologne
1—From Wiesbaden
1—From Frankfurt
2—From Munich (Vienna)
2—From Vienna
1—From Budapest
1—From Budapest [*sic*]
All my letters together would make a great stack.

Insel Verlag—in reading over lists of romances and novels one is impressed by number of translations from foreign tongues—especially French and English.

In a book window opposite museum I counted 570 books—many of them in editions.

Tomorrow—Go to picture gallery again and gallery opposite it, and City Park.

At the [*Fine Arts*] museum again this morning—Modern pictures very bad—of the Hungarian School—Some spectacular pieces by the Germans viz.—The Sphynx with great evil living breasts kissing a man who sinks exhausted in her embrace—one or two Lenbachs—a picture of Mme. Lenbach by Munkácsy with vast vulgar breasts.

If we consider separately the works of the writers at present most sought after in Europe, we will not find any remarkable breath

35. The English-Hungarian Dictionary and the Hungarian edition of *Hamlet* are still in Wolfe's library. So are three of Jean Paul's works, *Flegeljahre, Levana,* and *Meine Kindheit,* but there is no indication as to which one he purchased at this time.

[*sic*] or universality in their selection of subjects. *Viz.* Zola, Dickens, Tolstoi, Dostoievski.

A Hungarian shoemaker—supposedly best in the world.

Bookshops in Budapest—[*list of all bookshops he knows in Budapest*]—Who buys the books?

Thurs. Nov. 15—

[*Bookshops on*] Lantos Ut—Modern German, French and Hungarian books—about 125.

Szechenyi Könyvkereskedés [*bookstore*]—on main street going to bridge—about 200 in window.

Kleine Anzeiger [*Little Notice*]

Widow, 33 years old, from good family, speaks English and French well, desires honorable companionship with young professional man—preferably law, surgery, or engineering. Can furnish photograph on request, and will be glad to exchange letters.[36]

36. Wolfe wrote Mrs. Bernstein the day after he returned to Vienna and included a version of this notice, which he said he concocted from many he had read. "Today—November European weather—grey, dismal thick and heavy. No wonder they get ahead so slowly. And everywhere! Everywhere! The interminable coffee house—they are doped and their dreams are such poor ones—to sit in the coffee house and dream and dream—what? To read perhaps one of the thousands of little want ads—soliciting for prostitution, worded with preposterous elegance—and to dream it may be true: 'Elegant and beautiful young widow, aged 32, from fine old family, with assured income of 600 schillings a month desires honorable companionship with young professional man—law or medicine preferred. Exchange of letters and photographs desired with meeting in coffee house as a result. Only the highest references considered. Address PXZ Kleine Anzeiger 426,' etc. I have made this up myself, but it is typical of thousands." Letter to Aline Bernstein, November, 17, 1928.

## *Pocket Notebook 6*

## *November 16, 1928, to December 7, 1928*

*Wolfe bought this notebook in Budapest and began making entries in the railroad station as he was leaving the city. He went on to another sojourn in Vienna and finally departed for Florence, shortly after hearing from Maxwell Perkins that Scribner's was interested in his book. His intense absorption with Viennese life is reflected all through the notebook, not only because of his state of mind but also because of his plan to set part of "The River People" in Vienna.*

---

[*Written on the inside of the front cover:*]

Things Seen in Budapest in 2 Weeks:
The Zoo
The Picture Gallery—3 times
The Parliament
The Castle
The Coronation Church
The National Museum
The Ernst Museum
Aquincum
The Ethnographisches Museum
The Industrial Museum
Mezökövesd
The Agricultural Museum, etc.
Divers churches, theaters, book shops, restaurants, etc.
The Schwabenberg [*Svábhegy*], Johannisberg [*Jánoshegy*], Margueriten Island
Also extensive personal investigation

Friday, Nov. 16—

In station at Budapest getting ready to leave—4:30—The last two weeks have been crowded and interesting—I believe I have captured a very real impression of this city which may be of use to me—Today, home about 4 a.m. after a last circuit through Great Boulevard and main streets noting book windows—In the train yards at Budapest the great continental expresses waiting their time—Istanboul, Belgrad, Budapest—Budapest, Wien, Berlin, Hamburg—Budapest, Bucharest, Constantinople—outside of B. P.—the bright scattered lights—the open fields—the road on the extreme outer girdle—the trains plying across the country—outside of town—the factories—these things among the present realities of Europe.

A mystery explained—The great blaze of light I saw coming in two weeks ago is really the heart of Budapest—the Gellert hill—and the quai—what we do from the station is make a curve around the outskirts of the city, cross the Danube lower down and come up behind the hills on the Buda side (Budapest-Kelerbold).

[*Sketch of the river, city, train station, and the sweep of the railroad toward Vienna.*]

We left at 4:35—man has just come by for tickets 4:45—8:57 in Vienna.

Today—Got up, went to the Passport Office across the river where I paid two dollars more for letting my time run over—It probably was not necessary—and my stay here has certainly been worth the extra two dollars—Went into bookshop opposite and bought several French books and looked over their stock—They had the Tauchnitz, the French books, a wall full of Reklams, the Art books, the blue books, the Göschen's and a wall full of technical books, but they showed me the same costume books and wanted the top price for them—as well as for the little folders of motifs.

Went back to Travel Bureau where I had hard time getting away from queer woman—wanted me to sell articles for her in New York—Describes herself as a "guide"—woman of intelligence forced to these expedients to earn living—will introduce you to merchants in order to get commission.

Reached Gyor seven o'clock after a solid run of 2:30 without stop—Sisters got out—Hungarian station in November—Uniformed men inside station moving about—queer rumblings and hisses from the bowels of the 3rd class carriage—Tracks stacked up—Rather Dismal lights, etc.—Soldier still with us—Has begun to carve loaf of bread—Sausage will presently appear—Yes.

Border Hegyeshalom—7:45–50.

Two cops stand outside train—to keep people from escaping, I suppose.

[*Wolfe returned to Vienna on Friday, November 16.*]

I was still too shaky when I told my lie to make it convincing. I should like to know what it is that made you doubt it; because in this way I might be able to find the strange gap which separates the real from the imagined. I still have confidence in my power to lie, but I lose that confidence when I write to you—I think I have never told you an important lie without soon after giving you the truth; but I have usually felt you knew when I lied anyway. I do not know why the death of this old woman should seem "a story." Death would now be a natural circumstance—she must be past 75. Perhaps there is a belief in us that all death is unnatural and melodramatic. There was also a desire in me to finish my story—to make this affair in Munich an episode with a beginning and an end. The old woman strung on somehow like a loose end—I wanted to complete and end her in my experience just as I had other people.[1]

Saturday [*November 17*]—

Last night at Oesterreichischer Hof—this morning to Cook's—found 2 letters (in 2 weeks!) from Aline—also letter from man and letter from Scribner's.

Dear Mr. Peters: [2]

I have been in Budapest for several weeks, and your letter, which was sent on from Munich, has waited here in Vienna for me.

1. Draft of a letter Wolfe wrote to Mrs. Bernstein on November 17, the day after he returned from Budapest. This paragraph concerns his report of Mrs. Richards' death, which he had included in the account he sent Mrs. Bernstein, and which she had questioned. In the letter immediately preceding this selection Wolfe wrote: "You say the part about Oberammergau is a good story. I hope so. I should like to get something out of it. As you indicate in your letter, the part about the old lady dying is a lie."

2. It is now amusing to see that Wolfe began the draft of his first letter to Maxwell Perkins, who was to become so important in Wolfe's life, by calling him Peters. Perkins had written Wolfe on October 22 telling him of Scribner's interest. (For the text of Perkins' letter, see *Editor to Author, the Letters of Maxwell E. Perkins*, ed. John Hall Wheelock [New York, 1950] p. 61.) Though the letter is typed, there is no typed signature. Perkins signed his usual signature, and at a casual glance it might be mistaken for Peters. At least Wolfe read it that way, for the same day he wrote Mrs. Bernstein: "I came here from Budapest last night. Today at Cook's I found two letters from you. Also news from home, and a letter from a Mr. Peters (I believe) on [*sic*] Scribner's. His letter had words of praise and admiration—with reservations indicated—and he would like to see me." Wolfe then proceeded to write this draft, which he further revised. For the text of the letter he actually sent Perkins, see *Letters*, pp. 158–59.

I am coming back to New York from Italy in December, and I shall come to see you within a day or two after I arrive.

Your letter gives me hope and confidence. For six months now I have not looked at the book. I was very cast down about it; I have written part of a new one abroad, but I have been to too many places to work steadily. I have made several books of notes, learned to read German, and got my nose and head broken.

I have had almost all of Europe I can stand at present. I am coming back to America to go to work.

People sometimes do damage by too much praise, but sometimes they do damage by not enough. Your words of praise in your letter for the parts of my book you liked have been worth more than their weight in diamonds.

Nobody realizes better than I do, now, how unreasonable it was to expect publication from the manuscript as it now stands. It has been almost six months since I looked at it. But I believe I could come back to it now with a fresher and more critical mind. I know it is far too long, and that obscene passages—which did not really seem obscene to me at the time—must come out.

Your letter gives me hope that you are seriously interested in the book, and might consider it seriously if *several important revisions* were made in it. I want you to know that I am eager and willing to make these changes. I think you already know one of my difficulties—I know something about writing and I have a great deal that I want to say—but I write too much. I can criticize wordiness in others but I am not always able to criticize it in myself.

I know that eventually one can depend only on oneself, but I have always hoped that I would someday meet an older person, with a good critical mind, who would tell me *exactly* what he thought good and what he thought bad in my work. I know this is a large order; but most people say "it is too long," or "some parts were interesting and others dull," and other generalities which do not help me at all.

Is there someone on Scribner's staff who might be interested enough in my book to *argue* with me? On many points I am sure he would not have to argue at all. But it would be wrong for me to say "Yes, sir," to everything in a spirit of weak agreement.

Herder & Co.—Wollzeile—A Catholic place [*followed by a list of books in the window*].

What writers in America today? Dreiser, Mencken, O'Neill, Lewis, Cabell, Anderson, Stein, Pound, Hemingway, Wilder.

Germany: Thomas Mann, Ludwig, Kaiser, Wassermann,

Schnitzler, Hauptmann, Sudermann, Hoffmannsthal, Sternheim, Hasenclever, Heinrich Mann, Agnes Günther, Eulenberg, Courths-Maler, Walter Von Molo, Von Aurak, Alice Berend, Julia Stochhauser, Graf Keyserling, Bruno Frank, Feuchtwanger, Alfred Neumann, Franz Werfel, Stefan Zweig.

France: Gide, Anet, Farrère, Romains, Rolland, Dekobra, Vautel, Bourget, Courteline, De Robert, De Régnier, Bordeaux, D'Houville, Tinayre, MacOrlan, Giraudoux, La Rochelle, Soupault, Montherlant, Lenormard, Cocteau, Duvernois, Courteline, Leon Daudet, Mme. Colette, Duhamel, Barbusse, Les Margueritte, Escholier, Mauriac, Bourdet, Larbaud, Carco, Morand, Jacques de Lacretelle, Paléologue, M. Rostand, Maurois, Jaloux, René Benjamin, Roger Martin du Gard.

English: Shaw, Wells, Bennett, Edgar Wallace, Somerset Maugham, Conrad, J. M. Barrie, Galsworthy.

H. L. Mencken—"Die Deutschen Amerikaner"—in *Der Rundschau*—a German Review.

Sunday—

Schubert Celebration all this next week—It began yesterday.[3]

Went to Siller's for coffee—Magnificent day—cold blue and sparkling—Donau Canal gleaming—Diana Bad bright in sunshine—Vienna curves along stream right to the hills which look very close. [*Small sketch of the scene.*]

On quotations—The practice of 19th century "good" writers was to decorate their compositions with neat little patterns of quotations.[4] That practice still persists in a great deal of the correct writing of the present—viz., the essays and leading articles of The *Atlantic Monthly*, the *Spectator*, *Harpers* and the *Century*, The *London Mercury*, etc. The quotation habit is generally a vicious one, since more often than not it has not even so worthy a design as to borrow from stronger and greater people an emphasis and energy and clearness that we have not, but rather serves as a sort of diploma to certify our culture—said culture consisting in our ability to quote scraps from Lamb, Dickens, John Keats, Browning, Dr. Johnson, and Matthew Arnold. The distortion this works upon the original sinew of the mind

3. The Schubert celebration honored the great Viennese composer on the centennial of his death, November 19, 1828.

4. "At La Regénce:" is written above this paragraph, and the whole passage is used on page 679 of OT&R.

is incalculable—writing becomes a waltz of pseudo-courtliness, neatly designed to arrive before Lamb with a bow and to be handed by Dickens to Lord Tennyson with a graceful flourish. The phrase "apt quotation" is one of the most misleading phrases ever invented. Most quotations so far from being apt to any purpose, are distinguished by all the ineptitude a politician displays when, having spoken for twenty minutes on the Nicaraguan question, says: "That reminds me of a little story I heard the other day. It seems there were two Irishmen whose names were Pat and Mike"—then proceeds to a discussion of the Prohibition issue after his convulsed audience is somewhat recovered.

A man who in the America of today can rely for his spiritual support, and take his vision of life from the 19th century English Victorian writers, although he may please himself on his rounded wisdom, and on the correct vision he has of life, is yet only a little mean fellow—a mean pretender to a scheme that only at its rare best was good, and at its average was mean and little.

*Neues Wiener Tagblatt*—that's the one on Sunday with 40–50 pages of little advertisements.

Schubert Feier [*celebration*]—Today over all—Saw the fountain unveiled—or rather waited in great crowd to see it—Then to City Hall 5:30—after dark—Gothic spires and traceries lighted from within with elec. and from without with searchlights.

The character of the Wiener Coffee House—Tonight (Sunday, Nov. 18) ate at Coffeehouse next to Burgtheater—People here are mostly more or less respectable mistresses, rather liberal and fast modern families, etc.

*Arbeiter Zeitung* [*Workers Newspaper*] for Sunday—Page and a half in small print of announcements of social democratic meetings in different sections of the city—"The Sexual Problem and The Proletariat Frau," "Russia's Problem," "Hungary and The Little Entente," "Hat Making," "The Sexual Problem of The Proletarian Child"—etc.

Schubert—Schubert everywhere—ceremonies at his monument, masses in the churches, songfests before the Rathaus—and the soft sensitive faces of the people—the poor people—as they listened to the music—Music in an open place is only the great ghost of music.

The "American" in the Budapestian operetta.

The Germans are not good story tellers—their novelists of the 19th century—Storm, Keller, Heyse, etc.—were *local* writers. Such a story as *Immensee* or *Der Grüne Heinrich* belongs to the German character and is interesting chiefly to them.

Best story tellers are probably the French. After them the English. The character of the French language lends itself to the telling of a story. It is clear, distinct, and rapid. Clearness and simplicity of structure are qualities that have been emphasized by the French. Renan said that he was grateful for the narrow confinement of the French language, since it had disciplined him, and forced him to win whatever success he had won within its comparatively narrow limits.

If a man who lived a solitary life in some primitive place, but who nevertheless spoke and read English easily, must form his entire opinion of the modern world—which he has never seen—from reading daily *The Times* newspaper or *The Telegraph*—What sort of picture would he get?

First—page after page of classified advertisement: Flat, St. John's Wood £125 per annum, Furn. £50, etc. Headmaster of Successful Prep. School wants £1,000, etc.

Then the News—Suicide and Murder case—Coroner's Reproof—Cruel and Cowardly Letter—etc.

Story of ship catastrophe.

Wills and Bequests—Brewer's Million.

Day in Parliament—Snowden, Baldwin, Sir ——, and Lt. Col. Sir ——, Socialist Jeers, Conservative Cheers, etc.

Sale at Sotheby's: Kipling Letter—Thackeray and Dickens letter—Kelmscott Chaucer.

Theaters and Music.

Court and Society.

Borah on Coolidge's Speech.

French Reaction to Premier's Statement.

Prince in South Africa.

Correspondence—Smoking in Theaters.

Dean Inge's Speech.

Meetings and Events Today.

[*Vienna, Sunday, November 18, 1928*]

Dear Aline:

Today was winter. It was beautiful and bright and sharp as we often have it in The Stytes, but as they rarely have it here. I went down first thing in the morning—that is, a little before noon—to the Danube Canal. All the buildings along the water had caught the sparkle of the day. The dingy faded poverty of this poor town was wiped out by the sun. And the hills of the Wiener Wald were bright and clear beyond the river—they seemed very near, and are. Do you remember when we first came here—the glorious weather, and all the gay people—they forget everything if the sun shines and they have the price of a coffee or a beer. For miles the Donau Canal was crowded with people bathing—all of them the honey-blonde color of Maria Jentzen. I thought they were the happiest, handsomest people I had ever seen, and this the most glorious place.

It is a glorious place, and the people are naturally good—but it is a sad place, and a terribly poor place.

The World Figures: Shakespeare, Goethe, Voltaire, Dante, Dickens, Dostoievski, Strindberg, Ibsen, Hamsun, Balzac, Heine, Jack London, Upton Sinclair, H. G. Wells, Dreiser, Shaw, Wilde, [*Maurice*] Dekobra, Edgar Wallace, Galsworthy, Lagerloef.

In *The Telegraph* today one little ad. caught my notice—Family will receive guests—or some such nausea—also added—young people dancing, going about in vicinity—I get a picture of it for a moment—Jolly, comrady—cheerio old gal and old boy stuff—of course, perfectly frigid—Even if anything ever happens between them I would not believe it—or if I did I would feel sorry and ashamed for them—I would feel rather ashamed and dirty—like walking into old maid in the bath tub.

Are there any *luscious* Englishwomen? I am told they can "go quite mad"—and all that—but I always see lantern jaws and false teeth.

English ad—"To clean your false teeth"—etc.

There is always the moment when we must begin to write. There are always the hundreds, the thousands of hours of struggle, of getting up, of pacing about, of sitting down, of laborious uneven accomplishment. During the time of actual work, what else besides ourselves can help us? Can we call to mind then the contents of 20,000 books? Can we depend on anything other than ourselves for help? [5]

5. Wolfe used this passage for Eugene's notebook in OT&R, p. 678.

Schubert Festival—Today—Monday—7:30 tonight Grosser Musikvereinssaale—Fest Kenzert of Wiener Männergesangverein—Ticket agency—Right side of Graben.

---

[*It was Wolfe's good fortune to be in Vienna during the Schubert Festival. Since he was probably stung by Mrs. Bernstein's remark that his taste in music was "cheap," he availed himself of this opportunity with an interest he seldom showed in music but usually reserved only for art museums. His reaction to this musical feast is given in a letter to her written November 25.*]

This has been Schubert week—he died one hundred years ago and the ceremonies in his honor this past week have been endless. I have attended three or four of them—my old fatal weakness of being a hundred desires and only one body, one active pair of legs, and one brain has kept me from seeing *all* the things and being in all the places. But I stood in a huge crowd last Sunday wondering what it was all about—finally the crowd dispersed having seen no more than I had. I walked up the street and found a new memorial which had been unveiled in his honor that afternoon—a statue, and as foolish and meaningless as most statues are—a naked lady sitting down a la Rodin with her head bent over. The relation of all this to Schubert's music failed to pierce my dull hide, but all the people stood there patiently, full of their devotion. Their devotion to him is astonishing—his picture is everywhere, books about him are everywhere; he has been sung, played, memorialized in churches, opera, concert houses and public places all this week—and always to great crowds. I think Schubert has become a great symbol to these people, standing for all that was best and greatest in "the good old time." He is Vienna incarnated—the thousand pictures of him showing him playing his pieces in warm looking 1825 drawing rooms, with lovely women and intelligent sensitive looking men around him; they show him walking through the rich old streets of the town with his friends; or sitting at a table in the court of a wine tavern in Grinzing composing a song, while young people make love at nearby tables, and so on. Schubert stands for what was fine and affectionate and tender in the life of Vienna—the people know this and he is rooted in their hearts forever. Last Sunday after dark I went to the Rathaus. A huge crowd of people was gathered outside, the great Vienna Men's Chorus was assembled on the steps, singing his songs. Most of the people were poor, shabbily dressed, but with that elegance and delicacy that I have never found in any comparable degree elsewhere—and as the great choir sang his songs, a strange and radiant tenderness shown in the faces of all the poor people—this is the only place where I have seen the religious emotion. What it is I do not know, but I know it comes only with pain and hardship and poverty, and that in America we do not know what it is, and should not. This music in the open air at night was glorious—the great men's chorus is a marvelous instrument, the director plays on it as on a great organ. Its single great voice whispered against the Rathaus, then it would rise like a wind, and be given back again. The Rathaus was all lighted in and out among its Gothic traceries and the effect was very beautiful—like illuminated lace. Later I went to hear this same chorus in the big concert hall—they sang a dozen of Schubert's songs. The music was simple and tender and grand; in addition, he had sense enough—which is rare in a musician—to choose great poetry for his songs.

---

Summoned by the song.

Estensische Mus.[6]

Ananda—Buddha Des Unendlichen Lichtes.[7]

"Alle schuld zu tilgen, und alles gute zu wirken." [*To nullify the guilt and originate the good.*]

"With the greatest tolerance Buddhism, which had already Indian and Chinese godhood in itself united, took also into itself the uncountable Japanese gods."

Masks: 1. For Tempelherren, 2. For No-Plays, 3. For New Year's Fest, 4. Personae.

Turkey—waterpipes—splendid shoes [*sketch*].

Siberia—skins—Costumes of a primitive people—Magnificent boots of soft skin with beadwork designs.

Magnificent Goldfisch fassen with horrible dragon-looking white wings.

Tang Dynasty—600–900—Mandschu Dynasty—1650–1900.

Whoever more for another does, does more for himself; whoever gives more to another, evenso richer is he—Lao Tse.

6. What Wolfe means is the Este Art Collection (Estensische Kunstsammlung), which formed a section of the Art History Museum. The collection formerly belonged to Archduke Franz Ferdinand von Österrich-Este, whose assassination at Sarajevo in 1914 touched off World War I.

7. This note and those immediately following were made on a visit to the Ethnographical Museum. Ananda was Buddha's first cousin and one of his principal disciples. Some of Wolfe's scrawled museum notes are illegible and have been deleted.

Taoismus, Buddhismus, Confeucinismus.
Little dumpy figures above Greek grave urns.

[*A list of plays then running in Vienna, theaters, and times of performance.*]

To get an idea of the state of culture of Europe one must come to central Europe. The German peoples have an enormous documentary and collecting power. They have egoism, but not the absurd vanity of the Frenchman, and they collect unto themselves the best—or at least the most reputed—things on earth. Thus, if you gaze long in their windows, you will sell your soul to hell, you will want, and your soul will break under the leaden weight of desperation; but you will find there, among all the horrible jungle of their books,—you will find there the skeleton of the world literature.

Oliver crying out loudly and standing against the glass of the bookshop windows.

That which I once held dear
Is lost
Only the jungle here.[8]

That which I loved and knew is far away; it stifles, it burns me —my loneliness
Only who has gone through it, knows what I grieve.

Yes, I have seen a star.
But I have not known it
Near to the eye but far
Too far to own it
Who made us stars has given
Only the seeing
Only the sight of heaven
Far from our being
Only the little skull
And the [terrible, *marked out*] thirst and the dust
And the heart overfull
That can [not burst, *marked out*]
The visions too great for us

8. This entry and the two following are trial lines for a poem Wolfe was writing.

The wisdom too late for us
The food that gives hunger
The wine that gives thirst
The jungle, the desert
And no end to our pain.

---

[*Wolfe continued to work on his poem until November 29, when he sent it to Mrs. Bernstein with an explanatory letter.*]

In my last letter which I sent off to you this morning I believe I threatened to send you a poem. Here it is—I have decided there is no use in trying to polish the unpolishable; so I send it to you about as it was at first. It is not much of a poem, but it may show you a little of what I have been feeling here recently. In the first act of Faust as they play it here he goes up out of his old Gothic chamber on to the roof of his house where he looks through a glass at the stars, falling prostrate at length at his inability to go farther than he has. I think this scene—and of course the whole play of Faust with its statement of my *own* trouble —worked on me unconsciously and resulted in the poem. I hope you are able to read it—the last lines in particular are for you alone. You will see that I do not agree with Robert Browning about stars and their heart-opening habits; but if his eminent Shade is troubled he has the satisfaction of knowing that although my lines may have more truth, his have certainly more beauty.

[*The poem bears the headnote:*] This is my poem. Don't know what to call it—It is for you.

Who only has seen a star
  Never has known it.
  So near to the eye, but far—
Too far to own it.

Who made us stars has given
  Only the seeing—
Only the sight of heaven
  Far from our being
Only the prostrate brain
  The loaded heart,
Only the toil, the pain,
  The fruitless part.

Only the flaming wish,
  And health to fan it.
A spirit too great for the flesh
And too small for a planet
  Too great for its little cage
  Too small for a star,
The grand heart beats hope into cinders, youth into age,
  Waging vain war
Searching till it goes blind
  The barren quarries;
Eating the Earth to find
  What a star is.
We who are men are greater than men
  And less than our spirit.
Climbing half-heavenward, falling to earth again
We starve in the jungle and die in the plain
  Seeing heaven, but too weak to near it.

If starmaker made the man,
  He made him small;
Puny in reach and span,
  Thirsting for all.
Little of skull and bone,
An exile, a stranger, alone,
With a vision too great for him,
And wisdom too late for him;
And the bed that's in wait for him
  Under a stone.
  —That is his bell,
  Not that he fell;
But that, like a god half arisen,
  He can look upon stars from his prison
  And find no help for his pain
But death in the jungle, the wind and the rain.

Who only has seen a star
  Never has known it.
All that *I* know of a certain star
  Is—it is far.
I do not own it.

(END)

Tues.:

City Historical Museum, Reit Schule [*Riding School*], Liechtenstein or Harrach Gallery, Krypt.

Akt Photos—Wiedner Hauptstrasse 116.[9]

Jeder Mann Ein Casanova.

Tuesday [*November 20*]:

City Historical Museum—In the Rathaus—Interesting—as a memorial—Grillparzer's working room and library.[10] Anzengruber, Suppé—etc.[11] The pictures and prints of old Wien—Photographs of 1858 etc.—The strange real yet shabby look of things photographed when cameras first came in.—Then to lunch in Rathaus Keller—Then to Cook's, stopping in at church at head of Kohlmarkt—bought cigarette holder on Graben—Then to Cook's. Found cable from Fred, letter from Mrs. Roberts, Don MacRae's wedding invitation, then up Kärntner Strasse to Anne Gasse—lovely old houses there. Pfarrkirche of St. Anne there. Then to Akt Museum—to steamship offices—to book store—to Cafe L'Europe—and to hotel.

Grillparzer's Library: Shakespeare's Plays, Beaumont and Fletcher, Classiques Latins, Fichte's Werke, Novellai Italiano, Aristotles, Flavius Josephus, Comedia di Calderón.

The head waiter in Cafe L'Europe (Vater ?).

*Till Eulenspiegel*—Burg [*Theater*].

*Simplicissimus*—Two or three very funny comedians—Last act —one act play—very funny and very dirty. Little Jew Komiker—Moses—took the part of a middle-aged Jewish fairy.

Coffee house on Rotenturmstrasse where women came at night —usually by pairs—men also here by pairs.

9. *Akt* is a painting term which means the whole figure of a nude model.

10. Franz Grillparzer (1791–1872), dramatist, was the first Austrian writer to achieve an international reputation.

11. Ludwig Anzengruber (1839–89) was an Austrian writer, and Franz Suppé (1819–95) an Austrian composer.

Nur wer die Sehnsucht kennt,
Weiss, was ich leide! [12]

In Wien this time: Kunsthistorisches, Naturhistorisches, over Belvedere, Schönbrunn, Estensische, Albertina, Stadtische Mus., Czernin, Hofburg, Volkskunde.

[*The following pages were torn out, and much of the material was used for Eugene's Paris notebook in* Of Time and the River.]

Books wanted: *Till Eulenspiegel, Dichtung und Wahrheit,* Heine's *Lieder,* Goethe's *Lieder,* German Lyric Poetry.

The Ring, Kärntnerstrasse and Graben between 5:30 and 6:30 —then all the women are on the street hurrying home—but with many an easy look.

Sind sie allein, oder sind sie rein? [*Are you all alone, or are you clean?*]—I made this up all by myself.

The people who say they "read nothing but the best," are not, as some people call them, snobs.[13] They are fools. The battle of the spirit is not to read and to know the best—it is to find it—The thing that has caused me so much toil and trouble has come from a deep rooted mistrust in me of authority.[14] I hunger for the treasure that I fancy lies buried in a million forgotten books, and yet my reason tells me that the treasure that lies buried there is so small that it is not worth the pain of disinterment.

And yet nearly everything in the world of books that has touched my life most deeply has come from authority. I have not always agreed with authority that all the books called great are great,

12. The opening and closing lines of Mignon II from Goethe's *Wilhelm Meister:* "None but the lonely heart / Can know my sadness." When Wolfe attended the Schubert concert of the Vienna Men's Chorus, this old favorite was one of the renditions. He wrote Mrs. Bernstein on November 25: "Two or three of the songs were written by Goethe and one of them is one of the most beautiful lyrics I have ever read. Here it is." He then proceed to write out the entire poem in German and added, "It is all lovely, but the part 'Ach, der mich liebt und kennt—Ist in der Weite' touched me most of all."

13. Wolfe later wrote "At La Régence: Semaine de Noël, 1924" above this paragraph to conform to the setting in time and place of OT&R. The entire passage appears on page 668.

14. "All cultural" was later added before "authority."

but nearly all the books that have seemed great to me have come from among this number.

I have not discovered for myself any obscure writer who is as great a novelist as Dostoievsky nor any obscure poet with the genius of Samuel Taylor Coleridge. But I have mentioned Coleridge, and although my use of his name will not, I believe, cause any protest, it may cause surprise. Why not Shelley or Spenser or Milton?—It is here that my war with authority—to which I owe everything—begins again.

There are in the world of my spirit at present certain gigantic figures who, although great as well in the world of authority, are yet overwhelmed often by other figures, and in some places loom as enormous half-ghosts—hovering upon the cloudy borderland between obscurity and living remembrance.

Such a man is Samuel Taylor Coleridge. To me, he is not one of the great English poets. He is the Poet. To me, he is not to make obeisance to the throne of any other monarch—he is there by Shakespeare and Milton and Spenser.

[*End of the loose pages.*]

Buchhandlung Theodor Hahn—Mariahilfer Strasse—nothing in windows I had not noticed before.

Thursday:

Must buy Koffer [*trunk*], overcoat, order suit of clothes, books, cable.

Neubaustr—Book Shop—investigate.

Wednesday [*November 21*]:

Today I have tramped the town and accomplished little. After going to Travel Bureau for estimates, ate, went to Belvedere, found it closed, went to big church above Under [*Lower*] Belvedere on the Rennweg, went up to Fasangasse, went along Fasangasse to Girdle near Süd-Bahnhof, took taxi, rushed down Favoritenstr into the Wien, cut through Wien, up poor looking street into Gumpendorfer street, climbed hill and came into Mariahilfer just behind Mariahilfer Church—went into church, saw Haydn Denkmal [*monument*], went to Siller's Coffee House, went out to Gut Freund's Kaffee House—later to Allguter, examined trunks, took none, went into book store, walked along Neubau Gasse, went into café, read papers for theater, looked at bookshop opposite, took taxi to Theater an der Wien, saw *Artisten*,[15]

15. By Gloryl Watters and Arthur Hopkins, with music by Werner R. Heyman. This German translation was staged by Max Reinhardt.

took taxi to Schöner's, and am now at little cafe above the square above Siebenstern Gasse.

The two best restaurants in Wien are at the Sacher Hotel and at Schöner's in Siebenstern Gasse—Go to Schöners at 11:30 after the theater—you will find powerful cars in the quiet little street outside, and inside beautiful whores and well fed looking men. Food is superb. Vienna gives its lure to you almost at once—but its vast plan opens up on you slowly.

How hard it is to rush things; to try to get too much in too short a time. Tonight I am tired and nervous, and my stomach full of pains—due to diseased red wine (I believe) that I drank a few days ago at the Excelsior on Rotenturm Strasse—I feel *up here* tonight—in this quiet street, at this luxurious place—and my hotel and the Inner City and all *that* seems down there—as a matter of fact it is—one mounts, one mounts with few intermissions all the way out to the Wiener Wald.

The Schöner is in one of these old buildings—Came into passageway leading to The Hof—Restaurants on each side—Rooms low rich, elegant—Polished wood half way up, dark tapestry paper, small rich ceiling chandeliers.

The elderly women in the Café Siller this afternoon. How they gossiped and went on! They had the broad yet gentle, coarse yet delicate [mean?] quality full of tenderness, easily capable of vulgarity and humor and liking a dirty joke.

Writing by [comparative?] cliché—"he admitted grudgingly" —how often have I seen that.

Thursday:

Up, to Cook's, to tailor's, to Sacher Bar, to lunch. Tailor in Seilerstätte.

"Leave my wife alone, Jaimy. She needs to rest."
"Then why don't you leave her alone?"
"I have the right. I'm her husband." etc. (*Artisten*)

Of course, the thing that gets me so damned nervous in Europe is the time required to transact simple business—The business of theater tickets—if one gets there even at a reasonable hour before the opening one is told that there are no more 6 or 8 schilling seats—that one must take a 20 schilling seat or stand, or nothing at all. I have tried two of the theaters today—Opera and Academy—and found both of them bought out.

On reading Galsworthy's *Swan Song*—the reason I am not convinced by his stories of the young people—and their adulteries and near adulteries—is that he himself is not.

Friday, Nov. 23:

Went to see Strindberg's great play *Der Vater* tonight in the Carl Theater in the Prater Strasse. Although I could follow only about ⅔ of the German text, the horror and impotent blood-lust the play aroused in me when I first read it came back. As for the audience, there was a sense of fear and spiritual sadness over them that kept them from applauding loudly or vigorously. The play is one of the most astounding things in the world. It is insane and logical—I feel the madness, the insanity in it, but when I try to speak I can not answer its terrible mathematical certainty. It is like a horrible nightmare which we yet fear may be true. People speak of the artist and say that he creates beauty. To pretend that this play is beautiful is simply to pretend, simply to trust words, to argue. That *Der Vater* was written by a great genius I haven't the faintest doubt. What a great genius is I do not know—but whatever he is, Strindberg is one. He is also a monster. The play is the work of an inspired monster.

What "good" does such a play do? I doubt that it does any. I can more easily believe that it does evil. Certainly if pain is evil, as Socrates said, then this play has done much evil, for it inflicts a wound upon a sensitive spirit from which it is never likely completely to recover.

But I believe it also enlarges and deepens the power of the spirit. It makes us richer, but whether that wealth is good or bad wealth, again I do not know.

Saturday:

Up, Ask about clothes, go to Cook's, cable, Harrach Gallery, Albertina, books, theater.

Saturday:

Henry Berenger—Aline Bernstein, Civic Repertory Theater, New York City.

Sailing Naples [Almost, *marked out*] Broke Have You two fifty.

Sailing Naples December Need Two Fifty. Tom.[16]

The book store today—the English books—shelves full—then Malory, Shakespeare, Schiller, Die Blauen Bucher, the red books on artists, the bookcase full of French books, the Insel Verlag books (Ricarda Huch).

German universities: Bonn, Köln, Frankfurt, Berlin, Leipzig, Munich, Kiel, Heidelberg, Dresden, Jena, Danzig.

Swarthmore, Penn, Oregon, Michigan, Harvard, Indiana, North Carolina, Vanderbilt, Tulane, Missouri, Wisconsin, Williams, Maine, Columbia, Cornell, North Dakota, Princeton, Yale.

Saturday night:

I went to Wolf's first—It cost me 12 schillings and it was not very good—a little ugly. [*Sketch.*] Floor of a horrible dirt—mottled plaster or stone—chairs white—[*sketch*]. Tables covered with cloths more or less white in a triangle. A light empty not overclean room. [*Half-page sketch of "chair."*]

Schönbrunner Str., Favoriten Str., Wiedner Haupt Str., Rennweg, Mariahilfer Str., Grinzing: Allee. I know these.

A mixture of waiters: the first has charged 1.50 for 2 wines straight—the second .90 for the same wine. Then I called the first again—he brought a better wine in a [*sketch of wine glass*] 1.50. (dishonesty obvious)—The waiter smarter than I—he guessed right—the first three were ordinary heuriger—(1.50). Then a second waiter not wise to game (.90). The 1st waiter polite—accusations (on my part)—vulgar.

Student talk—Now they are playing Strauss—"Beautiful Blue Danube"—I am a King it said.

1.50 [*five perpendicular marks*] Have had as much as 10? [*check mark*]. [*Oriental writing*] (Persian).

For a later time—but I do not feel so [confident?] as in the foregoing.

16. Drafts of a cable to Mrs. Bernstein.

Aha! aha! aha! [*illegible word*]. They are, they are dancing, dancing, DANCING.

[*Sketch of a face?*] Brownish softish roundish [whiteish?]—all around—a very little hair—but only to the side.

It is ONE o'clock. Now they are going out—I am rather drunk —and waiter made a speech effect of which I was not starting in but to get out (shadows passing me).

At 1 o'clock in November they get out (???).

At 1:04 I made a bad/ a false/ movement/.

I am drunk—now is the time to beat it—The shadows downwards are passing past me.

[*The passage becomes more incoherent and the handwriting becomes more illegible. An indecipherable list of book titles is included.*]

Sunday [*November 25*]—

Akademische Buchhandlung (where last night or this morning I tried to put down the names while drunk). Here are a few of them: [*A much more legible list, six pages long.*]

[*Sunday night, November 25, Wolfe saw* Faust. *There are no notes on the play in this notebook. It is likely that the notebook he lost contained some* Faust *notes. However, the following day he wrote Mrs. Bernstein about it. Since the Faust theme is of special significance to Wolfe—he included it in* Of Time and the River, *and he personally identified himself with Faust—the following excerpt from his letter is included here.*

"Last night I went to see *Faust* at the Burgtheater here. The play began at 7 o'clock and continued until past 11 with only one short pause. I must add it to one of the good things for which we can forgive the rest of life. I had a copy of the text, but in the darkness I could not follow it. But I understood ⅔ of the German, and the course of the play is well known to everyone. I can not speak of its philosophy or the greatness of its poetry—but I can say that as entertainment it is magnificent. Four hours of it—and I was never bored! Your heart lifts up out of all the weary dust—you feel yourself a god because another man was great enough to create all this. Faust's own problem touches me more than Hamlet's—his problem is mine, it is the problem of modern life. He wants to know everything, to be a god—and he is caught in the terrible net of human incapacity. The acting was magnificent—the man who played Mephistopheles was a great actor—and the mechanism of the great stage was grand and interesting."]

Monday:

Cook's, overcoat, Schubert Museum, church in Salvatorgasse, books, museum, theater.

Monday night:

Accomplished very little today and bought no books.

Wednesday [*November 28*]—

Got coat today on Mariahilfer Strasse—It fits beautifully—also looked at clothing material—bought copy of *Nibelungenlied* [17]—went to Kunst-historisches Museum—Have had no answer to my cable yet—Tomorrow—Cable again if no answer—Go to library in morning, also Reitschule and Landgewerbe (?) Museum in Wipplinger (?) Strasse. *Oktobertag* advertised for opening tonight—also *Chicago—Macbeth* at Burg Theater.

Books to be bought yet: *Dichtung und Wahrheit, Akt Studien,* Plays, *Üppige Weib* (?).

The Faust business again today—too much to see—We learn restraint too slowly.

At least my chances have been as good or better than most. At least the difficulties life offers me she offers to many. Today as I was going through Kunsthistorisches again, I thought this:—The loafer is respected in Europe—he is not respected in America. All culture has at its bottom an art of loafing—often of loafing outwardly, while undergoing the most terrible labor of the mind within—work that is not visible and *profitable* is not recognized in America. Even a man with much money who desires to do nothing must develop a certain callousness—the atmosphere is not right—A European with just enough money to loaf on would probably stop working and his neighbors would think him a very sensible fellow, and envy his lot. This is not true in America—But, despite this, over an equal period in recent time —*viz.*, since 1910, I believe America has easily held its own creatively with Europe. The astonishing fact is that so much of what modern Europe has built with an eye to beauty is very ugly, and so much of what America has built with an eye to commerce is very beautiful. The opinions of modern Europeans on America today are usually less than worthless. When they are not simply foolish, they are weak echoings of what Mencken is saying forcibly—As for the French, although

17. A clothbound copy in German edited by Karl Simrock (Leipzig, 1924) is in the Wisdom Collection.

they have begun to write travel books, it seems hopeless ever to expect them to see the rest of the world sensibly—A Frenchman's account of a voyage to London reads like an account of a visit to Mars, and his account of life in New York like the visit of a 17th century explorer among the aborigines of South America. (*viz.*)—Article I read in *Revue des Deux Mondes* (1886 ?) on Frenchman's visit to New York. See G. Lowes Dickinson's *Modern Symposium.*[18] (Avenue du [Arquebusiers—Broad?], etc.—Belgian newspaper—My boy, dit il, in the same time chewing gum mechanically and spitting for emphasis from time to time, we have the money—we have the men—we shall win—etc.

I am 28 years old—⅓ of this time I have spent in sleeping—the other ⅔ in eating, studying, dreaming, sometimes working.

I am steadier in spirit since coming to Vienna than for months.

Tonight—writing this at Kaiser's *Oktobertag.* Little theater Die Komödie is very pleasant, elegant, and warm looking.

SWINBURNE[19]

The death of all things living
The life of all things dead,
New birth to crime and killing
Cutting of flesh and filling
Bunkers with bitter bread.

If all the different editions and volumes of the works in a great German library were counted up, how many would they number?

Goethe, Shakespeare, Schiller, Dostoyevski, Wieland, Abelard, Kleist, Chamisso, Korngold, Anzengruber, Grillparzer, Dickens, Balzac, Dumas, Tolstoi, Freytag, Keller, Wundt, Karl May, Busch, Hauff, Grimm, Storm, Stifter, Courths-Maler, Voltaire, Plato, Cicero, Titus Livius, Burckhardt.

Fontane, Kant, Schlegel, Hebbel, Körner, Herder, Homer, Th. Mann, Hein. Mann, Wassermann, Sudermann, Luther, Gregorovius, Agricola, Kotzebue, Heine, Gerstäcker, Heyse, Thoma, Schopenhauer, Jack London, Galsworthy, H. G. Wells, Theodore Dreiser, Hauptmann, Lessing, Kaiser, Hegel, Wolf.

18. (New York, 1905). The thirteen members of the Seekers Club discuss modern life, especially American life. Wolfe was familiar with the work through selections in *The New World,* ed. Harold Bruce and Guy Montgomery, which he discussed with his students in Freshman English.

19. After having revised Browning in the poem for Mrs. Bernstein, Wolfe now tries his hand at Swinburnian verse.

Wagner, H. Löns, A. Berend, Sternheim, W. Von Molo, Eulenberg, Marie Grazie, Klopstock, Dante, Sophocles, Aeschylus, Curwood, Grey, Twain, Emerson, Rolland, Colette, Baedeker, Griebens, Byron, Chaucer, Nibelungenlied, Hasenclever, Dekobra, Thackeray, Jonathan Edwards, Shaw.

Chesterton, Wilde, Cervantes, The Holy Bible, Pascal, Victor Hugo, A. France, Upton Sinclair, Sinclair Lewis, Rabelais, Calderón, Lope De Vega, Ibañez, Jókai, Molnár, [Sigmund?], Szabó, Mihály, Ovid, Demosthenes, Theocritus, Bourget, Flaubert, De Maupassant, Bulwer-Lytton, Hector Malot.

Captain Mayne Reid, Paul Féval, Paul De Koch, Motley, Gibbon, Darwin, Haeckel, Euripedes, Stevenson, Conrad, Berta M. Ruck, Beatrice Harraden, ? Mrs. Edwards, Ibsen, Björnson, Lagerloef, Undset, Hamsun.

Tonight at Hungarian Restaurant—In before me in sport roadster—Reading*Times*, those two little whores (masc.) who go all over Europe with 2 men and 1 woman.

Ah, but we all must eat (2½ hrs.). Yes, and we all must sleep (7½ hrs.) and we men almost all work, love, play (12⅓ hrs.).

Wednesday [*November 28*]—

Got money today.[20] In morning to Cook's, to coffee house, to bank, to Dorotheum (great auction house),[21] to two book stores, to

20. In October Mrs. Bernstein had written Wolfe wondering whether he was getting money from Olin Dows. (He was not.) She further stated that she had just been paid $750.00 by the theater, and, though that was all she had, she would be willing to send him up to $500.00 to come home on, if he needed it. His cable was evidently in response to her generous offer. On November 27 she sent him a draft on the Wiener Bank-Verein for $350.00, with the message, "Your cable delayed." He immediately wrote her on November 28: "Today I received 350 dollars by cable from you. I cabled the other day and said I would need 250. This is very generous of you—I do not think I have been extravagant, but I had only 180 dollars of my own left. I have bought an overcoat and books here—I think I will let Cook make my route for me to Naples—I hate to do this, but my time is limited, and I might waste both time and money if I tried to do it myself now. Cook's gave me an estimate that was complete down to what I should have for breakfast, and which would land me aboard the boat, where—says their estimate—'our responsibility ends.' The whole thing, for a little over two weeks, including railway fare, hotels, bus rides, excursions, and all my meals, was about $115—to Naples. This seems to me fair enough, since Naples is a long way off."

21. The Dorotheum, the state-owned auction, moved Wolfe to comment at length in a letter to Mrs. Bernstein on November 29: "I went to a fascinating place yesterday—a huge building in a narrow little street that you have to hunt for. The building is called the Dorotheum, it was probably once an immense private palace—now it has been made into a gigantic auction house. I climbed

hotel, to old beer house, to Kino [*movie*], to Augustiner Keller, to Sacher, to cafe, to hotel (&) to L'Europe.

Last night saw *Oktobertag.*[22] In the papers reviews of *Chicago*, *Oktobertag*. Thornton Wilder is in town—interview in paper.[23]

There are some books which have a first place among the books of a year, and even of ten years. Then they seem old and old fashioned. The critics of the newer period smile at them, or ridicule them, where once they praised them, as many men now ridicule H. G. Wells and Barrie, and smile at Galsworthy. There are other books which seem to rise triumphantly above this.

Why is it that we hear men saying that Galsworthy dates? But we never hear that about Fielding or Dostoievsky.

(Melange)

But who only has seen a giant on the earth has never known him. There are giants among the Plains of Hungary, where the gypsy makes a song for dirty shepherds. Chamisso on his trip around the world saw giants in Papua. And sinning men with frozen shanks in hell, yet burn their toes. The heroes with gobbets of dripping flesh upon their spears were great men.

Tuesday night, Dec. 4—

All arrangements made at Cook's today—Leaving for Italy tomorrow—Terribly distressed over the loss of my last notebook—Con-

---

from floor to floor, from one enormous room to another—in a dozen places auction sales were going on. The rooms were crowded with shabby looking people who were obviously habituées—they sat on benches or around a railed enclosure and made bids. There were three auctioneers in each room—and things were sold with amazing speed."

22. Wolfe enjoyed the play and recommended it to Mrs. Bernstein in a letter, November 28: "I do not know if it has been done, or is being done in a New York theater, but if it hasn't why don't you speak to Miss LeGalliene about it? I bought the play in Munich and had read it before I saw it. Both in the book and on the stage it seemed to me a very real and moving play—modern in spirit, but with no eccentricity in the writing or production. [*Georg*] Kaiser is the best of their Expressionist writers; but this has none of the expressionist *foolishness* to it. The structure, the dialog, the whole action is set forth very briefly and simply—it is astonishing to find such a spare form in a German thing. I am bringing the play home and will tell you about it." His paperback copy (Potsdam, 1928) is in the Wisdom Collection, unmarked but with all the pages cut.

23. Wolfe wrote Mrs. Bernstein: "He said that he had come to Vienna to see the Breughels in the picture gallery—I naturally feel that you and I have discovered Breughel and that Wilder has heard of him through us."

vinced it was left at Thomas Cook's, as that is the only place I remember taking it out.

Here are my movements for day—Up late, went to coffeehouse, read *Herald*, went to Theater Book store, bought two plays, went to Kunsthistorisches Museum, went to library, bought post cards there (and believe I put them in notebook—they too are gone), went to coffeehouse for lunch, went to Cook's—made payments and here remember taking notebook out—went from Cook's to Wechsel Stube [*Exchange room*], from there to bookseller on Stefansplatz, from there to Gilhofer's Bookshop, from there to cigarette booth on Graben, and from there to L'Europe where discovered loss—went back to Cook's —it was late but found manager there—he couldn't find it—went to Stefansplatz Bookshop and yelled thru window at them—they said they didn't have it—after careless look—went to Gilhofer's—said they didn't have it—then to coffee house on Rotenturm Str., then to big coffee house—nowhere.

I am convinced I left it at Cook's—they promise to send it on to me if it is found.

I made no notes yesterday or today—My last notes in this book apparently are on Wednesday night—that means I have lost notes for Thursday, Friday, Saturday, Sunday—but very full and copious ones.

Between Thursday and Sunday—where: Plays—To *Ida Popper's Karriere*,[24] To *Der Präsident*,[25] To *Oktobertag*, To Theater Die Komödie.

Saturday wasted day with $2-a-day American.

Sunday—walk in IX and XVIII Bezirks [*districts*]—hunting up rooms—Interiors in the Berg Gasse, etc.[26]

First several pages of book had scrawled script of my poem. Must recover part of what I lost—not that it had great value, but that it represents notes made on the spot.

24. This was simply a part of Wolfe's avid theater-going; he had not anticipated it with much relish: "I am going tonight to a play called *Ida Popper's Karriere*—and I fear the worst. The piece was written about 1904. *Chicago* went on the other night and is apparently a hit here—it confirmed their worst suspicions."

25. Also by Georg Kaiser.

26. The Berggasse contained some significant interiors. No. 19 was then the home of Sigmund Freud.

The awful feeling of having lost something.

*Ida Popper's Karriere*—play poor—not very good—but woman in lead magnificent, play had been written for her—two men who sat by me—woman behind—Later [*breaks off*]

Tone of head waiter in answering questions—Kindly, but somewhat as if he were instructing child.

Standard of *living* in America—they say—is higher than anywhere else. But the standard of *life?* (One piece in the lost note book—was difference between people today and people 50 years ago.) One difference is this (etc.).

European does not care.

Then a list of things and books and people that are interesting to me, and of those that are not.

The people at L'Europe and at Rotenturm Str. coffee house might have been invited (said I).

Then list.

Or beastwise where the cellar brew is strong
With beast to hew and grapple in the dark.
—mud
—blood etc.[27]

I had rather own a copy of Heine's *Lieder* than a fake Titian—other than that the fake Titian might be sold and my Heine's *Lieder* and other books bought with the money.

[*Six pages of figures on currency exchange and travel costs, in which he figures how much Cook's is making on him for* "2nd Class railway fare to Naples, 16 nights in hotels, 16 breakfasts, 8 transfers, 8 transfer tips."]

[*Wolfe finally left Vienna reluctantly on Wednesday, December 5, to go to Italy, where he would board his ship for the return voyage to America. After an overnight stop in Venice he arrived in Florence on December 6. He was drawn to Florence largely by its great art treasures, and his first morning there he went by Cook's to pick up his mail and then headed for the Uffizi Museum without taking time to buy a new notebook. He went immediately to see the "Foreign*

27. Wolfe seems to be attempting some versifying about the fight at the Oktoberfest.

*Schools," where he could find his favorites, the Flemish and Dutch Masters. Though this present book was well filled, he jotted notes of his Uffizi visit wherever he had a blank corner or margin in the last pages of the notebook. These Uffizi notes have been assembled at the end where Wolfe would have placed them if he had had any more blank pages.*]

UFFIZI

1212 P. Brueghel ["*Ascent to Calvary*"].
1459 Cranach—"Adam."
1458 " "Eve."
1087 Holbein ["*Portrait of Richard Southwell*"].

1871 Rembrandt ["*Self portrait of the artist as an old man*"].
1864 Rembrandt ["*Portrait of Rabbi Saul Levy Morteira*"].

Watteau—all that doesn't interest me.

3192 Hugo van der Goes' great picture—"Adoration of the Shepherds."

Van Der Goes room—1065—Nicholas Froment D'Avignon—"Resurrection of Lazarus"—Strange dark greenish look of disciples—one elegant, holding cloth to his nose and making a face.

1036–8405—Man and wife [*Pier Ant. Baroncelli and wife*]—Unknown Fiammingo [*Flemish*].

Bordone, Moroni—beginning—Palma—16th century.

But John Bellini, Crivelli, Mantegna—15th cent.—good.

Voluptuous golden Helen, naked woman—Titian ["*Venus of Urbino*"].

Italian XVII century! 914 Tintoretto—"Apparition of St. Augustine"—looks almost like Greco.

Room of Bronzino.

Michaelangelo—"Holy Family"—(1456—no [cuckold?])

744 [*Scuola di*] Tiziano—"Ritratto Di Papa Sisto IV"—great portrait—The effeminate prettiness of the great pope—1706 [*Raphael*]—a gay man.

Piero Cosimo—a good painter—510 "Andromeda Liberata da Perseo."

Filippino Lippi—"Ritratto di vecchio"—good.

8344—Giotto—great—picture of "La Vergine col Bambino."
Piero Della Francesca—Portrait of Montefeltre and his wife.
Cimabue—8343—Se XIII—"La Vergine col Figlio."

## *Pocket Notebook 7*

## *December 7, 1928, to December 20, 1928*

*This notebook records Wolfe's stay in Italy. It begins on his first day in Florence and includes his week in Rome and his brief stopover in Naples before boarding his ship to return to America. It contains copious notes on what Wolfe saw in the art museums and only a few lists of books, most of which have been omitted. Since he was nearing the end of his European tour, he became reflective about what he had experienced and thought in Europe, and he set down a great many generalizations about the European nations and made many comparisons with American culture.*

*The notebook itself is falling apart, partly because Wolfe tore out a number of pages to help form Eugene Gant's notebook in* Of Time and the River. *Wolfe had bought it in Florence and, still annoyed at losing one in Vienna, he wrote on the inside of the front cover:* "Property of Thomas WOLFE."

---

Florence Friday [*December* 7].

Today—up, left hotel shortly after 10 o'clock—to Cook's—then to the great Uffizi gallery—Stayed 2½ hours—then a trip around town in carriages—above town—and back—First went to Medici chapel—then across river and up hill—then back to grand and gleaming church of Santa Croce [*design*]—Then to stone mosaic works and to leather shop—and back to Cook's—a full and wonderful day.

*Se la luna mi porta fortuna*—Campanile.[1]

Bought a pair of shoes—the only pair that fitted me[2]—for 90 lire—This is probably only 15 or 20 lire above their regular price—I brought him down from 105—and found I was wasting too much time —It has been only two days since I left Vienna—but they have been

1. A recently published novel by Achille Campanile, who was the same age as Wolfe. The title means "If the moon brings me good luck."

2. No wonder, especially in Italy. He wore size 13 with a wide last, and he even had difficulty finding shoes to fit in New York.

loaded with travel and seeing—I will try to make notes of the most important things.

The Medici Chapel—Grand in size—the smaller chapel with the famous Michaelangelo statues meant little to me.

For Saturday: Up, write hotel, go to Pitti Palace, lunch, books, Duomo [*cathedral*], etc.

In Italy—Depression
In France—Despair
In Germany—Honor
In England

Florence, Amiens, Boulogne, Budapest, Frankfurt, Köln, Bonn, Wiesbaden, Mainz, Oberammergau, Rome, Naples.[3]

I've seen Budapest; Aline has seen Berlin.

PITTI PALACE

Bronzino—pretty good portrait painter—but not interesting.

Andrea D'Agnolo [*also called Andrea del Sarto*]—The critics would talk about his color—enough.

Floris—Adam and Eve by starlight.

313—Tintoretto—"Madonna e Bambino"—Like Greco.

Titian, a good portraitist—but nothing here yet to touch the one in Vienna.

Titian—"Ritratto di Tommaso Mosti"—Great fault of Italians is their sweet false prettiness—Perhaps it is the way they really look—not the artist. I think this likely—Titian's picture of old German Duke in Vienna is not this—it is a grand picture of the powerful old swine.

Corridor full of the little delicate pictures—kind you examinate [*sic*] with a microscope to see how perfectly a fly has been painted on the rose leaf.

Cornelio Poelemburg, landscapes with ruined castles.

364—Jacopo Bellini, "Madonna with Child."

355—School of Botticelli [*Luca Signorelli*]—Woman's picture —a *good* picture.

3. A list of the cities he has visited for the first time on this trip, including the two he expects to visit before sailing.

372—Ditto [*Andrea del Castagno*]—Man's picture.
343—Fra Filippo Lippi, "Madonna & Child."

Sir Peter Lely—"Oliver Cromwell"—408—Good (But good partly because the sitter was good).

Pourbus—Several pictures of great Medicis.

Tapestries—Triumphs of Zeus, Mars, Venus, and Minerva—with elephants and camels, Neptune with seahorses.

Sodoma—"S. Sebastiano," 1590—celebrated—not excited by it.

Raffaello—"Leone X con i Cardinali"—This is a good picture.

67—Titian—"The Magdalene."

The innumerable "Sancta Familias" and Madonna con Bambinos.

Guido Reni—"S. Pietro in lacrime"—Ah, but it's *typical*—that is to say "bella."

Next to it is a Raffael—"The Holy Family"—The painting is much better, but the picture is just as bad—dull, gluey, sobful sweet.

Titian—"Ritratto di Andrea Vesalio"—Damned good picture. Above "Ritratto di Gentiluomo."

Ah—the belle Rubens—among its compeers—Guido Reni and Raffael—"The Consequences of War"—and it shows a fat naked lady with blond bejeweled hair being conveyed away by a bearded gentleman in a helmet and armor to the knees—Entwined and beflown about by nice little cupids with the old boy with a torch before—Bella bionda bella [*pretty blonde pretty*]—and clouds and wailing women and everything.

Also Cigoli—"Ecce Homo."

Also in the Sala di Giove—the belle Rubens—"Ninfa sorprese da satiro."

Fra Bartolommeo—"St. Marco" (1469–1517)—great grandfather of baroque.

Paris Bordone—"Ritratto Muliebre"—good.

Tintoretto—"Ritratto di Vincenzo Zeno"—good, 131.

Sustermans—119—old woman, good. ["*Portrait of Elia.*"]

Raffaelo—61—portrait, "Agnolo Doni"—good. 59—portrait—"Maddalena Doni"—good.

Raffael—"Portrait [*of*] Tommaso Inghirami"—good.

Raffaello—"Madonna del Baldacchino"—of course he could paint and he is very dear—but god, how dull.

Raffael—Portrait of Cardinal Dovizi da Bibbiena—*good* picture.

Andrea D'Agnolo—he's all over the place with Holy Families and Madonnas—this one (172) called "Disputa sulla Trinita" [*"Dispute on the Holy Trinity"*]—Pictures in great gilty barok frames.

Barok ceilings all gold with wall paintings of ladies on clouds, in blue—and naked men and women all gilt etc. In the first hall—the Sala dell' Iliade—by the door there is a small portrait by Josse Van Cleeve ("Portrait of a Man"—223) not a great picture nor even a very good one, but compare its strength and intelligence with the pictures around it—A great Andrea del Sarto beside it—"Assumption of the Madonna" (225)—the bland gestures, the red draperies—the foot upon the step, the natural-unnaturalness of the outstretched hand—the interesting-uninteresting variety of expressions on the faces of the saints—with Mama sitting on a cloud upstairs, hands clasped before her, and little fat boys all around.

R. del Ghirlandaio—woman's portrait—224, good.

Guido Reni—"La Cleopatra"—oh but this is good.

Dolci, Carlo—Figure it out for yourself.

Vries, Abraham De—"Ritratto D'homo"—Among all the Renis and Dolcis—the keener intelligence and strength of the old Dutchman.

Tintoretto—"Portrait of Andrea Frizier."

1555—Giovanni (Mannozzi) da San Giovanni (1590–1636), one of the Terrible School—"La Prima Notte Di Matrimonio." A young man naked in bed with a look of holy rapture on his face. Simpering lady being drawn and egged on by eager mockers—mother with an expression of pious sorrow.

*Das Russische Theater*—Joseph Gregor & René Fülöp-Miller.

Ghiberti's doors of the Baptistery—Florence.

A man should be a great deal more afraid of victory than of defeat. When I tell my story of the Oktoberfest I hesitate to say that I was fighting with three men because it sounds like only the cheap boasting most of our people do. Nevertheless—that is true—otherwise I can not strut it or give myself airs. I was so drunk I could not tell the faces of my opponents and would not know them if I saw them. I fought very badly and clumsily and was hurt worse than any of them (I am sure of this and am on the whole glad of it). The only thing I can congratulate myself on is the endurance and pertinacity I showed —but this was probably the result of drunkenness and my almost complete insensitivity to pain at the time—I must have been knocked down at least four or five times; I always got to my feet again and continued to fight and even the blow that broke my nose did not stop me for a second. I fought until the others were fought out, and at the end I was on top of the sole remaining man trying to kill him—his wife was on my back. This is the true story after 2½ months time. But it is not an American story—the small change fellows like the one in Vienna ($2 a day) who try to find out how I got the scar on my head, tell me of their own fights and how they lied about them and routed people twice their size, etc. They have no truth and no greatness in them. I have, I think, now that my spiritual torment regarding the Oktoberfest has died down, on the whole a feeling of increased confidence. Before that, a certain fear of people—my "crowd neurosis"—caused me to bristle up, and to be pugnacious. This comes more from a sense of fear than otherwise. But, now that I have shed blood, and have got a scar, a new confidence and balance seems to have come to me, I feel kindlier towards people. I do not want to jostle them out of the way—if they want to take up more room than belongs to them and to be loud and hostile, I will give way—up to a certain point. But I am not in the least afraid of them. I do think that my spiritual humility at present keeps me from doing full credit to myself—I think that another person telling of my adventure at the Oktoberfest might treat me much more generously than I have treated myself.[4]

Ristorante Melini—Firenze, via Calzaioli, 13—all red and white and good.

A proud and poisonous whore.

Saturday [*December 8*]—

Today up, left hotel at 11—to Pitti Palace—Rightly named—it is more than a pity; it is a catastrophe, a tragedy. It should never have been. The good pictures are bad, the bad ones horrible—Among the good pictures were [*breaks off*]

Politeáma [*Theater*]—Via Nazionale—Theater La Amánte Del Signore Vidol—Luigi [Venendi?].

4. A straightforward account of the Oktoberfest fight, and an appraisal of its effect on him—including, perhaps, some wishful thinking. Wolfe was keenly aware of his fear of crowds. In a brief autobiography—probably prepared for Scribner's use in promoting LHA—he candidly states this fear. "He is alone at least 20 hours out of the 24: he has been afraid of people in groups and crowds since his childhood. He almost never goes to parties." "River People" ledger, p. 98.

Rum, Tum and Rumble dum
The scum, the scum, the double scum.

Books: Ernest Renan, Galsworthy, Maugham, Nietzsche, Tolstoi—all in Italian. [*List of Italian books.*] P. G. Wodehouse—*Avanti, Jeeves;* Jack London—*La Valle della Luna.*

What can not be used is not good.
What is not interesting is not beautiful.

Italy—The trouble with it is that it is too beautiful—There are too many beautiful things—much of it therefore ceases to have meaning.

If we could imagine a living organism—a living man—whose flesh contained all the diseases there are—the man might poison the world yet live forever—like Rappaccini and his daughter—they were proof against their own poison.[5]

If one kind of poisonous snake—a copperhead—should sting another kind—a rattler—would the rattler be poisoned?

People say that beauty is a rare thing and must be sought after. This is not true. Perhaps *our* beauty—these things that we *see* as beautiful—is rare—but the number of beautiful things is infinite.

Beauty is a very common thing. In Italy there are thousands and thousands of very beautiful things.

How can we say that a man is great who reproduces himself hundreds and hundreds of times as do painters like Rubens, and Titian, and Veronese and writers like Dumas and musicians like Schubert and most of the poets. At a Schubert concert I read "opus 127"—and he died at 30-something[6]—of course it is sad and ridiculous. People will say Shakespeare—yes, he had enormous fertility and enormous power—he wrote 3 dozen plays—but if you consider the sonnets, they belong to a single thing.

All discussions as to whether art is for "the few or the many" seem to me foolish. Some art is for the few and some is for the many—some artists have pleased and interested a few and some have pleased and interested a great many—it is stupid and provincial to say that a man is a bad artist because only a few know and like him, and it is stupid and foolish to say that man is bad because many like him.

5. A reference to Hawthorne's short story "Rappaccini's Daughter."

6. Schubert died two and a half months before his thirty-second birthday. His life was six years shorter than Wolfe's was to be.

Dickens and Dostoievsky have been for the many.

Donne and Verlaine and Stendhal and Coleridge have been for the few.

Uffizi—Sunday [*December 9*]—

Ignoto Toscano [*unknown Tuscan*] (Sec XIV) First Room.

Jacopo Del Casentino (St. Bartol. E Angeli)

Cimabue—8343—"La Vergine col Figlio"—one of the greatest pictures in the world.

Andrea e Jacopo Orcagna—"St. Matteo"—3163.

8344—Giotto—"La Vergine col Bambino e Angeli"—The Giotto has lovely clear color—the Cimabue is covered with a marvellous gold rust. Giotto far and away the greatest painter—his colors beautiful and fresh still, but Cimabue the greatest artist—Cimabue one of the greatest artists that ever lived—The convention of their heads. [*Sketches of four pairs of heads.*]

452—Good—Simone Martini e Lippo Memmi—"L'Annuciazione."

Uccello—Good battle picture ["*The Battle of San Romano*"].

3rd room:

Domenico Veneziano—good—Virgin with Bamb. e various Santi.

Baldovinetti—a good painter—483—"L'Annuciazione."

All these are early Florentines:

Fra Filippo Lippi—a good painter—8352—"Incoronazione della Vergine."

881—Ghirlandaio—"Virgin with son and various saints"—good.

8388—Ghir. ["*Virgin enthroned, with SS. Dionysius and Thomas Aquinas*"].

The marvelous fair delicate colors of Filippo Lippi.

Next room, the Leonardos and Verrocchio.

Pollaiuolo here—Pollaiuolo's strange women figures here—Temperance, Prudence, Justice, Charity, Faith, & Hope.

What a great drawer Leonardo was!—"L'Adorazione dei Magi."

Next room, the Botticellis.

Botticelli, Filipepi Alessandro—"Vergine col Bambino."

Sandro Bott.—"Birth of Venus," "Spring," "Minerva and the Centaur"—"Annunciation." [7]

Lorenzo di Credi—1482—small portrait of man—good.

Last big room of this section. XVI Cent. Florentines. Lorenzo di Credi, a good artist, also Piero di Cosimo, D'Agnolo, Fra Bartolommeo, Andrea del Sarto, Albertinelli, Ghirlandaio.

Lorenzo di Credi—"Venus," 3094.

Next Section—Umbrian and Sienese schools. Se XV.

Perugino—1435—[*"Virgin enthroned, with SS. John and Sebastian"*].

Vecchietta, Lorenzo di Pietro (1424–82)—[*"Virgin with child and various saints"*]—good but not much color).

Signorelli, Luca ("Sacra Famiglia").

Perugino, 8366, "Assumption of the Madonna." The famous one, holy rapture, etc. "Aesthetics course."

Bronzino, 741—man's portrait [*"Bartolomeo Panciatichi"*]—Good!

Vasari was *not a bad* portrait painter.

793, 748—Bronzino, women. 1475, child with bird, good.

Lorenzo di Credi, a good painter (N. a Firenze 1459–1537). Room with little portraits, fine. 1603, 1604.

Fine picture of "Perseus liberating Andromeda"—great diagram by Piero di Cosimo—an interesting painter.

Two good small pictures—one by Filip. Lippi—one of woman.

Michelangelo, 1456, "Holy Family."

1706 Raffael—young man, a little sweet but good.

Pontormo, good portraits.

Granacci—good for masses and numbers. 3908.

Francia, 1444, "Portrait of Scappi."

Araldi, Alessandro—3548, woman's portrait, good.

Ambrogio di Predis, man's picture—good.

This ends the first corridor.

7. Wolfe apparently did not realize that Sandro Botticelli and Filipepi Alessandro Botticelli were names for the same painter.

Cross the end part here and enter Venetian School.

Titian—two pictures of Venus, 1431, 1437, several portraits—good but—!

Giorgione—"Cavaliere di Malta"—942—good picture.

Veronese school—Portrait of Guidobaldo da Montefeltro—Elizabetta Gonzaga—Good.

Paris Bordone, Moroni, Sebas. del Piombo, Palma Vecchio—939 "Giuditta" [*Judith*]—good portraitist.

Then room with Tintorettos, Veronese.

Then Sala da Tiepolo.

Salvator Rosa [Rather coarse?], Domenico Fetti, Luca Giordano.

Then Franc. Guardi, little Venetian man and Rosalba Carriera, woman—like both.

Then room with Rosa, Giordano, Crespi, Tiarini, Magnasco (and he). Crespi interesting.

921, Tintoretto—[*"Portrait of Admiral Venier"*].

3192—Van der Goes, "Adoration of the Shepherds"—Fine.

1036–8405—Fleming unknown [*Bruges Master—portraits of Pierantonio Baroncello and his wife*].

1643, 1644—Van Cleve—[*Man and wife*].

Rubens Hall.

Foreign Schools:
1212—"Ascent of Calvary"—Pieter Brueghel
Rembrandt, Cranach.

Baroque Hall.

Hall of Niobe.[8]

Piazza della Signoria—that's the famous one with Vecchio Palace and Loggia and Neptune's fountain, etc.[9]

8. A collection of fourteen ancient Roman copies of a Greek group, Niobe and her children.

9. Once the forum of the Florentine Republic, it has remained much the same since the fourteenth century.

Fiesole—Got there in time to see Florence all smokey in the late light of evening.[10] [*Rough sketch.*]

Politeama Fiorentino—music; Teatro Della Pergola—Dramma; Teatro Nazionale—Dramma—Circo [*circus*] Kludsky.

What I have seen in 3 days at Florence: Theater 3 times, Pitti Pal. 1, Uffizi 2, Santa Croce 1, Duomo 2, Battistero 2, Loggia 2, Fiesole 1, Santa ? 1, Looking over town 1, Medici Chapel 1.

*Who* does like anyone else, anyway?

Young Italians fellows dress, gang up, and look very much like young American rowdies—Neither race is capable of solid study or prolonged reflection—American movies all over Italy apparently—Tom Mix in Venice—nigger comedy, Bessie Love, [*John*] Barrymore and [*Dolores*] Costello here.

The officers in the Italian uniform must spend a terrific amount for uniforms. And O la la, how they get dressed up, and how they swagger. What fun the American ladies must have!

---

[*After his hurried tour of Florence, Wolfe arrived in Rome on or about Monday, December 10. Like all people who received a good grounding in the Classics, he was anxious to see Rome—especially the structures and sites about which he had read and studied. Since he had wasted much time in aimless wandering in other cities, and as his time before departure was now limited, he planned his sightseeing more systematically than usual. He purchased a Griebens guidebook,* Rome and Environs, *and in this printed list he circled the sights he intended to see (a thing he did not often do in his guidebooks). Those which he circled are starred with an asterisk in the list which follows. He visited places he did not circle, however; the Borghese Gallery is not marked, but he has notes on it.*

SUITABLE PROGRAMME FOR AN 8 DAYS' STAY

First day. *Forenoon:* St. Peter's,* Vatican Museum of Antiques.*
*Afternoon:* Palatine and Colosseum.*

10. Fiesole was once the home of Robert Browning and is where he probably wrote "My Star," the poem Wolfe had in mind at the time of his own efforts to write the poem for Mrs. Bernstein.

Second day. *Forenoon:* Vatican Gallery and Library,* Raphael's Stanze,* Borgia Apartment,* Sistine Chapel.*
*Afternoon:* Villa Umberto I and Borghese Gallery.
Third day. *Forenoon:* Capitol Museums and Gallery.
*Afternoon:* Passeggiata Archeologica * (Archeological Zone), Baths of Caracalla.*
Fourth day. *Forenoon:* The Forum Romanum.*
*Afternoon:* Roman National Museum (Baths of Diocletian).
Fifth day. *Forenoon:* National Corsini Gallery and Farnesina.
*Afternoon:* National Gallery of Modern Art (Valle Giulia).
Sixth day. *Forenoon:* Basilica of Santa Maria Maggiore,* Basilica of St. John's Lateran,* Baptistery, Scala Santa, Basilica of Santa Croce in Gerusalemme.
*Afternoon:* Church of Santa Maria del Popolo. Castel Santa Angelo.*
Seventh day: *Forenoon:* Lateran Museums.
*Afternoon:* Basilica of St. Paul's. Outside the Walls Protestant Cemetery.
Eighth day. *Forenoon:* Palazzo Venezia, New Museum in the Palazzo Venezia, Monument to Victor Emmanuel II,* Doria Gallery.
*Afternoon:* Church of St. Agnes outside the Walls and Catacombs of St. Agnes.*

*On December 15 Wolfe wrote his mother:* "I've seen a great deal of Rome but I'm half dead with a cold caught in their miserable rain."]

---

Is there a horn which blows in Rome that I do not hear? Too-oo-ot! Too-oo-ot! The little irritating things.

Ristorante di Roma—Gang of Fascisti came in to eat—my table is moved away from me in order to make room for them. I am left sitting in the middle of the floor with a knife and fork in each hand.

A beer table, 5 in a row. [*Sketches of heads.*]

I knew them with a vision that was beyond knowledge, beyond the finding of knowledge, beyond all the wearisome and horrible labor of this world which leaves us nothing but the ashes and the [*breaks off*]

The Baths of Caracalla—Tonight, dearest, I shall be waiting near the Catacombs.

The Coliseum looks to God
The Coliseum moveth not
And Romans live and Romans die
In all the dens of iniquity
  They rot.

Something with grease upon its hair
With liquid languor in its eye
Clenches the sword and breathes the air
And swings the cape, and invites the Fair
  With it to lie.

But the Coliseum moveth not
The little men go up and down
The fingers shaken in my face
Haggle and faun and show the race
  And I think of home
  And this is Rome.

The Italian land—what is it about Italian earth that seems strange and familiar and wonderful—consider the mountains—the intimate hills of Italy from Venice to Florence—and from Florence to Rome. And especially the Roman Campagna—what is the Roman Campagna? Is it flat? No, for there are hills, and some of the land rolls. Is it bare? No, for there are trees—but most is bare—We feel that every part of this land has been lived on—in a hundred *suggestive* ways we see that the land has been manipulated thousands of times by men—that the land has come to belong to man rather than to nature—in a hundred ways outside of Rome we get these strange and baffling suggestions of the enormous city greater than either New York or London today—that this country held. At the time of the Emperor Septimius Severus the population of Rome may have been about 11,000,000.

Rome and New York—I must have a culture that has life—What in God's name can I get from Ludwig of Bavaria and all his horrible castles—or from Baroque—or from *modern* Rome? Rome and New York—they are for me symbols—the rantings of their opera singers here about the re-creation of Rome mean as much to me as the painting of a modern Hungarian "in the manner of Raphael"—Remember the guide and his picture that was by a young fellow who is called "the modern Raphael."

"The Modern Raphael"—that is to say, modern Italy, Pagliacci, Victor Emmanuel Monument, the uniform, Celeste Aida, the newstand, etc.[11]

I can live neither upon the dead nor among them—The Italians can do both.

Gestures of Mich. Angelo's God and Adam—Is that glorius majesty modern Italians' head-and-finger-talk?

Theaters: Teatro Adriano—dramma, 9 o'clock. Teatro Quirino—revue, 9 o'clock. Teatro Argentina—operetta, 9 o'clock.

Sat. night [*December 5*]—other side of Tiber:

*My* Roman Circus

The angels of peace and of darkness
Have laid us to rest
This is Rome—she is dead and was taken.

Before the thunder lifts the dawn
And triumph rolls away
Proud thronging hordes of Hungary
Have swept the plains of Lombardy.

O Umbrian land that rests on my hills.

What is the color of a Roman column—all bestained with triumph of dead time.

The chariot and the slave.

Connection with *Paris*—Small towns of America—Cocky, smelly, butty, fucky, powdery, Southerny—belle-by-lottery—Paris fashions, through Ginsberg's, New York models, purchased by Paris' own agent, Mr. Abe Schwartzberg of The Fashion Palace, who goes to New York Personally every 4 weeks.

11. "Celeste Aida," an old favorite, had soured for Wolfe. On November 17 he had written Mrs. Bernstein from Vienna: "You once said that my taste in other things seemed good, and in music cheap—that I was always humming Celeste Aida, or Samson and Delilah, and so on. You wrong me. I hate Aida now, but S and D isn't half bad.—But as for most music, good or bad—I am no longer sure that any of it—the grand opera—grand composer kind—is good."

Thus here in Rome I see the reach, the thrust of Europe into North Carolina.

Cosimo Medici was the son of a Florentine banker. His people for four generations had been Florentine bankers. Before that they had been peasants.

Behind the walls of an Italian house (We must learn the picturesque and dirty—I mean the houses in outer Florence toward Fiesole. Rather ugly lumpy things—What's in them?)

Are there any Italian women who won't fuck other men (Italian men) other than their husbands—if given a chance?

(At 28 I think of these things when looking at women—at 48? What?)

How we see the faults—the "old fashionedness" today when reading such writers as Richard Harding Davis, etc.—Yet—D'Annunzio.

But what about D'Annunzio! No one has ever said to me, "D'Annunzio is a great writer." Yet D'Annunzio enjoys a fame greater than many great writers.

Myself, I think D'Annunzio is not a great writer—is not always a good writer.

But (say they) there's the man!

That makes [*sic*] nothing—we're talking of writers.

Sunday, Reg. luncheon, 2 wines; Sat. Reg. Dinner, 2 wines; 1st Day—reg Supper (?), 1 wine.

Sunday [*December 16*] (the last Sunday), Brought sunshine—cold better, but still with me—Up very late—out to Veagh—Gin Fizz—Back to Hotel, lunch, two bottles of wine.

Through the arches of the Coliseum—the blue sky—no clouds. Writing this from the Arch of Constantine.

Livia's House.[12]

12. The house of Livia, mother of Tiberius and later wife of Augustus, especially interested Wolfe. He has a full page sketch of a column, and in his guidebook he underscored the description of the *Triclinum*, which had been the dining room.

Via Tritone—Book shop: *La Rome Antique* and many other guidebooks.

[*Borghese Gallery*]

369—[“*Entombment*”] Christ being lowered away from Calvary—by Raffael—one of their treasures and of course quite uninteresting.

74—Pontormo—Many pictures, not bad.

434—“Leda with swan” (Scuola di Leonardo)—Fine lustful looking swan.

Carpaccio—Head—450—good.

In the big book store: I bought *Rome*—Gabriel Faure—also *Wonders of Rome.* Books, Books, Books. *Roma Sacra*—and dozens of other books in French, English, and German on Rome and Italy. Grazia Deledda, Dekobra, *Decameron*, Mazzini, the Nelson Series in French, Have—*Walks in Rome*, *Roma—Scultore*, *Roma—Pittore*, Tolstoi, Balzac, Dickens.

Buy several of the Italian classics in little 5 lira vols. before you go home.[13]

De Musset, Shakespeare, Joyce, Tinayre, Du Gard, etc.

[*Though subdued by his severe cold, Wolfe spent his week in Rome. On December 17 he left for Naples, his port of embarkation for the homeward voyage.*]

Naples—Tuesday morning [*December 18*], Have had breakfast and got lunch and went out.

Now: Cook’s—mail, check steamer Cunard Line. *Vulcania*, Friday 21, Embark 11 o’clock.

Buy: Extra note book, pocket knife, underwear, socks, 2 shirts, Guide book to Naples (?).[14]

13. The only Italian books now in Wolfe’s library in the Wisdom Collection are Dante, *Divina Commedia* (Firenze, ?) and Petrarca, *Le Rime* (Milano, ?). Both are clothbound editions.

14. He did buy one—Griebens’ *Naples and Environs.*

Did all these things today according to plan in spite of feeling rotten. In addition luncheon over on the other side of basin by fortress, where later walked.

Tomorrow—Pompeii and Vesuvius—179 lira.

Movietone people coax two Italians into doing a piece. Little ragged scrap of a man—about 50—stubble of grey beard on his face—burlesque of frightfully dirty quality—and the little young Italian girl who giggled at first—then acted up her part.

The Americans and the Italians—the little dudey director—plump pleasant little face—good natured and hard boiled together—The rawboned movietone man—Young college kid.

"How was my courting, Mr. Ellis?"

"Very very rotten" etc.

The camera man, "Fred." The melting Italiano in spats and oh-so-dandy clothes and all the lousy ragged filthy wonderful people.

*New York Herald-Tribune*—Paris edition. The International Disgrace—Particularly the book section—The snotty little fellows highhatting their betters at home.

NATIONAL MUSEUM—NAPLES

Some of the statues and bronzes from Pompeii show signs of the evil and profound luxuriousness of the place.

Look up Titus—Face that of a voluptuous and evil man.

Vespasian—some heads with mouths part open—a little revolting—Another that of strong thoughtful man.

Scipio Africanus Maggiore—bronze. Another lean powerful Yankee face.

A Drunken Bacchus on a wine bag.

Two young men in bronze—Lottatore (wrestlers) very handsome, strong, and graceful.

Pompeio Tempio D'Iside. 976—a very beautiful thing—a little statue of Isis.

Antoninus Pius—Head of a good man.

Julius Caesar—Lean, calm head, lines around mouth, humor, intelligence, power.

The long thin nose of Euripides, the flat fleshy one of Socrates.
Vittoria—statue of—why are they so often headless?
Apollo (IV Century—in heavy black stone)—voluptuous.
Half man, half woman.

"Artemide d'Efeso" [*Diana of Ephesus*]—(6278)—a very strange thing—a [mummy?] column—with a dozen or more beast shaped ornaments—goats, lions, sphinxes, swans winged woven around the body, neck, and head.

Satyr and Maenad (Relief)—She's got him by the beard, and with her other pretty hand seems to be clutching for his privates—but he holds her by one hand and grasps her beard-pulling arm with another.

[*The following notes refer to ancient frescoes taken from the walls of Pompeii and Herculaneum.*]

Little wall paintings—very interesting. 9514—A little port basin —fire all around piers—boats with sails down—columns and cornices.

9003—Someone crowned with laurels—who could pass for Napoleon.

11059—Man feeling a woman's breast—her delicate hand is bent above his head—jewels, bracelets, rings—impression of great luxury—man is usually painted with brown sun-dark skin—woman's much lighter.

9193

9207—Cupids playing and dancing with volcanic looking mountains in distance.

8968—Voluptuous looking man—emperor or lord—with fat white arms—arrayed in gorgeous silken robes—with wine bowl in hands being supported on his cushioned couch by old naked slaves.

Four tempting forms that glimmer through the shade of centuries.

A hunting scene—with little springing horses—men on horseback—nobles, trees and ruined columns with a black boar springing through the trees, and a great dappled deer—like a giraffe with two highpointy horns—like Cranach's in Vienna 111479—a magnificent thing.

A springing horse—and a young man or woman being drawn backward from it by the hair by naked man.

Europa and the Bull.

Mosaic side—The great mosaic of battle between Alexander and Darius—the thing I saw in history books as a child—magnificent reproduction—Darius in chariot with strange headdress—his manner likewise—[picture?] was almost obliterated at left part—perhaps Alexander—the wonderful spears like Uccello.

COLERIDGE

The angels of peace and of darkness
The dear dark guardians of breadth
Have covered him over with darkness
With silence and peace and death.

5:50 Café Gambrinus:

People say there is "little to see at Naples outside of the scenery"—I think there is probably to be seen the most indescribable filth, poverty and vice in Europe there—after Vienna—here all this swarthy loud animation—this not-very-good Latinity—the somewhat poisonous and untidy strumpets.

Among the poor I am sure they can go to depths we can not believe because they have no sense of filth. I am sure there are dung-eaters among them—people who would think nothing of eating bread soaked in urine.

The point is that filth means something to us—something terrible and unutterable—It means little to the Latin. The way the men sit around with hats on in gangs in the cold cafés—there is something loutish and (sorry) American about it—You see it in New York—among the Irish and the Italians.

[*Here begins a series of loose pages from which Wolfe took many entries to use for Eugene's Paris notebook in* Of Time and the River, *pp.668–72. He made no revisions except to change Italian references to French ones. He clipped the pages together with a yellow scrap of paper on which he had written some words to place the material in Paris. They appear on page 668 and begin the whole sequence:* "At Le Régence: Remembering the whore with the rotten teeth that I talked to last night on Rue Lafayette."]

The great myth that the Latins are "romantic" people—The Latins have qualities and standards that we do not possess—Hence we overvalue them.

There are many places in the world where life attains a greater variety, interest, or profundity than in Paris (viz. New York, London, Vienna, Munich). Yet a great many Americans make their homes in Paris because they are sure it is the center of the world's intellectual and cultural reputations.

It is easier for a writer to secure a reputation in France than in any other country. Many French writers have very respectable reputations who would be laughed at in other countries. For example, Henry Bordeaux—some Americans who study French literature think he is a distinguished writer. His name has a solid respectable sound to it. On the covers of all his books is printed "member of the French Academy." But you could hardly find an intellectual in America who would say a kind word for Harold Bell Wright. Yet Harold Bell Wright—poor as he may be—is a better writer than Henry Bordeaux. If you don't believe it, read them. Americans are very unfair about this.

This is what is horribly decayed and dying about Naples—the brilliant lights, the Mediterranean—all that should make for light, life, and gayety at night. Instead the dead (suppressed) streets—the air of sober quiet and slumber for tomorrow's work—and within simply thrust out of sight—the enormous monstrous crime—organization of vice.

Tomorrow—

Up, breakfast (Get enough sleep tomorrow), Cook's (Cable Aline and Mama, mail address).

Museum.

Eat at Via Roma (see Guide book), after lunch go for "visit" there 4 or 5—7 o'clock.

Socks (Get box from Gutteridge), shirt.

Big Book store (album of Naples, bloody books, newspapers and cheap books, Tauchnitz).

Trinkets (?)—Something for Aline.

On seeing a ragged whore in Rome—My dirt is not as dirty as your dirt. My clean-ness is cleaner than your clean-ness. If I have a hole in my sock—that is cunning. If you have a hole in your stocking love flies out the window. Why are we like this?

Boredom is the bedfellow of all the Latin peoples—The English, in spite of the phrase "bored Englishman," are not bored. The Germans are eager and noisy about everything they are told they should be interested in. The Americans are interested in everything for a week—

a week at a time—except sensation; they are interested in that all the time.

I have heard a great deal of the "smiling Latins," the "gay Italians" etc. I have seen few indications that the Italians are gay. They are moody—they are really a sombre and passionate people—the Italian face when silent is rather sullen.

A little bar near Via Torino at 12:30 at night—The descendants of Julius Caesar and Cosimo Medici came in—Gang spirit—swarthy, pasty, poisonous-looking fellows in jazzy clothes.

What has happened, Clio? Speak!

Italy in winter is about the most uncomfortable place I have ever been in.

In New York the opportunities for learning, and for acquiring a culture that shall not come out of the ruins but belong to life, are probably greater than anywhere else in the world.

This is because America is young and rich, and comparatively unencumbered by bad things.

Tradition which saves what is good and great in Europe also saves what is poor, so that one wades through miles of junk to come to a great thing.

In New York books are plentiful and easy to get; the music and the theater is [*sic*] the best in the world.

The great trouble with New York is that one feels uncomfortable while enjoying these things—In the daytime a man should be making money. The time to read is at night before one goes to bed. The time to hear music or go to the theater is also at night. The time to look at pictures is on Sunday.

Another fault comes from our lack of Independence—I am sure some of the most knowing people in the world about the arts are in America. I can not read a magazine like The *Dial*, or The *Nation* and The *New Republic* without getting frightened. One man wrote a book called *Studies In Ten Literatures*—which of course is foolish.[15] We want to seem knowing about all these things because we have not enough confidence in ourselves.

We have had niggers for 300 years living all over the place—but all we did about it was to write minstrel show coon stories until two or

15. *Studies from Ten Literatures* (New York, 1925) was written by Ernest Boyd, husband of Wolfe's agent. Wolfe later satirized Boyd as Seamus Malone in **W&R.**

three years ago when the French discovered for us how interesting they are. We let Paul Morand and the man who wrote *Batouale* and Soupault do it for us—then we began writing stories about Harlem, etc.

Instead of whining that we have no literary traditions, or that we must learn by keeping constantly in touch with the European models, or by keeping away from them, we should get busy telling some of the stories about America that have never been told.

An immense amount of writing is being done in America today, but most of it is according to a stupid pattern. For example, there are dozens of cheap fiction magazines with a cowboy and a smoking gun in his hand. Most of the stories in them are about the Double X Ranch, and so on. There are others about the Northwest Mounted; others about sea life.

A book like *Main Street* which made such a stir, is like Main Street. It is like "I've seen all Europe" tourists who have spent two days in each country in a round-the-town-bus.

In a magazine like The *American Mercury* the stories are also too much of a pattern—it is all about how the Deacon screwed the Methodist minister's wife at the same time having the town prostitute put in jail for coming to church on Sunday and mixing with the good folks.

When you hear people saying about *Babbitt*—that it is not the whole story and that much more can be said, you agree with them. Then they begin to talk about "the other side" and you lose hope. You see they mean by other side—Dr. [*Frank*] Crane and Booth Tarkington.

So far from being "another side," there are a million other sides. And so far from *Babbitt* being too strong, the stories that may be written about America will make *Babbitt* an innocent little child's book to be read at the Christmas school entertainment along with *The Christmas Carol* and *Excelsior*. The man who suggests the strangeness and variety of this life most is Sherwood Anderson. Or was I think, he's got too fancy since *Winesburg, Ohio*.

A French writer who said there was no real variety in the life of the French because they all had red wine on the table, sat at little tables in cafés to gossip, and had mistresses, would be called a fool. Yet an American will criticize his country for standardization on no better grounds—namely that most of them are Methodists or Baptists, Democrats or Republicans, Rotarians or Kiwanians.

*Babbitt* is a very interesting book. But I believe it would be possible for a German writer with a talent similar to Sinclair Lewis' to write a book called *Schmidt* or *Bauer* which would be just as sweeping a portrait. Do you want to know what the gentleman looks like? He is much easier to describe than Babbitt.

Morality—If a man has a mistress in America it is a sign he is a Bohemian, a rebel against society, etc.

In France such a man is the average Bourgeois. Sexual intercourse in America is considered normal and natural in only one way. In France they write dozens of books describing dozens of ways. Any French whore will use her mouth—usually by preference—and no one ever thinks the act is perverse.

MOCK LITERARY ANECDOTES[16]

One day as Whistler was standing before a shop window in St. James Street observing some prints of Battersea lodge, he was accosted by Oscar Wilde coming in the opposite direction.

"Gad, Jimmy," said Oscar with generous impulsiveness, "I wish I had said that."

"Don't you just?" remarked the inimitable James imperturbably adjusting his monocle.

One day in June Anatole France went to Rodin's studio for luncheon. The talk having turned to early Greek primitives, Rodin remarked:

"Some writers have a great deal to say and an atrocious style. But you, Dear Master, have a delicious style."

"And you, Master?" queried France ironically, allowing his eyes to rest upon the torso of The Thinker, "Since when did you become a Critic?"

In the burst of laughter that followed this thrust Rodin had to admit himself floored for once.

16. Wolfe revised these somewhat for Eugene's notebook, and they appear in OT&R pp. 663–64. He also provided a little introduction, which ends this way, "A certain kind of mind collects these—pale, feeble, rootless, arty, hopeless, lost—Joel Pierce tells them too. First time I heard them at Harvard what sophisticated raconteurs I thought them!—God, how green I was! "You will, Oscar, you will," and all the rest of it!—Today, sitting on terrace at Taverne Royale, I made some of my own. Here they are:"

A young actor who had, it must be confessed, more ambition than talent, one day rushed excitedly up to Sir Henry Irving, during a rehearsal of *Hamlet*.

"It seems to me, sir," he burst out without preliminary, "that some actors ruin their parts by overplaying them."

"And some," remarked Sir Henry during an awful pause, "don't."

One day Sir James Barrie observed Bernard Shaw staring somewhat disconsolately at an unsavory mass of vegetables that adorned his plate while he was lunching at the Atheneum.

"I hear that you are working on a new play," remarked Barrie whimsically, eyeing the contents of the platter.

For once, G. B. S. had no answer ready.

Why won't these do?

Young American writing book reviews for *New York Times* in classical, simple, godlike manner of Anatole France:

"The new book of Monsieur Henry Spriggins, which lies before me on my desk, fills me with misgivings. The author is young and intolerant of simple things. He is full of talent, but he is proud, and has not a simple heart. What a pity! (etc.)"

Sculpture—"There's a big gallery full of it here. Why doesn't it interest me more? The trouble is that sculpture must have begun more as a form of commemoration than as an art. Roman men and matrons had their portraits done in stone so that "eternal" Rome could look at them for centuries.

# *PART THREE~*

# *PUBLICATION AND FAME*

## *Pocket Notebook 8*

### *December 20, 1928, to January 26, 1929*

*This smudged and dog-eared notebook comes at a turning point in Wolfe's career, when Scribner's accepted his novel for publication. The notebook contains very little, however, only an account of Wolfe's bad-tempered voyage back to the United States and his notes on changes to be made in his manuscript before publication.*

*Inserted in the end papers are the following items:*

*1. A receipted dining room bill from Macpherson's Hotel Britannique in Naples.*

*2. A telegram from Madeleine Boyd to Wolfe on January 9, 1929, saying,* "CALL UP AT ONCE VERY IMPORTANT."

*3. The final examination of Dean Munn in English 55 (Bible) at New York University given on January 22, 1929.*

*4. The address of Desmond Powell in Colorado Springs.*

---

[*Naples, December 20.*]

St. Lazar Picture House. Via Chiaia.

Big Perfumery shop just opposite picture house on the same side as picture house about the 5th or 6th place from movie.

Gambrinus again—Boat does not leave until five o'clock (or later) tomorrow—Leave hotel at 4.

[*Sketch of a man's profile entitled* "Why the Ladies come to Italy" *with comments:*]

The bear's grease begins here.
1½ inches of Forehead.
The full wet Lips.
That dark O-so-Romantic Color.

The vicious stupid life of the [streets?]—how bad and dull it is —and what infinite boredom is in it.

The Italians, I am sure, are tired of their own gestures.

The business of this afternoon—the vaccination and haircutting, although it was done with the greatest good humor, has left me with an ugly feeling. Why? I am sure that millions of Italians trying to get into America have gone through things a thousand times worse.

[*Sketch of man's head.*] An old gambler at the Gambrinus.

Handbook [*and*] cigarette seller. [*Sketch.*]

Cook's: tomorrow morning.
(1) Ask questions about my [insured bag?]
(2) Buy Aline coral [thing?]
(3) Buy Books (and perhaps candy)
Return to hotel by ten o'clock and pack. [*All items marked through.*]

It is eleven-thirty now in Gambrinus. Orchestra still here, but most of the people gone or going—Those fat, throaty voices, full of hock and spittle—Middle-aged or older men going home now to greasy wives.

In the square outside—bareness—cold light—sporty young wop with his slut walks by.

On the other side I know are the Taxis, the [Hookmen?], the innumerable pimps, "guides," and whorehouse touts ready to swarm over you at moment's notice.

The young wop author—the poet—in the bookshop this afternoon, who made me a copy of his work. I was touched. It was kind and gracious.

11:35 orchestra leaving—Me too—*Up* from this frayed red plush—*Out*—of this ghastly tomb. Away! Away!

The desire to do some work that can be seen. I have taught. Yes; but I can not *see* the effects of it.

The soul sinks at the thought of all the work that has been done in the world.

Where are the men who built the Forum?

Before some of the great monumental buildings of Italy—even new ugly ones—you feel not only puniness of your flesh but puniness of spirit. How many thousand men have sweat to build this?

Don't feel this about [America?]—I think it is [because of the?]

machine—You feel that machines have done the work—that one man with a machine is worth a thousand.

[*The poem about the star appears again here.*]

Chesterton's Cheese and Beer—I have been to England, and I know it is bad cheese and bad beer. That's the trouble.

[*On Friday, December 21, Wolfe boarded the Cunard Line's* Vulcania *and sailed for home, occupying Cabin 455C. Exhausted from his frantic touring, and sated by what he had seen, he faced an uncertain future in America. But there was a gleam—Scribner's was interested in "O Lost."*

*He made no further notes in this notebook until the day after Christmas.*]

Wed., Dec. 26—

Today we are opposite the Azores—weather bad and almost everyone is seasick. The air is damp, steamy, and heavy—the sea all ugly grey and still with no big waves, but with a treacherous roll that keeps the ship creaking and heaving every second.

Yesterday was Christmas, but there was little Christmas spirit aboard. They fed us prodigously last night—two wines (Capri and Spumante) after which the Franciscan [1] got up and made an impassioned baroque speech which he wanted me to follow—I didn't, of course. As for me, I am bored by the sea, I am bored by these poor dead, sullen, stolid, swarthy, murderous wretches who sit so dumb and peasantlike on the ship's new chairs. My arm is still sore and badly inflamed from the vaccination. On the third day (Sunday) according to medical prophesy, I had fever and stayed in bed good part of time. It is ugly, nasty and unpleasant. I have made few notes in this book recently. None, I think, since leaving Naples.

The sea had a bad effect upon my concentration. I am torpid, sleepy,—a little touched today, I believe, by seasickness, although I have none of the more unpleasant symptoms—But this is the physical log of the voyage:

Friday night 11:30—Left Naples—I went on deck and watched the elfin witch lights of Naples and the bay recede. Saw the ship go out of the breakwaters of the inner harbor, and then saw Vesuvius a great

1. The priest was a fellow passenger who ate at the same table with Wolfe.

black cone supporting another great black cone of smoke turned upside down—So [*sketch*].

That was practically the end of Europe for that time.

Next day, Saturday (about noon), we went around the end of Sardinia.

Sunday I was sick and did not go on deck much, but heard we could see the coast of Spain.

Monday morning (about 3:30) we went through Gibraltar—I did not see this.

Monday at lunch we saw the last of the Spanish and Portugal coasts—grand blazing cliffs of chalk and "nobly nobly Cape St. Vincent."[2]

Tuesday (yesterday) was Christmas—full Atlantic, but good weather.

Today—much fuller Atlantic, bad weather, sick passengers.

I have tried to reach Aline twice by radio[*gram*]—Yesterday, Christmas Day, I tried to get a message through, but was told it was useless. Will try again today. Have thus far heard nothing from her in answer to my cablegram.

English: 512—Wallace, 518—Wodehouse, 498—Millin.[3]

Thursday night [*December 27*]—

I do not like a voyage in the modern liner. It is a perfection of boredom and torpor. I have no money: I travel second class—I am weary to the roots of my soul of these sick sullen swarthy faces—when I see the Italian women and children puking upon the decks I almost hate them.

And I do not feel well. I am torpid, slow, weary—I eat too much—and am subtly diseased by the sea.

Here I am tonight mid-way over from Europe to America—but a little nearer America—and I wonder if I could ever have thought these creatures "quaint" or "picturesque" in their native habitat—Italy or Greece, or wherever they came from.

A great many of them have suffered the softening grace of my own native land, and I found them equally detestable—loud checked caps, cheap clothes, tan shoes—Also they "spik Eenglis."

2. "Nobly, nobly Cape Saint Vincent to the North-west died away" is the opening line of Robert Browning's "Home-Thoughts, from the Sea."

3. Books in the ship's library by Edgar Wallace, P. G. Wodehouse, and Sarah Gertrude Millin.

I am tired of the fat Franciscan and his interminable Italiano mouthings and eatings and drinkings and sickenings. And of the two doctors, the woman and the man—from Chicago. Perhaps they are living in adultery, but good god! how dull, how dull! who cares.

High spot of glory and joy today came just at lunch when boy brought radio[*gram*] from Aline to my cabin. I had sent her one not a half hour before. There was a moment of light and glory then.

Also, the sea this afternoon—all bright and windy and strong and blue. The ship swinging powerfully up and down—all around me now the smooth steady jar of the vibration—the polished smoking room wood creaks like leather—the smooth dynamo drive of the engines.

Saturday Night—

Today has been the stormiest weather we have yet had—afraid it has slowed the ship down considerably. Sea has been marvellous—sky sunshiney—terrific gale blowing—mountainous waves exploding in clouds of smoke—emerald green wake—The ship's stern rolls and lifts, and plunges upward into air like toy rocket—the huge waves come under the hull, and she bumps over them in a distressing way—I am enormously bored with these Italians—I feel horror and disgust and meanness at their sullen dark uncleanliness.

But most of all with the fat priest and his unending complaint, his unending eating, his unending tales of dieting.

The young sporty Italo-Americans play cards for a nickel or 3 cents and curse each other. The cur-snarl "What th' hell you want to know for what I got?" etc.

Of what I shall find in New York; of what life I shall lead there nothing yet. That must wait.

The shrilling of the radio in 2d class smoking room—1st class orchestra playing. Now for movies.

Sunday Night [*December 30*]—

One unending, interminable, wearisome day—and Naples-New York (Europe-America).

The sea has spared us nothing today. The gale has lasted since yesterday morning—today the ship was standing on its nose—most of them sick. But sea incredibly beautiful—walls of smoke, mountain high exploding against ship. Tonight (10:30) we are not far from Nantucket and the sea seems to be abating.

Tomorrow at 2 or 3 o'clock (they say) New York.

The two doctors—man and woman—that strange, dull, adulterous pair!

The Hungarian Girl.

The Sailor Men (Jansen and Brother Benn Frank).

The Barman with The Broken Nose.

Tonight at our storm tossed dinner: Chateau Lafite (Bordeaux) instead of the French Stuff.

The two old Salts—The Captain and The mate—Big thick limbed, thick featured man—The one a Lithuanian, the other a Norwegian.

The Mate's Stories of His Life: Passenger Ship Bergen to Newcastle-on-Tyne—Norwegian Navy—War of Independence—Now Vacuum Oil Co.

The owner's son (of Cosalido Line) aboard here.

Recollections: Streets of Naples—those winding, winding, climbing up to the hills—the little narrow streets sloping up and down into Via Roma—sensation of slum, vice, hanging wash, multitudinous small shops. Via Chiaia.

[*The remainder of this day's reflections were used, with slight modifications, for Eugene's Paris notebook in* Of Time and the River, *pp. 67–80.*]

Europe and America are still too far apart—the "interminable" day is far too long—for the speeding ships—*new* impression with which I passed over Italian border—we must bring them closer together.

*Results*—Things that matter in our life can not be *resulted* so easily. I have lived deeply, intensely, vividly, on the whole unhappily for six months. Some people say that is all that matters. I do not think it is. But things can not be tallied up so easily.

Aline—I am wandering in a vast *vague* about her. I love her, I think of seeing her again with a sense of strangeness and wonder; but I have no sort of idea what it will be like, or what has happened. Why can we not remember the face of anyone we love? Never has the many-ness and the much-ness of things caused me such trouble as in the past six months—But never have I had so firm a conviction that our lives can live upon only a few things, that we must find them, and begin to build our fences.

All creation is the building of a fence.

But deeper study always, sharper senses, profounder living: *Never* an end to curiosity!

The fruit of all this comes later—I must think. I must mix it all with myself and with America. I have caught much of it on paper. But infinitely the greater part is in the wash of my brain and blood.

Shaw makes a fool of himself when he writes of Napoleon, because he hates Napoleon and wants to make him ridiculous. But Shaw makes a hero of himself when he writes of Caesar. Shaw's Caesar is the best Caesar I know of. It is like Caesar looks. I am sure Caesar was like this.

But it is a mistake to suppose that Napoleon got his hair in the soup.

Sunday Night—

At about 8:30 tonight the sea began to abate—the ship's heavy pitching was lessened. Now (about 12 o'clock) it is a great deal better —there is a rocking movement, but not bad—glorious night—cold gale blowing still, brilliant half-moon, steely water, occasional light of fishing boat.

In smoking room two or three groups still playing cards—Venetian wall motifs—how far away here!

Venetian wall motifs—Japanese lanterns over lagoon—Masked woman (courtesan?) in red with black cape, mask, and naked breasts —To her bowing pantaloon (or some other). With her, unmasked woman in cockade hat (Is it Commedia dell' arte?).[4]

Monday [*December 31*]

Smooth sea—cold bright day—we land in New York during afternoon. The customary hokus-pokus of landing cards, herding about, etc. has already begun.

This boat too is America—this swarthy stew of Italians, Greeks, and God knows what other combinations. This morning they are "spikking Eenglis" (How are yew, Mister? etc.) and going about in their new cheap American clothes.

4. Commedia dell' arte is a very old type of Italian popular comedy in which actors performed stock parts with improvised dialogue. The "pantaloon" was usually a foolish old man, frequently a cuckold.

Tomorrow's Ocean (will be small).

This poisonous dropsy (great fat fellow).

When I'm in America I see some of the worst of it. When I'm away from it I think of the best of it.

A man belongs to his country as an arm belongs to its socket. Any permanent separation from it is an amputation.

What now! What now!

Good feeling of a lucky day—The calm sea—the steady drive of the ship's motors—the smoke of a freighter—the feel of the mighty earth, the mighty city, of life beginning and awaking, the smoke and smell of 90 million breakfasts in the air. This is a good thing in life.

America still means Hope and Life to me. I am the True Immigrant. It means Youth. I am 28.

One morning at the close of 1928 a ship was approaching the American coast at her full speed of twenty knots an hour. She was the *Vesuvia*, of Italian registry—she was a vessel of 25,000 tons and this was her first voyage. She carried 70 passengers in the first class, 120 in the second, and over 400 in the third. Her port of departure was Trieste; her destination was New York—she was due to reach New York at four o'clock of this same day.

There was reason why the *Vesuvia* was urging her engines forward at their capacity. It was the day before New Year's, the ship had promised delivery of passengers in New York on that day, it was her first voyage, and she was anxious to prove her worth. For two days she had fought with a terrific storm which had pounded at her hull from the Banks of Newfoundland to Nantucket lightship.

Among the second class passengers of this ship was Oliver Weston.[5]

[*Wolfe landed in New York on December 31. The momentous days following his arrival are best described in his long letter to his "spiritual mother," Margaret Roberts, in* Letters, *pp. 162–72. The next day, New Year's, was a holiday, and he could do nothing about his book. But on January 2 he called Maxwell Perkins and was invited to come for an interview. It is both prophetic and appropriate that the first entry in his notebook after he touched American soil is the address of Scribner's.*]

5. This passage was intended for "The River People," but, after many drafts and considerable shifting, it eventually became the beginning of Chapter 17, "The Ship," in W&R.

Scribners 597—5th Ave.

Civic Rep. Theatre—Chel. 0054.[6]

Circle 8080—Hotel Warwick—Theresa Helburn.[7]

1. Landlord (Money, lease, key) [8]
2. Gas and Electric—(15th St. and Eighth)
3. Truckman.

Marcus—6th Avenue and 21st Street. Go at Five o'clock.[9]

Notes: [10]

I propose to correct and revise the mss. 100 pages at a time, and if possible to deliver 100 pages every week.

Proposal for Condensation

First, to cut out of every page every word that is not essential to the meaning or emphasis of the writing—If I can find even 10 words on every page this will be 10,000 or more in entire mss.

Then, to cut out the introductory part, and write a new beginning.

To shorten the child-in-the-cradle scenes.

To shorten St. Louis scene save for Grover's death.

To correct all unnecessary coarseness in language, and to cut out unnecessary pages and passages scattered through the book.

6. Mrs. Bernstein was at this time associated with the Civic Repertory Theatre.

7. Miss Helburn, managing director of the Theatre Guild, was a close friend of Mrs. Bernstein's.

8. Wolfe had rented a new apartment at the rear of the second floor of 27 West 15th Street.

9. Marcus C. S. Noble was a friend who graduated from the University of North Carolina in 1921 and also studied at Harvard. He had accompanied Wolfe, Frank Graham, and Benjamin Cone on a tour of the Chateau Thierry battlefield in 1924.

10. Wolfe had his first interview with Maxwell Perkins on Wednesday, January 2. Although Perkins had virtually made up his mind to accept "O Lost," with his usual caution he would not commit Scribner's until all details could be agreed upon. Consequently, he made a number of suggestions to Wolfe and told him to think them over for a few days. These notes were made by Wolfe in preparation for his second interview with Perkins, which took place on the following Monday, January 7. At that time Perkins agreed verbally to publish "O Lost."

To revise Newport News scenes, and to omit scene with woman on the boat.[11]

To shorten State University part as much as possible—and further, in the university scenes to keep Eugene's relations with his family uppermost.

Questions:

—What about several pages that list all the smells and odors?

—What about child's fantasies?

—What about the seduction scene with the waitress in Charleston?

—What about paper-boy scenes, and especially that one with negress?

Scribner's suggests unity of scene so far as possible.

What about Julia's various trips to Hot Springs, Florida, New Orleans, and so on?

Proposal to Scribner's:

If I can get some definite assurance of their willingness to publish the book—if revised—I will set to work immediately.

The first thing I will do will be to write new introduction and omit the present beginning.[12] I can have this ready and delivered one week from the present interview.

Jan. 7th, 1929

T. W. A. B.

On this day Charles Scribner's and Son, Pub., accepted the *mss* of my first book.

Jan. 9, 1929

On this day I got letter from Scribner's confirming their acceptance of my book.

ALINE BERNSTEIN [*her signature*] THOMAS WOLFE

11. A dark-haired woman invites Eugene aboard ship for sexual relations.

12. "O Lost" began with two little boys, W. O. Gant and his brother, standing by a road in Pennsylvania watching Lee's troops pass on their way to Gettysburg, and continued with a long discussion of the Gant ancestors and the life of W. O. Gant prior to his arrival in Altamont. Perkins later wrote: "for years it was on my conscience that I had persuaded Tom to cut out that first scene of the two little boys on the roadside with Gettysburg impending." *Harvard Library Bulletin*, I (Autumn, 1947), p. 271.

Friday, Jan. 11

Dear Dean Munn: [13]

I'll keep coming in until I find you. I know you're very busy, but I want to talk to you a few minutes.

Came in this morning but you were occupied elsewhere. I have become [*sic*] to quiet down a little after the excitement of the other day, and I am beginning to work on the revision. Nevertheless, I'm still very happy.

TOM WOLFE

Melville Cane—Bryant 8126—28 W 44th St—16th Floor.[14]

Bottle Acidopholous Milk, Worcestershire, Lettuce, A-1 sauce, Guldens mustard.[15]

Jan. 24—

At Steve's—Letter from Don MacRae at Harvard Club tonight (from Buffalo)—he had heard from Asheville about book (from mother) and of course she had everything garbled.

Sat. Jan. 26—

Butter, Bread, Pork Chops, Endive, Delmonico Steak, Asparagus —Can—Best.

13. James B. Munn, Professor of English and Dean of Washington Square College at New York University, befriended Wolfe on various occasions and had read the manuscript of "O Lost." Munn's belief in the book, "I would not change a single word," encouraged Wolfe during the dark days of the rejections the previous spring.

14. Mr. Cane, an eminent attorney and poet, is an authority on theatrical and publishing contracts. Wolfe met him through Mrs. Bernstein, and he later became Wolfe's attorney. He reviewed the contract with Scribner's, wrote Wolfe's wills, and was friend as well as lawyer for the rest of Wolfe's life.

15. This grocery list is in Mrs. Bernstein's handwriting. Acidophilus milk is milk fermented by bacteria of the species *Lactobacillus acidophilus* and is used therapeutically to change the intestinal flora. Mrs. Bernstein was then on a diet which required this special milk, and it appears frequently on Wolfe's grocery lists.

## *Pocket Notebook 9*

## *February 4, 1929, to March 21, 1929*

*Wolfe had arrived in New York broke and with no immediate prospects of a job. But the acceptance of his novel brought him an unexpected windfall, an advance payment of $500.00 from Scribner's. Less his agent's fee, this netted him $450.00. On January 11 Perkins had written him: "I sent the contract and check to Mrs. Boyd yesterday. She said she would immediately get in touch with you. I look forward eagerly to seeing the first section of the revised manuscript. You can certainly be sure that your novel will have the greatest personal support and interest in this establishment." While this amount was most welcome and would sustain him for a while, he did not know how long the process of revision and publication would take, so he turned to his friends Professor Watt and Dean Munn once more.*

*Professor Watt had already filled all the positions in his own department for the semester beginning in February, but he managed to get Wolfe a job teaching one class of Freshman English in the Department of Architecture in the new College of Fine Arts. This would pay him $300.00. The class was a small one and met only twice a week, but Wolfe took his responsibility seriously and gave it his best efforts as a teacher. A few of his teaching notes are contained in this notebook.*

*Dean Munn was currently teaching a large class in Literature and the Bible and employed Ralph Beals, then an instructor in the English Department at N.Y.U. but later chief librarian of the New York Public Library, as his reader. Munn decided to use Wolfe as a second reader because, as he wrote Watt, he wanted to spare Beals' eyes "and give Tom a little more money." This arrangement brought Wolfe an additional $300.00.*

*Although the bulk of this notebook is filled with notes on Dean Munn's lectures and other academic jottings, only the notes on the first lecture have been included, as a sample of this material.*

---

Monday Night Feb. 4:

Went to Kensico today with Aline and Woodsend, the architect.[1]

1. Mr. and Mrs. Bernstein were building a country house on Whippoorwill Road, Armonk, N.Y., and the architect was Hy E. Woodsend.

Work at N.Y.U. starting tomorrow.

Ate at Blueribbon tonight.

Tea at Aline's this afternoon—Alice Baker there.[2]

Thinking tonight of conversation with Volkening other night —I said "Fritz" Gottlieb—knowing Gottlieb's name was Hans.[3] Why? Because vaguely—no fault to him—he was associated in my mind with painful scenes and events of last year—I did this to appear forgetful, indifferent, etc.

Dean Munn: [*Tuesday, February 5*]—1st Lecture:

*A Student's Philosophy of Religion*—Wright—Macmillan, 1923. Chapters X–XIII.[4]

Gospels—Synoptic: Matthew, Mark, Luke, John.[5]

Purpose of Course:

First Term—Went over Old Testament of Judaism—Second term—How the develop. from Judaism—Christianity—and it conquered world of England—how it affected lit[*erature*]. Certain elements in Judaism—every one of which present in Christ.

Religious fervor [*page torn*]. Religious differences can always flame up—but we can discuss them more easily now.

Second term—1st—a rapid review of New Testament—Jewish students will be surprised at similarity of Judaism and Christianity—many people say Christianity only Judaism.

Wright: 10—Judaism
11—Catholicism
12—Mod. Judaism & Christianity.

Chronology:

Babylon, Assyria—Fell about 540 BC—Persians came in [*page torn*]—Was Jesus cognizant of divine mission at time of Capture? *Yes* —Something supernatural accompanying it.

In Apocryphal books (which have been rejected) stories of little clay birds which Jesus made fly, etc. The paternity of God—his

2. A friend of Mrs. Bernstein's who sublet the quarters on 8th Street while Wolfe was in Europe in the fall of 1926. Miss Baker and Ruth Albert were proprietors of an antique shop at 11 East 8th Street.

3. Hans J. Gottlieb was an instructor in the English Department at N.Y.U. Henry T. Volkening had been an instructor in English at N.Y.U. from 1926 to 1928, but he left to join a literary agency.

4. The text in the course was by William Kelley Wright, Professor of Philosophy at Dartmouth College. Wolfe's copy, now in the Wisdom Collection, is unmarked, and some of the pages in the last chapters are uncut. The titles of the four chapters assigned are: "Judaism," "Ancient and Medieval Christianity," "Modern Christianity," and "Christianity and the Conservation of Values."

5. Wolfe is mistaken. John is not one of the synoptic gospels.

friendliness and love. Spoken of by Hosea and Amos—Therefore no significance in 12-year-old *temple* Jesus calling God father.

Jesus very ordinarily brought up [*page torn*] and Jesus' parables are [*page torn*] common-folk stories—and hominess—one reason why Jesus' words have had such enormous influence.

In the many conflicts between letter and spirit Jesus invariably sided with spirit—notable case of woman taken in adultery.

*Temptation* again—Satan—symbolized Adversary to Jesus who appears as in our bitter moments.

Jesus like all the prophets [*page torn*]—goes back to desert—fast 40 days—Oriental custom—Jesus has been baptized and knows he is divine. Adversary says—If you are the Son of God, what's the use of fasting?—Man is not completely an animal as you and your kind seem to think—Adversary takes him to Jerusalem and sets him on a temple—If you are Son of God, why not prove it, and spare (Psalm 91—XI–XII) yourself [agony?]

*Again*—"devil takes him up into an exceeding high mountain—showeth him all the kingdoms of the earth"—Devil says—Only bow in the Hour of Remorse (obey power and flesh) and I'll stay by you. Jesus says—not by might and not by power but by God's Spirit.

Jesus has marvelous power of homely illustrations.

## THE FEELING OF POWER [6]

At the Age of 27, I estimate that I have eaten more food than have most men of fifty, and that there are not two dozen people in Europe and America with a subtler or more delicate taste than I have. In addition to my refined gluttony I am blessed with one of the most powerfully exquisite sensory organizations in the world—there may be other men of finer and more delicate gourmandism, but they can only be seduced through the length of their bodies of 5 feet 8 or 10.

In addition I have enjoyed over 900 bottles of good wine, and the bodies of more than 100 women, more than 20 of whom have given themselves to me without charge.

In addition I have read, since my fifth year, I have read parts in about 50,000 books and plays, and about 15,000 in entirety.

6. Since Wolfe gives the narrator's age as 27, this is apparently the beginning of a fictional work—perhaps something along the line of the sketch that he later called "Gulliver."

Some of the nicest things in the world: [7]

The pictures of Peter Breughel
The Wiener Wald
Alte Nussbaum
L'Écrevisse in June
Der Rheinreise [*The Rhine trip*]
The Cherbourg-Paris Express diner—good bottle of red wine looking out on the fair plump land of France
Stadt park in Bonn on summer's day
First meal (in France?) after getting off the boat (in Boulogne)
Summer's afternoon at the Régence
Henriette
Foyot and Fouquet
Valentin Sorg's in Strassburg.

English I—Feb. 11:

*Writing*—Make it as simple and clear as possible for them—get the main things first.

The Word (precision, concreteness, definiteness). Give examples. All writing begins with the word.

The Sentence.

The Paragraph.

Discuss these two:

The World Court and The League of Nations.

Is the World Court A Better Means For Adjusting International Disputes than the League of Nations?

[*Theme*] TOPICS FOR NEXT WEEK

(1) The Most Exciting Moment In My Life
(2) A Process Exposition
(3) One Natural Advantage of My Home Town

7. Of the thirteen European pleasures that Wolfe lists, nine of them concern eating. In addition to the first meal in France and the Paris Express diner, he lists seven of his favorite restaurants, some of which he includes in his fiction. Paris restaurants L'Ecrevisse, Régence, Henriette, and Fouquet are mentioned in OT&R, p. 688, and La Régence was made the heading for many of Eugene's notebook entries. Foyot, a left bank establishment, and Valentin Sorg's in Strasbourg were longtime favorites, but the Alte Nussbaum in Budapest was a recent discovery.

(4) Is Speed A Sign of Progress?

(5) Why I Prefer The City (The Small Town) To the Small Town (The City)

(6) Why I Prefer the Big University (The Small College)

(7) To The Small College (The Big University)

(8) Why We Should (Should Not) Envy Our Grandfathers.

Assignments In Grammar and Essay Book (Jargon).
Essay on Jargon [*by Arthur Quiller-Couch*].

Another part of the forest:

The Romans marching up and down with J. Caesar. Caesar at a table before his tent (dictating memoirs to his secretary).

*Caesar*—Have you got his letter there?

—Yes.—It is very long, Caesar.

*Caesar*—(wearily) Let's have it.

—Your soldiers have pillaged our cities, raped our wives, deflowered our virgins, and burned our grain.

*Caesar* (sharply) What's that? Who did that? Burned his grain, I mean.

—(impatiently) No one, of course. [*Marked out:* That's nothing like the usual palaver.] The beer-bellied old bastard is just getting wound up. As for deflowering his virgins [*breaks off*]

Books of Harvard Club: [8]

Shakespeare plays
Shaw's Plays
Leslie Stephen
Shelley's Poetry
New English Dictionary
Ward's English Poetry
Synge's Plays and Writings
*Encyclopaedia Britannica*
New Testament
*Who's Who*
Lives of Bernard Shaw

8. The Harvard Club, 27 West 44th Street, was Wolfe's favorite retreat, and it often supplied him with necessary services. He usually had his mail sent there to protect the anonymity of his apartment address, and during the period he lived in the loft building on 8th Street, he used the Harvard Club for his baths. He also enjoyed browsing in the club library among the books and periodicals.

Works of T. Roosevelt
Works of W. Bagehot
*Cambridge History of English Literature*
Max Beerbohm
*Oxford Book of English Verse*
Tolstoy
Russian Lit.
Africa Travel
New York Travel
U.S. Travel.

The Corp's lieutenant rose and with a few graceful, if somewhat formal, words, welcomed to the newcomer into the brotherhood, managing with perfect propriety to make a few sly insinuations as to the charms of German womanhood, an allusion which was not lost upon the audience who laughed with hearty appreciation and pounded their approval on the table. All of this was done without a suggestion of coarseness—no word that might offend the most delicate taste was uttered.

Mr. Gant replied with a few simple and well chosen words, stressing the ties of blood and culture which bound the two great nations, and skillfully avoiding all mention of the Rhine question, the Ruhr, and the painful subject of the last war. Rather he spoke of the great brotherhood of youth and sport which formed the most enduring hope for the peace of the world. The speaker also won the hearts of his listeners by frequent references to German Culture—reciting, without the trace of an accent a few stanzas of *Die Wacht Am Rhein*, embellishing his address with copious quotations from Goethe and Schiller, and referring frequently to Heinrich Heine, Adalbert Stifter, Gustav Freytag, Theodor Storm, Friedrich Von Kotzebue, Karl Immermann, Franz Grillparzer, Jean Paul Richter, Hermann Sudermann, Freidrich Von Lessing.

All winterwild, All blown is their hair.

Alain Fournier (*The Wanderer* (?))[9]

9. *The Wanderer*, an English translation of Fournier's *Le Grand Meaulnes*, had recently been published and had been favorably reviewed by the New York press just prior to Wolfe's return to the U.S. *The Wanderer* is the story of an adolescent's search for an ideal, which draws heavily on scenes and episodes from the author's own youth in rural France. Place names and personal names are used with little or no change. Both the theme and the autobiographical nature of the novel would have struck responsive chords in Wolfe, especially at the very time he was revising "O Lost" for publication.

[*Life-size drawing of index finger with bitten nail—probably a tracing of his own—across which is written:*]

That day we read in the book no more.[10]

On "the Passion For Condensation." It may be a very bad passion. Probably what we need is a passion for expansion. What most of us mean when we say we have a passion for condensation is simply that we haven't very much to write about. Perhaps *The Bridge of San Luis Rey* is a better book than *Of Human Bondage*, but it is certainly not a better book simply because it is shorter. If the story of San Luis Rey can be told in 200 pages well and good. But that does not mean that all stories should be cut to 200 pages. As a matter of fact, the long novel can easily hold its own against the short one. Even if we attempt to choose the best novels written during this century it seems to me that most of them would be long ones. To name a few:

| | |
|---|---|
| *Jean Christophe* | *The Old Wives Tale* |
| *Of Human Bondage* | *Buddenbrooks* |
| *Ulysses* | *The Magic Mountain* |
| *Sons and Lovers* | *The World's Illusion* |
| | *An American Tragedy* |

Olin Dows
c/o Vincent Astor
130 East 80th Street
[Can you come to tea Mrs. Bernsteins today, *marked out.*]
Call me Watkins 3882 today at four-thirty.

TOM WOLFE

[*Teaching notes for Freshman English:*]
Definition
Detail
Comparison
Contrast
Division
Repetition
Example
Awe—Terror

10. This famous line of Francesca da Rimini occurs in Canto V of Dante's *Inferno*, where she recounts the beginning of her illicit affair with her lover Paolo. It apparently struck Wolfe as a good potential title. Later that year or the next he wrote in "The October Fair" miscellaneous ledger, "Title: They Read in the Book No More," for the story of Stephen Hook in his publisher's office seeing a workman fall from the top of a building.

Joy—Happiness
Materialist—Idealist
Prettiness—Beauty
Temperance—Abstentiousness
The Pedant—The Scholar

[*Theme*] TOPICS

What Is Courage?
What Is A Gentleman?
What Is A Snob?
What I Understand By "Education."

[*Name and address not in Wolfe's hand: James Lewis Mandel, 701 Cratona Park North, Tremont 2700.*[11]]

George Stevens, W. W. Norton, 70 5th Avenue, Algonquin 4659.[12]

ENG[LISH] COMP[OSITION]

Paragraph structure p. 53 Grose.[13]
Effectiveness p. 54.
*Topics* (also topics on Popular Fallacies)
Write a paper illustrating differences between:
(1) An Interesting Lecture And A Dull One
(2) A Liberal Education And A Technical Education
(3) A Good Newspaper And A Poor One

11. Mandel was the student in Dean Munn's Bible class whom Wolfe employed to type revised portions of "O Lost." He has described his association with Wolfe in "Thomas Wolfe: A Reminiscence," *Thomas Wolfe at Washington Square*, pp. 93–103.

12. An Atlanta-born publisher who graduated from Harvard the same year Wolfe left. At this point he was vice-president of W. W. Norton & Co. Later, as editor of the *Saturday Review of Literature*, he was personally to review *The Web and the Rock* and put Wolfe's picture on the cover (June 24, 1939).

13. The textbooks in the course Wolfe was teaching were *Freshman Readings*, ed. Roger Sherman Loomis (Boston, 1927) and George Benjamin Woods, *A College Handbook of Writing* (Garden City, 1928). For his classroom preparation, however, Wolfe drew upon a text he had used in previous courses, Howard B. Grose Jr., *College Composition* (Chicago, 1926). Wolfe's copies of these textbooks, including two of Grose, are in the Wisdom Collection.

(4) Coney Island In February And In July
(5) Broadway By Day And By Night.

Charles, Cavanaugh's, Alice McAllister, Luchow's, Siegel, Italian Rest. (12th St.), Sam Broad's, Longchamp's, Geneva, Blue Ribbon, Lobster, St. Regis, 3 Star, Chop Suey (Columbus Circle), Rosoff, Grand Central, Solowey (Penn Stat.), Keen's (35th), Constantinople, Sardi's, [*Dinty*] Moore's.

March 3—Sunday 2:45 in El going from 14th to 42nd:

This near end of winter—young March sunshine—glorious day—The winter sunshine is all in the sky—far off beautiful and unwarm—It paints the cheap redbrick buildings beautifully and thinly (Yet of course it is warmer today).

THE WOMAN'S CLUB ROMANCE

(Cleveland-Indianapolis Unvisited)

A Rival to Richard Halliburton and Professor Erskine and young [Waugh?] the Englishman—A drive in the luxurious little roadster out to her lodge in the pine woods.[14]

(He thought with pleasure how fine he would look in his evening clothes, boyish yet beautiful and dignified—after the lecture—he is kidnaped by three beautiful matrons all contending for his favors).

How the district around the hotel looks at night (11:15 of winter's eve).

Estimating population of N.Y. as 6,000,000 and *half* as females. 3,000,000 women—of which between ages of 20–35 perhaps 750,000. Do I see one in 750 that I want. *No!* There are not over 1500 women in N.Y. who could be physically desirable to me.

For example N.Y.U.—see what happens there.

14. These notes for a parody or satire were never developed in published form. Richard Halliburton (1900–39) was an intrepid traveler and author of adventure books whose name was synonymous with romantic adventure to Wolfe's generation. John Erskine (1879–1951), a professor of English at Columbia University, wrote satiric modern versions of famous legends in addition to serious scholarly works. The young Englishman who would add old-world sophistication to this trio was probably Alec Waugh (1898——), novelist, travel writer, and older brother of Evelyn Waugh.

*Consider this*—In Germany meeting with German professor who will give me accelerating medicine which will enable me to read all the books.

The Varieties of Human Experience (In literature)
Wealth—[*The Count of*] *Monte Cristo*
Love—Romeo & Juliet, Sappho
Adventure—*Moby Dick*, Dumas, Young Wild West, *Quentin Durward.*
The Heart and Soul—*Crime and Punishment, Jean Christophe*

[*Two pages of figures comparing enrollment at German universities with that of American universities*]

[*Whole page of sketches of faces.*]

Will you send me a ticket?
*Sent* you a *tick* et.
And I did.
What about your girl friend?
I suppose you found you better go.
I don't know how it's going to turn out—that's one of reasons.
That's *absolutely* true.

(Another)
I saw her—willing to travel.
(The Same) I said what's the matter with so-and-so—is she choosy? She said yes.
I said no I don't think so. I don't think she is.
(The subject of these two talks were women, living with men, hotel rooms, girl friends, and so on.)

Dean Munn, Tuesday, March 11 [*12*], 1929 [*Lecture on the Reformation in England.*]

Dean Munn, March 14, 1929 [*Lecture on puritanism in the American colonies.*]

[*Theme topics*]
I—Selection of Details and Point of View:
1. A House
(a) A Purchaser

(b) An Insurance Agent
(c) An Architect
(d) A Person who wanted to Recognize the House when He Saw it Again
(e) A Builder who had Undertaken to Estimate The Cost When Bidding

2. A Landscape (as seen by)
(a) A Farmer
(b) A Surveyor
(c) An Artist
(d) A Commuter

3. A City Snow (as seen by)
(a) A Taxi Driver
(b) A Street Cleaner
(c) A Man Who Lives in The Country
(d) A Literary Man

II—Write a brief description of some person in the school of architecture who has marked characteristics. Write about him in such a way that he can be recognized without being named.

Amplification of General Statement:

"The World Is Too Much With Us"[15]

"The future is only the past again, entered through another gate."[16]

We judge a man partly by the company he keeps.

[*March 20:*]

THE FAST EXPRESS[17]

Make it (this whole section) about 60–80,000 words long—end it with talk between two women (Helen and Eliza).

15. Title of one of Wordsworth's best-known sonnets.

16. Arthur Wing Pinero, *The Second Mrs. Tanqueray*, Act IV.

17. This is the first mention in Wolfe's notes of "The Fast Express." While thinking about "The River People," Wolfe was led somewhat astray by the autobiographical character in that novel, and he planned a section to include several autobiographical episodes (items 2, 3, 4, and 5 of his outline) which he had already written. The last item of the outline was to be the talk of Helen and Eliza as Eugene waited for the express to carry him north. After many shifts and revisions it would eventually become the opening scene of OT&R.

Outline
1. Meeting at Twilight
2. Eugene's fantasies and life in Boston
3. Emerson Pentland, and all the other Pentlands
4. The Girl in Medford
5. Promenade of Mr. E. G. Faust
6. Gant's Death
7. The Fast Express
8. The Two Women

An Autobiographical Sketch (500 words)
What College Means to Me
My Favorite Study
Why I Have Chosen Architecture As A Profession
My Last Year In High School

# *Pocket Notebook 10*

## *March 21, 1929, to June, 1929*

*Though Wolfe's restless mind was active with ideas and ambitious plans for new writing projects, he had a busy spring with the tasks at hand, and this notebook reflects all of his principal activities. Like many teachers of freshman composition, he continued to use a former textbook for suggestions, but he enriched that material by drawing on his own writing experience. Since his classroom preparation thus suggests certain of his creative interests, we have included more of his teaching notes than usual. We have deleted, however, his notes on eleven of Dean Munn's lectures, keeping only the dates of the lectures and an indication of their subject matter.*

*Wolfe's main concern was still the revision of his manuscript, and it was during the period covered by this notebook that most of it was readied for the printer. The length and the editing of that manuscript have spawned numerous anecdotes that have long since passed into literary legend, with all its exaggeration and distortion. Wolfe himself contributed to the legend when he gleefully wrote his friend George McCoy the following August:* "When they accepted the book the publishers told me to get busy with my little hatchet and carve off some 100,000 words. . . . I did get busy, and in a month or two cut out twenty or thirty thousand words, and added fifty thousand more." *Even the impeccable Maxwell Perkins has added to the prevailing misconception while trying to clear up some of the confusion. Almost two decades after the fact, Perkins—in a notable lapse of memory—wrote in the* Harvard Library Bulletin *essay that was left unfinished at his death: "The extent of cutting in that book has somehow come to be greatly exaggerated. Really, it was more a matter of reorganization." Despite these widely circulated but misleading statements by the two principals involved, it was not a matter of reorganization; the problem actually was one of cutting.*

*When submitted to Scribner's, the manuscript was 1,114 pages long and contained approximately 330,000 words. In the process of revision it was reduced by about 95,000 words, but Wolfe added some 5,000 more, mostly for new transitions, so that the net reduction was roughly 90,000 words. This compression was achieved by 147 cuts in the manuscript, two-thirds of which are listed in the latter part of this notebook and indicate how the reduction was accomplished.*

*This cutting caused Wolfe considerable pain, even though he recognized its necessity. In May he complained to his sister Mabel:* "I am working every day with the editor of Scribner's, Mr. Perkins, on the revision of my book. We are cutting out big chunks, and my heart bleeds to see it go, but it's die dog or eat the hatchet." *His protest was more bitterly expressed when he roared at his agent,* "Those sons of bitches, they are taking the balls off me."

---

Thursday, March 21:

Bought this book today.

Read in *London Mercury* today piece about radio taken from *American Mercury*.[1]

Ignatius Phayre—writes for English *Quarterly Review*—a bitterly Anti-American writer—but very skillful and unobtrusive.[2]

Henry Williamson—in the light now (Read his novel).[3]

Mrs. B. and Edla in my place all afternoon working on Follies while I slept.[4]

Getting papers (Bible), finished up—Taking them back next Tuesday.

We believe in Hardy's writing because in their structure we feel what is good, and because in his plain but not familiar style, touched a little by stiffness and difficulty, we feel that the language too had a masonic weight and will endure.

There is too much fluency about Henry James. I shut my eyes and look at his books and I am looking at a thicket. I shut my eyes and

1. "Station B-U-N-K," by H. LeB. Bercovici, was reprinted in the March, 1929, issue with the editorial note that the article "illustrates, amongst other things, the advantages of the English system of financing Broadcasting." It had first appeared in the *American Mercury* the previous month.

2. A recent article, by Phayre, "The 'Big Navy' of the United States," had appeared in the January, 1929, issue.

3. Williamson (1897——), an English novelist, had received the 1928 Hawthorndon Prize for *Tarka the Otter*. His novel *The Pathway* (1928) was Book IV in an autobiographical tetralogy, which was given the collective title *The Flax of Dream*. This fact undoubtedly held special interest for Wolfe, who was even then planning a series of his own. The March, 1929, issue of the *London Mercury* contained a portrait of Williamson that brought him to Wolfe's mind at this time.

4. Edla is Mrs. Bernstein's daughter.

look at Hardy and I see stones with nothing growing to or between them.

Loot a few cells of this my swarming brain.

For Henry Volkening: [5]

Bamburger Hof—G. G.—Tom.

Wurtemburger Hof—Simply delightful—Ethel.

Grand—N. G.—Aline.

Rothenburg—There's a charming Hotel but I don't know its name.

Nuremberg—to Bayreuth—to München—Munich through Bavarian Alps to Garmisch-Partenkirchen to Innsbruck—to Salzburg.

Esplanade in Prague—Excellent Hotel.

Munich—Vier Jahreszeiten—don't fail to eat there if you go to Munich—Best food in Europe—Neue Börse—A very pleasant place to eat.

Budapest—Stay at the Hungaria—or in hotel on Margaret Island —or at the St. Gellért—Eat at Hungaria—at Alte Nussbaum—at Spolarits—Finest Hungarian restaurant there—Drink Tokay—but only for desert—Go to the bookstores and ask for books on Hungarian costume and folklore—Go out into country to Mezökövesd on Sunday.

From Salzburg to place called Ischl (some of the most beautiful country in world there).

Munich—Alte Pinakothek (The Dürers, Grünewalds, etc.)—Deutsches Museum—Staatsgalerie for a few moderns.

Italy—Read Sinclair Lewis' latest book—*Dodsworth*.

Via Roma—Naples—chief shopping street—Gutteridge—an English store for merchandise—Use horsedrawn vehicles—Thomas Cook owns the railway up Vesuvius, make arrangements there—See if you can arrange at Cook's for sailboat or motor boat for trips in Bay of Naples—Go up the coast past Vesuvius, Pompeii, Sorrento, Capri, etc. —Gambrinus—in the great Piazza [*San Ferdinando*]—the best café—also, probably a good restaurant.

5. Volkening and his wife were planning an extensive European tour and had asked Wolfe for suggestions. For an account of his enthusiastic response see Henry T. Volkening, "Penance No More" in *The Enigma of Thomas Wolfe*, pp. 38–39. Though most of the list came from Wolfe's recent travels, the second and third items are comments by Mrs. Bernstein and her sister, Miss Ethel Frankau.

Investigate some of the little narrow sidestreets—walk down along Old Port—Visit National Museum—eat at Bertolini's.

Rome—Go up on Capitoline hill after going through Forum. Buy the best maps and reconstructed pictures possible to study Forum. Study the Capitol hill carefully—the ruins of Caligula and Nero's palaces, Lydia's house, etc.

Use the buses.

England: London—Wells—Bath—Bristol—Torquay—York—Lincoln.

Waldo Frank: We must beware of people who call for definitions, standards, precise meanings. They are often the most inexact and murky thinkers—under a great patter of ugly and difficult words they propose to point out the chaos and incoherence in the work of other people. If we are to go to such people as Mr. Waldo Frank for clarity we may as well go to Hollywood for intelligence and beauty. "What I said precisely was this," said Mr. Waldo Frank. But Mr. Frank has very rarely said anything precisely: he has only *said* he has said something precisely.[6]

About the papers I am correcting for Dean Munn: It never occurs to most of these people in answering the question "Was the repentance of the Prodigal Son sincere?"—that sincerity may have its seat in the belly as well as in the heart, and that the prodigal's bitter cry "my father's servants have bread and to spare," does not indicate false contrition or hypocrisy: the use of certain words in these papers set off constantly in antithesis to each other shows an unthinking habit of classification which has no relation to people as they are—Such words are "spiritual," "material," and so on.

Thus, I read dozens of times, that the prodigal's repentance is material rather than spiritual, whatever that may mean. What does it mean? Of what must the prodigal repent? His repentance is over his folly. In what did his folly consist? In making a fool of himself. Did he do it deliberately? No, of course not. No one deliberately makes a fool of himself. What had he done? He had taken the money his father had given him and wasted it on riotous living. Why? To me this is one of the essential and most fascinating aspects of this intensely human story.

6. Waldo David Frank (1889–1967), a New Jersey-born novelist, essayist, and critic, frequently advised his countrymen in his controversial works. His latest analysis of the U.S., *The Re-discovery of America: An Introduction to a Philosophy of American Life*, had just been published by Scribner's.

Yet, not one, I believe, of these 130 papers were interested in the Prodigal until he came running home to his father. Yet all of us have seen the Prodigal hundreds of times. He was young, suddenly he had money—What did he do? He went in search of pleasure, gayety, and love. Is the search for these things criminal or sinful? I think not.

[*Ralph*] Beals—How long will he be at N.Y.U. today? Could he leave his book with someone who will be there? If not, I'll come for it this morning. Does he want to see the papers before I return them? Shall we return them tomorrow or hold them?

People touched by commonness—There is multitude, there is no vanity—The American who writes for *transition,* his mind is as common and dull as the ordinary fictioneer.

Proposed Titles for New Book:

The River People—For the whole
The Fast Express (Train)
Mr. (Mister) Faust.

Construct a Theme For The Student. First of all Should National Prohibition Be Abolished? Has National Prohibition Been Successful? What's Wrong with this, etc. (Turn over 2 pages).

Denotation and Connotation. The Word—p. 204. My own examples: pomegranate, dagger (stiletto), Father, Scrape, boy, Babylon, The Hebrides, Speed, Star, Prince, Hobo, etc., etc.

1. Limitation of Subject.

2. Arrangement of material (Joe is a bootlegger, what does he look like, how does he transact his business, what does *he* think about prohibition). Effects of Joe on the neighborhood. General reflections on the validity of national prohibition.

(1) Joe as a person—his appearance, physical and mental traits, background, etc.
(2) Joe as a Bootlegger—What he did previously (?), how he carries on business, his relation to neighborhood, police, to society.
(3) What Joe thinks about it.
(4) General conclusions.[7]

7. Wolfe later developed this outline into a description of the owner of the speakeasy to which George Webber took Esther Jack to celebrate his twenty-fifth birthday, W&R, pp. 351–53.

In other words, we go from the particular to the general and keep within our actual knowledge.

Now—What questions?

1. To what class of reader is this paper addressed? (Concrete and homely words, specific words as against technical and general words.)
2. How shall I divide my paragraphs?
3. Are my sentences well constructed?
4. Are my words precise, concrete—do they properly convey my meaning?
5. The theme as a whole—does it hang together—have I said what I want to say?

For Discussion In Class: Make out a list of American characteristics—general traits or facts about Americans that distinguish them from the peoples of other nations.

For today: The ______ ______ spring wind ______ softly about the eaves. The first flowers were ______ through the grass.[8]

Draw up a list of six subjects upon which any member of the class might be expected to write without previous preparation. Submit to class.

P. 417, 418—Sentences.[9]

[*At*] 30:

O Lost—3 novels
The Fast Express—2 novels
Welcome ) 1
Mannerhouse )
Other Stuff ) 1
The River People )

"Great" American Poets of the Period 1914–1929:

| | | |
|---|---|---|
| Masters | Sandburg | E. Wylie |
| Frost | Pound | Millay |
| Robinson | T. S. Eliot | Jeffers |
| Crane | G. Stein | E. E. Cummings |
| Lindsay | Amy Lowell | |

8. Wolfe's own word choice is given in LHA, p. 205: "Warm sporting gusts of wind howled faintly at the eaves; the young grass bent; the daisies twinkled."

9. An exercise in which the student was to "point out and correct faults of rhythm or euphony in the following sentences." Grose, *College Composition*, p. 417.

During that period only a few novelists have achieved anything like the same high praise—Yet the novelists have, I believe, a greater average talent than the poets.

| | |
|---|---|
| Dreiser | Wells |
| Cabell | Bennett |
| Cather | V. Woolf |
| Lewis | A. Huxley |
| Hemingway | Galsworthy |
| Hergesheimer | |

[*Munn's*] 1st Lecture after Easter—April 2, 1929 [*on George Herbert*].

[*When Scribner's informed Wolfe that "O Lost" was not a satisfactory title for the novel, he began searching for a new one. The list on which the definitive title first appears was compiled about April 3. Among other considerations, he was interested in the number of letters in the title. The first item on the first list, the title of a Matthew Arnold poem, became the subtitle of Wolfe's novel:* Look Homeward Angel: A Story of the Buried Life.]

The Buried Life [*marked out*]
Exile (*m.o.*]
(An) The Exile's Story [*m.o.*]
The Exile's Youth (?) [*m.o.*]
The Stranger's Youth [*m.o.*]
A Lodging [*m.o.*]
The Lost [*m.o.*]
The Childhood of Mr. Faust [*m.o.*]
In A Strange Land
Far Wanderers
The Wilderness [*m.o.*]
The Sea Floor [*m.o.*]
The Wanderer's Song [*m.o.*]
The Wanderers
Alone, Alone [*circled*]
Naked and Alone
The Prison of Earth
The Lost Boy [10]
Remembering Home

10. Though Wolfe was obviously thinking of Eugene at this point, he later employed the title "The Lost Boy" for the story of the death of his brother Grover published in *Redbook Magazine* (November, 1937), later included in HB.

P. 224 Gant The Far Wanderer, etc. Change to page 77 (?).[11]

How shall I sing of my deep breasted Helen?
The halters of earth are broken, the feet of the wind are shod.

For The Fast Express: Train Scene—These quartette voices in the evening air:

Old Black Joe
Sweet Ad-o-line
Old Kentucky Home.

The Hill Demon
Child's Land
The Lost and Alone
Alone and Lost
Under the Earth
The Lost Boy
The Haunted Boy
The Magic Earth [*m.o.*]
Lost Angels [*m.o.*]
(In) A Strange Land (Country) [*m.o.*]
The Far Wanderers [*m.o.*]
The Lost Land [*m.o.*]
Look Homeward, Angel 17
*The Sun Also Rises* 15 [*m.o.*]

Good Titles:

*The Posessed* [*sic*] 11—Russian
*Vanity Fair*—Eng.—10
*Moby Dick*—8—Amer.
*War and Peace*—11—Russian
*The Egoist*
*The Return of the Native*—20
*Sons and Lovers*

11. "Gant the Far Wanderer" was a portion of Chapter XIV, the awakening of Altamont. Perkins felt that this stream-of-consciousness passage lost some of its effectiveness by being placed in juxtaposition with the dawn antics taking place in Uneeda Lunch No. 3. Wolfe accordingly transferred the passage (pp. 224–38 of his typescript), and wrote an introductory paragraph of transition; the section then became Chapter VII of the published novel. The passage logically followed Chapter VI, which ended on p. 77 of the typescript, and was obviously misplaced where Wolfe had it. This shift was one of the two major changes which Perkins suggested in the editing of "O Lost" and was the only transposition made.

*The Three Bright Pennies*—21
*The Sun Also Rises*
*The Voyage Out*
*The Magic Mountain*
*The World's Illusion*
*Bleak House*
*The Sentimental Education*
*Penguin Island*
*The Gods Are Athirst*
*Tono-Bungay*—10
*Dead Souls*
*The Man of Property*
*The Nigger of the Narcissus*—23
*Nostromo*
*The Kings in Exile* (Daudet)
*Of Blood, Pleasure, and Death*
*Jude The Obscure*
*Point Counter Point*

The Lost Language
The Lost Music [*m.o.*]
The Kings In Prison [*m.o.*]
The Gods In Prison [*m.o.*]
The Boy In Prison (Exile) [*m.o.*]
The Ghosts in Exile (Prison) [*m.o.*]
Toward
Prison Pent [*m.o.*]
Dawn In Chaos [*m.o.*]
Dawn In The Jungle [*m.o.*]
We Are Lost [*m.o.*]
We Have Come Far [*m.o.*]
Lost and Far [*m.o.*]
Far and Lost [*m.o.*]
We Are Strangers [*m.o.*]
They Are Strange And They Are Lost [*m.o.*]
It was Far and We are Lost [*m.o.*]
The Dance of The Lost (Boy) [*m.o.*]
The Search of the Lost Boy [*m.o.*]
There was a Boy [*m.o.*]
The Dance of the Far and Lost [*m.o.*]
The Far and Lost [*m.o.*]
The Dance of The Blind [*m.o.*]

The Web of The Lost [*m.o.*]
In A (The) Strange Land [*checked*]
The Dance of the Lost [*m.o.*]
The Strange and Buried Men [*m.o.*]
They Return In Flower and Leaf [*m.o.*]
The Lost and Far
The Lost Boy [*checked and m.o.*]
We Have Come Far [*checked and m.o.*]
Far and Lost [*checked*]
The Lost Boy's Story [*m.o.*]
New Lands
The Far Wanderers
Prison Pent [*m.o.*]
We Are Lost [*m.o.*]

Thursday, April 4, 1929 [*Munn's lecture on Crashaw, Vaughn, and Herrick*].

In the great works of literature society has frequently come under the merciless scrutiny of the artist's eye. It is doubtful if the South would willingly accept such analysis from an artist within her bounds—it can not, I think, be seriously maintained that the South has ever been receptive of new ideas or has intelligently received sharp criticism.

The idea that Northern publishers are hostile to books which do not continue to present the life of the South in terms of the Old Marse-Uncle Mose tradition is, of course, preposterous.

An aristocracy does not grow up on fried food, moonshine whiskey, and the works of such writers as Joel Chandler Harris, and W. G. Simms. The independence, the carelessness to what others thought or felt about one's conduct, the reckless individualism which has always characterized members of the genuine aristocracy, has never found disciples in the South where the upper crust have always exhibited a thoroughly middle class correctness.

Kleist—*Käthchen von Heilbronn—Euphorion.*[12]

Dodd (riding along from Newton): The female bee devours the male—all nature fructifying and destroying itself in the sexual act.

12. A reference to an article by Spiridon Wukadinovic on the most optimistic of the plays of Heinrich von Kleist (1777–1811), "Über Kleists Käthchen von Heilbronn," *Euphorion*, 1895, Erstes Ergänzungsheft, pp. 14–36. Wolfe first encountered Kleist at the North State School, and he later listed

"My father," he said slowly, "was an educated loafer."
(Eugene thinks poem up.)
My father was an educated loafer,
My mother was an alcoholic bum,
My sister's name was Nelly, she had a lovely belly,
Aside from that she was a dirty scum.[13]

Pull up the flowers, and then pull up the flowers. The tender easy flowers pull up, pull up.

And pull mandragora O pull the mandrake shrieking from the earth.

I have gotten the earth with child.

The argent waters curve into the shore.
Buttressed against the oak the ivy crawls.
I heard things fall and dive into the silvered lakes.
The wet cold body of the other divers.
The Ostrogoths have never marched in woods like these.

New England woods are wild and fleet—they brood, but things skim fast in them.

French woods—Papa in shirtsleeves, paper on the grass, the wine bottle greasy with a dozen hands, or *La Vie Parisien*, or Monsieur Feuillet.[14]

Tuesday, April 9 [*Munn's lecture on intellectual thought in eighteenth-century England.*]

---

Kleist's comedy, *Der Zerbrochene Krug*, as one of the German stories read by Eugene Gant (LHA, p. 319). However, while he was in Germany the previous year, Wolfe had developed an interest in Kleist, and just before he left Munich he jotted in Pocket Notebook 4 a list of books to buy, with the first item "Something by Kleist." A German edition of *Penthesilea* is in the Wisdom Collection. In "The River People" ledger, p. 213, under the heading "A Modern Movement that Will Really Be Modern," Wolfe has a list of its "explorations," one of which is "A Study of Heinrich von Kleist." In this instance Wolfe's interest in the tragic Kleist was avant-garde; though Kleist has long been a classic of German literature, he was not generally appreciated abroad until the Second World War.

13. For the character Hugh Dodd, Wolfe drew upon his 47 Workshop friend Frederick L. (Fritz) Day. Dodd makes a brief appearance in OT&R, but Wolfe transfers this doggerel quatrain to Eugene's musings about Dinwood Bland, p. 678.

14. Octave Feuillet (1821–90), French novelist and dramatist. In the list of French writers that begins Chapter LXXV of OT&R his name is first. An illustrated paperback copy of Feuillet's *Histoire d'une Parisienne* (Paris, 1925) is in Wolfe's library.

Notes for Book:
Change *Jeannerette's* name
Look up *Belvedere* (Brunswick)
Insert (from other copy) *Exeter scene.*[15]

The complaint you make against my book is not that it is untrue —but that it is painful and ugly. But surely you can not deny that there is much in life that is painful and ugly.

You take the traditional posture of the professional Southerner —you are unable to see my book as a book: you see it as an "attack" upon a segment of geography and the life it includes called "The South." I have absolutely no interest in writing a polemic against the South or anything else.[16]

Dark Star [*m.o.*]
Leaf and Stone
Wind Grieved Ghost [*m.o.*]
The Phantom Years
The Only (True) Voyage [*m.o.*]
The Happy Land [*m.o.*]
The Forgotten Faces
Deathless Ben [*m.o.*]
Over Us All
Pride Will Pass
The Sunken River
When Can We Forget
No More
The Dark Virginians
The Strange Voyage
The Window [*m.o.*]
The Stranger's Window

15. The name of Louis William Jeanneret, the Swiss watch-maker who rented space in W. O. Gant's marble shop, was changed to Jannadeau. The Belvedere, a boarding house across the street from Dixieland, was changed to Brunswick on pages 196, 202, and 429 of LHA but remained the Belvedere on page 189. The Exeter scene, Eugene's first visit to a brothel, was one of four scenes that Wolfe took from his ribbon copy of the typescript and gave to Madeleine Boyd in the hope that they could be made into magazine stories, but they were not accepted. The Exeter scene appears in LHA, pp. 404–12.

16. Wolfe anticipated that his book would receive an adverse reception in his hometown and wrote several drafts of a projected reply to unfriendly critics, of which this passage is one. For a longer, published draft see *Letters*, pp. 176–77.

The Hills Beyond Pentland
Embarkation
The Stranger's House
(5) Embarkation 11
Look Homeward, Angel 17
(2) The Hills Beyond Pentland 22
(1) The Stranger's House 17
The Stranger's Window [*m.o.*]
The Visitor's Window [*m.o.*]
(3) Fear No More 10
The Rebel Powers [*m.o.*]
Sinful Earth [*m.o.*]
The Phantom Years [*m.o.*]
(4) Leaf and Stone or (Stone and Leaf)
The True Voyage [*m.o.*]
The Happy Land [*m.o.*]
The Forgotten Faces [*m.o.*]
The Sunken River
Over Us All

Thursday, April 11 [*Munn's lecture on eighteenth-century poetry and prose*].

[*Teaching Notes*]

Description:
Aim of Descript:—Two purposes
(a)—Information
(b)—Suggestion
Make out a list of smells.
Degree of Specific—Enter Clay a boy of Twenty—enlarge.
[*Grose, p.*] 261—Sensations.
Make a list of things.
Describe:
A Room In a City Boarding House
A Country Railroad Station
A Kitchen In A Farm House
A Student's Room.

In the street a dray wagon ______ ______ over the cobble stones. A ______ spring wind ______ gently around the house. A cowbell ______ ______ in the wind. Far off there was the long ______ of a train whistle. The boy at the desk _____ over his work, _____ intently, in an _____ effort to concentrate. But it was _____ from the _____ expression on his face that his mind was _____ _____. Outside the young leaves of May _____ in the wind. A woodpecker _____ against the trunk of a _____ tree. Buds were _____ from the earth. The trees were a _____ of _____ _____ green.[17]

A lonely place on a moonlit night described by:

(a) one who enjoys solitude
(b) a painter
(c) a naturalist
(d) one who is afraid.

Describe *taste, smell, sound*—page 261—Additional Topics—Those by contrast and comparisons—A Room In Greenwich Village.

Tuesday, April 15 [*Munn's lecture on sentimentalism in the eighteenth century*].

THE ORDEAL OF YOUNG WILD WEST [18]

Young Wild West As Young Man—Beautiful Arietta—Yuba Bill—Then his education—changes in physical action—Sexual relations with the Beautiful Arietta—Finally Young Wild West at 30—the "modern."

1st Scene: Young Wild West on The Prairie.
2nd Scene: Young Wild West at College.

17. Wolfe intended this paragraph as an exercise for his students, but it is taken from his own work. An expanded version had been written for the picnic scene with Laura James, LHA, p. 451.

18. The *Wild West Weekly: A Magazine Containing Stories, Sketches, Etc. of Western Life* was a popular dime novel series published by Frank Tousey from 1902 to 1928. The first issue was "Young Wild West: The Prince of the Saddle, by an Old Scout," and subsequent issues carried Young Wild West through many adventures: "Young Wild West and 'Gilt Edge Gil,' or Touching Up the Sharpers," "Young Wild West Wrests Cowboy Challenge," "Young Wild West and the Arizona Boomers," etc. During his boyhood Wolfe was an avid reader of the weekly adventures of Young Wild West, and he later listed this series first among the dime novels read by Eugene Gant, LHA, pp. 102–103. At this point, however, Wolfe had begun to think of developing Young Wild West as a character in his own work. At the end of a narrative passage in "The River People" ledger, where Eugene thinks about his boyhood reading, Wolfe has the note: "Here use The Ordeal of Young Wild West (vision of the defeat of The Undefeated)," p. 268. He continued to toy with this idea, and he later considered making Young Wild West the boon companion of Monkey Hawke. Scenes written for "The October Fair" in which Young Wild West appears show him to be very amusing, and it is unfortunate that Wolfe abandoned such a hilarious character.

3d Scene: Young Wild West as a Young wild poet (playwright, dramatist, etc.)
4th: Y. W. W. begins to grow up.

The softness of the hard ones—Hemingway and his imitators. He is far the best of his imitators.

Silly talk about sentimentality and the lack of it.

"the lost generation"—what has it lost in America?

Put into final scene of book: "Look Homeward, Angel, now, and melt with ruth." [19]

Thursday, April 18 [*Munn's lecture on the pre-Romantic poets*].

Over the Train Wheels: Then you'll re-member You'll re-meh-heh-heh-heh-hemb-er me.

Take all the *mags* in Brentano's window—divide into groups—and burlesque.

*Clayhanger*—700 pages.
*The Case of Sergeant Grischa*—450.[20]

[*Drawing of a hand.*]

A Book by a *Dial*-ly young Jewess named Gertrude Diamant (change to Gertrude Sternbaum) going on endlessly like this:

She had been pregnant too long. When you touched it there it hurt. She lay down on the bed.

"No longer be afraid, but yield her hand to them."

The planes of light came down shifted, mixed, caressed her where it hurt there.

[*Grose*] page 262—Sounds by contrast and comparison.

The scene beggars ______. Silence ______. Pandemonium ______. Last but not ______.

19. The quotation is line 163 of Milton's "Lycidas." Wolfe had selected *Look Homeward, Angel* as the title of his book, but he never did carry out his intention of working this idea into the final scene.

20. Wolfe was still concerned with the length of his manuscript. The 1910 edition of *Clayhanger*, the first of Arnold Bennett's trilogy, has 698 pages. Arnold Zweig's *The Case of Sergeant Grischa*, published in 1927, is shorter but is still a long novel.

Dialog—page 328 [*An example from the* Pickwick Papers].
Topics:[21]
How I Earned My First Money
The Bravest Act I Ever Saw
A Vacation Adventure
A Strange Coincidence.
Incidents: [22]
A Student Finds A Proof Sheet Of An Examination Which He Must Pass In Order To Remain In College.
A College Student Determines To Tell The Whole Truth And Nothing But The Truth For A Day.
A Man Crossing A Railway Trestle Suddenly Sees The Fast Express Bearing Down Upon Him.
A Steel Worker Working On The Fourteenth Floor Looks Up And Sees Three Tons Of Steel Plunging Towards His Platform.
Five Minutes Before The Hour Set For His Execution A Murderer Is Informed That The Governor Has Granted Him A Reprieve.

"He's a b-b-b-bit p-p-pale, don't you think," the sailor stammered, barely conscious of what he was saying.

"Just a moment!" said Horse Hines quickly, lifting a finger. Briskly he took a stick of rouge from his pocket, stepped forward, and deftly, swiftly, sketched upon the dead gray cheeks a terrible rose-hued mockery of life and health.

"There!" he said with deep satisfaction and stick in hand, critically attune, like a painter before his canvas, he stepped back into their staring ghastly silence.[23]

Tuesday, April 23, 1929 [*Munn's lecture on Wordsworth and Coleridge*].

Holliday Book Shop, 49 E. 49: *Moby Dick*, *The Scarlet Letter*, *The Red Badge of Courage*, one of James, one of Dreiser, one of Lewis, *My Ántonia*, Harry Leon Wilson.

The Modern Writers: Hemingway, Dos Passos, Gertrude Stein.

21. Selected from a list in Grose, *College Composition*, p. 301.

22. The first two are selected from a list in Grose. Wolfe supplied the other three.

23. This passage was added to Luke's and Eugene's visit to the undertaker's. LHA, p. 571.

Wednesday [April 23]:

Narration:

Starting From Action (last time)
Starting From Setting
" " Character
" " Idea.

Setting: A Deserted Garden, overrun with weeds.

An old house, falling to pieces, set back from a lonely road, in a grove of trees.

A rotting pier on the waterfront at night.

A lonely beach on an island in the tropics.

Starting from character: a college student, good humored, lazy, expert in avoiding work.

A mischievous little boy.

An old woman who always suspects the worst, delights in malicious gossip; and has many imaginary aches and ills.

On The Transport (page 18): "The deck now slanted down in front of him, now rose so that he was walking up an incline."

"He had never been to a dance. He had no dress suit, and no notion of dancing." (Bennett, p. 130.)

"The dreaded doctor was an immoderately tall man, lean and wiry, carelessly clad in a long loose coat of no colour, loose trousers, and huge shoes." (Meredith, p. 33.) [24]

The work on the pier—Eugene finds work there for himself and Sinker Jordan.[25]

Thursday, April 25, 1929 [*Munn's lecture on Tennyson*].

No book is better than the man who makes it.

On reading French book on flagellation—the "perverse" here is often only what I dreamed of in days of puberty.

"People in a small town talk."

24. These last three items are the beginnings of three selections in *Freshman Readings*, ed. Roger Sherman Loomis. "On the Transport" comes from *Three Soldiers* by John Dos Passos. The second, entitled "Denry and the Countess," is taken from Arnold Bennett's *Denry the Audacious*. The last, "Dr. Shrapnel," is an excerpt from *Beauchamp's Career* by George Meredith.

25. The published account of this scene, LHA, p. 518, is a condensation of the manuscript version, as is generally true of the Norfolk material. Many of the details of Eugene's work there were deleted or summarized.

In The Sunday Paper—The Theater, Books, Radio, Business, Real Estate, Politics, Murder, Prohibition, Society, Sports.

The Turks, The Dagoes, The Rooshians an' such.

Some of these days—

Ladies and Gentlemen—Mr. Oscar Wilde, of The Happiness Boys, will now sing, "I Cant Help Lovin' That Man."

[*Teaching Notes*]

What, Why, When, How, Where, Who.

Expand: He was a late riser, and the period between 8:15 and 9 o'clock in the morning was a mad scramble from bed to school.

Yesterday afternoon two young men entered the jewelry store of S. Goldman at 579 Lexington Avenue, held up the jeweller and his assistant at the point of a gun, and escaped with over $40,000 worth of jewelry.

Jenks, who had been for thirty years the company's bookkeeper, paused timidly a moment at the door to the manager's office. His shoulders were narrow and bent. His hair had grown grey and thin.

A man, 35 years old, wife and 4 children, out of work, found a wallet containing $15,000 and the card of J. T. McGregor, President of the Providence Trust Co. He returned the wallet to Mr. McGregor who rewarded him for his honesty with a $10 bill.

The rescue of the men from the sinking freighter and their transfer to the liner was accomplished with great danger and difficulty.

For Reading (For Exam): [26]

Marco Polo—Eileen Power—p. 397

The Fight—William Hazlitt—p. 61

The Keeper's House—Thomas Hardy—p. 27

The Costume Warehouse—E. Ferber—p. 29

The King's Camelopard—M. Twain—p. 164

Topics: Write a biographical sketch of some person you know, limiting your treatment as far as possible to a single trait of character.

Write an account of some interesting incident using dialog as much as possible.

A man dines elaborately at a restaurant, making a great impres-

26. These selections from Loomis are Eileen Power's account of the famous traveler in *Medieval People*, Hazlitt's well-known essay, the description of the keeper's house in Hardy's *Under the Greenwood Tree*, an account of the warehouse from Edna Ferber's *Cheerful—By Request*, and the King and Duke episode in *Huckleberry Finn*.

sion on the waiters. When time comes for paying bill, he tells the waiter he has no money.

Now beats the heart in iron cage
The guts are queazy, breath uneasy
Gather [*breaks off*]

Title of next book—Faust and Helen.[27]

The woman who has baby is maid in Helen's house (Helen's maid?)—conversation in morning at hospital with woman.[28]

On writing "The Book About New York"—How silly this is. Who has ever written the Book about London, the Book about Berlin, the Book about Paris?

Thursday, May 2 [*Munn's lecture on Browning*].

[*Early in the year Scribner's had asked Wolfe for the completed manuscript by the first of May. Through Wolfe worked diligently at the job and by the last of April had finished the revisions listed in his proposal in Pocket Notebook 8, the manuscript was still too long and needed additional cutting. At this point Perkins began daily sessions with Wolfe, and the following lists of specific revisions resulted from their conversations.*]

Cuts 62—The Pentland Family.[29]
All about Henry cut out.[30]

27. Wolfe was considering the possibility of writing a novel based on his love affair with Mrs. Bernstein, and at this point he called the female character Helen, though her name would finally become Esther Jack. The title "Faust and Helen" eventually was given to the last section of OT&R.

28. Ever since Wolfe witnessed the birth of a baby at the Manhattan Maternity Hospital on July 10, 1927, he planned to use the experience as fictive material. Here he is considering making the mother a maid in the house of Helen (Esther Jack).

29. One paragraph describing the idiosyncrasies of the Pentlands was deleted from page 62 of the typescript. For a discussion which categorizes the following cuts, see Francis E. Skipp, "The Editing of *Look Homeward Angel*," *Papers of the Bibliographical Society of America*, LVII (First Quarter, 1963), 1–13.

30. Four pages of typescript containing a portrait of Henry Pentland were cut from the description of the Pentland family in Chapter I of LHA. Wolfe developed this material into *A Portrait of Bascom Hawke*, his prize-winning short novel, which still later became the account of Bascom Pentland in OT&R.

Gant's House—condense.
73–74—the lean and the fat [*years*] etc.—all cut.[31]
He was acutely aware—fire p. 27.[32]
With that naivete, 28—no speech, 30.[33]
Then it was gone—a door—p. 31.
Page 66—The reading?[34]
Change name of Colvin.[35]
All of them were—p. 68–70—Gant was a great man.[36]
Isaacs—change name.[37]
227–228—Bull-humans.[38]
230–231—This is the heart.[39]
232 top of page—make transition shorter.
90—Bowels and Bladder.[40]
92—Fire dept. scene.[41]
93—Firemen's tournament.

"I must say I have been surprised at many things I have found here," she said. (It was as if she had been waiting for the question and desiring it.) "I have met some nice Americans" (Eugene winced as he

31. Two pages of typescript, discussing America in the 1890's and summarizing the activities of the Pentland family, were deleted from Chapter II.

32. One third of a paragraph about the infant Eugene was cut.

33. Two pages of typescript describing the precocity of the infant Eugene were omitted. The following entry also concerns another minor deletion.

34. Helen's recitation was kept and appears on page 62 of LHA.

35. The Colvins were neighbors of the Wolfes on Woodfin Street. He changed the name to Duncan.

36. Four paragraphs of direct authorial comment to the reader about old Gant were omitted. They immediately preceded the paragraph beginning, "Gant was a great man . . . ." LHA, p. 64.

37. This notation reflects a curious feature of Wolfe's writing. The Israels were Woodfin Street neighbors of the Wolfes, and their son Max was Tom's favorite childhood playmate. In the holograph manuscript of "O Lost," Wolfe usually calls his characters by the actual names of their prototypes; thus the neighboring families of Colvins and Perkinsons appear in both the holograph and typescript manuscripts with their real names. Wolfe, however, changed the name Israel to Isaacs and used Isaacs in almost every instance in the holograph. This note is evidently a reminder to check the typescript to make sure that he had been consistent. If he was considering a further change in the name, he decided against it, for the name remains Isaacs.

38. A small deletion was made in Gant's musings (LHA, p. 73) concerning the transplanting of bull organs to man.

39. A page-and-a-half parody of tourist-guidebook prose was omitted from the book.

40. A short section about how Eugene wet himself in the second grade was deleted.

41. This scene (LHA, p. 90) was shortened, and the following account of the Altamont annual fireman's tournament was eliminated.

had many times in England—the crisp intonation of the word, with the sharp accentuation of *mer* seemed to have in it something hostile, full of dislike) "but I have met a great many more who were not. And oh the English they speak! Among educated people! It was shocking. Sometimes," she said, "when they speak to me I don't know what they mean. I think they are being sarcastic."

"I was talking to one man the other night," (she was breathing more rapidly now, with a sharp quiet indignation). " 'Well, at any rate, there's one thing you've got to admit, Mrs. B—' he said, 'This is the richest country in the world today. That's the reason you English are jealous of us.' Yes, I said, and how did you get that wealth?"

It was, he saw, a hopeless business. How could this little woman ever adapt herself to this vast chaos, arrogant and indifferent to all she knew.

In spite of her false teeth, he wanted to possess her—she had none of the elegance and perfection of body that American women had, but she had a sincerity and simple courage which they lacked. That story she told about the Arabs, for example. Although these English women were homely, he liked their crisp manner, their way of smoking a cigarette—with a few touches of her hand she had made the tea look so lovely—there on a clean dish cloth, with a light red strip under it, lay a square of honey, a plate of bread and coffee roll, and the tea, brown and strong.

Against this national bitterness and hostility of the English—he had observed it in New York—was it not very similar to his own neurosis, his going over in his mind of what "he said" and "she said," his own panting with indignation. Was it altogether a neurosis? Was it even at all a neurosis?

Every Englishman is England, but no American is America.

A host of niggling annoyances eating up her sanity—(the English woman).

Mr. Gant stared drunkenly at the ruined mouth of copesmate Julius, then turned away to the coffee urn wiping a reflective palm strongly across his mouth.

The red haired waitress, white stockings, milky skin. O Tender, Tender.[42]

The Czech girl, small, square-round face, full jawed, thick wings of hair tied in a voluptuous knot behind her. She turned, her

42. This passage was evidently intended for Chapter XXIV of LHA but was not included in the final version.

small shoulders were white and square, her back as flat as a board. She stepped forward with an easy drowsy movement of strong round buttocks.

| The "Modernist People (In English) | | "Modern" People |
|---|---|---|
| Joyce | V. Woolf | Hemingway |
| Stein | A. McLeish | Lewis |
| Sitwell | Thayer | Anderson |
| Cummings | M. Moore | Dreiser |
| Crane | R. Graves | D. Garnett |
| Pound | Laura Riding | A. Huxley |
| Eliot | K. Burke | R. Firbank |
| Gillespie | W. C. Williams | Sandburg |
| Geddes | Herbst | Calla[g]han |
| Tate | Diamant | Lytton Strachey |
| Cowley | Herrmann | Conrad Aiken |
| Paul | Wyndham Lewis | |
| Jolas | K. Boyle | |

When Mr. Pope went calling in the City
Like paper cuttings frozen in the air
With cold upcurve like frozen foam O ver ben;d in! G [*overbending*]
The Alps lean over Tours
No time was, Sudden, clear
Il trene di Milano comes into this SilencE . .[43]

---

MISS MONA FUCHS[44]

Boston is an Irish city. Boston is run by the Irish. The Mayor is an Irishman. All the policemen are Irishmen. Most of the city officials, street cleaners, court attendants, firemen, and building inspectors are Irishmen.

The largest department store in Boston is Ervine's. It is called

43. Wolfe was apparently manufacturing a "modernist" poem—with suggestions of Tate, Eliot, Pound, and Cummings.

44. Wolfe began developing this character in a ledger and continued in his notebook. This first portion of the sketch is taken from "The River People" ledger, pp. 169–71.

Ervine's because it is owned by a man named Isadore Fuchs. Mr. Fuchs is not Irish.

Mona reads and talks foreign languages. She talks French. She can talk French good. The French like to hear her talk their language with "cette accent adorable," as they call it. Whenever Mona is a little drunk she talks French. It is most amusing to hear her. She will coax the orchestra for just one more *tiny* little tune. "Juh pawnse," she says, "qu'ill fote oncore day mooseek."

Mona has travelled. She has been to Europe several times and has lived in England for a whole year. She adores the English, and subscribes to *The Spectator, The New Statesman, The London Mercury, The Quarterly Review, The Tatler* and *Punch.* Sometimes she writes an article and gets it published in one of the English periodicals.

When Mona lived in England that time she got to know some of the celebrated people of the day. She got to know Lytton Strachey and Clive Bell and Rebecca West and Virginia Woolf and Roger Fry and Hope-I-May-Die, and T. S. Eliot and Papa's-Not-Well-Yet, and I don't know who-all.

Mona went into a bookshop and ordered several books to be sent to various friends. She was always sending people books. She sent the poems of Beddoes to her friend Mrs. Rita Weinberg, the stage designer, in New York. She sent the poems of John Donne to a friend who taught in the English Department at Smith. She sent a copy of William Beckford's *Vathek* to Miss Henrietta Pettigrew, of Louisville, Kentucky. She sent a copy of the poems of William Blake to Mr. Snobscott Pillivowel, the dramatic critic.

And how much did it come to? $35.20. How much *is* that? Oh, about seven guineas! It was so hard to get used to this absurd American money.

She had written a note to her brother, editor of the *Stag and Ibis,* asking him if any "interesting men" were contributing to the magazine. She had written a note to Mr. Francis Strudwick, saying she did hope he would come and see her soon, and were there any "interesting men" writing plays.

---

Mona was just back from London. She had been there for a whole year. During that time she had been analyzed by Sir Ernest Jones. She had a neurosis. She had read all about them in books for years. Several well known lady writers in the modern movement had the same trouble. Mona had been in love with another Lady, a teacher at Smith College. But she wasn't any longer. Sir Ernest Jones had fixed all that, and now she was going to be Very, Very Happy.

But, she was thinking, should I have gone to Sir Ernest Jones. After all, he is a Freudian and Freud's becoming déclassé. Everyone's going in for Jung now. But what, her tortured mind was telling her, if Jung too is getting old-fashioned. Then there is Adler. There is—there is—In anguish she repeated the names of half a dozen possible successors to Sigmund.

Must she then spend the rest of her life being analyzed by different authorities only to see their authority vanish?

Ah, she thought sadly, the Victorians had an easy time of it after all. Only appendices and gout—what a happy age *that* had been.

Rita Weinberg in New York had been analyzed by one of Jung's disciples. She must ask Rita what that had been like, Rita kept having a terrible dream—O a terrible dream. She dreamed that she was coming apart, disintegrating. She would blow her nose (in a dream) and all the bones in her nose would fly out of her head. Then she would have no bones in her head, and her nose would be just like rubber. She would pull it, it would stretch out eight inches in front of her face and snap back again with a plopping noise like a rubber ball. It had taken Rita and the analyst almost two years to get at the bottom of this.

She would begin to tremble violently and an arm would drop off: a violent shudder, and three ribs would rattle on the pavement. A sigh—her pelvic girdle would slip around her ankles. A cough—her guts came welling up like boiling oil.

She wrung her hands—only to pluck off her fingers like ripe bananas. She stamped her foot—only to have her toe nails strewn on the ground.

As much let me put down here as you may need
To make a picture of its maker's clay
The broken statue pieced together stands—this finger was true marble, this his nose, here runs the lower thigh—the arm and size is thus [*breaks off*]

George Herbert
"sap and juice" [*"The Jews"*]—The Church Porch
"Rain, do not hurte my flowers" [*"Providence," line 117*]
"Strongly and sweetly" (shall the rivers run) [*line 2*]
"Thy cupboard serves the world: the meat is set" [*line 49*]

(Bird, come to my finger-crook, Fish to my hook)—(mine) [*paraphrase of line 51*]

("On it (poore paper) my heart doth bleed
As many lines as there doth need
To passe itself and all it hath to thee.") ["*Obedience*"]
Saw angels, grave and golden, in the wood (mine).

May VI:

94 Cut Coleridge Stanza.[45]
95–96 Bessie and Brother Jack business cut.[46]
99 Meanwhile Eliza had begun, etc.[47]
101–102 Drown a Jew and hit a nigger.[48]
104—All the inherited [*prejudice of caste*] etc.—104.
107—Hen-mistress.[49]
109—Niggertown description.
114—Another series was more generous—chivalry.[50]
115—the sword its sheath etc.[51]
118–120 Richard Devereux.[52]
124 Or as the wizard surgeon.[53]
[*125*] Or in bullish madness etc.
127 How strong you are Eugene etc.
[*128*] Or perhaps Happiness in the Valley.

45. A stanza of Wolfe's favorite poem, "The Rime of the Ancient Mariner," was cut from what is now the break on page 91, LHA.

"Like one, that on a lonesome road
Doth walk in fear and dread,
And having once turned round, walks on,
And turns no more his head;
Because he knows, a frightful fiend
Doth close behind him tread." (lines 446–51)

46. Otto Krause's bawdy notes to Bessie Barnes and a swim in a polluted river with Jack Barnes were cut.

47. A short passage about Eliza's dream of owning Dixieland was eliminated.

48. This statement was retained (LHA, p. 96), but the remainder of the paragraph, a discussion of the effect of prejudice on human relations, was cut. The following item also concerns a deleted paragraph on inherited prejudice.

49. A passage concerning the practice of one of Eugene's playmates was deleted.

50. Two paragraphs on the fantasies of the youthful Eugene were omitted.

51. A passage of phallic symbolism was deleted.

52. A two-page episode of Devereux's experiences with the Mexicans is omitted from Eugene's literary adventures given on page 108, LHA.

53. This item and the following one refer to additional fantasies that were omitted.

Page 128—books.[54]
138—In all their life together, etc.[55]
*139 Thus save for Ben etc. (*Rewrite?*) [56]
151 We believe reader etc.[57]

Tuesday, May 7 [*Munn's lecture on Browning continued*].

162–163—All the Riverside Park Scene.[58]
186 Nightmare.[59]
193—to get a smell.[60]
197 he was paralyzed with disgust.[61]
201 About Daisy.[62]
207—on—Put in more dialog—Gant's sickness etc.
210 Upon the hill, etc.[63]
210–211—School scenes in Hot Springs.
[*211*] "Son" said a lank debauched Southerner etc.
222 Dotted about, etc.
223 In the Bijou Cafe etc.
[*224*] Rewrite statistic business of Gant, and son Ben—night time, daytime, etc.[64]
240 Shorten and make more natural Horse Hines.
[*248*] How about one on halitosis of the bunghole? [65]
Think up some more names for Tugman's burlesque—255–265.

54. A long list of Eugene's reading was left out.

55. A paragraph was deleted from the description of Luke (LHA, p. 117) which emphasizes the lack of rapport between Luke and Eugene.

56. The revised paragraph (the first one that begins on page 118, LHA) considerably softens Eugene's hatred of parental demands and his self-proclaimed righteousness.

57. A brief paragraph of direct authorial comment to the reader was omitted.

58. A two-page description of Eugene's visits to the Altamont amusement park was eliminated.

59. Eugene's recurring nightmare of being crushed by a train but never killed was omitted.

60. This phrase was changed to "hardly out of didies yet," LHA, p. 147.

61. This reaction of Eugene to Steve's attack (LHA, p. 150) was deleted.

62. The cut portion gives a general assessment of Daisy's character, painting her as rather weak and lacking the originality and boldness of Helen and Luke.

63. This passage, which refers to the library in Memphis, and the following four were all deleted since they only added further details to those already in the narrative.

64. The statistical paragraph about Gant, with very slight revision, is used in LHA, pp. 70–71. The passage about Ben, unrevised, is on page 165.

65. This phrase was changed to "pyorrhea of the toe-nails," LHA, p. 176.

[*267*] Mose Extinct business—Can this come at end of Chapter?[66]

[*269*] Cut in Beaumont Castle, etc.[67]

FAUST AND HELEN

Book I	The "Story"
Book II	Faust and Helen
Book III	The Fast Express

The train! The train!
Eliza talking here!
The train! The train! The train!
Eliza talking here!

p. 281–282 "Because the murder of Abel" etc.[68]

288 But the mistakes [*Julia made were few*] etc.[69]

289—Jim Pentland had perhaps etc.[70]

291 In later years etc. Early part of Simon More.[71]

308—Plan street, etc.[72]

313—So on the hairline [*of million-minded impulse*]—all the rest of it cut.

315 Her thin face etc.[73]

319–324 The history of the Leonards.

327 Smiling with vacant lust etc. and seducing himself—328.[74]

338 Blair Logan etc.

337 et seq.—Leonard's wig.[75]

Will Pentland made [*secret donations to charities*]—346.

348—[*a passage describing Eugene's fear of the crowd*].

66. The incident of Mose's death is given in LHA, pp. 184–85, but the poem "Mose Extinct," a satire of T. S. Eliot, was cut. For this amusing parody of "Sweeney Among the Nightingales" see Kennedy, *The Window of Memory*, p. 154.

67. A bawdy satire of horse fiction was cut.

68. A paragraph that traces a chain of causes back to Cain and Abel was excised.

69. Additional comments on Eliza's property transactions were cut.

70. Information about Jim Pentland's fortune was cut.

71. Additional details on the early life of the crazy millionaire, LHA, p. 198, were omitted.

72. A paragraph describing Helen's graduation from the Orange Street school was cut.

73. This paragraph about Mrs. Leonard was retained, LHA, p. 213.

74. Two short deletions were made that refer to John Dorsey Leonard.

75. One page that describes Eugene's horror on learning that Mr. Leonard wears a wig was deleted.

349 Years later, it seemed to have.[76]
356—Washington all cut out.[77]
Tomorrow we'll go to *500*—that's half of it.

Wed., May 8:
Scribner's today—Cutting book with Mr. Perkins—on way to Harvard Club saw Little Johnny Lowes—the Harvard Prof.[78]

The essence of our thinking about life is less changed by science than scientists assert. The overthrow of the Ptolemaic system by the Copernican is often cited as the revolution in man's thinking about the universe. He no longer, says the scientist, thinks of himself as "the centre of the universe." Alas, a very short examination will show us he has gained no such modesty. The most extravagant egotisms of the Romantic movement came after Copernicus—if we want a modest estimate of man's place we must go to Plato rather than to Hegel or Bergson.

Thursday, May 9th [*Munn's lecture on Hardy and World War I poets*].

365—You little freak etc.[79]
367 There was nothing that Steve.[80]
384—For Pearl Hines the adventure.[81]
384 She did not know etc.
385—not like to beg.
391 What about the bushes, Luke? [82]
394 Demon, monster, etc.[83]
396 The whole page.[84]

76. An indictment of schools was omitted.

77. Seven pages of typescript were cut—a description of Eugene's trip to Washington with Eliza to witness Wilson's inauguration.

78. John Livingston Lowes (1867–1945) was professor of English at Harvard from 1918 until his retirement in 1939. Wolfe had two courses with Lowes, Poets of the Romantic Period and Comparative Literature, while Lowes was writing his famous study of Coleridge, *The Road To Xanadu,* which he read to Wolfe's class. This work greatly influenced Wolfe and helped to spur his voracious but indiscriminate reading in an attempt to fill his own "deep well of unconscious cerebration" with all kinds of lore that could later be summoned by the imaginative faculty in the creative process.

79. This paragraph was kept, LHA, p. 238.

80. A passage that compares Steve unfavorably with his father was cut.

81. This item and the two following refer to omitted paragraphs about the Hines family.

82. "Gushes" was substituted for "pushes," LHA p. 256.

83. One paragraph on the family automobile was omitted.

84. A satirical passage on Southern virgins was deleted.

397 Luke—has nothing physically to do with women.[85]
398 make this clear.
397–398 Revise these pages.[86]
(413—In summer a tall spire etc?) [87]
Or when I have des[*troyed the Japanese armies*].[88]
418–422 God hears.
Spruce Street change.[89]
448—The clank of a chain.
455 The opinion, he found [*was wide-spread*].[90]
461—Lifted by his success etc.
466–67 Eliza looked—here and there.[91]
XXI—467.
469–470—Her vision was obscured etc.—The Methodists.[92]
472 It was an age of marvellous discovery.[93]
482—At this moment mine host.[94]
488—494.[95]
498–500 Guy Doak [*a schoolmate of Eugene's*].
505–507—Miss Amy's party.
512–523 cut.[96]
523–525 cut (who's going my way).
543–44—English speaking people.[97]
551 Patroness of all the arts etc.[98]
555 Judge Walter C. Jeter was deeply moved.[99]

85. The passage except for this statement is in LHA, p. 259.

86. These two pages appear, with only slight revision, in LHA, pp. 259–60. The four-letter words were replaced by synonyms.

87. This passage was retained, LHA, p. 271.

88. This item and the following refer to a four-page heroic fantasy of Eugene's that was cut.

89. Spruce Street was changed to Spring Street, LHA, p. 275.

90. A passage on sexual relations between the white paperboys and a middle-aged Negress was omitted.

91. A passage about Eliza's developing interest in real estate was cut.

92. A passage which attributes certain limitations of Margaret Leonard to her Methodist heritage was cut.

93. A tribute to "The Rime of the Ancient Mariner" as "the greatest romantic poem that has ever been written in English" was left out.

94. A deleted passage on eating was written in mock-Elizabethan style.

95. A long passage about Eliza's visit to her brother Will's family in Florida was cut.

96. This item and the next refer to a long section cut from the walk-through-the-town sequence in Chapter XXIV. It reveals George Graves's Mexican descent, Mexican-baiting by the boys, and their attitudes toward various residents of Altamont.

97. A one-page parody of Anglo-American relations was deleted.

98. The revised paragraph appears on page 345, LHA.

99. A satire on Judge Jeter's background, and politics generally, was omitted.

Laboring People—Italians, Mill People etc.—"in town" shopping—sallow gaunt women staring suspiciously, curious but unwilling at goods, drawing back.

The cheap stores on 14th street on Saturday afternoon.

*Arrowsmith:* 450
450
———
22500
1800
———
202500 [*words*].

563 They were lifted up—O God of Voyages etc.—as the war developed.[100]

566–568—It's no use, mater.[101]

568–570—Mrs. Pert.

578–580—Mr. Bowden's Funeral.[102]

587 He thrust his knee.[103]

590 They went into a bar.

Shakespeare.[104]

614 Hugh Barton merited the frantic devotion [*of his mother and sister.*]

If men have lost their God, or discovered that they have never had Him, they may in time be able to create him.

From Jack Loeb's frog to the God of the Jews is perhaps not such a Big Jump. If they can in time create a Big Old Man who lives a million years, and looks over the world, they could do something vaster than the Baptists ever imagined.

[*Final examination on*] Thursday, May 23, 9:30—12:30.

628–629—Gant and Eliza [*were more interested in scholarship.*]

657—He sought back etc.[105]

100. The first item refers to a deleted satire of the Leonards' attitude toward England—the emotional response to the First World War of people who cherished the literature of England. The God of Voyages passage is a two-and-a-half-page lyric summary of Wolfe's European experiences that was also cut out.

101. A parody of a sentimental English war letter from the front was omitted.

102. This deleted passage contains an unrestrained outburst against Christian burial customs.

103. A part of the scene with Louise was omitted from page 363, LHA.

104. The Shakespeare section was retained and forms the beginning of Chapter XXVII.

105. A passage giving Eugene's thoughts and sense of guilt at the moment he enters the brothel in Exeter was cut. The next item refers to a description of his brothel experience, which was also deleted.

662—whole description.
676–682—The Food—Going to Sidney to see women.
686—The best fabulists.[106]
688—

Books
*The Grandmothers*—Glenway Wescott
*Java Head*—Hergesheimer
*Babbitt*—Sinclair Lewis
*An American Tragedy*—Theodore Dreiser
*The Sun Also Rises*—Ernest Hemingway
*Winesburg, Ohio*—Sherwood Anderson
*The Cream of The Jest*—James Branch Cabell
*My Ántonia*—Cather (*The Song of The Lark*)
*Ruggles of Red Gap*—Harry Leon Wilson
*Show Boat*—Edna Ferber
*Scarlet Sister Mary*—Julia Peterkin
*Round Up*—Lardner
*The Bridge of San Luis Rey*—Wilder

771–775—Cut.[107]
778–784.[108]
788–792.[109]
809–810.[110]

*Aspects of the Novel*—E. M. Forster.

People I know in New York:

Aline
Olin
Abe
Munn
Watt
Varney
The Volkenings
R. Williams
Bergum
Emerson

106. This passage praising Voltaire and Swift was kept, LHA, p. 422.

107. A four-page deletion made at the beginning of Chapter XXXII includes a portrait of a Canadian drill-master, a satiric passage on the president of the University, and comments on the war by fellow students.

108. A description of the family of Harold Gay and Eugene's visit with them in Sidney was cut.

109. Additional details and anecdotes of student life were omitted.

110. Eugene's remorse because of his drunkenness was cut from what is now the break on page 498, LHA.

Perkins
Wheelock
Meyer
Beer
Mrs. Boyd
Mabel Egg[*leston*]
Steve
Margaret (Hotel Albert)
Percy Grant
Miss F.[*aulkner*]
Ed
Stott
Greenleaf
Old Greenleaf
The Greens
Muriel Moore
Roland Holt
The Lewisohns
The Workshoppers
N. Mobley
Dollard
Troy
Tyndall
Carpenter
Martin
J. Brown
Doris Ullmann
M. Cane
Miss Arthur
Miss Morgan
Lily
Miss Willcox (her brother)
D. Powell
Middlebrook
Gorham
Terry
Miss Maurer
Mrs. Miller
Cimmalucha
White

"ring the bells backward"—Charles Lamb.
"Sweet funeral bells . . . . as I lay moored"—DeQuincey.
My own vision of the single street of life etc.

OKTOBERFEST

or THE OKTOTERFEST
or THE OCTOBER FAIR.[111]

Your Uncle Will was going on with some of his foolishness.[112]

May 29 [*a grocery list*].

111. This is the first appearance of the title that became Wolfe's favorite for a number of years. At this point "The October Fair," or its German equivalent, was simply to be a book about his wanderings in Europe, but after he abandoned "The River People" he began to lump all his various projects into one book, which was to be entitled "The October Fair." This title was retained as the book kept expanding through the years. The first half was finally published as OT&R in 1935, though Wolfe still planned to use the original title for its sequel and so announced it in the "Publisher's Note" to OT&R.

112. This statement of Eliza's was evidently the key to an episode Wolfe planned to work on later. He has the identical statement written inside the back cover of "The River People" ledger.

Books Written or Planned
Pub. when I was 28—Look Homeward, Angel
29—The Oktoberfest
30—Faust and Helen
31—The River People
33—A Woman's Life.

Dashiell—Lunch—Tues., June 4.[113]

To this hill will come the city
Then the jungle, waste, and death
Desolation, love and pity
A million lives shall draw their breath
When we lie buried underneath.

In this paper wrap my breath
In this paper wrap my heart
Let it lay there after death.

Stone will last when body's dust
Our faith, our hope, our love, our trust.

## A WORM CROSSING [114]

W.

In this paper wrap my breath
Stone will last when body's dust;
So shall stone die ere the death
Of faith, our hope, our love, our trust.

Buried in the walls my spirit
Through the stone will speak to her.
No one in the house will hear it;
No one in the house come near it
But she whom it was written for.

113. Alfred S. Dashiell was then Managing Editor of *Scribner's Magazine* and later was to hold the same position at *Reader's Digest*. He and Wolfe became friends; Wolfe usually refers to Dashiell by his nickname, Fritz.

114. Just under the title Wolfe wrote and then scratched out, "Put this near her in her house."

# *Pocket Notebook 11*

## *June 11, 1929, to October 15, 1929*

*Wolfe spent the summer preparing* Look Homeward, Angel *for the press. He corrected proofs, wrote a brief preface, and selected quotations for the dedication page and title page. He also saw his first story, "An Angel on the Porch," appear in* Scribner's Magazine. *But he looked ahead as well as back. His plans for "The Fast Express" began to develop further, and details about "The October Fair" began to appear.*

*Much of this work was carried out in a cottage at Ocean Point, Maine. In August, Wolfe visited Quebec and Montreal and then returned to New York to begin teaching once again at New York University. Before classes opened, he took one more journey home to Asheville; it was to be his last for seven and a half years. He returned to New York quite worried about how his book was going to be received in his home town, for* Look Homeward, Angel *was scheduled to be published on October 18.*

---

June 11—Tues.—

Out in Westchester with Aline and Woodsend. The wind, [unswerved?] unfoliaged, strikes out sick thoughts and desperate fantasies.

Nous n'allons plus au bois.
Les lauriers sont coupés.[1]

"Merciful God!" howled Gant. "What in the name of Jesus have you done?"

"I've trimmed 'em fer ye, Mister Gant," said Reese. "I done just like I thought ye wanted. I reckon ye'll have plenty o' sun on yore side after this." His slow lout's face broke into a gap-toothed grin of idiot satisfaction. "You damned mountain grill," bawled Gant. "You've ruined us all. He'll bring suit against me for this, and get judgment, too."

1. "We go to the woods no more./The laurels are cut down." Lines from a French folk song.

Not standards—limits.

Well, I said to him—No I guess not. I got enough to live.

*As a Child:* A terrific rain—the grocer's wagon—the poor beast of a horse standing in the street, forehead adroop, with torrential rain playing across his body—the foaming gutters (how as a child I loved it!) Think of all that has gone between—how much breathing and sweating and reading.

How old are you?
I'm past twenty.
How old are you?
Please—well I'm past 30.
I know damned well you are—how much?
Now will you tell me something?
Don't ever do it. Don't ask me now.
(About the bus boy)
This boy's getting riper and riper—he'll get it soon. He's almost ready to drop, said the waiter.

Now what do you think about *that?*
You're going back and sleep with her etc. etc.
Put me in a cab and send me over there. I'll go.

Can the fish read the language of the diver?

I understand there may be millions of universes. (How interesting! You say the beer is 25 a glass?)

"The story of New York has not yet been written" (True, true, I murmur, why don't you write it?)

The post-war generation has lost its faith in God (By way of agreement, I glance towards heaven with a cynical smile.)

"These Latin men have something—a *finesse*, an approach—something I cannot describe that Anglo Saxons lack" ("I know what you mean," I murmur helpfully.)

"It seems to me your own approach toward life is more that of a Latin than an American" ("I think you may be right," I say "I have often felt like that myself.")

"When I first saw you I took you for an Italian" ("Not really!" I whisper softly and smile with pleasure, "In Paris they take me for a Russian—'un Russe,' you know.")

When I come to the town again I shall come a stranger—No one will know I have come—No one will be there to greet me. And, somewhere in the town she will be sleeping?

I have built no house here since my brother died.

Categories of the Novel

The English Country House (10,000).

The Bar X Ranch (10,000).

The French Provincial Town—Wife-Lover-Monotone (10,000).

The Tauchnitz-Victorian—The Rector's Daughter—It was a Lover and His Lass Affair (3,000).

The Younger-Older Generation Novel (3,000).

The Russian I'm-A-Fool-But-Christlier-Than-My-Wisers (1,000).

49th Street Grill (Tuesday, June 17—Hellish hot):

Everyone in New York has a grievance—I listen to the people around me—tonight (I got my proofs today) I feel at peace—but I listen to the people all around me talking of their friends and acquaintances—one is a fool, one is a grafter, one a liar and bluff—their mean little smiles are full of venom.

"Do you suppose he's living off his friends?"

"They're millions like him."

"What is he—a big wind?"

"O you can't tell me it's all an affectation—(the shy little girl)—she's not that."

I worked on the Chicago Tribune—there's millions like him—English accent and all, etc.

Compare Aline with these people—her sweetness and belief—how did it come [*to*] her in New York?

Aren't you a comfort. You never saw such notices in all your life. It embarrasses me to think of it.

And besides, I realize, Peg has no real interest in those things (Peg evidently is the one she hates).

"You've got me all hot and bothered."

(Barbara and Peg)—"If Barbara ever found out I was anti-Peg she'd be all off me" etc.

"She doesn't like me—I know that."

"She's a very strange girl."

"I said, 'Peg How many boys are you stringing along?' "

"She got hurt then—she got terribly hurt then."

"Never kick an alley cat."

"I only said it jokingly."

"Oh she just burned up."

"In the fertilizer business—in Akron" (etc, etc, etc) (They laughed at this—the city fellows).

No, this is exactly what she said.

Since then he's been round the world.

Kennedy came in, and Murdoch.

"And everything started going (very fast talk) I crawled upstairs, didn't know what I was doing, etc, etc.

"He must have money, though, somewhere" (etc, etc.)

"She's very well off" (the flat Chicago voices).

[*two sketches of heads*]

"Is he a friend of yours?"

"Do you remember—we were having fits wondering if we'd find a filling station open?"

"Bermuda ranks third in honeymoons."

"We—Mildred said—I said—" (the loyal married tricksters—nauseous).

"With married people—you can flirt with the husband. You know it's all in fun—but as soon as one single person comes in it's different."

"It was a cartoon for the *New Yorker*."

"She isn't—she isn't that way. She isn't with me"

"She isn't with you."

(Finally they didn't order anything for an hour and a half).

Ocean Point, C. W. Snow Cottage, c/of Mrs. Benge.[2]

Sunday July 1 (?)—Eating at Child's 5th Ave—

But I mention as a few interesting and new phenomena—

—The Nature Cults in Germany with their numerous semi-pornographic mags.

—The dominance of the criminal in politics and business in this country.

—The Rise of the Labor Party in England.

2. Wolfe planned a vacation trip which included a stay on the edge of the sea at Ocean Point with Mrs. Bernstein. Here he would correct the proofs for LHA. Later he would make an excursion into Quebec.

—The Rise of The American Empire

—The American Woman (i.e.—what should be done with her? Is she worth saving, or should the next war be directed toward her extermination and the nation recruited with German, Austrian, and Scandinavian women?)

—The Collapse of the Mother Myth.

There is too much "frank talk" about fornication in America and too little frank fornication. It is all right to write words about fornication but when one begins to write articles for *Harpers, The New York Times Book Review,* and *The American Mercury* on the subject, matters are bad.

[*The following quotations reflect Wolfe's search for a suitable epigraph to place on his title page and for some appropriate lines to include with his dedication of the book to Mrs. Bernstein.*]

"I wonder by my troth, what thou, and I
Did, till we lov'd? were we not wean'd till then?"
(*The Good-Morrow*—DONNE)

"Or if, when thou, the worlds soule, goest,
It stay, tis but thy carkasse then,
The fairest woman, but thy ghost,
But corrupt wormes, the worthyest men."
(*A Feaver*—DONNE)

"O wrangling schooles, that search what fire
Shall burne this world, had none the wit
Unto this knowledge to aspire,
That this her feaver might be it?"
(DONNE—*ibid.*)

"Then, as all my soules bee
Emparadis'd in you, (in whom alone
I understand, and grow and see,)
The rafters of my body, bone
Being still with you, the Muscle, Sinew, and Veine,
Which tile this house, will come again?"
(DONNE—*A Valedictorian: Of My Name in the Window*)[3]

3. Wolfe selected these lines to accompany the dedication "To A. B.," and he marked them in his copy of Donne's *Complete Poetry and Selected Prose.* Mrs. Bernstein had given Wolfe this book, which was her own copy of Donne's work, and it became one of his most treasured volumes.

"Doth not man die even in his birth? The breaking of prison is death and what is our birth but a breaking of prison?"

(DONNE—*Sermon XV 1st Friday in Lent*)

John Donne
*Complete Poetry and Selected Prose*
Nonesuch Press, Bloomsbury 1929.

SONG

Dear, again back recall
  To this light
A stranger to himself and all;
Both the wonder and the story
Shall be yours, and eke the glory:
I am your servant, I your thrall."

(JOHN FLETCHER)

There is a lady sweet and kind,
Was never face so pleased my mind;
I did but see her passing by,
And yet I love her till I die.

(*Anonymous*)

"With thee conversing I forget all time,
All seasons, and their change—all please alike.
Sweet is the breath of morn, her rising sweet,
With charm of earliest birds"—

(*Paradise Lost*, Bk. IV, p. 614)

Gant—"You'll laugh out of the other side of your mouth—etc.

"A lovely lady, garmented in light
From her own beauty"

(SHELLEY—*The Witch of Atlas*)

"A lady richly clad as she
Beautiful exceedingly"

([COLERIDGE]—*Christabel*)

"The rainbow comes and goes,
And lovely is the rose"
([WORDSWORTH]—*Intimations of Immortality*)

"And beauty born of murmuring sound
Shall pass into her face"
([WORDSWORTH]—*Three years she grew—etc.*)

"To see her is to love her
And love but her forever"
(BURNS—*Bonny Lady*)

"At one time the earth was probably a white-hot sphere like the sun"—
(TARR AND MC MURRY) [4]

Thursday, July 10—Preparations for Maine.
Friday: 1) Get Lottie [5] to empty all the food.
2) Buy moth balls for clothes.
3) Buy two flannel shirts, khaki trousers, socks. (Look at old shoes—get them soled if need be).
4) Buy sweater (?)
5) Get Preface Typed—arrange with Scribners about proof, etc.
6) Take only two bags if possible—small green one (or big black one) and brief case—
7) Take Sheets to Maine.
8) Call up Eastern Steamship Comp.
9) Pay bills—or take them to Maine.

Trains to Bath [*Maine*].
8:30 A.M. Boston. 12:14—Bath—Boat for Boothbay 12:33–2:05.

Stop here my friend and cast an eye.
As you are now so once was I.
As I am now so you must be.
Prepare for death and follow me.

4. From the first page of *A Complete Geography* by Ralph S. Tarr and Frank M. McMurry, Wolfe's grammar school textbook. He has marked the passage in the book, which is in the Wisdom Collection. Wolfe selected this statement to use as an epigraph on the title page of his novel.

5. Lottie Brown, a cleaning woman.

Sugar maple
Betula Lenta (Sweet Birch)
Liquidambar Styraciflua (Sweet Gum)
Koelreuteria paniculata (N. China) [*golden rain tree*].

Send fifty Thomas Cook Quebec Monday Sending Check Home Wednesday.

TOM

Quebec—Sunday, Aug. 4—

Lunch at Kerholn's—22 Rue de la Fabrique—good lunch—Interesting how French hold native traits after 300 years here. The woman in the pastry shop out front—shrill servile little French voice "Oui-i" like a pig squealing—haggling over phone with women over prices—"a dozen petit fours—no—impossible. Well, to make you a better price, etc."

Monday—Aug. 5—

Got wire with money—grey day—went to Rue St. Pierre 83—cashed it—back later—now drinking in little Tavern in rather charming square opposite Notre Dame Des Victoires (*ascenseur* presently up hill). Looking at my hand holding cigarette—The long brown bony structure—the fingers curled—how grand.

Hotel Blanchard—in a little square opp. Not. Dame des Victoires—Good Pub—rough place with booths.

Quebec—Aug. 5—

At desk in my hotel room—thinking of Aline—it seemed strange to think that she ever came to wake me in the morning—yet that was only 3½ wks. ago—and will be again before this summer's over—Thinking thus—thought of DeMaupassant when I first began to masturbate—Picture—"Every morning before he was up she came and slipped into bed beside him"—etc.—picture showed woman with drawers flounces getting in beside moustached Frenchman (get page of this in new book).

States I've Seen
New York—12,000,000
Penn.—10,000,000
Mass.—4,000,000
Conn.—3,500,000

N.C.—3,000,000
Georgia—3,000,000
S.C.—2,000,000
La.—2,000,000
Maine—800,000
Md.—2,000,000
Va. —3,000,000
Tenn.—2,500,000
R.I.—800,000
Vermont—700,000
[*N.H.*]—600,000
Mo.—4,000,000.

New Places This Summer:
Maine, Vermont, Canada.

It is like paying attention to smart Jews like L. Lewisohn and Waldo Frank—they have too many bright ideas—What they are interested in is having bright ideas and not in getting at any essential unity.

Conversations with Joel Pierce—

It is better to be a pork packer with a poet's mind than one who passes for a poet, but has a pork packer's mind.

The only real ruling unity is in the mind and in the soul—I shrink back before your essential trivial nastiness—Your minds stink—no matter how often you bathe your feet or take cold showers.

Unless one can be first and best, or among the best and first, there's no point in going on writing—unless, finally, one cannot help writing.

Cathedral—Montreal.

Tu Es Petras et Super Hanc Petram.[6]

Montreal—the bright sun, a dusty street down hill, the hot sun falling on dreary slate roofs—garages, oil tanks, and factory towers—a junk shop—the ragged ends of cheap fiction for thirty years—O God! O God! O God! (The newstands with the American mags: *War-Birds*, *Ace High*, et al, et al, et al.)

6. The words of Jesus to Peter: "You are Peter and upon this rock [I will build my church]," Matthew 16:18.

130,000,000 acres of commercial forest in old Quebec—Exhibit grains, woods, etc. in Montreal station O God! O God!

The Editor,[7]
Dear Sir:

I regret very much the delay in answering your letter of July 29th—I have just returned to New York from Canada, and have just finished reading your letter. I wish to give you my warmest and most grateful thanks for the generous interest you show for my work, and to assure you that no praise and commendation could be of higher value to me than that of my own people.

But I must respectfully decline your friendly invitation to write about my book. I think you will readily understand my reasons after I have set them forth: I am a young man and an unknown writer—although the event of my book's publication is an important one in my life and has made me very happy, the book is only one of thousands that are being published every year. My publishers, Charles Scribner's Sons, hope that it is one of the better ones, but that, of course, can not be known until it has been published. Certainly, it seems unwise to me for a writer to advertise his first work before it has been seen by the public. And probably, for a novelist, silence—outside his own books—is best. I mean he should let them speak for him.

Like most young men I am thirsty for praise and desire the respect and attention of intelligent people for my work. It is only stupid to pretend any grand detachment or disinterest on this score. It is one of the powerful springs of the creative act. But I feel it is useless to try to get it in any other way than by the work itself.

You say that since reading my book much has been made plain about which previously you were in doubt.[8] I wonder if such subtle penetration of motives is necessary to begin with. It is best to begin with the simple things—and some of them have not been made plain to you. Apparently you did not value or believe in my devotion and loyalty to you during these years—a devotion and loyalty which up to now has remained steadfast, although embittered by reports brought to me of contemptuous and unfriendly things you had said about me.

7. This is perhaps a draft of a letter to one of the Asheville papers. The *Asheville Citizen* had carried a notice of Wolfe's "An Angel on the Porch" when it appeared in *Scribner's* and had announced the forthcoming publication of his book. But since Wolfe was given to making up occasions for letters to the press, it is probably only a projection of the imagination.

8. This appears to be a preparation in self-defense for an attack that Wolfe was anticipating from some Asheville friend or relative.

Find out about trip to Lachine Rapids.
Visit McGill.
Visit Art Museum.
Make purchases, if any.

25—Goya [*Portrait of Altamirana, Judge of Seville*].
4—Tintoretto [*Portrait of a Lady*].

Montreal, Wed. afternoon:

Went to Museum and McGill University Library—have never seen so large a city with so few good things in it—Museum filled up with junky pictures—a good portrait by Goya—one or two good Daumiers—a room full of what is called "Canadian Art"

Feeling here for Americans is not hatred, but dislike. Nevertheless—or because—their city's imitation-American through and through.

The Scotch woman in the museum—the best thing I found there—Ye must excuse me sir-r-r—I don't speak English guid—talkin' to a stranger—but it's my auld home there—the place where I was barn in Scotland.

[*When Wolfe's story "An Angel on the Porch" appeared in the August number of* Scribner's, *he began to get some response from friends about it.*]

Dear Miss Rosen:

Thanks very much for your interesting letter. I wish I had time to answer it as it deserves. But I am very busy at present on the proofs of my book.

I hope you will read the book when it appears, and also like it. Several of the questions you ask about the characters are answered, I believe, in the novel.

Thank you again for writing me.
Yours Faithfully,
THOMAS WOLFE

I hope you may be wrong in thinking what I have written may distress members of my family or anyone else.[9] Certainly, I would do anything to avoid causing any one pain—except to change the book fundamentally. I am afraid, however, that if anyone is distressed by

9. A draft of a reply, August 11, 1929, to Mrs. Roberts' letter about "An Angel on the Porch." See *Letters*, pp. 197–99. A similar argument is found in the Foreword to LHA, "To the Reader."

what seemed to me a very simple and inoffensive story, their feelings, when the book comes out will be much stronger. And the thought of that distresses *me* more than I can tell you.

Nothing, however, may now be done about this. You say in your letter that you never knew many things about my life when I was a child and that many more you did not discover until years later. I am afraid there are still other things that you are yet to learn—a thousand words leap to my tongue, words of explanation, persuasion, and hope—but they had better rest unsaid.

Silence is best. More and more I know that the grievous and complex fabric of human relationship may not be explained by language. However our motives or our acts are judged or misjudged, we can only trust to the belief of other men that we are of good will.

About my book the only apology I have to make is that it is not better—and by "better" I mean that it does not represent by any means the best of which I am capable. But I hope I shall feel this way about my work for many years to come. But there is much in this first book for which I hope I shall always continue to feel affection and pride.

I can not go into explanations of the creative act. That has been done many times by other people, and much better than I could hope to. I can only assure you that my book is a work of fiction, and that no person or no act or event has been deliberately and consciously described. But I think you know that fiction is not spun out of the air, it is made from the solid stuff of human experience. Dr. Johnson said a man would turn over half a library to make a book; so may a novelist turn over half a town to make a figure in his novel. This is not the only method, but this is illustrative, I believe, of the whole process.

Jonathan Daniels [10]—Sacramento 7961.

Saturday—Aug. 18—

Up late—phone call from E. Simpson [11] in Flushing—uptown—to Harvard Club—then to Blue Ribbon—then to Hippodrome for prize fight picture—then to Harvard Club—then to Jack Kennedy's

10. Journalist, author, and member of the White House staff under Franklin Roosevelt, Daniels was at this time a young reporter for the *Raleigh News and Observer*. He and Wolfe were fellow students at the University of North Carolina and remained friends until he wrote a review attacking LHA for its treatment of the South. See his memoir *Thomas Wolfe: October Recollections* (Columbia, S.C., 1961), which describes their train journey down to Asheville at this time, just before Wolfe's book was published.

11. Wolfe had apparently met Mrs. Edith Simpson on his voyage to Europe in 1928. He continued to see her from time to time in New York.

Chop House—Read *Point Counterpoint* [*by Aldous Huxley*]—better than I thought.

"Half dozen best critics" according to various writers:

Mencken, Nathan, Lippman, Krutch, Boyd, Canby.

W. Frank, G. B. Munson, E. Wilson, K. Burke, M. Cowley, A. Tate.

Carl Van Doren, H. Brown, Harry Hansen, Max Eastman, W. L. Phelps, Mark Van Doren.

Van Wyck Brooks, Elliot Paul, E. Jolas, W. C. Williams.

Henry Hazlitt, Herschel Brickell, Herb. Gorman, Cuthbert Wright—et al, et al, et al.

| | |
|---|---|
| Dreiser | Fitzgerald |
| Lewis | Hemingway |
| Cabell | Westcott |
| Cather | Wilder |
| | Wolfe |

Sunday afternoon—Aug. 18—

Home late last night from Harvard Club—E. Simpson had already called—Up late today—called E. Simpson said I could not come to Flushing because of my proofs—Her voice was sour, got better later—Eating in Child's Cafeteria 5th Avenue—Young girls with young girl boobies and sweet vicious fifteen-year-old faces arouse my lust.

[*The following entry is the draft of a letter in which Wolfe is thanking John Hall Wheelock for the gift of a copy of* The Bright Doom. *See* Letters, *pp. 201–202. Wheelock's inscription in the book includes lines from his poem "Noon: Amagansett Beach":*

"for Thomas Wolfe
in friendship and admiration
'Loneliness—loneliness forever. Dune beyond dune,
Stretches the infinite loneliness—pale sand and pale sea-grass,
Pale beaches, mile upon mile. In the immensity of noon
A hawk moves upon the wind. Clouds darken and pass.'

JOHN HALL WHEELOCK
August 26, 1929."

*Wolfe was especially moved by Wheelock's poem "The Dark Memory" because it suggested aspects of his own situation with Mrs. Bernstein. The poem opens:*

"It was our love's Gethsemane, and you wept.
Around us, in the drab twilight, the little room
That had known our love, that had known our tears and
  laughter, kept
Shamed silence. Silently 'round us rose the gloom. . . ."]

I am—or am trying to be—a story-teller—perhaps I like poems best that tell a story: I will only say that "The Dark Memory" is one of the most moving poems I remember to have read in years—the music in it is grand and sad, and twists at the heart.

You are a true poet—you have looked upon the terrible face of Patience, and the quality of enduring and waiting shines in every line you have written. The poets who are dead have given me life; when I have faltered, I have seized upon their strength: now I have by me living poetry and a living poet, and in his patience and in his strong soul I shall often abide.

I am honored in knowing you, I am honored in having you call me friend, I am exalted and lifted up by every word of trust and commendation you have ever spoken to me.

Classes at N.Y.U. start September 24th.

Asheville, N.C. Train leaves Penn. Station 1:05 Standard—2:05 D.S.

Lower 10 in Car 29
Fare Round Trip $45.

For Henry Stevens.[12] Call up 114 In Asheville—ask Mr. Ingle to wire H. S. about fare. $350 or $275 etc.

---

[*Just before leaving for Asheville, Wolfe bought another large accounting ledger and began to make some notes for future projects, especially "The October Fair." We have included several of these notes here in conjunction with his diary entries about the Asheville visit. The last of these notes, some phrases and statements of his mother's as she reminisced about her childbearing and miscarrying, show Wolfe's first consideration of material that developed into the short novel* Web of Earth.]

12. An old Asheville friend whom Wolfe used as a model for the character Robert Weaver. He was the central figure in a long section, "The Man on the Wheel," in Wolfe's abortive novel about a train, "K 19." He later appeared in OT&R.

What I remember about trains:

"Miss" Eliza's story of Paul Hester—on his way back from St. Louis to Altamont—at New Market, Tennessee.

Old Engineer on the Big Trunk line—"never had but one accident in all my fifty-four year"—"I've been workin' on the railroad all the livelong day."

On my way to Washington—one-armed engineer who explained the way train runs—eccentric strap breaks.

Pity? How can we avoid it? There they are with wigs, false teeth, and a cancer flowering in their vitals—talking above the dinner cups. How grand! Mrs. John De Peyster Chamberlain entertained at a dinner dance.

"Well, Mother," said Greenberg, as he came in, "have you finished having that baby yet?"

Cimmilucca's dark merry face was bubbling with little wells of laughter. "Boy!" he cried "What a cinch that was! She—" he was unable to go on for a moment, and sat down weakly, laughing.

"Numbah 39—Train fo' Black Mountain, Ole Fo't, Maw-w-gunton, Hick-o-ree, Statesville, Sawls-berry, Greens-boro, Dansville, Ro-an-oak, Wash-in-ton, an' aw-w-ll points East."

(chooka-a-lucka, chook-a-lucka, chook-a-lucka.)

Sept. 6—

Make something out of this [13]—Left New York for Asheville—Writing this as the train leaves Trenton—Bridge over river—depressing grey day—and the flat ugly Jersey country—rank with weedage—with heavy wilted August leafage.

Outside of Elizabeth—the magnificent 4 ply Pennsylvania roadbed—The other train raced us on the other roadbed—a magnificent experience—The big engine thundering slowly up on us at 50 miles an hour—I rush to the platform—Young engineer and fireman slide slowly by me—two feet away grinning—everyone pleasant gleeful and boyish—Young Engineer goggled, strong white teeth with one gleaming gold molar (or canine)—That strong pleasant untough face

13. Wolfe first developed the episode for "K 19"; later used it for "The Train and the City," published in *Scribner's* in May, 1933; and finally incorporated it into OT&R, pp. 407–11.

—then the rival conductors and porters grinning pleasant with gentle irony at us.

Then—O strange and wonderful vision—the inside of a pullman as we slipped up on it—as it slipped up on us—an old man weary and meagre, dressed in thin expensive clothes—the two old veined hands folded on his legs—a lovely young woman—blond haired cross legs, silk legs and the long white tapering hand with tips curved inwards toward her belly where she fumbled with a chain—the porters making faces at each other—Finally our train gathers terrific speed and begins to slip by the other which is on the inside track and according to our porter "not supposed to make the time we are"—as we go by the rival engine the engineer has given up the race—and has turned to shout something at his fireman who stands arms akimbo on the floor—there is about them an air of having finished—it was all a joke mixed with seriousness—they now grin pleasantly while their big engine *bucks and rocks loosely along, slowed down.* Their manner seems to say, "Well we gave you a run for your money, at any rate"—and above it all—our train and theirs—there is the magnificent sense of expertness that I love —American expertness—the big steel coaches, the enormous engine— the vast careless dinginess and dullness of the color—but the magnificent color within—America—America.

The bright yellow flowers among the drear towns—the ruined [strength?]—the rough unfinished land.

*The October Fair*—Characters

Eliza
People on the Train
The Engineer
The Schoolteachers
The Dutchmen (on Shipboard)
The Hotel Albert People
The 8th Street People
Abe
The Instructors—Burgum, McCullough, Dollard, Carlton, Manley, Carpenter, Martin, Terry, etc.
The Students
Munn
Watt
The Night Watchman on 8th Street
McKee—his wife

Grant
Stott
The Neighborhooders—the Lewisohns, Morgan, Arthur, Carrol, Edla, A. Beer, etc.
Olin Dows
Mabel Eggleston.[14]

Saturday, Sept. 7—at night, very weary—Asheville—[15]

Arrived this morning—Mabel, Mama at Station—Spruce St.—Breakfast with Mama ("I've a good ear of corn on that stalk for your dinner next week")—Mabel's for lunch—Mrs. Wheaton—older—more paralysis of tongue—but marvelous shape for 84—"Dom—what do you think of women in politics?" etc.—Mama's long reminiscence of Colonel Lash—her life a series of reminiscences—Dine—"the Scribners friends of ours"—Ralph—little or nothing at station—the Honess wedding party—then through town—G. McCoy—Gooches—Home—Mr. Colvin—Mabel's—Supper—the quarrel incessant with the Wheatons begins ("Are there any of those brown biscuits, Helen?"—"I'll get them for you in a minute—I'm doing as many things as I can at one time"—then Ollie, Effie, Louise—then the Salters—then Mama, home.

Wed.-Thursday, Asheville—3 A.M. morning:

The vast and even noise of the night things—Spruce Street—front room.

Got back from Anderson [*South Carolina*] with Fred [*Wolfe*] tonight about midnight—suffering now from corn whiskey melancholia combined with night noise—(other sounds: a low rumble on the rails as in book.)

Cause of distress: Left Effie and Anderson—that hot dismal town—ever the same—the pretty drawling girls with bribing word of rape, red clay, cotton, bigotry and murder.

14. Miss Eggleston, who appears frequently in lists of people whom Wolfe considered for character models, had come to know Wolfe during his first year in New York, when he was living at the Hotel Albert. Later, in her letters to him, she claimed to be his oldest friend in New York.

15. Among the people mentioned in the following entry are Ralph Wheaton, Mabel Wolfe's husband; Mrs. Wheaton, Ralph's mother, who lived with them; Elizabeth Honess, who married Charles Cane on September 7; George McCoy, Tom's schoolmate from the North State School and now a reporter on the *Asheville Citizen;* James Colvin, a Scotch-American who lived across the street from the Wolfe's when Tom was a child; Ollie Wolfe, Tom's first cousin and son of Uncle Wesley; Effie Tugman Wolfe, his wife; and Louise Wolfe, their daughter.

Then Greenville [*South Carolina*]—Fred Gambrell[16]—the Mill district—the red-clay unpaved street—the corn liquor—the nigger shacks—the mill—Poinsett Hotel—the "good-fellow" clerk—the men with straw hats wise-cracking—the gaily uniformed nigger bellhops—the coffee shop—the laughing, smiling, and grinning girls—the sniggering men—Leaving town—sadly, sadly the sun—the rolling land, the red clay—the ice-plant—the man with the son at Ga. Tech.—Freshman—football team—then at length the country—memories of jail—then corn and cotton—Paris with the foothills—then Old Man Hightower and wife—the palaver—the corn liquor—then the glorious hills—then night—O noble and vast night—and drinking the corn liquor.

Then Hendersonville—the Coffee shop—the boy—the order—then Fred, "Did he insult us? Did you hear what he said?" I hadn't. Fred kept it up: "He said 'I'm not drunk' when he knocked vase over. I'd like to know what he meant by that"—"Everyone will take a drink now and then" etc.—Called boy up, questioned him, asked him what he meant by it; seemed to me he abused him—Kept asking me if he thought boy has insulted us—Boy seemed very nice to me—I felt bad—boy insisted he had intended nothing—I asked Fred if he thought it brave for two men to beat up a young boy like that—said we should hunt up Asheville cops or grown men—not to abuse servants—Finally recalled boy—took him out and gave him liquor.

Set off to Asheville—Fred raised question of "insult" again—said is so often I got tired and said, Yes—the boy had insulted us—called us sons of bitches—Fred turned round and drove back to Hendersonville at fast rate—I said nothing—He got nervous at length—asked if boy had used word "son of a bitch." I said I had not heard him but since he (Fred) felt insulted and kept talking of insult—boy probably *had* said it—Told him if his honor was insulted I would stand by him in any trouble—I was very bitter and ironic—Fred argued out of it—parked in front of shop—backed out and went back toward Asheville—we talked at random—finally I said nothing—near town broke out on him and said By God I was ashamed of him and of myself, etc.—Looked at him suddenly and saw he was crying—I made him drive up to curb near Biltmore Avenue—and I was crying too—Told him I was one of the family and couldn't get along with them—told him, he was a good fellow—and I knew his value—this made him cry—we drove round in Asheville—had coffee in Greek's place—I stopped Greek outside Wheaton's.

We drove through Grove Park and past Mabel's several times—

16. Wolfe's brother-in-law, who had married his oldest sister, Effie, and lived in Anderson, South Carolina.

back to telegraph office—long talk with young fellow there—Fred sent message. Bach home to O. K. H.—waked mama—gave Effie's present—found letter from Aline like message from another world—Told Fred goodnight—Went uptown to *Citizen*—reporters playing cards—Geo. McCoy away—went for coffee to Vick's and back home—the lights—the deserted streets—the same as I knew it (how well I *have* it!) Yet tonight seems strange and terribly sad and unreal—still feel all the country around, the vast rolling depressing Piedmont, South Carolina, corn-licker depression, the incident at Hendersonville—the tears, the neurosis, and O God the sadness, the sadness, the sadness and the loneliness of my life—to *what* did I belong, to *what* do I belong—*who* wants me? Mama's old weak eyes and face puckered fumily with sleep as she looked at us—No more do I belong!

O God, the sadness, the strangeness, the loneliness, (the young men playing cards there in the office) the pity, the pity, the pity of it all!

This written past 3 A. M.—vast brooding star-lit night—vast even night sound—far off a car—and thunder on the rails.

This same morning-night—a brief record:

Saturday—First day home—Mama—Mabel's.

Sunday—Mama's—Mabel's—church, etc.—Fred—Mabel's.

Monday—Mama's—Mabel's—Spartanburg—Chesnee—Greenville—Anderson.

Tuesday—Effie's—Fred—Hotel.

Wednesday—Hotel—Effie—Greenville—Fred Gamb.—Hendersonville—Asheville.

And so, and so to bed!

THE RETURN OF THE [17]

Well—as I say—I don't know why I'm here to tell it—

I had ten—

It was just like your papa if he'd been all stewed down to that shape.

The one at my ear kept whisperin' "Two" "Two"—the one at the window kept saying "Twenty" "Twenty."

Why—I'd just jump off the step.

17. Wolfe's theme of homecoming after long absence was frequently accompanied by the title "The Return of the Prodigal."

I said to Purefoy "it's two weeks before my time"—he said to me "that doesn't matter—it's your time."

He looked and said "My God! It's my image."

I certainly went through the mill in my young days—it's a wonder I'm here to tell it.

I took the children and was walkin' down by old Fort Marion near the Ponce de Leon when I felt it all break loose.

"like I told your papa—"

"I feel like my lower and upper parts are coming in two."

I had less married life than any woman I know—and I had all the children.

Mabel was the biggest child I had—Fred was the smallest—and look at him now.

I put it out on an old plate and stretched its arms out for your papa to see—when I came back its hands were folded over its breast like someone had done it—O I cried out it's some spirit—Pshaw said your papa it's nothing of the sort—it had life in it and when its muscles contracted—etc.

He took it out and buried it under a fig tree.

---

THE FAST EXPRESS

Leaving Culpep-puh.

Rock, reel, smash, and swerve—go it, go it on the curve—steady, steady does the trick—keep her steady as a stick—eat the earth, eat the earth—slam and slug and beat the earth—And let her whir-r-r and let her purr at eighty per.

(Across the Southern plain her cry wailed back—hoarse, high and doleful)

I am the Fast Express, eater of earth, slayer of distance, the World-Devourer.

Lean Death and Pale Pity went out for to take—a city a city, awake—Pale Death and lean Pity went out for a city, went out for a city, went out for a city to take.

Narrative Episodes in "The October Fair"

(each must be made as good as possible)

1) Nearing Land (invocation to Earth) Mrs. Kerr [18] and the

18. Wolfe had met Mrs. Edith Kerr on his voyage to Europe in 1928.

land—Plymouth harbor—"Well, here we are"—the Seagulls—Eugene and Cockney [19] embrace each other in their joy.

2) On the train—the race outside Elizabeth—all the train scene.
3) The hospital—child-birth.
4) Joel Pierce on Mrs. Annster's water closet.
5) The German girl.
6) Meeting Irene [20] on the boat.
7) The woman in the 6th Avenue Market.[21]
8) The Tubercular-Diabetic—The night Scene on 11th Street.[22]
9) Visit of Abraham Jones to 11th Street.
10) The "party" on 11th St (The instructor and the girls).[23]
11) Building Irene's house—Mr. Milesend (Lanesend).
12) The literary party at P. Moeller's.
13) The week-end at Chartres.[24]
14) The New Year's Dance at Webster Hotel.
15) The Summer in Maine.
16) The cottage in the Lake district.[25]
17) Wertheim's lunch at Ye Olde Cocke Taverne.[26]
18) Irene and Gene in Philadelphia—in Boston.
19) A walk, a talk, a visit from Varney.[27]
20) McKee, his French mistress and Dorothy.
21) Luke and the girl he loved too late (the New York Visit, etc.)

Well there now—well there now—well there now—listen.

You just foller that road around that there bend—he said in a

19. A character in "Passage to England."

20. One of the several names Wolfe used during the development of the character Esther Jack.

21. An episode that eventually appeared in W&R, pp. 457–58.

22. A sequence, never completed, based on Wolfe's friend Desmond Powell, who was diabetic before he was stricken with tuberculosis. Later references to it will be found under the titles "Early Sorrow" or "Hunger."

23. Two of the University instructors, William Tindall and Emmet Glore, visited Wolfe's apartment at 263 West 11th Street with two girls for a steak dinner. Mrs. Bernstein, passing the apartment, saw a woman's shadow at the window and, suspecting that Wolfe was up to no good, rushed up to investigate. When she found the whole group in the apartment, she left without creating a disturbance.

24. Wolfe and Mrs. Bernstein had visited Chartres in the summer of 1926.

25. Midsummer, 1926, when Wolfe, beginning to write LHA, stayed at Ambleside with Mrs. Bernstein. For a fictional treatment, see Aline Bernstein's *The Journey Down*, Chapter 2.

26. This episode became Eugene's first meeting with Starwick, OT&R, pp. 93–102.

27. John Varney, a poet and fellow instructor at New York University.

slow eager voice, pointing—until you come to a house set back from the road.

[*Sketch of a house on a hill with a "holler," a "red clay bank," and a field of "corn."*]

The folds—the "hills and hollers"

[*Sketch of a house with a sign on the roof, "D. R. Sluder Groceries & Feed," with the comment "False Front."*]

Grass—the hard paved road—the red clay mud—the thick coarse grassy weedy compost that covers the ground unevenly and coarsely.

The rough landscape of dull coarse green—the corn fields on the hill with the red clay ridges shining through—the crickety stitch of noonday in the high rank wet weed grass—a rusty can, a dirty white cur dog with red eyes and a hide streaked with clay and mange.

The ducks and chickens quacking and o-so-hasty clucking—the country men rattling by in Ford trucks—the little cheap houses half painted, half unpainted. In short the South.

The dog begins to wheel faster and faster for a fly that crawls and buzzes on his rump—he snaps highly and bonily for it.

All this near old Owenby place on Leicester road.[28]

This is the South—A few birds sing—mid September—the equinox beginning.

[*Sketch of a house with these explanatory words:*]

This is the South.

Two-family, cheap, drab, painted dingy light yellow—probably type of cabinet factory worker.

Red clay—black cinders—gully—coarse weeds and grass.

Shall I ever come back to my home, ever again?

During these years in New York the 8 million people therein planted their image on his brain several times.

K 19

Hot—The Philadelphia Gear Works—concrete frame and glazed windows—within a whir of glittering belts.

Hot—Outskirts of Philly—coming North—dismal little houses, each with two cone-shaped towers of rusty red tin.

28. The scene is northwest of Asheville. This road goes about ten miles to the small town of Leicester.

The Back-ends of Wilmington, Delaware. Then the old Victorian houses near the rails here and there.

Maxwell Perkins has hay fever (See the fields of goldenrod). Maxwell Perkins has hay fever. See the fields of goldenrod—goldenrod—goldenrod.

1) Why did poetry develop before prose?
2) What Is Epic Poetry?
3) Distinguish between Popular and Literary Epic.

A Young Fellow:

We-we-we-would not take a man into the club until we saw him drunk—until he was—out-out-out-of control—because-because-because-we could see what he was.

"definition."

But-but-but-if a man should say "you were drunk last night" I-I-I would resent it.

---

[*From The October Fair ledger*]

Sunday, Sept. 22:

An Unread Letter

1. That she has done all she could, that she can do no more—that if I have determined to leave her she will say good-bye (But we will meet Monday to talk it over).

2. That I am small and mean with low evil thoughts, that she is good and fine—that she will pay the rent on the studio and not see me again.

3. That she is dying, or going to die—Goodbye forever.

4. That I can call her when I want her—that she will not call me again—if this is the end "God bless you dearest, I will love you forever."

Result: What she said is a modification of several of the above, but subtler and more nicely calculated to reduce me to pulp. "I hope that whatever good you gain by the separation will weigh in the balance with my heavy heart."

Aye, but what of my own, the insults, the contempt before her friends, and the more insulting affection *two hours later* with me?

Remember the Maine!

These late skies of France, these late summer skies, that were suffused with such rich and delicate colors, sank gently and sadly into his heart with an immemorable sadness. As with all that is most deep and beautiful in men he could not speak the feelings they conveyed, but they evoked for him a sense of classic grief—of grave and beautiful men and women walking homewards down enormous aisles of noble trees—a sense of the tragic destiny of men that had in it none of the fierce colors—the great ball of sunset, the fierce glow of noon, the powerful and riotous landscapes, the unceasing hard struggle and violent action of his own land—no, even the sky, even the end, the death of day here was subdued, restrained, infinitely sad and remote.

That first visit to New York returned to him now in a vivid and strange picture from which all the confusion and chaos of an actual scene in the city had vanished. That first visit to New York had now become glorious and perfectly unreal. He had walked the streets many times since looking for the landmarks of that visit, and when he found them he had been shocked to see that the gold had turned to dingy brass.

It did not seem to him that she had any feeling for the country in which she lived, or that she ever thought very much about it. She was a New Yorker; she knew a great deal about New York and had known hundreds of its most celebrated and powerful people over a period of thirty years. But her knowledge of the country did not extend beyond the city.

By God, his father made the stone above his grave—it weighs six thousand pounds, his father chiselled it. It took ten years, eight surgeons, and a cancer like a sunflower to kill this man—now go where he lies buried and look about you: do you see other flowers so rich on other graves?

---

Write Louis Graves [29]

Give Gamzue's Poem to *Scribner's* Magazine.

29. Editor of the *Chapel Hill Weekly*, who was disturbed at the reference to the University of North Carolina when *Scribner's* described Wolfe's background in the August issue: "After attending a small Southern college he went to Harvard and worked with George Pierce Baker in the '47 Workshop.'"

Send copies of book to Mama, Mrs. Roberts, Mabel, Thomas Beer, William Troy—American University Union—Paris.[30]

The flowerlike face—This business of the flowerlike face is wearing thin—"My darling little Edla" (etc.) has the flowerlike face.

[*To My*] Mother[31]
[*Julia*] E. Wolfe
[*I*] present this copy of my first book with love and with hope for her happiness and long life.

TOM WOLFE
Oct. 15, 1929.

30. Thomas Beer, the biographer of Stephen Crane and literary historian of the 1890's, had met Wolfe through Mrs. Bernstein and had tried to help him find a publisher for his book. In his later fiction Wolfe based the character Stephen Hook on Beer. William Troy, a colleague of Wolfe's at New York University, was just beginning his career as a literary critic.

31. The side of the notebook page is torn off here.

# *Pocket Notebook 12*

## *October, 1929, to January 27, 1930*

*During the fall, Wolfe got his first taste of fame as the most promising young writer in America. His book was reviewed and generously praised all over the country, he was asked to lecture, he was invited to dinner, he began to receive a stream of letters from readers. As a result he began to alter the conception of his next book: he would go beyond dealing with his own life, he would try to give expression to all American life—with his own experience and observation as central and representative. His recent work on "The River People," especially that section called "The Fast Express," could be adapted to his new idea. More than this, his story about the love affair with Mrs. Bernstein, "The October Fair," and his profuse notes from his European travels in 1928 could somehow be combined with it all. In December, in applying for a Guggenheim fellowship, he tried to articulate these uncertain creative stirrings, saying,* "the book has a great many things in it, but its dominant theme is again related to the theme of [*Look Homeward, Angel*]: it tries to find out why Americans are a nomad race (as this writer believes); why they are touched with a powerful and obscure homesickness wherever they go, both at home and abroad; why thousands of the young men, like this writer, have prowled over Europe, looking for a door, a happy land, a home, seeking for something they have lost, perhaps racial and forgotten, and why they return here, or if they do not, carry on them the mark of exile and obscure longing." [1]

*This notebook not only contains evidence of Wolfe's desire to record American life in all its variety but is also filled with entries about two other areas of his life that occupied his mind. He again had a full teaching schedule of classes in both English Composition and in Ideas and Forms in English and American Literature. He was also jotting drafts and notations which reflect the response to his book, especially the scandal it caused in Asheville.*

---

1. *Letters*, p. 212.

Ann Bridgers[2]
43 West 93d St.

[*The following notes are apparently Wolfe's preparation for a lecture on the modern novel for the Woman's Club of Glen Ridge, New Jersey.*]

A modern house, a modern apartment, a modern steamship—we are generally accurate when we call *things* modern—What is meant by the word "modern"? It is one of the words most often on our tongue; it is used to express a great variety of meanings, and many times it is used with a very loose inexact sense of what the speaker wants to say.

Example of the Sunday-School teacher at home who had read [*breaks off*]

Who and what is modern? Astonishing thing is that some of the greatest moderns are dead—Plato, Rabelais, Voltaire, Swift, Donne, Blake, Melville—

"We are a part of all that we have touched"[3]—

I remember that someone said to me rather bitterly that "a lot of these modern writers were just trying to show off and act smart." In other words this man had been puzzled and distressed by things he had read—it seemed to challenge and upset the pattern of life he had come to believe in, and his answer was that the writers who caused him this distress were lacking in sincerity of conviction.

The Modern Mind: It is quite often a disillusioned mind. Disillusioned as to what? Dis. about many of the most cherished beliefs of a former generation—belief in war and glory, belief in patriotism (in the "my-country-right-or-wrong" sense), even profound disbelief in some of the most cherished conventions of social morality.

A Typical Modern—His name, let us say, is John Q. McGlick. Comes from Middle West. Goes To the war.

Reading References:

1) Phelps—August Fiction Number [*Scribner's*].
2) Hemingway—page 196–page 240.
3) *The Virginian* [*by Owen Wister*]—III 474–480. ?
4) *Inside of the Cup* [*by Winston Churchill*]—509–510.

2. A girl from the South who met Wolfe at a dinner party given by Dubose and Dorothy Heyward. She later wrote a profile of Wolfe, "Thomas Wolfe: A Legend of a Man's Hunger in his Youth," *Saturday Review of Literature*, XVII (April 26, 1935), 599–600, 609.

3. Wolfe frequently quoted the line from Tennyson's "Ulysses," "I am a part of all that I have met."

5) *A Farewell to Arms*—350–355.

I Introduction—comment on meaning of word modern.

a) exact formal use of word—"Modern" architecture etc.

b) Wider Literary use—anything that is of living and vital interest today—Plato, Donne, Blake, Samuel Butler, Swift, Voltaire, Dostoievsky.

c) Loose and derogatory meaning of word—with a connotation of indecency.

II Read Phelps extract—comment on it—

a) The two generations—Some of the difficulties of understanding—one came to maturity before the war, the other after. Beliefs of the older generation not held by younger.

b) Read Hemingway page 196 "I was always embarrassed" etc.[4]

c) Hemingway—page 240—a composite picture of the modern writer (thanks to Malcolm Cowley).

III Read extracts from Wister, Churchill, and Hemingway—conclusion.

Beautiful and Pretty Literature can not be governed or judged by the standards and capacities of 16-year-old boys and girls.

"To show the beautiful instead of the ugly in life," "to show what is clean and pure rather than what is ugly."

Perhaps the answer is that Life in itself is neither beautiful nor ugly, clean nor dirty—it is simply an enormous wave that is breaking over us all (Dostoievsky here).

They're a live bunch out there.

Memo—Get up at 8 o'clock—call Aline—tell her not to let papers and letters be destroyed by Lottie.

The Evening [5]

Called Cocke.
Met Bill Cocke at 6 at house.
Later C. B. Chase.

4. From *A Farewell to Arms*. Frederick Henry's statement about his distrust of abstract words such as glory, honor, and courage. The next quotation is Frederick's account of his jump into the river to escape the battle police.

5. This account of Wolfe's evening was written when he had been drinking heavily; thus the handwriting is difficult to decipher. William Cocke was a friend from Asheville. Cleveland Chase was a reader at Longmans, Green and Company. Robert McAlmon was a writer and a friend of Hemingway's. He stood for the portrait of Bill Gorton in *The Sun Also Rises*.

Later Jack Chase & wife.
Later McAlmon.
Later [Mina's?]—E. Boyd—McAlmon and others.
Chase's Insult—Mc. better than Wolfe or Hem[*ingway*].
Boyd's Insult.
My Reply.
Later—Back to Rooms, Talk.
My Grand Insult.
Chase said "I could write better novel than Wolfe or Hem."
I replied "You could do nothing—You're nothing but a dirty little [worth-nothing?] fellow—I know what you are."
Climax of Evening—After this, conversation on syphilis.
Their answers and [alarm?]—Home.

---

[*From the October Fair ledger*]

Monday, October 21:

Read first reviews of my book today. All from North Carolina. *Asheville Citizen* generous and sympathetic. *Asheville Times* bitter and grossly personal and unfair. *Raleigh News and Observer*—Headline says I turn in fury upon North Carolina and the South and "spit upon them." [6]

Live and learn, Wolfe. Upon the premise that my story is laid in North Carolina and the South, the critic builds a further premise that I do not like these people and write about them with "bitterness" and finally that I have spat upon that State and the South.

Dear Mr. Schorer: [7]

I got your letter this morning. It is the first letter I have had from a stranger about my book, although I have had several from old friends.

I am moved and honored by what you say about my book. It is quite a grand thing to know that what I have written has meant so much to someone I have never met. It is a beautiful and moving thing to know that what one has created leaps through the dark and makes, where only darkness was before, a light and a friend.

I hope, naturally, that I will have many other letters from

6. A review by Jonathan Daniels, October 20, 1929.

7. Mark Schorer, the critic and scholar, was at this time a graduate student at Harvard. His letter displayed an ecstatic response. ("It is the most magnificent book I know. This is the sort of book I have always wanted to write.")

people who liked the book as you did, but yours will always have a particular value to me because it was the first.

Faithfully yours,
THOMAS WOLFE

Uncle Gil

"The rest of us were all below. We weren't paying any attention to him—we all thought he'd gone on to bed and was sound asleep. All of a sudden there was the damdest noise upstairs you ever heard in your life. Your Aunt Mary said later she thought sure it was an earthquake, the house was shaking and trembling like a leaf, and Gil was cussing something awful. I've never heard such language in my life —they heard him way over on Chestnut St. When I got upstairs the place was damn near flooded. Gil had wrenched the bathtub off the floor and pitched it out the window clean into Orchard St. Gil was standing there with water up to his knees—cussing out the whole of creation:

'You lowdown sons of bitches,' he said. 'I'll drown every bastard living before I'm through. Why goddam you all to hell!' he said. 'What have you done with my licker? I'll ______ on you and drown you deeper than Noah's flood,' he said.

"Well do I remember," said Gant grinning faintly, and clucking in deprecation. "He very near wrecked the house before he was through."

Mrs. Hugh T. Barton, Sr.:
Gene:

Well Gene "Old Lady" Barton returned from Altamont yesterday where she had spent a delightful vacation with her dear son and daughter Hugh and Helen, but before she left a book arrived from a *Harvarde* graduate who I suppose thot he was doing something very brilliant but everyone in Altamont calls it a *low rotten* piece of work.

The most interesting thing I ever heard in the subway: "Guess what I found in my coffee this morning?"—then I had to get out.

The way Virginia looks in the morning—the confederate soldier with unseeing eyes—the carnival wagons on the tracks.

"I see," Dinwiddie [8] said, emphasizing the word heavily, "I *see* that you have a guest here. I say I *see* because I don't *see*. I can't *see*. I

8. The character called Dinwiddie Martin in Wolfe's early versions developed into the sinister blind man Dinwood (Rumford) Bland who appears in YCGHA.

hope your friend likewise is willing to lose his eyesight as I lost mine."

"You lie, you rotten syphilitic bastard. Don't you come here and try to ruin my reputation before my friends."

---

Dear Mama: I have not been able to write before because of school work and also work incident to my book's coming out. I have heard from Mabel a couple of times, and I have also had letters from George McCoy.[9]

I also read reviews in both Asheville papers about my book. I thought the one in the *Citizen* splendid. It seemed to me that the one in the *Times* was unfairly personal. George McCoy writes me that there is considerable excitement in Asheville over the book, and that many people try to read living personalities into it.

The book was written as any other book is written—it is a novel, the characters in it are of the author's own imagining, and it is being received and reviewed outside of Asheville in this light. It seems to me that I should be given fair treatment in the town of my birth as in the rest of the world.

But if people object to any part of my book, I should like to know what it is they object to. It seems to me and it seems to the people who have read and reviewed the book in New York that the people in it are very real, very human.

Dear Mrs. Roberts:

When I got your letter a week or two ago I took it up to Mr. Maxwell Perkins, who is the real head of Scribner's, and of whom you have heard me speak a great many times. He is a man of the finest and highest quality—brave, honest, generous and gentle—and my friendship with him is one of the things I value most in my life. I gave him your letter to read and left his office while he read it twice. When I came back he said "This is the letter of a very magnificent person." That is also the way I feel. There are many things in your letter that caused me deepest pain, but my feeling about you has been enhanced, if possible, by the letter. In view of the way you evidently feel about certain parts of my book—a feeling in which I want to say humbly I believe you are mistaken—your letter is very wonderful, and I will also say just and honest.

I do want to say two things that touch upon statements in your

9. George McCoy's fiancée Lola Love wrote the review of Wolfe's novel for the *Citizen* and treated it as a literary work rather than a scandalous revelation. McCoy reported to Wolfe the Asheville response and the gossipy treatment that the Asheville *Times* had given his book.

letter: First, that in one of the passages you mention, there is not the slightest hint of "illegitimacy" and that if the entire passage is read calmly and carefully it will be seen that this is true.

You are entirely right in saying that I will not write such a book twenty years from now. More than that, I would not write such a book now. One of the people in my book says that we do not live only one life—we live a dozen or a hundred. Since I began to write this book over three years ago I have lived at least one. And the sad part of it is that this life, including that other one that is wrought out in my book is over, finished.

At one place in your letter you seem to question my sincerity —"No one," you say, "can make me believe you were not sincere."

Lunch with Tom Beer Thursday at one o'clock Yale Club.

Go to Public Library and get copies of *Leslie's* for 1898–'99–00—also *Harper's* (?)

Which I did.

*Leslie's*—1895–1898 to 1900—Spanish War—Boer War—Floods in Arkansas (pictures of floods in little Am. town with walls ripped away, cheap cot, blistered dresser, and cast iron stove showing).

Easter Day 1895 (or 1900) (Meanwhile the German emperor! Der Kaiser—riding through a Berlin park—The horse at a proud fast trot—Somber city dignitaries—uncovered people—officers with thick square beards).

*Remember the Maine!*

Brooklyn navy yard on Christmas day—sailors—the grinning American faces eating—a bottle—a loaded cloth—a pyramid of fruits in center—bananas, oranges, etc. (the terrible permanence of that fruit).

(Meanwhile Gorewitz [10] reads *Creative Personality* beside me.)

The Paris Exposition.

American Ladies buying flowers near Gare St. Lazare Station.

O what can make lost moments live again?

(A man—two women—one ripe and good—49th grill.)

"a peculiar looking fellow."

"rather old fashioned for her to talk about people—out of date."

10. Wolfe's generic name for a grubby intellectual.

(Another:)

"I said well there's not another laugh like that in the world—so, I looks up and sees this guy."

"She knows Paris better than New York—she speaks French as well as English."

I don't think he cares anything about her. I think he's just got her on his hands and is trying to make the best of it.

She always talking about how rotten he is in front of him (a rich fashionable giggle).

But if you're going to have one I most assuredly am going to have one.

When Spring comes—a quiet *humming busy* dinning of rain on the roof—so comforting and quiet.

An old man listening to rain on the roof.

[*At this point Wolfe lists sixty-five individuals or groups he knows in New York.*]

Monday, Nov. 18, written at Child's 6th Ave.

To Bed at 3:30—up at 11:30—Aline called—I called Perkins—talked to him about Mad. Boyd—said to head her off—Sales now 3800 (one mo. after pub.) They say this is good—for me, too slow—hope Eng. pub. will pull it off—Mrs. Boyd says 15000 in England.

Tuesday, Nov. 19:

Grades, Architecture Papers (4), Give hell Mrs. Boyd, Speech at Arts Club.

Dear Albert: [11]

I got a tremendous thrill when I saw your name on a letter again. Neither of us, I am afraid, is a very frequent correspondent, but if I had written to you every time I thought about you these last six or seven years you would have a trunk full of letters now.

I shall certainly not allow you to spend good money on my book. By heaven, Sir, (this is only the effect of my O. Max Gardner [12] training)—by heaven, sir, you must not, you shall not, you will not taint me with your lucre. (Don't think, however, that I am *giving* the

11. Albert Coates was a classmate of Wolfe's at Chapel Hill. Later he attended the Harvard Law School while Wolfe was doing graduate work. They lived in the same rooming house briefly in the fall of 1921.

12. A North Carolina politician and one-time governor of the state. He had campaigned on the campus at Chapel Hill when Coates and Wolfe were students.

money back to you. I expect you to deposit this check in a solid New England Bank and call it The Coates Fund For Hungry Novelists.) I expect to visit the fair city of Boston later on, and I shall most certainly expect you to be on hand with your three dollars, prepared to banquet me at the best $1.50 dinner Boston can offer.

## WHY I WROTE MY BOOK [13]

I began to write it three years ago in England—Had been with friend—Left alone—Took rooms in the Chelsea district of London—Later Oxford—Every[*where*] alone. Had tried to write plays—Plays didn't succeed—Too long—Thought if I wrote a book I should at last find something long enough to fit. Then when I wrote book it was about five times average length of novel.

Book culmination of several years wandering around Europe—I had tried to settle down in Europe (France) but found I was unable to—Realized at end of year I was homesick for—America. Why? I did not know. Many other young men had also tried to settle there. Perhaps some did it successfully. But I could not. I wanted to come home. I came. Then, I wanted to go back again.

At end of period of wandering, began to write in England. Wrote first third of book there. Finished it in New York.

When I finished it I thought no one would publish it—Threw it in closet—Gave a copy to Mrs. Boyd—Went to Europe—In Vienna six months later heard from Scribner's—Came back—Work of cutting—They helped me—a great deal like a miracle—But miracles do happen—

What I feel about writing—Will not attempt to generalize—will only speak about myself. It seems to me that the life I have known has been quite rich and wonderful. I do not think it has been drab and dull.

What I want to write now and I imagine for some time to come comes pretty directly from direct experiences—from what I have seen, felt, thought.

I do not believe, for example, that all small towns are alike. I do not believe that most business men, clergy men, and realtors are alike. I have not found what life I have known throughout the country standardized. I do not mean to say that a book about these people would be beautiful—it might seem very ugly, painful and terrible—but it would not be drab or dull.

13. These could be notes in preparation for a lecture or talk to one of the various groups which Wolfe was called on to address, or they could be notes for the questionnaire from the Guggenheim Foundation.

WHY DO WE WRITE

Some people, I suppose, write for money, and know how to write for money. I think perhaps I should also write for money if I knew how. But I honestly do not know how.

Why then do we write? I suppose many of us still write for glory. But our ideas of glory change. I believe we would write if we knew there was an audience of only 2 or 3 for our work.

I know you don't want to listen to this stuff—This ain't good stuff—But give me a drink.

O go over to Jerry's place.

This is the only place I can get in.

"When a man from the high seas can't get a drink—it's terrible."

(In the hoarse, harsh business voice).

Kenneth Raisbeck
1335 Lincoln Boulevard
Santa Monica, Cal.[14]

Exile.

Where is the longing for the First of May?

[*Wolfe asked his freshmen to give oral book reports on biographies they had read. The following items are a sample of the many notes on student reports which he recorded here.*]

*Henry VIII*—Hackett—(Miss Weisberg)—Reads all of it C.

*Autobiography of Benvenuto Cellini*—(Greenberg) Speaks with some feeling and delivery—but does not get down to concrete facts very well C+.

Boswell's *Life of Johnson*—Makes very intelligent criticism of duty of biographer—Says Boswell allows himself to intrude too much B+.

*That Man Heine*—Lewis Browne—Sobinsky—Somewhat broken but intelligent and interesting C+.

14. On December 6, 1929, Raisbeck sent Wolfe a copy of his review of LHA, which praised the work highly ("not since the poetry of Walt Whitman has there appeared in American Literature a work which so voraciously savors existence"). Also about this time Wolfe gave Mrs. Boyd a copy of Raisbeck's play "Rock Me, Julie," and she sold it to a producer. It opened in February, 1931.

*Ariel*—Andre Maurois—Quite interesting and a bit broken—Criticism of book poor C+.

*Henry VIII*—Francis Hackett—Miss (Feinstein?)—girl with glasses—C+.

*King Henry VIII*—Hackett—all of them stress the matrimonial side—criticizes idea that Henry was not a Catholic—says Henry merely wanted to marry again C+.

*The Wind and The Rain*

This is not a review of a book, because the writer has never reviewed a book and does not know how.

"a story of lust rather than of love," "the modern taste for prurience," etc. William Allen Pherrick.[15] The terrible shadow of Leonard Q. Snodgrass[16] falls across the nation. He is given a book and he remembers a word—"whore" occurs on page 87, a man and a woman go to bed together on page 136. It does not occur to him that life is [*n*]either clean or dirty, inspiring or degrading, beautiful or ugly, no more than it occurs to a healthy man that he is delightfully free from pneumonia.

We have come, perhaps, to mistrust nobility. They are noble, and we are a little embarrassed. They are noble—and the result of their nobility is that Anatole France is "a dirty old man" and that A. S. M. Hutchinson has written a truly great, a truly inspiring play.

They are noble, and behind their noble mask is the rack, the rope, and the screw.

They are noble—for God's sake hang on to your watch, clutch your wallet, look about you for a means of escape, for they are noble, the nobles are coming, and you will be dispossessed before night comes, you will be ridden on a rail.

Tues. Dec. 3, 1929:

Up—to lunch with Salter—home—to McAlpin to meet Mrs. Schroeder[17]—to tea—to the tube—to the Harvard Club—letters to Jim

15. A name for a character who is a prudish literary critic, based on William Lyon Phelps, Professor of English at Yale and conductor of the book feature "As I Liked It" in *Scribner's Magazine*. In the August, 1929, issue, which contained an installment of Hemingway's *A Farewell to Arms* as well as Wolfe's "An Angel on the Porch," Phelps began: "In comparing contemporary literary fashions in England and America with those of thirty years ago, it appears that the most conspicuous advance in novels is the change from love stories to stories of lust."

16. Wolfe's fictional generic name for the repressed, middle-class American city-dweller.

17. Mrs. Jessie Schroeder, an Englishwoman married to a German who was now living in the United States. She was a member of the Women's Club of Glen

Boyd[18] and Bill Polk[19] Called Aline—Eating at 49th Street Grill.

Herald Square at 4:30 and at 5:30—A search for the bookman —the grey cold slush-muck underfoot—Sunday—the red-white lights decorated with college pennants—Harold Lloyd—Night club—The Hippodrome on Sunday—Sunday in New York.

The clams—their smooth hard bulk, dark brown and wet—He opened the valves with a knife, exposing their pink flesh, a clean murky mucous now dribbling across his fingers.

The heavy voices jar the air—the girl's hard clean voice cuts higher—the liquor has stolen on my flesh—the leg-scruf itches.

He ran his finger pulps over the slick paper—it was a little like a woman's leg.

His great long right leg, heavied with drink, crossed limp and close against his left.

He breathed luxuriously the smoke the other blew.

Dec. 4—The lust for theft may come from avarice.

Voluted to the nostrils heavily—the Armenian Jewish somewhat Assyrian party who came in, "What do you say Frank the Clank?"—they talked—one near—remember the collar [*sketch*]—the slick hair. The market—All right I'll lend you $500—if you'll split the profits with me.

(Another table—girls and man—one English) "Amerí-ican men throw money around so"—a cockney doing the stuff—Shame! Shame!

(Another)—Don't be sill-*lee*—how I saw man run over by a train, legs on one side, arms on another. I thought I'd die.

You must have a galvanized stummick.

Grace Cutler[20]
Main 6898.

---

Ridge who was eager to meet him. She wrote him a letter in which she praised his talk, saying, "Sie haben mir so viele aus der Seele gesprochen." Letter, November 1, 1929.

18. The author of *Drums, Marching On,* and other historical novels. Perkins had introduced Wolfe to Boyd and they became good friends. Wolfe asked Boyd to write a letter to the Guggenheim Foundation for him. Boyd said in a letter of March 27, 1930, that "it was like being asked to furnish a veterinary certificate for Pegasus."

19. William Polk was another North Carolinian who attended the Harvard Law School when Wolfe was in Cambridge.

20. One of Wolfe's friends in the circle of young Southerners in New York. She later married Wolfe's friend Beverly Smith.

Telegrams for Christmas

| | |
|---|---|
| Mabel | Hilda |
| Mama | Elaine |
| Fred | Kenneth R. |
| Effie | Edith Simpson |
| Geo McCoy | Mina Curtiss |
| Mrs. Roberts | Madeleine Boyd |
| Mrs. Ulmann [21] | Margery Latimer [22] |
| James Boyd (?) | Aline |
| Henry Volkening ? | |

Dear Mina: [23]

Why should I not wish you a quote Merry Christmas. Dear Mina I wish you a Merry Christmas Donne Eliot Joyce Blake.

TOM

(Ital. waiter)—She must have made a mistake. As soon as she came she asked if you were in.

She had dinner here. She had dinner with Mr. Smith, etc.

(The Ital. waiter) Mr. Smith was *in* here—She had dinner with Mr. Fletcher. (There was a pause).

(The drunken man) I am plastered etc. (pause) You goddamned sentimental bastard.

That's up to him. If I knew Horace (Liveright) [24] I know what I'd do.

(Drunkenly) Julian's a goddamned fine man—a damn good person—fundamentally he's all there.

If Horace stuck to that business he'd have a gold mine (pause).

I think I know more about that business than any one else—at any given moment.

You ought to know more about it than I do.

21. Doris Ulmann, a photographer, took a series of pictures of Wolfe for Scribner's when LHA was being promoted.

22. She gave LHA a highly favorable review in the New York *Herald Tribune Books*. Later she and Wolfe became friends.

23. Mina Kirstein Curtiss was a friend of Mrs. Bernstein's. She was an Associate Professor of English at Smith College and took a lively interest in modern writers and in her brother Lincoln Kirstein's little magazine, *Hound and Horn*. Wolfe had met her on board the *Olympic* in 1926 when he first encountered Mrs. Bernstein. She is the model for the character Lily Mandell in Wolfe's fiction.

24. The publisher to whom Wolfe had first submitted LHA. Wolfe was angry about the rejection, especially the weary tone of editor T. R. Smith's letter of rejection. Later he satirized Liveright as Mr. Rawng of the firm Rawng and Wright.

(This is the atmosphere of the literary "racket") [*with arrow pointing to above*].

Dear Mr. Adams: [25]

I am 29 years old. I have lived 10,765 days and nights. When your correspondent says "I should be interested in a novel by Mr. Wolfe not so closely related to his own emotional life" the writer will not have it. I have only these 11,000 days to go by. Mr. Wolfe, if he writes further, has at present eight or a dozen novels which come from his 11,000 days and nights. Since your correspondent is un-interested to the extent of writing 350 words and a quarter column about my book [*breaks off*]

Friday—Dec. 27—

Cold better—Aline came at 11:30—stayed 45 mins.—says Theo's [26] partners want him to come back in business—I said I was bitterly disappointed to see tragedy fall through—but better maybe—She had been to doctor for dose of thyroid medicine—Went to laundry for shirt—Miss Greenberg came for autograph—Talked of Wien—Türkenschanz Park. Out to Bank—payment had come on Mrs. Boyd's check from Paris—The Bank People.

The men working on building on 14th St.—a young cop grinning into police telephone. Eating at Charles—The Italian grocery boys with wheeled carts—Esposito's—young telegraph linesmen grinning and tough gathered round reel of huge cable in side street. Carpenters in khaki bearing wooden beams for 14th St. Building—a rattling concrete mixer with its uneven spill of concrete—Figures of workmen moving about in dark ground floor—a spieler selling a trick knife—cuts glass, corkscrew, etc.—on kerb—A man stepping up docilely to buy.

---

[*From the October Fair ledger*]

SCENES FROM LIFE OF THE CITY

1) The J. Walter Thompson Company.
2) The Maternity Hospital.

25. In his column "The Conning Tower" in the New York *World*, February 6, 1930, Franklin P. Adams had quoted a letter he had received from an unnamed Ashevillian about the furor which Wolfe's book had caused.

26. Mrs. Bernstein's husband Theodore, a stockbroker in the firm of Hirsch, Lilienthal, had suffered heavy losses in the recent stock market crash. Mr. Bernstein, born in Bad Ems, Germany, in 1873, had come to the United States at the age of sixteen and had had a successful financial career on Wall Street.

3) Scribner's.
4) Bergdorf-Goodman's (apartment upstairs).
5) The Harvard Club (1000).
6) 49th St. Grill and Louis Martin's.
7) Esposito's (the eternal richness of the earth: Antaeus).
8) Luchow's (present richness, past warmth).
9) Park Avenue People (30).
10) The Neighborhood Playhouse, Theatre Guild, etc. (150).
11) The Hotel Albert (700 days and nights).

My Servants:

Janitor who robbed me (11th St.)
Irish woman who married German (the lower depths).
Lottie (15th St.)
Joe (8th St.)

How when you want a washerwoman you go to the grocer who gives her address.

How when you want your landlord you call up an electrical shop on 6th Avenue.

Dramatis Personae—chauffeurs, cops, firemen, doctors, lawyers, thieves, prizefighters, students, instructors, nurses, tailors, bricklayers, masons, brokers, actors, actresses, theatrical people, swells, newspaper men.

Sometimes—the apple of this earth lay in his hand, ripe for his mighty palate.

He was one of the lords of language, and the swarming myrmidons of life.

So far away from all the earth that fed him, a great hunger and thirst devoured him—his mouth was a cavern, his teeth great granite rocks; he would drink off the rivers of the continent; reach from a mountain top, drain chill lakes in New Hampshire at a gulp; he would stall oxen in their tracks with a blow of the fist and roast them on the plains over a spit as big as a telephone pole. Finally he would throw great Scandinavian blondes into the wheat and strive gigantically with magnificent girls named Lindquist and Neilson.

His fantasy of the city's destruction returned at the fire on Park Avenue.[27] Huge churnings filled the sky, aerial ruin. Cloven in upper

27. On January 3, 1930, Wolfe was at a party in the Bernstein apartment in the Marguery, 270 Park Avenue, when a fire broke out and routed everyone from the building. He used the scene later for "The Party at Jack's."

air, the million-windowed towers split, fell with slow thunderings. Exultant, he watched until (No, surely not . . . O of course not . . . By God, there it goes . . . . Goodbye, New York).

Aline—on the phone—I'm going to walk over to Terry [*Helburn*]'s after supper—She's not coming here—Theo's feeling better —Maybe you'd give me a ring at Terry's, it's the Warwick Hotel, Circle ———. I think I've got a customer for the house—two men called. Theo up today—Nothing will (happen) though . . . It's better so . . . I'll give you a ring in the morning . . . It's your early day, isn't it . . . .

Would you like to come here to dinner tomorrow night . . . My cousin's coming to make onion soup . . . the French one . . . I thought maybe you'd like to . . . Do as you like, dear.

(When I went into steamship agency in 14th Street to ask for circulars, Aline stood outside with bitter look on face) . . . Well, that's your way of informing me, is it? (she began) . . . If you go away and leave me this time, it will be for good . . . I know you'll never come back to me, etc.

"I guess you weren't listening . . . I told you about it today."

---

Mr. Reeves,[28] Thursday, Jan. 9. Meet at Harvard Club at one o'clock.

| | |
|---|---|
| $4500 | $5000 |
| 440 | 2500 |
| 4940 | 7500 |

Personae, Personae.

I think that Longfellow mentions it—at least one of the biographers does—all that material is simply lifted from etc. etc. etc.

No she has talked to me a few times.

I thought that that was all very well handled etc.

Louis Martin's (Only one conversation—2 men—one of them quoting Kipling "For I knifed her one night cause she wished I was white"):

"You mean I said I'd rather have my *children* smoke and drink."

"Did you hear er-er what Misses Nevill sed?"

That's my French blonde.

28. A. S. Frere-Reeves, the editor of William Heinemann Ltd., Wolfe's publisher in England.

By God, she certainly did. I admire you—Listen, Jack never got drunk in his life—I admire you. They'll never ketch you.

Except last Saturday night—I passed right out.

You big bum I'll put you right under the table now—Do you want to go under the table (joke).

I travelled with that fellow for ten years.

(A woman—whisper whisper whisper) This gay fellow over here.

(A man) I don't give a goddam. There's going to be a fight tonight yet.

(The gold-digger tone to those men—patronizing flattery) Hello Bill—What's the matter Bill?

Where were you, in the kitchen?

(He had to catch the 10:21 for New Rochelle).

(To waiter) Listen Big Boy—He wants a Scotch high ball with plain water.

(Woman) Listen Bill, he doesn't want anything.

Listen Bigboy, I'm going to have a moderate high ball. . . .

. . . No, no, now *lissen, lissen,* Arthur.

You can tell your Big Brother I've got to go to see my friend Bill. Where's Bill?

Bill, I've been lookin for you for 2 days?

Meet Miss Heyward here and Mr. Rasmussen (laughter).

Bill, would you have any objections if I had a drink.

Allright, Cheerio.

Cheerio.

Bill, lissen I'm going to have a drink and charge it over to my table (a silence falls upon them—he is drunker).

I want to buy a drink—I want to buy *your* friends a drink.

I want you to meet Mr . . . . . Miss How'd ya spell it? S-y-r-u-p. No, no, that's molasses.

You don't know what I think of that old redhead over there . . . that old redhead son of a bitch.

Lissen, let me tell you something. I don't give a damn if anybody drinks with you.

Bill, George is here. Hank is here. In other words, Bill, in a little while we lose out (harsh bitter laughter).

Allright—allright—George—George—lissen, George.

. . . . . . Because I like you, Bill . . . . . . I heard about you before I ever knew you.

Jack, Jack, draw up a chair won't you, please.

No *Bill* I want to buy you a drink.

Nono, wait a, wait a, wait a, wait a minute.

I've heard a lot about you—lissen—Sit down—I'm gonna buy you a drink—all right—all right—lissen, sit down—See that redhead over there—he's the best fellow here.

Pick on Jack—Jack's a good boy—be picked on—Pick on Jack —*I'll* be picked on—Who's gonna *pick* on me.

(They were all I think, including some folks downstairs, salesmen here on some yearly meeting. The salesman with his New York women. Meet Mrs. Nevill, Mrs. Rosen—Salesmen's wimmen. I think they were Cash Register Salesmen).

Thursday, Jan. 9, 1929—

Eating at Charles 7:30 before going to 35 class—Lunch with Aline—went to Century Club later—talked to Mr. Walpole [29] and Mr. Reeves—Walpole very warm about book—I thanked him for his generosity—Said he wanted to meet me later for lunch—Then with Reeves to Park Lane—Talked together there—Read F. Tennyson Jesse's report on my book.

The Jews: Why is Aline a great Jew? Because she does not think she has a great mind. Emotionally and psychically they are the most interesting people on earth—intellectually they are sawdust and ashes.

To Abe: "What do you think I like about you, you big bum? Your great intellect?" said Eugene sneeringly.

Abe came in; he was silent. In a moment he burst out, "Gene, By God, it's just come to me. The Jews are a great race. They're the most low-down set of people on earth."

In the class-room they (the Jews) were like hot hounds around the bitch (Miss Greenberg).

Death in New York. Where do they go! Make scene out of this —Eugene in New York 4 years—never sees funeral—the daily obituary columns in newspapers (copy it).

Second by second over the city he heard the gentle terrible drumming of 8 million hearts—Fattied by drink and food, weakened by smoke and gas.

29. Hugh Walpole, the English novelist.

That strange unmistakable roar of the firetrucks through New York City that brings destiny with it, and that seems always coming to your home.

"All around the town" [*A list of twenty-four streets in New York follows*].

Under Madness: Put under *that* year in the book all that you can of the insane, the grotesque, the macabre.

"He found sanity now only at daybreak" (?) A moment of washed purity and lucidity—then cometh (hah) the great sun bringing putrefaction.

Madness—It is around us—all things so looked at become horrible.

The creation of a figure like Friar John of the Funnels (?) who shall stand for the Earth (Eugene—Antaeus). Could he be Aline's Uncle in Hartford? Or shall it be a complete Jew?

No—must have the Anglo-Teutonic earthiness.

Or shall he be a tobacco man (like Buck Duke)? [30]

Better perhaps (?) from among Olin's crowd (suggestions of Sheriff Bob Chamber) own a baseball club (?) racing horses, farms, ranches, ships.

"He said it's killing me," roared the Captain. "By God, son, it's been killing me for forty five years now."

"What are you saving yourself for?" roared the Captain. "Are you a prize or something?" You never got ripe, Mamie, you were pulled green.

"Who's looney now?" [31]

"You'll get no money of mine, you bitch," he roared "I'll see to that. I'll endow milk stations before you do. I'll give my money to the Anti-Saloon league. I'll endow the Methodist Church."

"Twenty-five years old," he repeated "and he's never ———!

30. James Buchanan Duke, who founded the American Tobacco Company and endowed Duke University.

31. Richard Walser informs us that this expression became a current phrase after it was used by John Armstrong Chanler (later changed to Chaloner) in a telegram to his rich brother, who had been double-crossed by a woman he had married. Earlier, the brother had had Chaloner committed to an insane asylum.

Twenty five years old. Great God! Alexander had conquered the world at that age. And *you!*"

Jim Boyd, Robert Norwood—Letter of thanks to each.[32]

---

[*From the October Fair ledger*]

Jan 15 (3:15 a.m.)—

A moment's respite from papers—Today—To University for conferences—Watt introduced my successor Mr. Krouse [33]—Home—H. Stevens here with friend, prying, spying, looking—Later to H. Club and 49th St. Grill—Wrote letters Miss Scarborough [34] and Dr. Norwood—Home by subway G'd Central—Young louts with girls shrieking with laughter as they watched little old drunk—his face twisting with alcoholic grimaces—In fear-ring circle the other subway—subway beasts look raptly gum-chewingly with rapt hatred-giving vacancy—the un-rich offal.

Through vast echoing station with its murmur of time—the starry roof the few sparse figures weave across the immense acreage of floors—From a train-gate a uniformed brakeman issues with tin pail—the baggage men gossip—the porters gossip—the newstand with its odor of fresh papers—its mechanic odor—Dark hawks hear as—Night, night—the dark void and universe of sleep, the fields of sleep—swift tired changeless—Night, night—the waste and lone immensity of night.

---

Dear Jim: [35]

You are a swell guy even if you do have decided theories of Form. It will be a proud day in my life when you wring my hand and

32. Robert Norwood, a clergyman and man of letters, was the minister at St. Bartholomew's Church in New York. He was a friend of John Hall Wheelock's, and, since he was enthusiastic about LHA, he arranged through Wheelock to meet Wolfe. He also wrote a letter to the Guggenheim Foundation in support of Wolfe's application.

33. Russell Krauss, a young man who took over Wolfe's classes at New York University in mid-year. Thirty years later Krauss wrote a venomous account of his dealing with Wolfe about this. See "Replacing Tom Wolfe," in *Thomas Wolfe at Washington Square,* by Thomas Clark Pollock and Oscar Cargill.

34. Miss Dorothy Scarborough wrote to Wolfe on December 23, 1929, asking if he would address the Writers Club of Columbia University on January 15.

35. Boyd had written Wolfe on January 9, 1930: "*Look Homeward, Angel* continues to grow in our mind, it has become one of our permanent possessions—though it contains things for which I denounce you before the throne of Form and Design (no doubt a mere certified public accountant's stool) it has the simple and undebatable merit of containing elements of greatness, and all of the formidable vigor of life."

say: "Son, the style and structure of your last book makes Flaubert look like an anarchist. I have done you a great wrong."

If I buy a set of false whiskers and revisit my native state, will you introduce me as your Irish cousin, Ernest?

Speakeasy Technic—They make the *third* drink stronger.

Cimmalucha [36]—(The ride to Brooklyn).
The Child's restaurant at 14th St.
Percy Grants' place.[37]

Christmas at the Hotel Albert—The cheap Christmas tree trembling with tinsel & colored lights—the painted and powdered and bravely smiling hags—(forever and forever and forever binding up and taking down their hair, like the hospital waitresses—on contrary—the husky Irish and Italian women leaning from windows as the trains thunder past)

The $20 Lives:

J. Benge [38]—110th St.
Middlebrook [39]—200th St.
The Dentists—Central P'k—93 94th St.
The Bernsteins—47–48th St.
Abe Smith—East Side.
Myself—11th St—15th St—8th St.

93d St.—167 W.—Single, large, front, privileges, both $6 up etc.
Stevens—16th St.
Wheelock—63d St.
Darrow [40]—86th St.
Helburn—Hotel (?)
Ulmann—100 P'k Avenue.

36. Probably a student of Wolfe's at New York University. His name appears several times in Wolfe's notebooks.

37. Although Wolfe probably knew Percy Grant at Chapel Hill, they came into contact once more through the University of North Carolina Alumni Association in New York, for which Wolfe worked briefly in the fall of 1923.

38. The woman from whom Wolfe and Mrs. Bernstein had rented the cottage at Ocean Point, Maine.

39. Samuel and Ruth Middlebrook were colleagues of Wolfe's at New York University.

40. Whitney Darrow was the business manager of Scribner's.

Park Lane Hotel
Roy Dock[41]—Fruit Mkts.
49th St Grill.
Volkening—25 Fifth.
Ritz Towers Hotel.
Fritz Dashiell—60th St.
Maurer[42]—B'klyn.
Miller[43]—New Jersey.
The Charles Street Police Station.
The Radio Building.

Last meeting—Archt. Eng. 1—Jan 17 1929:
Description: odors, sounds, sights.
Papers—comments.
Essays—Dean Inge.
Read Sam'l Butler character sketch—call for criticism.
Themes—Wooley & Scott [*College Handbook of Composition*].

Eng. 35—Give short information exam—Summary & conclusion.

On these tide winds and waters of men's sleep.

"Are you my little Jew?" he says. "Yes," I say, "Yes." "Are you my little Jew, doch?" he says. "Yes," I say, "Yes." "Can I bite your apple-cheeks?" he says. "Yes," I say. "Yes. But not too hard."

The Furs Man: Step right in, folks its going to be a cold winter. O yes, we're in for a sudden change in atmospheric conditions.

The circus—"He don't play with it, do he?"

At Salisbury—Mr. Cline[44] outside his engine—Fireman climbs up in cab—"All right, Mr. Cline, who's goin' to Asheville?"

41. Roy Dock was a classmate of Wolfe's at the North State Fitting School.
42. Marion Maurer, one of Wolfe's students at New York University, with whom he used to discuss LHA while he was writing it.
43. Mrs. Henrietta Miller, the principal of Lincoln High School in Lodi, New Jersey. She was continuing her studies at New York University and had apparently come to know Wolfe there.
44. Tom Cline was the locomotive engineer in LHA, Chapter XIV.

Jan. 17—the shackling-irons of memory and desire.

Jan. 17, 10:10—going uptown on Elevated:

Very cold—Today last day at University—Tired but happy—Coming out of house of 15th St. tonight the great fleet of trucks all ready for Philadelphia—Canvassed up—the clean white boxes bulging out behind—The green lights—The drivers cranking, tough and happy in the dark.

Men walked, motors whirred, traffic ran.
But propped on beds of amaranth and moly.[45]

Today on 15th St. about one o'clock—the Irish Cadets in front of their school—an old drunk—the pouches under his bloody eyes—perfectly violet-blue—Had he been hit? Or was it beginnings of canned-heat blindness—He stops young cadet-boys—shyly—with grinning horror—they circle, sidle, move away—walk on talking about it.

Good, good, good: the white thighs of our American women, cantaloupe, concord grapes, good American beef.

The young Kansas woman, Mrs. G—— —O good-good-good—This is ample Kansas—how can anyone suspect what is mean and petty here?

49th St. Grill:

Two men, two women, a kid—the kid, girl with the pert too-wise look of theatre children. I think they were.

Coffee?

No thank you.

Don't want anything?

No thank you.

We got a long way to drive.

I know we have.

You'd better go on the wagon—I know but you shouldn't.

No, no, don't ask me, honestly I *couldn't* eat anything more.

John (to call his attention) John—you can all sleep—I'm the only one that gets to stay awake (they're going out to country—cold night).

Did you make that noise? (the kid belches and laughs with rich burblesome giggle).

45. The second line is from Tennyson's "The Lotos-Eaters."

I notice during the last week or two that I have quit coughing —The terrific nervous tension has quieted since Christmas—I am probably smoking far less.

Periods (The Dean Inge School): The Renaissance—The 18th Century—The Romantics—The Age of Pericles—The Age of Augustus—The Victorian Age.

The smooth crafty waiter to those leaving "Well Kid Berg won another fight."

"Did Kid Berg win?—did you bet against him?"

"No I wouldn't bet against him—he's too good."

"Did he knock him out?"

"No—he's not a knocker—he's a punisher."

Walpole, F.P.A., Beer, Hansen, Eaton,

Thackeray: Scene between Rawdon Crawley, Becky Sharp, and Lord Steyne—Crawley throws diamond necklace at Steyne leaving a permanent scar, etc.

The Things: American hangings; the electric chair; the front porch; the swings; the rockers; men in shirt sleeves at telegraph tickers wearing arm-bands and green eye-shades.

Miss Hecks comes in, see. One of the biggest jobbers in New England, see. So I goes down to get my ticket—well he puts me in the committee with the Governor of Mass. and Mayor Nichols—well, we sells 10,000 copies.

Well Miss Hecks says—I want you to tell me all about the time you had and I hope you have a wonderful time. Drop in she says on your way to the South Station.

---

[*From the October Fair ledger*]

Jan. 17—Late at night (1:30 A.M. Jan. 18)—

My teaching days are over—I hope forever. Today my last classes at N.Y.U. Talked with White, walked away with Kissack[46]—Feel little rancor towards them—They are venomous and small and malicious, but they simply have no loyalties, no warm rioting affections

46. Hal White and Robert Kissack, instructors in English.

—Like weak people they band together against me—but these combinations are incessant—they will betray their closest friends, and have no sense of betrayal. Yet it is impossible to *villainize*, to *Mephistophelize* any of them.

And tonight coming home on Lex. Ave. subway—the great deaf mute and the little deaf mute talking upon their hands—the old trainman tired and dirty—the great grimed hands of a mechanic.

Yet when the day of his departure came, he felt little rancor. Having returned from his last class, he stood stupidly by his desk for a moment, opening and shutting the clasp of his brief-case several times. Outside the air was cold, sharp, and frozen with bursts of fierce gold upon the sky; there was the slamming racket of the riveting machines upon the building; high up the masons worked on their swinging platform. Within, the instructors sat, wheeling restlessly before their desks in swivel chairs conferring, quarreling with a stream of coming-and-going Weisbergs, Feinsteins, Cohens, and Grebenschicks.

Antaeus: Whoever goes through Libya must throw me.

Who comes? Who comes? A stranger who would pass. Then try the might that's in you. Whoever goes through Libya must throw me, and you can throw me fair enough, but every fall makes for my final victory.

Whoever stirs the giant's dust will get no rain.

O walled with steel and carpeted with stone, what plants have [*breaks off*]

As he lay upon that hill it seemed that his body had grown gigantic and covered the earth, and was being sucked into the earth, and was bent to the vast curvings of the earth. The great river swept by a mile below him at his feet, and he could feel the earth swing through its orbit under him. The sun burned richly on his back filling his flesh with molten gold.

Jan. 19–20 (Saturday Morning):

Up at 12:00—phone call from R. Williams [47]—bright bitter-cold day—washed, shaved, dressed in new-pressed clo'es—new shirt with collar—stinging ruddy alcohol on face—out to Union Sq.—subway to G'd Central—Columbia Club with R. Williams. The crafty face, unc-

47. Ralph Williams.

tuous voice—"Alfred Lunt was telling me" (O casually)—eyes glittering at details of my success—later Fritz Dashiell—then to Mr. and Mrs. Aley's with Fritz and Connie—Dubose Heyward, R. Nathan, Mr. and Mrs. Aley, et al.[48] Mrs. Aley—climber—black—the black hair coming down on neck—the somewhat worn sensuality—white naked arms with delicate veins and the raised arm pits with light-colored sensual hair—stirring of sperm—much talk—later home with Fritz and Connie —W. Rarebit and coffee and gin—then to H. Club—then home.

Monday, Jan. 20 (written Tues):

Aline for lunch—at Scribner's in afternoon—then to Holliday's Book Shop—then home—Aline returned from afternoon with Lily's[49] kid at Westport—then to Louis Martin's—Thayer[50] comes in and holds her hand—I leave her outside bitterly jealous—Then to 270 Park Ave—Then to Madeleine Boyd's until 5 o'clock.

Tuesday (written at night):

Awoke at 11 feeling sick from night-before tempest and Boydian gin—Aline came in—Bitter tears—The old sensation of being caught, caught, caught returns—Go to Architecture to give exams—later home—Aline comes in from Civic Rep. (remember M. B.'s saying —"always time to do work")—more tears—again we promise to part —she goes home—D. B. Heyward calls up asking me to dine Thurs.

Mad[*eleine*]: "Awake! Are you cr-r-razy? She's sleeping soundly as a baby. How do you think Esther keeps that complection? Anyone can look at her and see that she's a *very* healthy, very sane, very well-balanced person. She cries! Of course, she cries! The Jews love to dramatize their emotions. Besides she's at that time of life when women get hysterical. Aha! You didn't know about that! I can see there are still some things that you must learn.

Suddenly he understood the full meaning and necessity of the tone of voice—the burlesque-courteous, heavily accented with an exasperated sneer—that had become habitual to Ernest and that he had so often heard him use.

When Madeleine ironically asked: "Do you think you are the

48. Connie Dashiell; Dubose Heyward, the author of *Porgy*, whom Wolfe knew through his wife Dorothy Kuhns Heyward, who had been in the 47 Workshop; Robert Nathan, the poet and novelist, and a friend of Mrs. Bernstein.

49. Mrs. Bernstein's friend Lillian Wadsworth.

50. Sigourney Thayer, a theatrical producer, who had married Mrs. Bernstein's friend Emily Davies.

only person in the world who has ever had an affair like this? Don't you know that your own case is not unusual—although you would like to think it is," he answered with measured insolence: "I do not suppose, of course, that my affairs are completely unique in a world of 1800 million people but at the present time, unphilosophic as it may seem, I am exclusively concerned with my own belly-ache. You, of course," he went on bitterly, "are a philosopher and a psychologist—you have read books by Havelock Ellis and you know all about it."

---

The Literary Life—I know these 'uns:

| | | |
|---|---|---|
| Dubose Heyward | Hugh Walpole | Ernest Boyd |
| W. Rose Benet | Jim Boyd | R. Nathan |
| Lyle Saxon | Tom Beer | Van Dine [51] |
| [*Louis*] Bromfield | Struthers Burt | |

The Greek's name at 49th St is Nick.

"Come on, Nick. Sit in with us Nick, I want you to meet my brother. Won't you have a drink, Nick?

(All together, the vaudeville people):

His success means more to me than my own, see.

(Tenderly, cynically) Is that so?

Yes—well to make a long story short . . . so I gave this fellow a check for $2000.

Now wait—September 1st I got a certificate covering the 10,000 shares . . . and he makes me out his own personal check for $5000.

My check is (was) made out July 13, see—So get this: Last Thursday a man walked into my office—A very fine set up, fellow, he says, You're Mr. Rice. I says, Yessir. He says, Mr. Rice, my name's Dowdy. At that time I don't know who Kenneth Dowdy is but he's a multimillionaire . . . . He says, Mr. Rice, you're a gentleman, I want to come clean with you and all that sort of thing . . . . You tell Mr. Nash I want to have a talk with him, see . . . . I says, lissen, you tell Mr. Kenneth Nash he's got to get in touch with me.

The use of the present tense—make a character out of it.

51. Lyle Saxon wrote popular studies of the New Orleans area; Struthers Burt was a novelist and essayist; Van Dine was the pseudonym under which Willard H. Wright wrote popular detective stories such as *The Canary Murder Case.*

Dr. John has no vacation at all this year.

Didn't he have any? You know he had a slight shock when he came to Boston.

It didn't affect him that way, see . . . . He was just tired, needed a rest, see.

They got a little camp down there, down the cape.

Down the cape?

Yeh, they got a little camp down there—just a few friends down there, see.

So a friend of hers has a drug store right across the street—I says to him you call her up and just ask for Peggy, see.

You could'a *knocked my head* off with a feather.

. . . Besides we have a couple of very marvelous songs, do you see what I mean?

. . . So I don't know what to do about the car; so many people discourage me.

Do you like an Auburn?

Well, yes and no. The first Auburn I had went over 27,000 miles without ever losing a nut.

A Liberty-Cadillac, a Liberty-Cadillac, sort of radiates luxury, do you see what I mean? An Auburn—well—I went around . . . I saw that Club Sedan for $2600. Its a four passenger . . . Do you want some more beer? . . . Its far superior, its far superior in appearance to a regular sedan, do you see what I mean?

[*These notes on overheard conversation continue for several pages.*]

Miss Dorothy Scarborough
c/o Men's Faculty Club
Morningside Drive and West 117th St
New York City

Giving final examination New York University seven to ten Thursday night Deeply regret impossible to come dinner with you and Mr. Lindsay.[52] Please ask me another time. Would like to meet you and talk with you.

THOMAS WOLFE

52. Miss Scarborough had invited Wolfe to dinner on January 30 to meet Vachel Lindsay.

Stringfellow Barr [53]
Care of The Virginia Quarterly
University of Virginia

Impossible to accept your generous invitation at present Finish teaching at New York University this week but must get stories ready for Scribner's. Will have more free time this Spring. Am writing you next week.

THOMAS WOLFE

Vardis Fisher [54]—Algonquin for Breakfast Friday Morning.

On the Boston Boat—in the smoking room—

Of wandering forever and the earth again. From these dark tide winds and waters of our sleep on which a few stars sparely look, call up the strange dark fish, the swart eternal whisperings. O forested and far, through all the waste and lone immensity of night, return, return.

O night, now, night, and from dark fields and forests of my sleep, I hear an army marching, softly, softly, with faint tremendous thundering, they come, they come!

They come, my great night horsemen come.

And the great trains of America thunder through the night.

Through the vast earth in darkness rivers run. Do beasts from coverts come? Do beasts at rivers stare? All through the dark our life, our breath, our vast dark land is lessening.

Upon the sea, lit by the great spare stars, the sea is bringing glory in great ships. There ships ride steady on the vast dark sea: the *Berengaria*, the *Leviathan*, the *Majestic*, the *Bremen*, the *Vulcania*.

Above the steady mast and quiet throb, set in the lone and waste immensity of night, the lonely splendor of Antares shines.

I turn the page, and Rosenzweig bends at the rail to watch phosphoric glints along the ship's steep side. Within the shadow of the ship, men watch the water-snakes, they see the living fire.

In 8000 presspits pressmen scan the inkfresh sheets, the cylinders un-river white, and boys are waiting for their routes.

53. On behalf of the Committee on Public Lectures at the University of Virginia, Stringfellow Barr had written to Wolfe on December 18 (and again on January 16) inviting him to speak in Charlottesville. Barr later wrote a generous review of LHA in the *Virginia Quarterly Review*, VI (April 1930), 310–13.

54. Vardis Fisher, who was just beginning his career as a novelist at this time, had become an instructor in English at New York University in 1928. He and Wolfe soon became friends. In later years he wrote a memoir of Wolfe which had a facile psychoanalytic approach: *Thomas Wolfe As I Knew Him*, 1963.

And the great trains of American thunder upon the land, thunder at the river's edge (Too-Tooey-Tooey-Too-Tooey), Forge-flares upon the sky, and headlights fingering six miles of rail, white startled headlights at a crossing, and cars upon the roads of Virginia and North Carolina, following trains.

Who stares at his enemy's or his mother's house in the dark?

Leonard Q. Snodgrass gropes for chaste wedded thighs. O dark dark—What do they say—Later he cleans his teeth, and washes freckled fingers—The medicine cabinet.

Tomorrow, dear, you know you must go to see Dr. Collins.

"After I have been with my wife."

We have done all that thou hast commanded us to do, Dr. Collins.

Dr. Collins said that once every two weeks was a normal average for a healthy man and woman. Do you remember that joke he told.

O Leonard, that was the *aw*-fullest thing! Imagine a man like Dr. Collins saying a thing like that.

I had to laugh, though. You know you did, too, dear.

Because I couldn't help myself. It *was* kind of funny.

Young college boys stir nervously, full of fear and joy.

The polo players lie with one another's wives. "The Long Island Set doesn't care what it does," said Joel. "If they feel like going to bed together they do it."

Police Courts—Night courts—(Rollo Wayne's story).[55]

Come sleep and with thy sweet forgetting, give me rest.

Leonard Q. Snodgrass—25% of population.
Grebenschik—5%
O'Toole—5%
Mose—7%.[56]

The awful shadow of Mr. Leonard Q. Snodgrass fell over the nation—Brushes his teeth with Squibb's—Gargles with Listerine—The fourth was on Wednesday, and this is only the sixteenth and you know what Dr. Collins said.

Seamen with dim glimmers on their faces—dark pilothouses.

55. Wayne had been at Harvard in Wolfe's time.

56. These are more of Wolfe's names to represent groups in America—Jewish, Irish, and Negro.

And as the sleepers slant through city yards at night, brightenings on the rails beside, bright livid glares upon uneasy sleepy faces, and bells, bells, bells.

Green lights of boats going up the dark windy sound.

All night lunch rooms—The taxi-men—the cops—the crooks—those who wait wearily for morning trains—workmen with steel-cutters and goggles—the late subways—women cleaning up office buildings.

Melville—There is an island in every man's soul—let him beware—etc.[57]

Boston, Sunday, Jan. 26—

Up at 12—out to Elaine's at Jamaica—bright sunshine—the smoky dark Fenway woods—the land glittering with ice and snow—out, out out in the cold street car—the cold frosty people—Dinner at Elaine's—there until 8:20 tonight—Back to hotel—writing this at Pieroni's—

Last night at Hilda's [58]—she told me plot of her book—Read fragments of it—The astrological parts! Part of the Westall mania—Mama's phrenology!

---

[*From the October Fair ledger*]

Boston, Sunday, Jan. 26—

When I spoke of Hilda's astrology, "It comes from the feeling in our blood that we are fated," said Elaine.

THE MATERNITY HOSPITAL

Here life began! Here, on the sweeping approaches to the great bridge with its crawling tides of trains and cars and trolleys, its moving dots of men, the shrill of whistles, the violent swinging arm of traffic cops, the cursing truck men, the jar and screech of stopping traffic; here set in its fabric of untidy streets, of swarming Italian, Jewish, German, Negro, and Irish life, of brawls and clamor, of lust and drunkenness and love and murder; here by the enormous incessant

57. A reference to *Moby Dick*, Chapter 28.

58. Hilda Westall Bottomley, another daughter of Wolfe's uncle, Henry Westall.

river, churned and parted by a thousand boats and barges, lined with a million lights and cliffs of buildings, a thick slow wash in which the horns were baying; here in rich, cruel, blind and bloody chaos, life began.

Brains battered with a baseball bat smeared in doorways.

The great river bore steadily and incessantly seaward all our stains—thickened with our sewage, darkened by our dumpings, rich, rank, stinking, tainted, mighty, beautiful, and unending as life itself.

He thought of houses where young maidens lay alone, where without congealing fear, young thighs might cleave and open in the night—unpapad and unmamad, ungirdled, unprotesting, unafraid.

*Another method:* What is going on inside a dozen people.

*Mina:* In a rich pouty irritated voice: But why can't he die or something? Aline's so lovely. Why must she be driven mad by a hysterical weeping man?

The "insides" of these ten [59]: 1) Aline 2) Edla 3) Theo 4) Mina 5) Martin the driver 6) "Stephen Hook" 7) Ernest Boyd 8) Madeleine Boyd 9) Gorewitz 10) Kawamura 11) Hilda—(mixture of obscene sensuality and sentimental romanticizing)—"Sweeney"—Snodgrass—Fat Jack Harvey (Southern malice).

"Oh Nakuchi (she pronounced the word with a fat caressing sound Na-kootch-y, at the same time making a sensual movement with her fat hips) You should know him, Esther, he's darling—and a r-r-reel chenius."

Carroll.

At night—different people awake thinking: a fairy—wrote furiously upon a paper "I never want to see him again."

"Well, I hope he sees it! I just hope to God he sees it! And I'll tell Irene Lewisohn what I think of the way she's acted too."

"And when I walked on in the second act in that impersonation of Jane Cowl doing Juliet [60] wearing that red dress Esther designed for me, did I knock them out of their seats? And how! I hope he heard what Weisberg said when I walked off: 'Albert,' he said, 'honest to

59. These notes are the beginning of what became, seven years later, "The Party at Jack's."

60. A reference to Albert Carroll's impersonation in "The Grand Street Follies."

God you're better than the real thing. If you got any photographs in that costume, you got to give me one. You got it all over her for looks, boy. You got a throat like a young girl.' "

"And that big overgrown bum of a Gant scowling and glowering at me as if he'd like to murder me. He'll get his, all right, all right. Just let him keep on long enough and he'll get it good and plenty. Someone's going to sock that guy right on the beezer someday and when they do I hope I've got a seat right in the orchestra. And will I be sorry? Don't ask! When he was telling me about his mother buying all that real-estate tonight I had a good mind to ask him if he wasn't carrying a good part of it around in his fingernails."

Esther: [61] . . . I wish that I were with him now riding through the dark. I'd like to be inside him. I wish he could swallow me and carry me around inside him. Now he is riding through the dark. Is he asleep? No, he is awake. I can just see him staring out the window at the scenery. He is too big to sleep in one of those little berths. Is the moon shining in Virginia? I wonder if he ever thinks of me when he's away from me. Is he thinking of me now? I carry you around in my heart, you are dearer to me than anyone in the world, I am yours until death—Esther.

Esther: . . . "Long, long into the night I lay thinking of how to tell my story" . . . Could I write a story? That was the only time I ever tried. I thought that first line was lovely. But I never got any further than that. I wonder if he'll ever write a book about me. I'd love it if he would. He says he will some day. I wonder if he knows at all what I'm like. . . . Someday he'll know after he's gone and left me. You'll miss your little Jew then, won't you? Do you ever think of me when you're away from me? I think of you, I'm always thinking about you. I'm always talking to you, thinking up conversations with you. I'll bet you never do that when you're away from me. I like that new record Teddy's got: 'I'll get by as long as I have you.' I suppose its only a cheap song, but there's something lovely about it. The idea's right, its the way we all feel."

Boston, in my room late at night—Rich voice of a woman laughing in the snowy silent street by the State House. Will I remember this years later?

61. These notes are the first which build toward the character of Esther Jacobs (later Jack). "Long, long into the night I lay . . ." becomes her motif.

And suddenly, from Nowhere in the mind, there comes the memory of a woman's rich burst of laughter in a silent street when one was a child in 1915, and there comes the memory of a distant motor roaring through the night in the distance at that same moment—a Hudson 1914. And where is that lost laughter? Where has the motor gone? And where is our vanished boyhood? All the dead world awakens—and the million unrecorded sights and sounds—those we did *not* see—return, return.

Cops grinning brutally as faces laced with blood are taken away—he felt the town's harsh pain: the split skull, the crash of flesh on asphalt, the splintered cartilage of nose.

(This has it!)

I shall go away with him and we shall live together in a little house in London. Somewhere near Kensington, I think. He will come home every night about six o'clock and he will call up to me from the foot of the stairs, "Are you there, dear?" He will say "I have brought Lytton Strachey home for dinner. Come down when you can." Sometimes he will bring his friends Aldous Huxley and A. E. Coppard, and one time he will bring Clive Bell and Virginia Woolf. If I could write, I should like to write like Virginia Woolf. It is the way a woman writes. That place in *To the Lighthouse* where the wind comes in that old deserted house and noses around. It creeps here and there stirring things and rustling against them just the way I want to.

A scene with a tremendous *lift* to it (Love and Death).
The Birth Scene (later on the walk across the bridge?)
Powell's [62] Farewell Scene.
Parting of Esther and Eugene.
Eliza's death?
Percy G's death?
Fire on Park Avenue.
The Oktoberfest Scenes.
Death of Mrs. Richards.
Joel on Astor's W. C.
Meeting of Esther and Eugene.
The Literary Party.
Madison Square Garden.

62. Desmond Powell. See Pocket Notebook 15 for the material Wolfe developed.

Stein and Solomon's New Store.[63]
Gant's Death.
Luke.
Henry Pentland's Office.
The Leonard's Fortune.

The years slide by like water and one day it is May again. Shall we ever ride out of the ponderous gates of the West together, sons of men? I heard a woman's laughter in the streets one night and the throbbing of a distant motor. And then I slept and never thought of it till now when I heard a woman laugh and I am far from home: and that was eighteen sleeping years ago when the song they sang was "Love me and the World Is Mine."

---

Describe one of the following scenes in such a way as to emphasize some dominant impression—drabness, cheerfulness, utidiness, loneliness, etc.

1) A Student's Room
2) A Room In An East Side Tenement
3) A Country Barn
4) The Chemistry Lab
5) Back-Stage of a Theatre
6) A Broker's Office [64]

America by Moonlight.
Of wandering forever and the earth again.[65]

From these tide winds and waters of our sleep on which a few stars sparely look.[66]

How many eyes from windows seaward look? Or on the rivers from a hill how many eyes?

Do men stand in our forests like a beast?

63. This material, based on Bergdorf-Goodman's, became "Stein and Rosen's," Chapter 27 in W&R. Wolfe developed it from Mrs. Bernstein's anecdotes; her sister Ethel was a buyer for the store. For a full discussion see Paschal Reeves "Thomas Wolfe: Notes on Three Characters," *Modern Fiction Studies*, XI (Autumn, 1965), 275–78.

64. Since Wolfe had already met his last classes at NYU, this and the next list of theme topics were probably drawn up for the final examination.

65. This became the thematic motif of "The October Fair" and later was used in the proem to "No Door" (long version) and OT&R.

66. Part of the line is from Milton's "Lycidas": "On whose fresh lap the swart star sparely looks."

The wrecking crew goes out into the dark. And the land unscrolls in morning.

What little lights are burning on the land?

III. Write four hundred words on one of the following topics:

1. My First Term at College.
2. A Book That Has Influenced My Life.
3. Physical Courage and Spiritual Courage.
3. Can Progress Be Measured By Statistics? (Make Concrete references to Dean Inge's essay *The Idea of Progress*).
4. Expand one of the following incidents:
   a) The engineer of the fast express sees an automobile stalled upon the track.
   b) A man, having dined expensively at a restaurant, informs the waiter he has no money.
5. When I Thought My Life In Danger.

*The October Fair* (Chance)
I Paris Aug 14, 1925
II London Aug 18, 1926

Monday [*January 27*], 5 P.M. South Station Boston—

Crowds waiting to be let through—Smoothly magnificently The Merchants Limited slides in—"I put your bag back here, sir" "Are you goin' all the way, sir?"—how smoothly we slide out with a brief clanging between other trains in which people are sitting—in 5 hrs. we'll be in New York—Now in the yards other trains with mournful clangings going in and out—The yards snow paved and the dark tangle of tracks—a grey leaden sky—and air full of smoke puffs—tall chimneys Gillette factory—lights—signs—smoothly smoothly goes the train —The Arlington hotel (whores)—now slowing up for Back Bay.

On the B. Bay station—A uniformed nigger with long deliberate strides wheeling a truck on which is a big trunk.

A woman in red. The rows of dirty brick houses with their rounded bays—one looks down corrugated rows on other side Boston arena—The white glaring lights of Boston shine harshly on the snow —now the open spaces—Y.M.C.A., Opera House—The dingy plots of ground—Now the wooden houses grey and dingy of Roxbury—Back kitchen windows warm with light and most in dinginess. Now by a thousand kitchen stoves—The white land—the smoke dark trees— great ads—Camels, smiling teeth—a glare of blue light through glazed chemical factory windows—The elevated rushing in across the country—with smooth roar another fast train rips Bostonward—processional of cars down every street—snow feathery woods around the two- and three-family houses—and raw ordered squares dingy with square porches set in each—stained brownish shingling.

Lights within now few and far—the country snow—dark coming now—Tough clumps of frozen grass darken raggedly the snow—a town a town—The feathery smoke plumes of slowly shifting engines fade in grey darkening air. The trees small frozen and bare—dark on the frozen earth—small gnarled looking. With smooth green warmth we tear along through frozen winter—The open wintry country now. The stern land breaks roughly through the snow. The stubble of old crops—clods—piles of frozen dung—Ecstasy as we cross dark frozen streams high up—Other lines soar off at tangents—Cars in white snow at little stations—A village street—old squares—warm houses—cold so cold without.

On feathery banks and hillocks bushes grow.